the
MIRANDA
debate

**Law,
Justice,
and
Policing**

NORTHEASTERN UNIVERSITY   1898–1998

the
MIRANDA
debate

Law,
Justice,
and
Policing

---

edited by

Richard A.
Leo

&

George C.
Thomas III

Northeastern
University Press

•

Boston

Northeastern University Press

Library of Congress Cataloging-in-Publication Data
The Miranda debate : law, justice, and policing / edited by
Richard A. Leo & George C. Thomas III.
p. cm.
Includes index.
ISBN 1-55553-338-8 (cloth : alk. paper)
1. Confession (Law)—United States. 2. Police questioning—
United States. 3. Right to counsel—United States. I. Leo,
Richard A., 1963– . II. Thomas, George C. (George Conner), 1947– .
KF9625.M57   1998
346.73′056—dc21   98-9496

Designed by David Ford

Composed in Bookman by G&S Typesetters, Austin, Texas.
Printed and bound by Maple Press, York, Pennsylvania. The paper
is Perfection Antique Recycled, an acid-free sheet.

MANUFACTURED IN THE UNITED STATES OF AMERICA
02 01 00 99 98   5 4 3 2 1

To Jerome Skolnick, who first excited my interest
in the *Miranda* debate
—R.A.L.

To George C. Thomas, Jr., for all he taught me
about law and life
—G.C.T. III

Contents

CONTENTS

CONTENTS

CONTENTS

Editors' Note

The basic concepts in this book were influenced by the advice, guidance, critique, and just plain old arguments that we have had with students, teachers, colleagues, and friends. While we cannot name everyone who has been helpful, we must name Richard Boldt, Paul Cassell, Joshua Dressler, Larry Herman, Jon Hyman, Eric Neisser, Steve Schulhofer, and Welsh White. We also thank all of the authors who permitted us to excerpt their work. Finally, special gratitude is due to Yale Kamisar, who provided guidance and assistance along the way, and sympathy when the path proved less smooth than we had hoped.

In editing these materials, we sought to make the book as readable as possible while maintaining fidelity to the original sources. We removed most footnotes and reproduced those that remain as endnotes to each chapter. These we renumbered sequentially within each reading.

Furthermore, in the interest of stylistic consistency and as an aid to readability, we conformed the original sources to follow current rules about capitalization and form, as well as the Harvard Law Review Association's *A Uniform System of Citation* for note citations. In this process, very minor changes in the original were sometimes made. Richard Leo made very slight revisions in his article excerpted in chapter 15.

When editing these materials, we generally used ellipses to indicate internal omissions; we used asterisks if the resulting material seemed to lack a transition. Omissions of citations of cases are not indicated at all. Sometimes we added a bit of explanatory material or additional text necessary to a smooth transition. This material we set off in brackets and, if more than a few words, indicate our authorship with "Eds."

We of course also benefitted from practical, day-to-day help of several people. For research assistance, we thank Gail Spence, a Rutgers law student. For secretarial assistance, we thank Linda Thornton at the University of Colorado, and Gwen Ausby and Helene Wright at Rutgers. For editorial assistance we thank Ann Twombly at Northeastern University Press.

We thank the following copyright holders for permission to excerpt material from the original sources:

Equal Justice in the Gatehouses and Mansions of American Criminal Procedure: From *Powell* to *Gideon*, from *Escobedo* to . . . by Yale Kamisar. Reprinted with permission of the University Press of Virginia.

Homicide: A Year on the Killing Streets. Copyright © 1991 by David Simon. Reprinted by permission of Houghton Mifflin Co. All rights reserved.

From Coercion to Deception: The Changing Nature of Police Interrogation in America by Richard A. Leo, Kluwer Academic Publishers, *Crime, Law, and Social Change*, vol. 18, 1992, pp. 35–59. Copyright © 1992. Reprinted by kind permission from Kluwer Academic Publishers.

"You Have the Right to Remain Silent": *Miranda* after Twenty Years by Patrick A. Malone. Reprinted by permission of *The American Scholar* and Patrick A. Malone.

Reconsidering *Miranda* by Stephen J. Schulhofer. Copyright © 1987 by The University of Chicago Law Review. Reprinted with their permission.

Questioning *Miranda* by Gerald M. Caplan. Copyright © by 1985 Vanderbilt Law Review. Reprinted with their permission.

The Supreme Court, the Attorney General, and the Good Old Days of Police Interrogation by Lawrence Herman. Reprinted with permission of the Ohio State Law Journal and Lawrence Herman.

A Modest Proposal for the Abolition of Custodial Confessions by Irene Mcrkcr Rosenberg & Yale L. Rosenberg. Copyright © 1989 by North Carolina Law Review Association. Reprinted with their permission.

A Peculiar Privilege in Historical Perspective: The Right to Remain Silent by Albert W. Alschuler, originally published by the Michigan Law Review. Reprinted with permission of Michigan Law Review and Albert W. Alschuler.

Miranda's Social Costs: An Empirical Reassessment by Paul G. Cassell. Reprinted by special permission of the Northwestern University Law Review, Volume 90, Issue 2, 1996, pp. 389–95; 416–23; 433; 437–42; 445–46; 483–86.

Miranda's Practical Effect: Substantial Benefits and Vanishingly Small Social Costs by Stephen J. Schulhofer. Reprinted by special permission of the Northwestern University Law Review, Volume 90, Issue 2, 1996, pp. 501–15; 538–47.

The Impact of *Miranda* Revisited by Richard A. Leo. Reprinted with by special permission of the Journal of Criminal Law and Criminology, Volume 86, No. 3. Copyright 1996 Northwestern University School of Law.

Police Interrogation in the 1990s: An Empirical Study of the Effects of *Miranda* by Paul G. Cassell and Bret S. Hayman. Originally published in 43 UCLA L. Rev. 839. Copyright 1996 The Regents of the University of California. All Rights Reserved.

Plain Talk about the *Miranda* Empirical Debate: A "Steady-State" Theory of Confessions by George C. Thomas III. Originally published in 43 UCLA L. Rev. 933. Copyright 1996 The Regents of the University of California. All Rights Reserved.

The Changed and Changing World of Constitutional Criminal Procedure by Joseph D. Grano. Reprinted with permission of the University of Michigan Journal of Law Reform and Joseph D. Grano.

Remembering the "Old World" of Criminal Procedure: A Reply to Professor Grano by Yale Kamisar. Reprinted with permission of the University of Michigan Journal of Law Reform and Yale Kamisar.

In a Different Register: The Pragmatics of Powerlessness in Police Interrogation by Janet E. Ainsworth. Reprinted by permission of The Yale Law Journal Company and Fred B. Rothman & Company from *The Yale Law Journal*, Vol. 103, pp. 259–322, and by permission of Janet E. Ainsworth.

A Statutory Replacement for the *Miranda* Doctrine by Phillip E. Johnson. Reprinted with the permission of the publisher, *The American Criminal Law Review* © 1987, and Georgetown University.

Videotaping Interrogations and Confessions by William A. Geller. Reprinted with permission of William Geller of the Police Executive Research Forum.

Introduction

School children are more likely to recognize the *Miranda* warnings than the Gettysburg Address. Perhaps this is not surprising given that the warnings have thoroughly permeated our culture through television shows and movies: "You have the right to remain silent. Anything you say can and will be used against you in a court of law. You have the right to a lawyer during questioning. If you cannot afford a lawyer, one will be provided for you at no cost."

The U.S. Supreme Court decision in *Miranda v. Arizona*[1] also requires that a suspect voluntarily waive the rights contained in the warnings. Without proof of warnings and waiver, no statement given during custodial interrogation can be admitted into evidence against the suspect.

One study shows that 64.5 percent of adult parolees understood the *Miranda* warnings well enough to score either eleven or twelve correct responses on a twelve-item test of the meaning of the warnings.[2] Yet most post-*Miranda* studies also show that at least half of all interrogated suspects make incriminating statements to police. How can the *Miranda* warnings so thoroughly pervade our culture yet leave the confession rate around 50 percent? The warnings seem to make it crystal clear that speaking to the police is hazardous and that the suspect can consult with a lawyer who will be provided at no charge. Why, then, do 80–90 percent of suspects continue to talk to police, almost all without consulting with a lawyer?

Decided in 1966 by a 5–4 majority of the Warren Court at the height of its judicial activism, *Miranda* seemed to create a mechanism to empower suspects to resist the isolation, humiliation, and deceit that had become the hallmark of police interrrogation. The dissenting Justices on the *Miranda* Court claimed that the majority's warnings-and-waiver rule would handicap the police. And why would we want to handicap police who are trying to solve crimes? Most suspects are probably guilty of the crime under investigation, and many of these crimes—homicide, rape, robbery—are terrible crimes of violence.

Newspaper readers in 1966 will remember the firestorm of protest that greeted *Miranda*. Critics complained that the decision meant the death of confessions, that the forces of crime were on the verge of prevailing over the forces of peace. Richard Nixon railed against *Miranda* in his 1968 presidential campaign. Yet in 1993, four national police organizations and fifty former prosecutors filed a "friend of the Court" brief to ask the Supreme Court not to restrict the availability of *Miranda* as a means of reversing convictions on appeal. The Court ruled that *Miranda* should continue to be available in all kinds of appeals.[3] Why would *Miranda*, friendless among police and prosecutors in 1968, suddenly have their support in 1993?

Miranda was the high-water mark of the Warren Court's criminal procedure revolution. Republican Presidents Richard Nixon, Gerald Ford, Ronald Reagan, and George Bush would appoint the next nine Supreme Court Justices. The very survival of *Miranda* through the increasingly conservative Burger and Rehnquist Courts is enough of a surprise. Even more surprising is that *Miranda*'s reach has been expanded in some ways by these later Courts.

One expansion occurred in 1980 when the Court held that the *Miranda* warnings are required not only when the police ask explicit questions but also when police engage in any conduct likely to elicit an incriminating response.[4] A year later, the Court made plain that a single request for counsel barred the police from reapproaching the suspect to ask for a waiver of the *Miranda* rights.[5]

To be sure, *Miranda* has not been expanded along all fronts, as Part II of this book will show. Nonetheless, imagine a conversation in 1966 in which a reader of the bitterly divided 5–4 *Miranda* opinion is told that although Republican presidents would appoint the next nine Supreme Court Justices, *Miranda* would be generally endorsed and even expanded in some ways. It is a claim that would likely have been met with derision. Yet this has happened. The long-term success of the controversial *Miranda* doctrine demands an explanation.

Few areas of criminal law have so fascinated scholars, jurists, and the public as the law of confessions. From the Inquisition to the English persecution of the Puritans to the McCarthy Communist Party witch-hunts, the proper role of the government in obtaining confessions has occasionally roiled the political scene. No enduring solution to the question of government's proper role has been forthcoming. This book will examine the reasons the confession question remains unsettled. One obvious reason is the pragmatic reality that the politics of criminal procedure sometimes tilts in favor of crime control and at other times it tilts in favor of protecting the rights of the accused. The constitutional law of criminal procedure is constantly changing (though often in subtle ways) as it shifts along this continuum.

A second reason for the unsettled character of the law of confessions is that two different forms of skepticism affect its analysis. Accounts of police torture and brutality induce skepticism toward all "confessions" from suspects who do not appear penitent. Why would a suspect do something so very much against his own interest unless the police are somehow coercing him to do it? On the other hand, lacking evidence of physical abuse in a particular case, one can reasonably be skeptical of the suspect's claim that the "police made me do it." The suspect *could* have chosen to remain silent: There is no official requirement that anyone must answer police questions; there is no legal sanction for failing to answer. Thus, when the suspect answers police questions (at least in the absence of physical coercion or threats), it must be because he wanted to do so at that moment. In what sense, then, is the answer coerced or the confession tainted?

Miranda turned thirty years old in 1996. It is the current, though aging, answer of the U.S. Supreme Court to the question of how much pressure government should be permitted to bring to bear on suspects who are being interrogated. The purpose of this book is to collect in one volume the most important and incisive writings about *Miranda*. Our goal is to present an easily readable and intellectually compelling collection that explores the historical, policy, ethical, empirical, and political issues raised by *Miranda*. In compiling the only book-length collection of writings that examine *Miranda*, we took seriously the obligation to present diverse perspectives on the many issues surrounding the past, present, and future of what is undoubtedly the Court's most famous, influential, and controversial criminal procedure decision. We prepared three chapters—Chapters 1, 20, and 24—especially for this book.

The book contains four parts. Part I begins with a brief portrait of Ernest Miranda and his crime, as well as of the law of confessions before *Miranda*. It also includes an overview of the issues that are plumbed in more depth in the rest of the book: (1) whether *Miranda* is a legitimate reading of the U.S. Constitution, (2) whether *Miranda* works to relieve pressure on suspects in the interrogation room, and (3) whether it is appropriate to give guilty suspects a "right to remain silent."

Part II presents the ethical and policy dimensions of the debate. One view is that *Miranda* overprotects suspects who should instead be encouraged (though not coerced) to answer questions; only guilty suspects have to worry about the pressure to answer questions. A very different view is that interrogation pressure may cause some suspects to overstate their guilt or even, in some cases, incriminate themselves when they are innocent. Moreover, some argue, it is inappropriate for the authoritarian police to trick, cajole, and manipulate disadvantaged suspects even if they are guilty. A middle-of-the-road position supports *Miranda* as a compromise that makes suspects theoretically equal to their interrogators but does not seem to interfere too much with the success of police interrogation when suspects are, in fact, guilty.

Part III provides a close analysis of how *Miranda* actually works (or doesn't work) in the station house, including the debate about what the empirical evidence shows. We include two new empirical studies that have recently been published, along with a critical reaction to one of them. Again, legal scholars differ radically in how to interpret the few studies that exist on the effect of *Miranda*. The estimates of the effect of *Miranda* on police interrogation range from preventing confessions in 16 percent of all interrogations (Paul Cassell) to 4.1 percent (the top of Stephen Schulhofer's range) to no detectable effect (the estimate Schulhofer and George Thomas find most likely).

Part IV seeks insight into the future of *Miranda*. Will it survive the new attacks on its legitimacy? Is there a better way to police the police? Does *Miranda* ignore too many problems inherent in the power imbalance between police and suspects? Perhaps *Miranda* will be supplemented by another requirement (such as videotaping police interrogations). Perhaps it will be overruled as both unnecessary and too restrictive of the morally good enterprise of police interrogation. Perhaps it will be expanded to make the rules more difficult for police to evade.

At some point in the twenty-first century, scholars may view *Miranda* as a transitory solution to the confession problem. The crucial question is whether *Miranda* was a brave beginning to a better understanding of the interrogation process—of how coercion operates in the police station, of how to protect suspects from that coercion, of how (or whether) to help suspects retain their dignity and autonomy, of how (or whether) to equalize suspects in terms of knowledge of their rights and the ability to act on that knowledge. The other possibility is that *Miranda* will be viewed as an aberration in the centuries-old attempt to assess the "voluntariness" and reliability of each confession. What happens in the next few years may well dictate which road *Miranda* travels.

NOTES

1. U.S. 436 (1966).
2. Thomas Grisso, *Juveniles' Capacities to Waive* Miranda *Rights*: An Empirical Analysis, 68 *Ca. L. Rev.* 1134, 1154 table 3 (1980).
3. Withrow v. Williams, 507 U.S. 680 (1993).
4. Rhode Island v. Innis, 446 U.S. 291 (1980).
5. Edwards v. Arizona, 451 U.S. 477 (1981).

I

Overview of the *Miranda* Debate

Part I begins with an account by George Thomas of Ernest Miranda, his victim, and the 1963 crime for which he was convicted. After Miranda's arrest, the case against him quickly shifted to the interrogation room in the Phoenix police station. The rule that governed police interrogation in 1963 was derived from the constitutional guarantee of due process. As we will see in Chapter 1, the Supreme Court since 1936 has prohibited the use of "involuntary" confessions, reasoning that this violates due process of law. While determining which confessions are "involuntary" is often a substantial problem, the early cases focused on the use of torture or physical coercion. Later cases looked to the general characteristics of the interrogation—its setting, how it was carried out—and to the general demeanor and history of the suspect in an attempt to determine whether the confession was the product of the suspect's will or that of his interrogators.

The Constitution also speaks directly to the question of compelling someone to be a "witness against himself" in a criminal case. The Fifth Amendment contains this prohibition, which in 1963 was thought to apply only to *legal* compulsion to answer questions—legal requirements to answer or face a sanction (usually contempt of court) for not answering. Witnesses are legally required to answer in judicial or quasi-judicial proceedings such as a trial, a grand jury hearing, a legislative hearing, or certain types of administrative hearings. When a person is required to

1

answer, and the Fifth Amendment thus applies, the concern with compulsion is so great that the Fifth Amendment is understood to create a right to terminate questioning. This expansive right is recognized in the terminology used as a shorthand to describe the Fifth Amendment's protection—it is called a "privilege against self-incrimination." A "privilege" implies that the holder of the privilege has veto power, in this context the power to terminate questioning.

But suspects, unlike witnesses, are not legally required to answer police questions. They face no legal sanctions for refusing to answer. As a consequence, suspects in the interrogation room were not protected by the Fifth Amendment privilege against self-incrimination in 1963 but, rather, by the less expansive due process right not to be coerced into confessing. The Court thus developed parallel doctrines: A due process doctrine bars police coercion and is often called the "voluntariness doctrine" to distinguish it from the Fifth Amendment privilege against self-incrimination.

Why should the Fifth Amendment, with its right to terminate questioning, apply only when a suspect is legally required to answer? Chapter 2 presents Yale Kamisar's classic 1965 essay, published a year before *Miranda*, which asks this very question. In Kamisar's terminology, why are the rules so different in the "gatehouse" of the interrogation room than in the "mansion" of the courtroom? The mansion may be quite ornate and ostentatious but, as Kamisar notes, once a suspect confesses in the gatehouse, the proceeding in the mansion is a mere "show," its conclusion usually foregone.

To Kamisar, the proceedings in the gatehouse are often a *de facto* inquisitorial system in which the suspect is "game to be stalked and cornered," the "enemy" of the state, a depersonalized subject to be manipulated into confessing. "Here ideals are checked at the door, 'realities' faced, and the prestige of law enforcement vindicated."[1] The solution? Apply some version of the privilege against self-incrimination to the gatehouse where police interrogation occurs.

Readers today may not fully appreciate the revolutionary nature of the idea that the Fifth Amendment right to terminate questioning should apply to police interrogation. It is not as if this analytical move had been considered and rejected. Rather, *the Supreme Court had never considered it.* Albert Alschuler's insightful essay on the history of the privilege against self-incrimination, excerpted in Chapter 12, shows why the Court would not quickly or easily have considered applying the privilege to the interrogation room: No general "right to silence" existed until long after the Bill of Rights was ratified.

Whatever else can be said about *Miranda*, it changed the Fifth Amendment landscape in 1966, for the first time extending to police interrogation the privilege to terminate questioning. In Chapter 3, the editors briefly describe the law of confessions in 1966 on the eve of *Miranda*, the problems that *Miranda* sought to solve, and the problems that the *Miranda* solution created. Then we present excerpts from the Court's opinion, giving the five-member majority a chance to speak for itself. We also excerpt the dissents to show the rather bitter disagreement then existing on the Court. Justice White, for example, ended his dissent with the words: "In some unknown number of cases the Court's rule will return a killer, a rapist or other criminal to the streets. . . . There is, of course, a saving factor: the next victims are uncertain, unnamed and unrepresented in this case."

In Chapter 4, we present David Simon's compelling description of the interrogation practices and strategies he observed in the Baltimore Homicide Division in 1988. He presents the drama of powerful, clever police detectives interrogating the frightened but guilty murder suspect. Simon's account of how the police manipulate and trick the suspect into confessing is sometimes comic, but ultimately it raises in stark form a very serious question: Has *Miranda* done any good?

Deception used against suspects is seemingly limited only by the ingenuity of the police interrogators. One example Simon reports, from veteran homicide detectives in Detroit, is using the photocopy machine as a "lie detector" test. The "test" involved pre-loading three sheets of paper into the machine, the first two marked "Truth" and the third marked "Lie." The suspect would be told to put his hand on the machine; the interrogator would ask the suspect's name, address, and whether he killed the victim. When "Lie" came out of the machine on the third question, the detectives would say, "Well, well. You lying motherfucker." The technique apparently worked often enough to be used fairly regularly. If it's that easy to get a confession, if police interrogation is but a confidence game that now cleverly includes the *Miranda* warnings,[2] then why bother with warnings at all?

Richard Leo's essay in Chapter 5 on the changing nature of police interrogation provides a scholar's perspective on the ease with which police obtain confessions. According to Leo, police have become adept at manipulating suspects and eliciting incriminating statements without resorting to overt coercion. Thus, like Simon, Leo portrays suspects as relatively powerless vis-à-vis police interrogators. Police can seemingly get confessions in most cases if they want them. As Leo notes, the model for police interrogation now is not the inquisitorial third-degree but Peter Falk playing Columbo on television. Leo's perspective makes *Miranda* seem much less potent than the *Miranda* dissenters feared.

Leo also discusses the ethical questions posed by the new forms of interrogation. Manipulation, trickery, and deception when used in the interrogation room are "fraught with moral ambiguity." Everyone agrees that it is immoral to beat a confession out of a suspect, even if the suspect is guilty, but not everyone agrees that it is immoral to trick the suspect into telling the truth about a crime that he has committed. This ethical question—how much "soft" pressure can police use on suspects in the pursuit of a confession that will solve a crime—will be a focus of much of the rest of the book.

Readers should make up their own minds whether the techniques recounted by Simon and Leo are morally worthy, morally neutral (but necessary), or morally unworthy. For example, can it be morally wrong for the detective to characterize the evidence against the suspect in the way most favorable to the state? Perhaps the detective says, "Your partner just rolled over on you" as a more-or-less accurate way to describe the other suspect's admission that the two of them were at the crime scene together. It seems unlikely that the Constitution or our sense of morality would condemn conveying that information in such a way.

But if that slight exaggeration is morally permissible, what about a police officer telling the suspect that he left lots of physical evidence at the scene (assuming that the officer knows of evidence left at the scene and has probable cause to believe that it will be traced to the suspect)? From here, it may be an infinite regress to the phony lie-detector ploy, always assuming that the police have probable cause to believe that the suspect committed the crime.

We return to the question of *Miranda*'s effect in Part III—when we consider the attempt to obtain rigorous empirical evidence—but for the present, readers are advised to be skeptical of the claim that *Miranda* has wrought great harm in the investigation of crime. Suspects often do not seem to recognize that it is in their self-interest to exercise the twin *Miranda* rights to silence and to counsel, or perhaps they are incapable of acting on what they recognize. A prescription for our readers: Whenever it begins to seem that suspects generally act in their own best in-

terest and remain silent after being warned of the consequences of con-
senting to interrogation, reread Simon and Leo (Chapters 4 and 5).

Patrick Malone wrote a thoughtful retrospective on *Miranda* after it
had been the law for twenty years. In the Chapter 6 excerpt, Malone explains how *Miranda* is neither as bad as its critics claim nor as good as
many of its supporters would like. Malone's view supports that of David
Simon and Richard Leo, noting the power imbalance in the interrogation
room and the realistic possibility that suspects will agree to statements
that overstate their guilt. Malone provides disturbing examples of police
manipulation and trickery. One sample interrogation of a suspected sex
offender included offers of "proper help," representations that the suspect's refusal to come clean was "hurting" the interrogator, and the statement: "You're my brother, I mean we're brothers. All men on the face of
this earth are brothers, Frank, but you got to be completely honest with
me." Is it possible for an innocent person to confess to a crime? Yes, concludes Malone, and without *Miranda* the problem would be far worse.

Malone argues that the confession rate has remained virtually unchanged since *Miranda*; that even when *Miranda* is violated, suspects
rarely go free; that the Supreme Court has steadily chipped away at the
doctrinal foundation of *Miranda*; that the voluntariness of the *Miranda*
waiver has replaced the voluntariness of the confession as the real
test of a confession's admissibility; and that *Miranda* has been more
symbolic than substantive in its impact, essentially reflecting a debate
more about the kind of criminal justice system we wish to have than
about the technical rules of procedure we wish to impose on police
interrogators.

By the end of Chapter 6, the reader should appreciate the complexity
of the *Miranda* debate. It involves perplexing constitutional questions
about whether the Fifth Amendment privilege against self-incrimination
belongs only in the courtroom or also in the police interrogation room.
It involves the intensely practical question of whether *Miranda* does
anything other than encourage police to use less obvious pressure and
more trickery, manipulation, and deceit. It involves the policy question
of the proper relationship between authoritarian police figures and disadvantaged, often minority, suspects. Finally, it involves transcendent
questions of American values as we approach the twenty-first century.
How do we strike the appropriate balance between the autonomy and
dignity of suspects, and the right of law-abiding citizens to insist on
crime control? How do we balance requiring police to follow norms of

fairness that prevail generally in society, and permitting police to be more successful in solving crimes? How do we balance the freedom of suspects to make up their own minds whether to answer police questions, and the freedom of police to seek confessions from suspects they believe to be guilty?

NOTES

1. See Chapter 2, at page 30.
2. See also Richard A. Leo, Miranda's *Revenge: Police Interrogation as a Confidence Game*, 30 *Law & Soc'y Rev.* 259 (1996).

1

Miranda:
The Crime,
the Man,
and the Law
of Confessions
(1998)

•

GEORGE C. THOMAS III

The Man and the Crime[1]

Spring comes early to the desert that contains Phoenix, Arizona, and evenings in March are usually warm and breezy. The evening of March 2, 1963, was no exception. Shortly before midnight, Mary Adams[2] left the Paramount Theater where she worked behind the concessions stand. The old Paramount was located in downtown Phoenix, a city of around 450,000 people in 1963.[3] Rape was still a relatively rare crime in Phoenix: 112 rapes would be reported that year.[4]

Mary Adams was eighteen years old and lived on Citrus Way with her mother, sister, and brother-in-law.[5] After leaving work at the Paramount, she took the bus to 7th Street and Marlette, in Phoenix's central city. Though the area was populated by "little pastel-colored adobe houses" rather than the "taller, darker tenements [like those] in Harlem and North Philadelphia and Southeast Washington," it was nonetheless true that "poverty and discrimination and crime resided here no less than elsewhere."[6]

Mary got off the bus that evening, like many others, and "started to walk toward her home. She observed a car, which afterwards proved to be [Miranda's], parked behind the ballet school on Marlette. The car pulled out of the lot, and came so close to her that she had to jump back to prevent being hit."[7]

The car stopped and a man got out and approached Mary Adams. She did not pay much attention to him because people were often on the

7

street when she made her walk home late at night.[8] But what happened next was not commonplace.

The man grabbed her and said he would not hurt her. He held her hands behind her back, told her not to scream, and put his hand over her mouth. He pulled her to the car and put her in the backseat. After tying her hands behind her back, and her ankles, he put something sharp to her neck and said: "Feel this." The object, whatever it was, was never recovered.[9]

He got in the front seat, started the car, and drove for twenty minutes, while Mary Adams lay crying on the backseat of the car.[10] He repeated his promise: "Keep quiet, and I won't hurt you."[11] It must have been a very long twenty minutes for Mary Adams.

Finally, the man stopped the car somewhere in the desert and untied her. He told her to remove her clothes and, when she refused, he began trying to undress her. "Please take me home," she begged. He ignored her pleas. She cried while he undressed her, saying over and over, "Please don't."[12]

Naked, she wept as he lowered himself onto her. "Please, please don't do this," she sobbed. She continued to cry. He said, "You can't tell me you have never done this before." She responded, "No, I haven't."[13] He tried again, while she pushed against him "with her hands, screaming."[14] He penetrated her. She later testified, "I kept screaming, I was trying to get away but he was a lot stronger than I was, and I couldn't do anything."[15]

After his climax, he told her to get dressed and asked where she lived. She told him, and he drove while she dressed. He stopped where he had abducted her and started to let her out. She said, "Well, this is not where I live." He replied, "This is as far as I'm taking you." As she got out, he called after her, "Please pray for me."[16]

She ran home. According to her sister, she was "crying, and looking like she had been in a fight."[17] The family called the police. Ten days would pass before the police arrested Ernest Miranda.

According to the journalist Liva Baker, it initially appeared that the case might never be solved. Mary Adams was not able to offer a good description of the car, and her description of the man did not contain any identifying marks that would set him apart from many men in their late twenties in Phoenix. Moreover, the police were a little skeptical that she had been raped. She had no bruises or marks from the ropes. Doctors found sperm in her vagina but claimed she was not a virgin. She gave sufficiently inconsistent stories about how much she resisted the rapist and about the route back from the desert that the police asked if she would take a lie detector test.[18] One of Mary's brothers-in-law told police that her statements were inconsistent and vague because she had a low IQ. The lie detector results "were inconclusive. The police sergeant who administered the test said there was some question of whether or not [Mary Adams] had taken medication prior to the examination; there was also some indication that she had lied in answering some of the questions."[19]

A break in the case came because her brother-in-law began walking her home from the bus stop. On March 9, he noticed an old Packard cruising the area near the bus stop, and he got the license number. Mary Adams said the Packard looked like the car in which she had been abducted. Police traced the car to a woman who was living with Ernest Miranda.[20]

Liva Baker has researched Ernest Miranda's life. He had "[s]ix arrests and four imprisonments of one kind or another between the ages of fourteen and eighteen."[21] He also received an undesirable discharge from the army after serving six of fifteen months "at hard labor in the post stockade" for being AWOL and for a "peeping Tom" offense.[22] After the army experience, he served nine months for car theft, moved in with a woman who was separated from her husband, and had a daughter with her.[23] On March 13, 1963, he was arrested for the rape of Mary Adams.

The police officers put Miranda into a lineup with "four other Mexican males, all approximately the same age and height, build."[24] The Arizona Supreme Court reported that Mary Adams "identified" Miranda "as the one who had perpetrated the acts against her."[25] Liva Baker's account is more circumspect on this point; she reports that Mary Adams said that Miranda "had similar build and features," but she could not positively identify him.[26]

The officers immediately began to interrogate Miranda, and he soon confessed. The oral confession, as recounted by the officers is, in relevant part, as follows:

> He saw this girl walking in the street, he said, so he decided he would pull up ahead of her and stop. He stopped and got out of his car and opened the back door of his automobile. He said when the girl approached him he told her, he said "Don't make any noise, and get into the car," and he said she got into the car, he said, in the back seat.

After getting into the car, he said he took a small piece of rope he had inside the car and he tied her hands and her ankles, then he got into the front seat behind the driver's wheel and he drove to a location several miles from there in the northeast direction to the area of a desert. . . .

He said then when he got there he noticed that the girl was untied, and he got into the back seat and he asked her if she would, or he told her to take her clothes off and she said, "No, would you please take me home?"

He said then he took her clothes off for her. After he had undressed her, she began to cry, and started begging him to not do this. She said she had never had any relations with a man before.

He said he went ahead and performed the act of intercourse, and in so doing was only able to get about a half inch of his penis in and at which time he said he did reach a climax, but he didn't believe that he had reached a climax inside of her.

He said after the act of intercourse, he then told her to get dressed and asked her where she lived. . . .[27]

Shortly afterwards, Ernest Miranda wrote out and signed the following statement:

Seen a girl walking up street stopped a little ahead of her got out of car walked towards her grabbed her by the arm and asked to get in the car. Got in car without force tied hands & ankles. Drove away for a few miles. Stopped asked to take clothes off. Did not, asked me to take her back home. I started to take clothes off her without any force, and with co-operation. Asked her to lay down and she did. Could not get penis into vagina got about ½ (half) inch in. Told her to get clothes back on. Drove her home. I couldn't say I was sorry for what I had done. But asked her to say a prayer for me.[28]

The top of the form contained a preprinted warning of rights, with a blank for the name of the person making the statement. This one read: "I, Ernest A. Miranda, do hereby swear that I make this statement voluntarily and of my own free will, with no threats, coercion, or promises of immunity, and with full knowledge of my legal rights, understanding any statement may be used against me."[29]

Later, at trial, one of the officers testifed that he read Miranda these rights, but his testimony is vague about precisely when the rights were read. It seems likely, from the context of the testimony, that the officer did not read Miranda these rights until he had already confessed orally (as the Supreme Court would assume in its *Miranda* opinion). Moreover, as the defense lawyer noted in questioning the officer, the statement of legal rights did not include the right to counsel, and the officer admitted that he had not told Miranda he had this right. The Supreme Court emphasized this omission.

The officer was on solid legal ground in 1963 in describing what he gave Miranda as his legal rights. Indeed, Ernest Miranda received more information about how his statement would be used than the Supreme Court had ever required in any case.

The Law

To understand the revolutionary nature of what was to come in *Miranda v. Arizona*, it is necessary to understand the original narrow scope of the Bill of Rights. In 1833, the Supreme Court ruled in *Barron v. Baltimore* that the protections contained in the Bill of Rights did not limit the power of state governments.[30] The Court's opinion was written by John Marshall, who served as Chief Justice from 1801 to 1835, a period in which the Supreme Court established its power against other branches of the federal government but not against the states. The Bill of Rights, the Court wrote in 1833, "demanded security against the apprehended encroachments of the general [federal] government—not against those of the local governments."[31]

The Court's decision in *Barron* meant, for example, that states were not required to grant free speech, freedom of the press, or freedom of religion. If a state wished, it could in 1834 have established a state religion and criminally punished anyone who deviated from that religion (subject, of course, to limitations that might be found in the state constitution and state laws).

Many guarantees of the Bill of Rights relate to the criminal process. The Supreme Court's 1833 ruling thus permitted states to conduct unreasonable searches and seizures, to refuse to allow a defendant to have a lawyer in court, and to refuse to provide a jury trial. If a state wished, it could have required defendants to testify before a judge who had sole authority to decide guilt or innocence. Moreover, a state could have barred a defendant from cross-examining the state's witnesses or putting forth any defense. States were trusted sovereigns in the federal scheme in 1834, and the Bill of Rights limited only the powers of the feared central government.

Distrust of the federal government was gradually replaced in the 1850s and 1860s with fear of losing the Union. If the Confederacy was permitted to leave the Union, then why not the western territories? Or even New England? Faced with the prospect of a "United States" consisting of several countries, Americans fought a bitter, costly war that finally produced union rather than division and separation.

One of the legal manifestations of unifying the country was the Fourteenth Amendment. Enacted in 1868, three years after the Civil War ended, the Fourteenth Amendment provides, "Nor shall any State deny any person life, liberty, or property without due process of law." States were no longer as sovereign as they were in 1834. They were now yoked by the Fourteenth Amendment.[32] For example, states could no longer deny a criminal defendant the right to present a defense, for this would surely constitute a denial of due process of law.

Slowly, the Supreme Court began to apply the Fourteenth Amendment's due process clause to forbid different types of state action. The first rights recognized to be a part of due process were those in the First Amendment—the rights of free speech and freedom of religion.[33] The first criminal procedure right to be considered part of due process was the right to counsel. In *Powell v. Alabama*,[34] the state had failed to provide counsel to the Scottsboro defendants, nine black youths tried and sentenced to death for raping two white women.[35] The Supreme Court held that due process of law included the right to counsel in some capital cases—at least those in which the defendants were young and illiterate, and thus presumptively incapable of defending themselves.

The Court reversed all the convictions in *Powell*, a fortunate outcome because later events indicated that the defendants were almost certainly innocent of the crime of rape. In what seems to be evidence of racism, Alabama juries reconvicted five of the defendants even after one of the "victims" admitted that no rape had taken place. Luckily, none of the defendants was executed, and all were eventually paroled or pardoned.[36]

Four years later, in 1936, the Court once again found that a state in the deep South had violated the due process rights of black defendants charged with a capital crime. In *Brown v. Mississippi*, the Court held that prolonged brutal beatings of three black suspects, and the threat of more beatings if they did not confess, violated the due process right not to be coerced into confessing.[37] All three suspects maintained their innocence. According to the dissenting opinion in the Supreme Court of Mississippi, one suspect was hanged, let down, hanged again, let down, tied to a tree and whipped. Still proclaiming his innocence, he was released, only to be picked up later by a deputy sheriff and severely whipped, the deputy saying the whippings would continue until he confessed. The suspect "then agreed to confess to such a statement as the deputy would dictate." Two other suspects were whipped until their backs "were cut to pieces" by a leather strap with buckles. They were made

> to understand that the whipping would continue until they confessed, and not only confessed, but confessed in every matter of detail as demanded by those present; and in this manner the defendants confessed the crime, and, as the whippings progressed and were repeated, they changed or adjusted their confessions in all particulars of detail so as to conform to the demands of their torturers.[38]

The only difficult feature of *Brown*, at least for modern readers, is in understanding how the Mississippi Supreme Court could have affirmed the convictions based on these "confessions." It was a simple matter for the U.S. Supreme Court to impose its will on the state court in a case like this. As the Court put it, "Because a state may dispense with a jury trial, it does not follow that it may substitute trial by ordeal. The rack and torture chamber may not be substituted for the witness stand."[39] But the Court otherwise moved slowly in the criminal procedure area, as can be seen by the Court's admission in *Brown* that states could refuse to provide jury trials. Over a period of half a century, the Court held that due process did not include the Fifth Amendment right to a grand jury indictment (in 1884), the Fifth Amendment privilege against self-incrimination (1908), or the right to be free from double jeopardy (1937).[40]

The Court also proceeded tentatively in deciding what types of police interrogation to forbid. The reason is not hard to understand: Society must ensure that police observe a minimum standard of decency in interrogating suspects, but the question of whether to suppress a confession is more complicated than whether the police treated the suspect with decency. A rational system of justice might sanction the police officer who violated standards of decency, or provide damages to the mistreated suspect, and still admit into evidence a truthful, reliable confession. After all, what is more important to society's fundamental interests: keeping a killer, robber, or rapist off the street, or making sure that the police do not bully a guilty suspect into confessing?

As America's greatest evidence scholar, John Henry Wigmore, noted early in the twentieth century, confessions are usually "the highest sort of evidence."[41] Assuming the confession is reliable—that it is not induced from a suspect who suffers from irrational thought and is not induced by methods likely to cause a rational person to give a false answer—it is trustworthy evidence of guilt from the mouth of the suspect. In addition to being reliable evidence, a confession also admits personal responsibility for the crime. "[I]t carries a persuasion which nothing else does, because a fundamental instinct of human nature teaches each one of us its significance."[42]

Brown held that torture and physical coercion would render a confession inadmissible, but few other kinds of police interrogation were barred in the post-*Brown* period. In the 1941 case of *Lisenba v. California*,[43] for example, the Court held admissible a confession produced as follows: The first period of incommunicado interrogation continued for forty-two hours, until the suspect fell asleep in his chair; during this interrogation, which occurred on private property rather than at the police station or prosecutor's office, the suspect was slapped at least once; a few days later, another interrogation lasted ten hours and ended only when the suspect said, "Can't we go out and get something to eat—if you fellows will take me out to eat now, I will tell you the story." The state courts and the Supreme Court concluded that the detention of the suspect constituted a felony under state law. Yet the confession was held admissible as the suspect's "free choice." The Court stressed the suspect's "self-possession," his "coolness," his "acumen" during questioning, which were sufficient to demonstrate that he had not "so lost his freedom of action that the statements made were not his but were the result of the deprivation of his free choice to admit, to deny, or to refuse to answer."[44]

The law of confessions and the Court have often used the word *voluntary* as a synonym for "free choice." A conceptual awkwardness exists, however, in the terminology of "involuntary confession" because every confession manifests, at least to some degree, the will of the confessor. As Wigmore put it, "As between the rack and a false confession, the latter would usually be considered the less disagreeable; but it is nonetheless voluntarily chosen. . . . All conscious verbal utterances are and must be voluntary."[45] Aristotle also noted the peculiarity of using "involuntary" to describe acts that manifest the will of the actor, though he was less dogmatic than Wigmore about the linguistic usage. Aristotle recognized that some choices seem less voluntary than others. Discussing acts that cause harm to the actor, he wrote, "Such acts, then, are voluntary; but perhaps in a general way they are involuntary, since no one would choose any such act of itself."[46]

For decades following *Brown v. Mississippi*, the Court sought a typology of police interrogation methods that would create a hierarchy of voluntariness and thus permit courts to draw the line between acceptable and unacceptable police methods. What evolved was a laundry list of factors to be considered. The list includes characteristics of the suspect (age, intelligence, education, country of birth, race, prior experience with the law, knowledge of rights, medical condition, psychological condition, and levels of intoxication, hunger, and sleep deprivation); characteristics of particular questions and answers (whether violence was used or threatened, whether promises of leniency were made or implied, whether trickery was used, whether the suspect was told of his right not to answer, whether the suspect asked for the interrogation to cease or to consult with counsel or a friend or family member); and characteristics of the interrogation (length of each session, number of sessions, intervals between sessions, number of questioners, frequency of food and bathroom breaks, provision of cigarettes or drugs to alleviate withdrawal symptoms, isolation of suspect from family or friends or a lawyer, a lawyer's attempt to communicate with the suspect, moving the suspect from one location to another). In short, as Joseph Grano remarked with characteristic insight, the Supreme Court created a voluntariness test that makes "everything relevant but nothing determinative."[47]

Powell and *Brown* were thus watershed cases less in the precise nature of what the Court held to be part of due process than in the idea that some state criminal procedures could be found to violate due process. The Court continued to move very slowly toward any kind of national standards in criminal procedure. In 1942, ten years after *Powell* found a due process right to counsel in some capital cases, the Court made it clear that this right did not exist in very many cases—only when a "special circumstance" about the case made the absence of counsel "a denial of fundamental fairness, shocking to the universal sense of justice."[48] In 1949, the Court held that a state defendant had no right to have the judge exclude evidence obtained in an unconstitutional search.[49] The so-called exclusionary rule had been required in federal court for unconstitutional searches since 1914.[50] The Court's refusal to require states also to exclude evidence seized in violation of the Fourth Amendment indicates that, despite the limited due process requirements of *Powell* and *Brown*, states were still largely sovereign in criminal procedure as the 1940s ended.

But the 1950s and 1960s brought a fundamental change in American society. While this change was not as wrenching as the Civil War a century before, the autonomy and sovereignty of states were eroded once again. And as before, the cause was largely the refusal of some states to provide full rights to black citizens. The 1950s ushered in both the civil rights movement and a broader concern about poverty and social injustice. Though both movements were directed at overt economic and social inequities, many state and local criminal justice authorities also practiced a form of discrimination against suspects, who were, after all, disproportionately poor and nonwhite.

In the 1950s and 1960s the nation saw the bitter fruit of the Supreme Court's refusal to impose national standards on states in most areas of criminal procedure. Defendants charged with state crimes could not suppress evidence that was seized in violation of the Fourth Amendment, even if the police used highly intrusive means.[51] Nor did the vast majority of indigent defendants have a lawyer at trial; the state-paid prosecutor proceeded against a virtually helpless defendant. Finally, state defendants had little confession law on their side. Cases from the 1940s allowed police to question suspects in relays, sometimes for over twenty-four hours, and to deny requests to consult with counsel.[52]

In a culture that tolerated overt racism, as did much of the United States in the 1950s, the lack of rights in the criminal process weighed most heavily on blacks, and particularly southern blacks. In 1966, Herbert Packer wrote, "What we have seen in the South is the perversion of the criminal process into an instrument of official oppression. . . . Powers of arrest and prosecution have been repeatedly and flagrantly abused in the interest of maintaining an illegal, not to say unconstitutional, social system."[53]

Finding a solution to racial discrimination and oppression was an important national goal in the late 1950s and early 1960s. Solutions that varied from state to state were unacceptable; a uniform policy was required. State sovereignty once again would have to be sacrificed for the national good.

A uniform, national solution to racial discrimination began to take shape. *Brown v. Board of Education* held segregated public schools unconstitutional in 1954,[54] and pressure was building in Congress for laws guaranteeing blacks equal access to goods and services and the right to vote. During this period, the Court began to take another look at state criminal procedures. Federal defendants had the right to suppress unlawfully seized evidence, and indigent federal defendants had a right to appointed counsel in every case. Moreover, though not required to do so by law, the FBI warned federal suspects that they did not have to answer questions and could consult with a lawyer before answering if they chose.

If these rights and practices defined fair procedures in the federal system, why were state defendants deprived of similar procedures? The state sovereignty argument, powerful in 1834, had been steadily losing force. By 1961, only three years before the Civil Rights Act of 1964, state sovereignty did not seem as important as a uniform standard for at least some aspects of criminal procedure. That was the year the Court decided *Mapp v. Ohio*.[55]

In *Mapp*, the Court overruled its earlier case refusing to apply the exclusionary rule to the states. *Mapp* held that due process required the exclusion in state court of evidence seized in violation of the Fourth Amendment. Roughly half the states had rejected the exclusionary rule as an interpretation of their state constitutions.[56] Despite this demonstration of a contrary state view, the Supreme Court brushed aside state sovereignty in the interest of a uniform national policy about how best to remedy Fourth Amendment violations.

Two years later, the Court modified its course on the right to counsel, holding in *Gideon v. Wainwright* that every indigent felony defendant had an absolute right to counsel at state expense.[57] The next year, the Court overruled the 1908 precedent and held that the Fifth Amendment privilege against self-incrimination was part of due process.[58] States could not compel a witness to testify and later use that compelled testimony in a criminal case against the witness. This case involved what Yale Kamisar calls the "mansion" or courtroom application of the privilege against self-incrimination.[59]

The self-incrimination clause by its terms appears to apply *only* to the courtroom: "No person . . . shall be compelled in any criminal case to be a witness against himself."[60] Scholars and courts gave the words their natural reading, concluding that one is not compelled to be a witness in a criminal case unless one is compelled to testify *in the courtroom*. The police interrogation problem was governed by the due process "voluntariness" test, not by the Fifth Amendment privilege against self-incrimination.

Police interrogation remained nettlesome. From 1957 to 1963, the Supreme Court reviewed ten state court cases that had upheld convictions based on voluntary confessions.[61] The Court reversed eight of the ten cases,[62] indicating that it was not satisfied with the way the state courts were applying the voluntariness test. The problem was, at least in large part, the flaccid nature of the voluntariness test. In a world that recognizes the complexity of human will and the many overlapping forces that act on it, deciding when a suspect in a police interrogation room voluntarily confesses is sometimes a philosophical or psychological problem of the first magnitude. In 1961 the Court sought to clarify the problem in *Culombe v. Connecticut*.[63] Justice Frankfurter, acknowledged as one of the most intellectually gifted Justices, wrote a sixty-seven-page opinion intended to give guidance to the state courts. Frankfurter designed his voluntariness standard as a three-phased process that combined philosophy, psychology, and law:

> First, there is the business of finding the crude, historical facts, the external "phenomenological" occurrences and events surrounding the confession. Second, because the concept of voluntariness is one which concerns a mental state, there is the imaginative recreation, largely inferential, of internal, "psychological" fact. Third, there is the application to this psychological fact of standards for judgment informed by the larger legal conceptions ordinarily characterized as rules of law but which, also, comprehend both induction from, and anticipation of, factual circumstances.[64]

If this standard was not difficult enough for trial judges to apply, the problem did not end in the trial court. Appellate judges had to comb the record in search of the dozens of potentially relevant facts by which to evaluate the trial court's "imaginative recreation" and application of a fact-dependent rule of law. Frankfurter's effort to clarify matters was doomed to failure. One example is *Culombe* itself; only Justice Stewart joined Frankfurter's opinion announcing the Court's judgment. Moreover, to apply his framework to the facts of the case before the Court took Frankfurter thirty-four pages—nineteen pages to describe the phenomenological facts and fifteen pages to infer psychological facts and apply the legal standard.[65]

Chief Justice Warren, who would later write *Miranda*, refused to join Frankfurter's opinion, calling it a "lengthy and abstract dissertation."[66] Ironically, the case in which the Court sought to give guidance to the lower courts divided the Justices and put in high relief the problems with the voluntariness test. Three years later, in *Escobedo v. Illinois*,[67] the Court tried a different tack. Perhaps police pressure and overreaching could be controlled by a Sixth Amendment right to counsel during police interrogation. The facts of the case disclosed that Danny Escobedo was a prime suspect being interrogated by the police, that he asked to speak to his lawyer, that his lawyer was present and trying to see Escobedo, that state law gave Escobedo the right to speak to his lawyer, and that over a three-hour period the police consistently refused to let the lawyer talk to Escobedo.

The Court's opinion in *Escobedo* was filled with stirring phrases about the value of the Anglo-American system in which the government bears the burden of proving the guilt of the accused. Implicit in our "accusatorial" system is the principle that the accused need do or say nothing, and that the authorities should ideally build their cases without depending on confessions. As the Court put it:

> Our Constitution, unlike some others, strikes the balance in favor of the right of the accused to be advised by his lawyer of his privilege against self-incrimination.
>
> We have learned the lesson of history, ancient and modern, that a system of criminal law enforcement which comes to depend on the "confession" will, in the long run, be less reliable and more subject to abuses than a system which depends on extrinsic evidence independently secured through skillful investigation. . . .
>
> We have also learned the companion lesson of history that no system of criminal justice can, or should, survive if it comes to depend for its continued effectiveness on the citizens' abdication through unawareness of their constitutional rights. No system worth preserving should have to fear that if an accused is permitted to consult with a lawyer, he will become aware of, and exercise, these rights. If the exercise of constitutional rights will thwart the effectiveness of a system of law enforcement, then there is something very wrong with that system.[68]

Law prides itself on precision. Courts generally phrase the rule of the case narrowly to fit the facts. Although there was some dispute among scholars, the most narrow (and thus most likely) reading of *Escobedo* was that a suspect had a right to consult with counsel when

> (1) the investigation has begun to focus on a particular defendant and is no longer a general inquiry into an unsolved crime; (2) the suspect is in police custody; (3) interrogation by the police is aimed at eliciting incriminating statements; (4) the suspect has requested and been denied an opportunity to secure advice from counsel; and (5) the police fail to warn the suspect effectively of his constitutional rights to remain silent.[69]

If that was the rule of *Escobedo*, Ernest Miranda had no right to counsel in the Phoenix police station interrogation room on March 13,

1963.[69] The Arizona Supreme Court agreed, reading *Escobedo* narrowly: "It will be noted in the discussion of these cases—particularly the *Escobedo* case—the ruling of the court is based upon the circumstances of the particular case. . . . The *Escobedo* case merely points out factors under which—if all exist—[a confession] would not be admissible." The court then noted, "Each case must largely turn upon its own facts," and held that the facts of Miranda's case did not show a constitutional violation.[71]

Escobedo had been an attempt to prevent what the Court saw as unfair police interrogation. The Court clearly thought it unfair to deny a suspect's specific request to consult with his lawyer. In the Court's view, this refusal smacked of incommunicado interrogation and police overreaching. Police and prosecutors were concerned that courts would read *Escobedo* broadly and require lawyers in many, or most, interrogations. But the Arizona Supreme Court (and virtually all other courts) read *Escobedo* narrowly, the way courts usually read precedent. If the U.S. Supreme Court wanted to open the police interrogation room further, if it wanted to minimize what it saw as trickery, deception, and pressure that traded on the ignorance and fear of poor, mostly minority suspects, *Escobedo* would have to be expanded.

The case of Ernest Miranda gave the Supreme Court precisely that opportunity. But what theory would the Court use? *Escobedo* was based on the Sixth Amendment right to counsel, but it was quite a stretch to apply the Sixth Amendment to the police interrogation room. The Sixth Amendment by its words applies to "all criminal prosecutions." How could it be a "criminal prosecution" to interrogate suspects who (in the vast majority of cases) have not been charged with a crime?

The *Escobedo* Court held that the "criminal prosecution" requirement was satisfied because the police investigation had "focused" on Danny Escobedo, making interrogation analogous to a criminal prosecution. But none of the Court's other Sixth Amendment cases had ever suggested that a criminal prosecution could begin without some sort of document that accused the defendant of a crime. Moreover, the "focus" test of *Escobedo* invited endless litigation about whether suspects were the focus of police investigation. Did "focus" depend on an officer's subjective belief about whether a suspect committed a crime, on the objective facts about the stage of an investigation, or only on the facts known to the police? Did it matter whether other suspects existed? Did "focus" require probable cause or a lower standard of probability? Did a suspect have to be aware that he was the focus of an investigation? If more than one officer questioned a suspect, did it matter if some but not all of the officers had focused their investigation on him?

The standard test for confessions in 1964 was whether the suspect "voluntarily" confessed. As we have seen, one reason the Court was looking for a new test was that the "voluntariness" inquiry often did not produce clear answers. Not much about arrest and interrogation is voluntary; on the other hand, if the police do not coerce a suspect to answer questions, his decision to answer seems voluntary, at least in the sense that he chose to answer rather than remaining silent.

If the Court was to regulate police interrogation more effectively, it needed a clean test that did not require litigation about "focus" on the suspect or the often excruciating metaphysical inquiry into whether the suspect had confessed "voluntarily." A right to counsel for all suspects being interrogated might do the trick. To retain the "focus" requirement of *Escobedo* would likely create a doctrine as complex and baroque as had resulted from the voluntariness test. But to abolish the "focus" requirement would sever the conceptual link to the Sixth Amendment (which applies only when the process has become a "criminal prosecution"). Even the Warren Court of 1966, at the height of the "due process revolution,"[72] was too conservative for such a bold move. Courts have institutional authority to interpret, not make, the law. Federal courts are particularly loathe to limit what state courts can do; they must find a justification in the U.S. Constitution. If the "focus" requirement from *Escobedo* were abandoned, the Court could no longer rely on the Sixth Amendment right to counsel.

What the Court needed was a new test and a new constitutional justification. The justification was handed them in 1965, a year after *Escobedo*, when Yale Kamisar published his classic essay, "Equal Justice in the Gatehouses and Mansions of American Criminal Procedure."[73] The key to the new approach was in recognizing that police interrogation often makes irrelevant the constitutional protections that attend the trial.

Once Ernest Miranda's trial began, the rules about asking him questions were very different from the rules governing the police interrogation. In the courtroom, he had a right not to testify, a right to have a lawyer offer him advice about testifying, a right to have a lawyer keep the state from taking advantage of him if he did testify, and a judge to oversee the questioning. In the police interrogation room, Ernest Miranda had none of these rights. He had the right not to be forced into giving an involuntary confession, but nothing more. The Court had *never* directly applied the self-incrimination clause to the interrogation room.

But why not?

NOTES

1. Except where otherwise noted, all the facts presented in this section come from the opinion of the Arizona Supreme Court in State v. Miranda, 401 P.2d 721 (1965). I will cite a specific part of the court's opinion only when quoting from it.

2. This is not her real name, which does not appear in the public court records.

3. Statistical Abstract 25 (Dep't Commerce 1980) showing population in 1960 as 439,000 and in 1970 as 582,000).

4. FBI Uniform Crime Reports 155 table 49 (1963).

5. Liva Baker, *Miranda*: Crime, Law and Politics 3, 5 (1983).

6. *Id.* at 5.

7. 401 P.2d at 722.

8. Baker, *supra* note 5, at 1.

9. 401 P.2d at 723.

10. *Id.*

11. Baker, *supra* note 5, at 4.

12. 401 P.2d at 726.

13. This dialogue is from Baker, *supra* note 5, at 4. That Mary Adams said she had never had sex with a man before is stated in 401 P.2d at 726.

14. 401 P.2d at 723.

15. *Id.*

16. This conversation was attributed to Ernest Miranda by the police interrogators. *Id.* at 726.

17. *Id.* at 723.

18. Baker, *supra* note 5, at 5–7, 9.

19. *Id.* at 7–8.

20. *Id.* at 8–9.

21. *Id.* at 10.

22. *Id.*

23. *Id.* at 11.

24. 401 P.2d at 726.

25. *Id.*

26. Baker, *supra* note 5, at 12.

27. 401 P.2d at 726.

28. *Id.*

29. *Id.* at 727.

30. Barron v. Baltimore, 7 Peters 243 (1833).

31. *Id.* at 250.

32. Two other Civil War amendments also limited the power of states, though in much more discrete and narrow areas. The Thirteenth Amendment prohibits "slavery [and] involuntary servitude, within the United States," which obviously includes all states. The Fifteenth Amendment protects the right to vote from being "abridged by the United States or any State on account of race, color, or previous condition of servitude."

33. Gitlow v. New York, 268 U.S. 652 (1925).

34. 287 U.S. 45 (1932).

35. The trial judge appointed the entire local bar to represent defendants, and then permitted an out-of-state lawyer to assist in the case. The Supreme Court characterized this appointment of counsel as "little more than an expansive gesture, imposing no substantial or definite obligations upon any one." *Id.* at 56.

36. One of the defendants escaped from prison in 1947 and was apprehended in Michigan three years later; Michigan Governor G. Mennan Williams refused Alabama Governor Jim Folsom's request for extradition. For an excellent account of the many trials, reversals, retrials, and prison time served by five of the defendants, see James Goodman, Stories of Scottsboro (1994).

37. 297 U.S. 278 (1936).

38. *Id.* at 282 (quoting the dissent in the state court opinion, 161 So. at 470–71).

39. *Id.* at 285–86.

40. Hurtado v. California, 110 U.S. 516 (1884); Twining v. New Jersey, 211 U.S. 78 (1908); Palko v. Connecticut, 302 U.S. 319 (1937).

41. John Henry Wigmore, A Treatise on the Anglo-American System of Evidence §866 (2d ed. 1923).

42. *Id.*

43. 314 U.S. 214 (1941).

44. *Id.* at 241.

45. Wigmore, *supra* note 41, at §824.

46. Aristotle, Ethics Bk III, §1 (A. E. Wardman & J. L. Creed trans., 1963). I have previously called this conundrum "Aristotle's paradox." See George C. Thomas III & Marshall D. Bilder, *Aristotle's Paradox and the Self-Incrimination Puzzle*, 82 J. Crim. L. & Criminology 243 (1991).

47. Joseph D. Grano, Miranda v. Arizona *and the Legal Mind: Formalism's Triumph Over Substance and Reason*, 24 Am. Crim. L. Rev. 243 (1986).

48. Betts v. Brady, 316 U.S. 455, 462 (1942).

49. Wolf v. Colorado, 338 U.S. 25 (1949).

50. Weeks v. United States, 232 U.S. 383 (1914).

51. To be sure, physically intrusive searches could violate due process and require suppression of evidence without regard to the Fourth Amendment. In Rochin v. California, 342 U.S. 165 (1952), police choked Rochin to keep him from swallowing contraband. When that failed, they took him to the hospital and ordered his stomach pumped. The Supreme Court held that this physical intrusion "shocked the conscience" and thus violated due process. Most Fourth Amendment cases fall far short of the *Rochin* standard.

52. Lisenba v. California, 314 U.S. 219 (1941).

53. Herbert L. Packer, *The Courts, the Police, and the Rest of Us*, 57 J. Crim. L. & Criminology 238, 240 (1966).

54. 347 U.S. 483 (1954).

55. 367 U.S. 643 (1961).

56. *Id.* at 651.

57. 372 U.S. 335 (1942).

58. Malloy v. Hogan, 378 U.S. 1 (1964), *overruling* Twining v. New Jersey, 211 U.S. 78 (1908).

59. See Chapter 2.

60. U.S. Const. amend. V.

61. Haynes v. Washington, 373 U.S. 503 (1963); Lynum v. Illinois, 372 U.S. 528 (1963); Columbe v. Connecticut, 367 U.S. 568 (1961); Rogers v. Richmond, 365 U.S. 534 (1961); Blackburn v. Alabama, 361 U.S. 199 (1960); Spano v. New York, 360 U.S. 315 (1959); Crooker v. California, 357 U.S. 433 (1958); Payne v. Arkansas, 356 U.S. 560 (1958); Thomas v. Arizona, 356 U.S. 390 (1958); Fikes v. Alabama, 352 U.S. 191 (1957).

62. The two cases not reversed were Crooker v. California, 357 U.S. 433 (1958), and Thomas v. Arizona, 356 U.S. 390 (1958).

63. 367 U.S. 568 (1961).

64. *Id.* (opinion of Court by Frankfurter, J.).

65. See George C. Thomas III, *A Philosophical Account of Coerced Self-Incrimination*, 5 Yale J. L. & Human. 79 (1993).

66. 367 U.S. at 636 (Warren, C.J., concurring).

67. 378 U.S. 478 (1964).

68. *Id.* at 489–90.

69. Yale Kamisar, Police Interrogation and Confessions 161 n.26 (1980).

70. There were two grounds to deny Miranda support from *Escobedo*. One was that Miranda's interrogation took place before *Escobedo* was decided. The other, which the Arizona Supreme Court used, was to distinguish *Escobedo* as not being applicable to the facts of Miranda's case.

71. 401 P.2d at 733.

72. Fred Graham, *Miranda:* The Self-Inflicted Wound 157 (1970).

73. See Chapter 2.

2

Equal Justice
in the
Gatehouses and Mansions
of American
Criminal Procedure:
From *Powell* to *Gideon*,
from *Escobedo* to . . .
(1965)

•

YALE KAMISAR

. . . I proceed on the premise that we can know the bad without knowing the perfectly good; we can spot injustices "without committing ourselves to declare with finality what perfect justice would be like."[1] If, for example, important consequences flow from a suspect's request for counsel, all suspects should be made aware that they may make such a request. This, it seems to me, is the force of the doctrine that fundamental rights are only to be waived "understandingly and knowingly," "unequivocally and specifically." If, to take another example, Supreme Court precedents or bar association clamor or public opinion preclude shutting retained counsel out of the interrogation room, systems must be devised to enable a member of the public defender's staff or other assigned counsel to enter, too. At least with regard to a matter so important, so pervasive, this is the point of "Fourteenth Amendment equality." That we can never achieve absolute equality between rich and poor is hardly a good reason not to strive for proximate equality.

The Show in the Gatehouse vs. the Show in the Mansion

Back in the early 1940s—and that is the stone age as far as the history of American constitutional-criminal procedure is concerned—even as far back as then, the Supreme Court of the United States was finding

2 5

support for its "involuntary" confession rule in the image of the accusatorial, adversary trial:

> The concept of due process would void a trial in which by threats or promises in the presence of court and jury, a defendant was induced to testify against himself. The case can stand no better if, by resort to the same means, the defendant is induced to confess and his confession is given in evidence.[2]

In another case the Court said:

> It is inconceivable that any court of justice in the land, conducted as our courts are, open to the public, would permit prosecutors serving in relays to keep a defendant witness under continuous cross-examination for thirty-six hours without rest or sleep in an effort to extract a "voluntary" confession. Nor can we, consistently with Constitutional due process of law, hold voluntary a confession where prosecutors do the same thing away from the restraining influences of a public trial in an open court room.[3]

Measuring the performance in the "interrogation" room against the standard of a public trial may be a stylish way to write an opinion once the matter has been resolved in favor of the defendant, but until now, at any rate, it has not been the way to resolve the matter. If it *were*, if the image of the accusatorial, adversary trial were the basis for judgment, not merely the language of decision, then all the due process confession cases which have reached the Court would have been reversed *per curiam* [a short opinion "of the court," used in cases that do not raise difficult issues—Eds.]. For amid all the sound and fury one point is plain: In the absence of judge and jury, law enforcement officers can—and without hesitation do—resort to methods they would never consider utilizing at the trial. . . .

In the courtroom, the conflict of interest between the accused and the state is mediated by an impartial judge; in the police station, although the same conflict exists in more aggravated form, "the law" passes it by. In the courtroom, a reporter takes down everything; in the police station, there is usually no objective recordation of the events, leading to inevitable disputes over what the police did, or what the suspect said, or both. In the courtroom, the defendant is presumed innocent; in the police station, the proceedings usually begin: "All right—we know you're guilty; come through and it'll be easier for you."

In the courtroom, now that *Gideon* is on the books [*Gideon v. Wainwright*, 372 U.S. 335 (1942), guarantees the right to counsel in felony cases—Eds.], if and when the defendant takes the stand, his lawyer is at his side, not only to shield him from oppressive or tricky cross-examination which angers, upsets, or confuses him, but to guide him on direct examination; in the police station the suspect neither has nor (usually) is advised of his right to get counsel. Indeed, leading police manuals emphasize that generally it is unnecessary for an interrogator to warn an offender of his constitutional rights before obtaining his confession.

In the courtroom, not only need the accused answer no questions, he may not be asked any (unless he chooses to take the stand); in the police station, even if the suspect is that rare and troublesome type who *knows of* (he is not likely to be told) and *insists on* his right to remain silent, his interrogators simply will not let him: "The problem . . . is to get him to talk, to convert him into a willing subject . . . to find the reason for his reluctance or inability [to talk] and overcome that reason."[4] One technique is to pretend to concede him the right to remain silent and then, after some "psychological conditioning" and after pointing out "the incriminating significance of his refusal to talk," to ask him "innocuous questions that have no bearing whatever on the matter under investigation. . . . As a rule the subject will answer such questions, and then gradually the examiner may start in with questions pertaining to the offense."[5]

In the courtroom, we are much concerned about the inability of the accused—going it alone—to tell his story effectively; in the police station, evidently we are untroubled that the "subject" may never be given a real chance to tell his story, albeit in his own fumbling way; his adversaries are trained to allude to a particular piece of incriminating evidence, then "cut off immediately any explanation the subject may start to offer at that time . . . for [otherwise the subject] is putting the interrogator on the defensive and this should never be permitted to occur."[6]

In the courtroom, to prevent a defendant's lawyer from guiding him on direct examination constitutes a per se violation of "fundamental fairness." Why? "The tensions of a trial" may make him "unfit to give his explanation properly and completely" without the aid of counsel.[7] Even though he has consulted with counsel *before* he takes the stand, even though his lawyer and family and friends are present, "when the average defendant is placed in the witness chair and told . . . that nobody can ask him any questions, and that he may make such statement to the jury as he sees proper in his own defense, he has been set adrift in an uncharted sea with nothing to guide him"; he may be "overwhelmed by his situation, and embarrassed"; "it will not be surprising if his explanation is incoherent, or if it overlooks important circumstances."[8]

In the police station, to prevent a "subject's" lawyer from guiding him on "direct examination"—to say nothing of protecting him from improper cross-examination—is not to violate "fundamental fairness." Why not? Torn from his home, his friends, and his neighbors, feeling himself "at the mercy of . . . custodians [who] have strong incentives for seeking a quick solution of probative problems by pressing [him] to acknowledge his guilt,"[9] never allowed to "bolster his confidence,"[10] advised that his interrogators have "all the time in the world,"[11] warned that he "can't win,"[12] the tensions are surely no less, incomplete and incoherent explanations hardly more surprising.

Indeed, as the late Justice Jackson (unsuccessfully seeking to sustain the products of a thirty-six-hour interrogation) readily admitted, "of course" custody and detention of a prisoner—even "for an hour"—is "'inherently coercive.' . . . Arrest itself is inherently coercive, and so is detention. . . . Of course such acts put pressure upon the prisoner to answer questions . . . and to confess if guilty."[13]

For a long time, too long, we have operated on the premise that, as Professor Arthur E. Sutherland recently put it, "a man with his life at stake should be able to surrender an ancient constitutional right to remain silent, under compulsions which in a surrender of a little property would obviously make the transaction void."[14] Asks Professor Sutherland:

> Suppose a well-to-do testatrix who says she intends to will her property to Elizabeth. John and James want her to bequeath it to them instead. They capture the proposed testatrix, put her in a carefully designed room, out of touch with everyone but themselves and their convenient "witnesses," keep her secluded there for hours while they make insistent demands, continual or intermittent, weary her with contradictions of her assertions that she wants to leave her money to Elizabeth, and finally get her to execute the will in their favor. Assume, further, that John and James are deeply and correctly convinced that Elizabeth is unworthy and will make base use of the property if she gets her hands on it, whereas John and James have the noblest and most righteous intentions. Would any judge of probate accept the will so procured as the "voluntary" act of the testatrix?[15]

Writing for the majority in a famous confession case some fifteen years ago [in 1949], Justice Frankfurter assured us:

Ours is the accusatorial as opposed to the inquisitorial system. Such has been the characteristic of Anglo-American criminal justice since it freed itself from practices borrowed by the Star Chamber. . . . Under our system society carries the burden of proving its charge against the accused not out of his own mouth. It must establish its case, not by interrogation of the accused even under judicial safeguards, but by evidence independently secured through skillful investigation.[16]

"Under our system society carries the burden of proving its charge against the accused not out of his own mouth." This is "the law" that students eagerly take down in their notebooks—those students, that is, "who do not wish to be confronted with the confused picture of what is actually going on."[17] "[N]ot by interrogation of the accused, *even* under judicial safeguards [emphasis added]. . . ." This connotes, and logic (if not justice) would seem to dictate, *a fortiori*, not by interrogation of the accused without judicial safeguards. But this is not, and long has not been, the case.

Police interrogators may now hurl "jolting questions" where once they swung telephone books, may now "play on the emotions" where once they resorted to physical violence, but it is no less true today than it was thirty years ago that

[i]n every city our police hold what can only be called outlaw tribunals,— informal and secret inquisitions of arrested persons,—which are, terminology aside, actual and very vigorous trials for crime. . . . Centering all upon the confession, proud of it, staking everything upon it, the major canon of American police work is based upon the nullification of the most truly libertarian clause of the Fifth Amendment. . . . The legal courts come into operation only after the police are through; they are reduced to the position of merely ratifying the plea of guilt which the police have obtained, or else holding trials over the minor percentage of arrested persons about whom the police could reach no conclusion. . . . The inquisition held by the police before trial is the outstanding feature of American criminal justice, though no statute recognizes its existence.[18]

The courtroom is a splendid place where defense attorneys bellow and strut and prosecuting attorneys are hemmed in at many turns. But what happens before an accused reaches the safety and enjoys the comfort of this veritable mansion? Ah, there's the rub. Typically he must first pass through a much less pretentious edifice, a police station with bare back rooms and locked doors.

In this "gatehouse" of American criminal procedure[19]—through which most defendants journey and beyond which many never get—the enemy of the state is a depersonalized "subject" to be "sized up" and subjected to "interrogation tactics and techniques most appropriate for the occasion";[20] he is "game" to be stalked and cornered.[21] Here ideals are checked at the door, "realities" faced, and the prestige of law enforcement vindicated. Once he leaves the "gatehouse" and enters the "mansion"—if he ever gets there—the enemy of the state is repersonalized, even dignified, the public invited, and a stirring ceremony in honor of individual freedom from law enforcement celebrated.

I suspect it is not so much that society knows and approves of the show in the gatehouse, but that society does not know or care. True, the man in the street would have considerable difficulty explaining why the Constitution requires so much in the courtroom and means so little in the police station, but that is not his affair. "The task of keeping the two shows going at the same time without losing the patronage or the support of the Constitution for either," as Thurman Arnold once observed, is "left to the legal scholar."[22] Perhaps this is only fitting and proper, for as Thomas Reed Powell used to say, if you can think about something that is related to something else without thinking about the thing to which it is related, then you have the legal mind.[23]

That the legal mind passes by or shuts out the *de facto* inquisitorial system which has characterized our criminal procedure for so long is bad enough. What is worse is that such an attitude leads many—perhaps requires many—to recoil with horror and dismay at any proposal which recognizes the grim facts of the criminal process and seeks to do something about them. . . .

As a judge of the Supreme Court of South Africa recently observed, despite "a great deal of emotional writing which elevates the privilege against self-incrimination to 'one of the great landmarks in man's struggle to make himself civilized,'[24] the most abundant proof" that it does not prohibit pretrial interrogation

is to be found in the United States. There the privilege is in the Federal Constitution and in some form or other in the constitutions of all but two of the fifty states. . . . But in none of the forty-nine jurisdictions does it apply to what happens in the police station. The police interrogate freely, sometimes for seven to eight hours on end. The statements thus extracted are given in evidence. There is the provision that only statements made voluntarily may be given in evidence, but that seems to be interpreted rather liberally, judged by our standards.[25]

Four score years ago, Sir James Fitzjames Stephen noted with pride that the fact that "the prisoner is absolutely protected against all judicial questioning before or at the trial . . . contributes greatly to the dignity and apparent humanity of a criminal trial. It effectually avoids the appearance of harshness, not to say cruelty, which often shocks an English spectator in a French court of justice." [26] Whatever the case then, one would have to underscore "apparent" and "appearance" in that statement today. Stephen also told us that "the fact that the prisoner cannot be questioned stimulates the search for independent evidence." [27] Whatever the case then, one cannot but wonder today how often the only thing "stimulated" by the inability of judicial officers to question a prisoner is questioning by police officers. One cannot but wonder how often the availability of the privilege (or, perhaps more aptly, the inability of the State to undermine the privilege), once the accused reaches the safety and comfort of the mansion, only furnishes the State with an additional incentive for proving the charge against him out of his own mouth before he leaves the gatehouse.

Is the Privilege Checked at the "Gatehouse" Door?

Those who would not narrow the gap between the nobility of the principles we purport to cherish and the meanness of the station house proceedings we permit to continue may:

(1) Cite the language in the Fifth Amendment which forbids compelling any person "to be a witness against himself" "in any criminal case" and contend that in the police station the "criminal case" has not yet commenced. But it is hornbook law that the privilege extends to all judicial or official hearings where persons may be called upon to give testimony, even to civil proceedings.

(2) Find some comfort in the assertion by the greatest master of the law of evidence, Wigmore, that the privilege against self-incrimination "covers only statements made in court under process as a witness." [28] As other masters of the subject have pointed out, however, this is an "obviously inaccurate" statement; [29] indeed it is in direct conflict with Wigmore's earlier declaration that the privilege applies "in investigations by a *grand jury*, in investigations by a *legislature* or a body having legislative functions, and in investigations by *administrative* officials." [30]

(3) Remind us (a) that the histories of the privilege and of the rule excluding "involuntary" confessions are "wide apart, differing by one hun-

dred years in origin, and derived through separate lines of precedents";
if the privilege, fully established by 1680, had sufficed for both classes
of cases, there would have been no need for creating the distinct rule
about confessions";[31] (b) that until recently, at any rate, the privilege
has never been applicable to police interrogation and "all of the decisions admitting coerced statements of incriminating facts not amount-
ing to a confession assume that the privilege is inapplicable, as does
the constant recognition of the accepted police practice which, in the
absence of statute, does not require that the accused be warned he
need not answer."[32] Here, as elsewhere, to look to "history" is to see
"through a screen of human values that gives importance to some
antecedents and relegates others to obscurity"; is to be less impressed
with historical facts "which do not fit into our theories . . . than [with]
those that do."[33] . . .

Nor should it be forgotten that for many centuries there were simply
no "police interrogators" to whom the privilege could be applied. Although what Dean Wigmore calls "the first part" of the history of the
privilege, the opposition to the ex-officio oath of the ecclesiastical courts,
began in the 1200s, "criminal investigation by the police, with its con-
comitant of police interrogation, is a product of the late nineteenth century";[34] in eighteenth-century America as in eighteenth-century England "there were no police [in the modern sense] and, though some
states seem to have had prosecutors, private prosecution was the rule
rather than the exception."[35] In fact as well as in theory, observes Professor Edmund M. Morgan, "there can be little question that the modern American police have taken over the functions performed originally
by the English committing magistrates [and at least by some colonial
magistrates]; they are in a real sense administrative officers and their
questioning of the person under arrest is an investigative proceeding in
which testimony is taken."[36] If modern police are permitted to interrogate under the coercive influence of arrest and secret detention, then,
insists Professor Albert R. Beisel, "they are doing the very same acts
which historically the judiciary was doing in the seventeenth century
but which the privilege against self-incrimination abolished."[37]

I do not contend that "the implication[s] of a tangled and obscure history"[38] dictate that the privilege apply to the police station, only that
they permit it. I do not claim that this long and involved history dis-
places judgment, only that it liberates it. I do not say that the distinct
origins of the confession and self-incrimination rules are irrelevant, only
that it is more important (if we share Dean Charles T. McCormick's

views) that "the kinship of the two rules is too apparent for denial"[39] and that "such policy as modern writers are able to discover as a basis for the self-crimination privilege . . . pales to a flicker beside the flaming demands of justice and humanity for protection against extorted confessions."[40]

NOTES

1. See Lon L. Fuller, The Morality of Law 11–12 (1964).

2. Lisenba v. California, 314 U.S. 219, 237 (1941).

3. Ashcraft v. Tennessee, 322 U.S. 143, 154 (1944).

4. William Dienstein, Technics for the Crime Investigator 98 (1952).

5. Fred E. Inbau & John E. Reid, Criminal Interrogation and Confessions 111–12 (1962).

6. *Id.* at 27.

7. Ferguson v. Georgia, 365 U.S. 570, 594 (1961).

8. *Id.* at 593–96.

9. John MacArther Maguire, Evidence of Guilt 109 (1959).

10. Inbau & Reid, *supra* note 5, at 27.

11. *Id.* at 109.

12 Dienstein, *supra* note 4, at 112.

13. Ashcraft v. Tennessee, 322 U.S. 143, 161 (1944) (Jackson, J., dissenting).

14. Arthur E. Sutherland, *Crime and Confession*, 79 Harv. L. Rev. [21, 37] (1965).

15. *Id.*

16. Watts v. Indiana, 338 U.S. 49, 54 (1949).

17. Thurman W. Arnold, The Symbols of Government 53 (Harbinger ed. 1962).

18. Ernest J. Hopkins, *The Lawless Arm of the Law*, Atlantic Monthly, Sep. 1931, at 279, 280–81.

19. If memory serves, this gatehouse (or was it outhouse?) and mansion terminology, or something like it, was utilized by Dean Claude Sowle in his remarks at a Northwestern University Law School conference on November 15–16, 1962. Unfortunately, on the erroneous premise that these remarks would later be published, I took no notes on the occasion, and when I began to prepare this essay I discovered that Dean Sowle had destroyed his.

20. Inbau & Reid, *supra* note 5, at 20.

21. Fred E. Inbau & John E. Reid, Lie Detection and Criminal Interrogation 185 (3d ed. 1953). The authors have dropped this graphic language from their later work.

22. Arnold, *supra* note 17, at 156.

23. So reported (in a somewhat different form) in Lon L. Fuller, *supra* note 1, at 4, and Paul A. Freund, *Rationality in Judicial Decisions*, *in* Nomos VII: Rational Decision (Carl J. Friedrich ed. 1964), at 116.

24. V. G. Hiemstra, *Abolition of the Right Not to Be Questioned*, 80 S. Afr. L.J. 187, 194 (1963). The reference is to Erwin N. Griswold, The Fifth Amendment Today 7 (1955), which, read in its entirety, strikes me as singularly *unemotional.*

25. Hiemstra, *supra* note 24.

26. 1 James Fitzjames Stephen, A History of the Criminal Law of England 441–42 (London, Macmillan 1883).

27. *Id.* at 442.

28. 8 John Henry Wigmore, Evidence §2266 (3d ed. 1940).

29. Maguire, *supra* note 9, at 15 n.2; Edmund M. Morgan, Basic Problems of Evidence 146–47 (1962).

30. Wigmore, *supra* note 28, at §2252(c).

31. *Id.* at §2266.

32. Edmund M. Morgan, *The Privilege Against Self-Incrimination,* 34 Minn. L. Rev. 1, 28 (1949).

33. Morris R. Cohen, The Meaning of Human History 114 (1947).

34. Note, *An Historical Argument for the Right to Counsel during Police Interrogation,* 73 Yale L.J. 1000, 1034 (1964).

35. *Id.* at 1041.

36. Morgan, *supra* note 29, at 147–48.

37. Albert R. Beisel, Control over Illegal Enforcement of the Criminal Law: Role of the Supreme Court 104 (1955).

38. Bernard D. Meltzer, *Required Records, the McCarran Act, and the Privilege Against Self-Incrimination,* 18 U. Chi. L. Rev. 687, 695 (1951).

39. Charles T. McCormick, Evidence 155 (1954).

40. *Id.* at 156.

3

Miranda
v.
Arizona
·

384 U.S. 436 (1966)

Editors' Introduction

Yale Kamisar's landmark essay on police interrogation and the privilege against self-incrimination (see Chapter 2) was published in 1965. The following year, the Supreme Court reviewed four confession cases from state courts. The Court had, for many years, relied on the due process voluntariness test to regulate police interrogation. Then, in the early 1960s, it sought to regulate such interrogations with the Sixth Amendment right to counsel. As noted in Chapter 1 (see page 20), however, the Sixth Amendment solution was difficult to defend as a reading of the Constitution. The Sixth Amendment right to counsel applies to "all criminal prosecutions." How can questioning before charges have been filed—in many cases even before a formal arrest has been made—be seen as part of a "criminal prosecution"?

Kamisar's essay showed the Court a way to avoid the problem of imposing a trial right to counsel into the early stage of police investigation. The new way was based on the Fifth Amendment self-incrimination clause: No person "shall be compelled in any criminal case to be a witness against himself." Using the self-incrimination clause to regulate police interrogation avoided the awkwardness of stretching the Sixth Amendment language ("all criminal prosecutions") to include police investigation. It also gave the Court a chance to approach the police interrogation problem afresh, without the baggage created by the voluntariness test. Clearly the Court hoped that the self-incrimination clause would yield a more workable solution than the metaphysical approach of the voluntariness test. The difficulties of knowing the precise moment when a suspect's will has been "overborne" by interrogation are manifest and difficult to exaggerate.

The Fifth Amendment solution carried its own set of problems, to be sure, but the Court must have viewed them as less troublesome than the problems with the voluntariness test or the Sixth Amendment solution. We will highlight some of the problems with the Fifth Amendment solution as a way of introducing the Court's *Miranda* opinion. At the level of constitutional interpretation, the self-incrimination clause, like the Sixth Amendment, seems concerned with trial rather than police investigation. The clause speaks of being a "witness" in a "criminal case." To make the Fifth Amendment solution work, then, the Court had to justify extending the self-incrimination protection to the police station, an analytical move that would be almost as bold as extending the Sixth Amendment to police interrogation.

Another problem with the Fifth Amendment solution was how to give meaning to the philosophically difficult notion of "compel." When a suspect answers a question that satisfies the due process voluntariness threshold, in what sense is the answer compelled? How would prohibiting compulsion be a better standard (clearer, more precise, more protective of suspects) than prohibiting questions that produce an involuntary response? And, perhaps more significantly, if courts find it difficult to determine when an answer is involuntary, how are courts any better equipped to decide when an answer is compelled? Thus, the *Miranda* Court faced the formidable challenge of developing an account of compulsion that overcame the conceptual and practical difficulties of the voluntariness doctrine.

The solution to this problem was a bold stroke indeed. The Court simply assumed compulsion is "inherent in custodial surroundings." If compulsion always occurs during custodial police interrogation, then courts do not have to look for it in individual cases. Perhaps this bold assumption was a reasonable accommodation to the realities of both police interrogation and the process of judging which confessions to suppress. But it immediately raised another problem: How best to avoid the inherent compulsion. At a minimum, someone should inform suspects of their legal right not to answer questions. But if the police interrogation process is inherently compelling, then how would suspects be able to act on the knowledge that they need not talk?

One way to permit suspects to take advantage of their rights would be to provide them a lawyer. Advice from a lawyer would presumably dispel the inherent compulsion of police interrogation because the suspect would have an expert at his side, rather than having to face the police alone. Counsel in *Miranda*'s analytical structure is not based on the Sixth Amendment right to counsel, which *Miranda* essentially abandoned as a solution to pre-indictment interrogation, but instead buttresses the Fifth Amendment right not to be compelled to answer questions.

At this point, the Court faced a momentous choice. Its view of the inherent compulsion of police interrogation suggested that suspects would always need the advice of counsel to decide whether to answer questions. But that would make the Fifth Amendment right to counsel virtually co-extensive with the Sixth Amendment right to counsel. It would also impose a huge burden on public defenders and private defense lawyers. And it might end confessions as a way of solving crime. As Richard Uviller put it, "Having taken us to the very edge of a confessionless abyss, . . . the Court swerved, unable in the crunch to renounce altogether the product of the station house 'inquisition.'"[1] "Swerving" in this context was to permit suspects to surrender their right to remain silent and to have a lawyer advise them. Oddly, the Court's view of the inherent compulsion of police interrogation still permitted suspects to make a free choice about whether to exercise the rights read to them by the police officer.

And there was yet one more problem with *Miranda*: its political and judicial legitimacy. Although the Court could find language in earlier opinions that stressed the right of suspects to make a free choice about whether to confess, and could cite as well some vaguely similar provisions in foreign jurisdictions, *Miranda* was truly without precedent in the United States. The Court had never before forced states to accept such a complex solution to a constitutional problem. As Fred Graham put it:

> With the Court riding the crest of its faith in the bold stroke and in the objective exclusionary rule, *Miranda* was destined to be an outsized example of both. Where its predecessors had been bold, *Miranda* was to be brazen—*Gideon v. Wainwright* had created a constitutional right to counsel in felony cases at a time when all but five states already provided it; *Mapp v. Ohio* had extended the exclusionary rule to illegal searches after roughly one-half of the states had adopted the same rule; *Miranda* was to impose limits on police interrogation that no state had even approached prior to the *Escobedo* decision.[2]

Graham was right: *Miranda* would prove to be the most controversial criminal procedure case that the Court had ever decided. It would also be the last major attempt by the Warren Court to impose uniform criminal procedure on the states. Now that we have sketched the Fifth Amendment solution and its problems, we present the Court's own words.

Miranda v. Arizona

MR. CHIEF JUSTICE WARREN delivered the opinion of the Court.

The cases before us raise questions which go to the roots of our concepts of American criminal jurisprudence: the restraints society must observe consistent with the federal Constitution in prosecuting individuals for crime. . . .

We start here, as we did in *Escobedo* [*v. Illinois*, 378 U.S. 478 (1964)], with the premise that our holding is not an innovation in our jurisprudence, but is an application of principles long recognized and applied in other settings. We have undertaken a thorough re-examination of the *Escobedo* decision and the principles it announced, and we reaffirm it. That case was but an explication of basic rights that are enshrined in our Constitution—that "No person . . . shall be compelled in any criminal case to be a witness against himself," and that "the accused shall . . . have the Assistance of Counsel"—rights which were put in jeopardy in that case through official overbearing. These precious rights were fixed in our Constitution only after centuries of persecution and struggle. And in the words of Chief Justice Marshall, they were secured "for ages to come, and . . . designed to approach immortality as nearly as human institutions can approach it." . . .

The constitutional issue we decide in each of these cases is the admissibility of statements obtained from a defendant questioned while in custody or otherwise deprived of his freedom of action in any significant way. In each, the defendant was questioned by police officers, detectives, or a prosecuting attorney in a room in which he was cut off from the outside world. In none of these cases was the defendant given a full and effective warning of his rights at the outset of the interrogation process. In all the cases, the questioning elicited oral admissions, and in three of them, signed statements as well which were admitted at their trials. They all thus share salient features—incommunicado interrogation of individuals in a police-dominated atmosphere, resulting in self-incriminating statements without full warnings of constitutional rights. . . .

Again we stress that the modern practice of in-custody interrogation is psychologically rather than physically oriented. As we have stated before, "Since *Chambers v. Florida*, 309 U.S. 227 [1940], this Court has recognized that coercion can be mental as well as physical, and that the blood of the accused is not the only hallmark of an unconstitutional inquisition." Interrogation still takes place in privacy. Privacy results in secrecy and this in turn results in a gap in our knowledge as to what in fact goes on in the interrogation rooms. A valuable source of information about present police practices, however, may be found in various police manuals and texts which document procedures employed with success in the past, and which recommend various other effective tactics. These texts are used by law enforcement agencies themselves as guides. It should be noted that these texts professedly present the most enlightened and effective means presently used to obtain statements through custodial interrogation. By considering these texts and other data, it is possible to describe procedures observed and noted around the country.

The officers are told by the manuals that the "principal psychological factor contributing to a successful interrogation is *privacy*—being alone with the person under interrogation." The efficacy of this tactic has been explained as follows:

> If at all practicable, the interrogation should take place in the investigator's office or at least in a room of his own choice. The subject should be deprived of every psychological advantage. In his own home he may be confident, indignant, or recalcitrant. He is more keenly aware of his rights and more reluctant to tell of his indiscretions or criminal behavior within the walls of his home. Moreover his family and other friends are nearby, their presence lending moral support. In his own office, the investigator possesses all the advantages. The atmosphere suggests the invincibility of the forces of the law.[3]

To highlight the isolation and unfamiliar surroundings, the manuals instruct the police to display an air of confidence in the suspect's guilt and from outward appearance to maintain only an interest in confirming certain details. The guilt of the subject is to be posited as a fact. The interrogator should direct his comments toward the reasons why the subject committed the act, rather than court failure by asking the subject whether he did it. Like other men, perhaps the subject has had a bad family life, had an unhappy childhood, had too much to drink, had an unrequited desire for women. The officers are instructed to minimize the moral seriousness of the offense, to cast blame on the victim or on society. These tactics are designed to put the subject in a psychological state where his story is but an elaboration of what the police purport to know already—that he is guilty. Explanations to the contrary are dismissed and discouraged.

The texts thus stress that the major qualities an interrogator should possess are patience and perseverance. One writer describes the efficacy of these characteristics in this manner:

> In the preceding paragraphs emphasis has been placed on kindness and stratagems. The investigator will, however, encounter many situations where the sheer weight of his personality will be the deciding factor. Where emotional appeals and tricks are employed to no avail, he must rely on an oppressive atmosphere of dogged persistence. He must interrogate steadily and without relent, leaving the subject no prospect of surcease. He must dominate his subject and overwhelm him with his inexorable will to obtain the truth. He should interrogate for a spell of several hours pausing only for the subject's necessities in acknowledgement of the need to avoid a charge of duress that can be technically substantiated. In a serious case, the interrogation may continue for days, with the required intervals for food and sleep, but with no respite from the atmosphere of domination. It is possible in this way to induce the suspect to talk without resorting to duress or coercion. The method should be used only when the guilt of the suspect appears highly probable.[4]

The manuals suggest that the suspect be offered legal excuses for his actions in order to obtain an initial admission of guilt. Where there is a suspected revenge-killing, for example, the interrogator may say:

> Joe, you probably didn't go out looking for this fellow with the purpose of shooting him. My guess is, however, that you expected something from him and that's why you carried a gun—for your own protection. You knew him for what he was, no good. Then when you met him he probably started using foul, abusive language and he gave some indication that he was about to pull a gun on you, and that's when you had to act to save your own life. That's about it, isn't it, Joe?[5]

Having then obtained the admission of shooting, the interrogator is advised to refer to circumstantial evidence which negates the self-defense explanation. This should enable him to secure the entire story. One text notes that "Even if he fails to do so, the inconsistency between the subject's original denial of the shooting and his present admission of at least doing the shooting will serve to deprive him of a self-defense 'out' at the time of trial."[6] . . .

The interrogators sometimes are instructed to induce a confession out of trickery. The technique here is quite effective in crimes which require identification or which run in series. In the identification situation, the interrogator may take a break in his questioning to place the subject among a group of men in a line-up. "The witness or complainant (previously coached, if necessary) studies the line-up and confidently points out the subject as the guilty party."[7] Then the questioning resumes "as though there were now no doubt about the guilt of the subject." A variation on this technique is called the "reverse line-up":

> The accused is placed in a line-up, but this time he is identified by several fictitious witnesses or victims who associated him with different offenses. It is expected that the subject will become desperate and confess to the offense under investigation in order to escape from the false accusations.[8]

[The Court described other strategies, including the "Mutt and Jeff" act in which one officer plays the good cop and one the bad cop whose brutality can be kept under control only if the suspect cooperates with the good cop. Another strategy discourages silence: "Suppose you were in my shoes and I were in yours and you called me in to ask me about this and I told you 'I don't want to answer any of your questions.' You'd think I had something to hide, and you'd probably be right in thinking that." Finally, one strategy discourages requests to talk to a lawyer or to a relative: "Joe, I'm only looking for the truth, and if you're telling the truth, that's it. You can handle this by yourself."—Eds.]

From these representative samples of interrogation techniques, the setting prescribed by the manuals and observed in practice becomes clear. In essence, it is this: To be alone with the subject is essential to prevent distraction and to deprive him of any outside support. The aura of confidence in his guilt undermines his will to resist. He merely confirms the preconceived story the police seek to have him describe. Patience and persistence, at times relentless questioning, are employed. To obtain a confession, the interrogator must "patiently maneuver himself or his quarry into a position from which the desired objective may be attained."[9] When normal procedures fail to produce the needed result, the police may resort to deceptive stratagems such as giving false legal advice. It is important to keep the subject off balance, for example, by trading on his insecurity about himself or his surroundings. The police then persuade, trick, or cajole him out of exercising his constitutional rights. . . .

In these cases [before the Court], we might not find the defendants' statements to have been involuntary in traditional terms. Our concern for adequate safeguards to protect precious Fifth Amendment rights is, of course, not lessened in the slightest. In each of the cases, the defendant was thrust into an unfamiliar atmosphere and run through menacing police interrogation procedures. The potentiality for compulsion is forcefully apparent, for example, in *Miranda*, where the indigent Mexican defendant was a seriously disturbed individual with pronounced sexual fantasies, and in *Stewart*, in which the defendant was an indigent Los Angeles Negro who had dropped out of school in the sixth grade. To be sure, the records do not evince overt physical coercion or patent psychological ploys. The fact remains that in none of these cases did the officers undertake to afford appropriate safeguards at the outset of the interrogation to insure that the statements were truly the product of free choice.

It is obvious that such an interrogation environment is created for no purpose other than to subjugate the individual to the will of his examiner. This atmosphere carries its own badge of intimidation. To be sure, this is not physical intimidation, but it is equally destructive of human dignity. The current practice of incommunicado interrogation is at odds with one of our Nation's most cherished principles—that the individual may not be compelled to incriminate himself. Unless adequate protective devices are employed to dispel the compulsion inherent in custodial surroundings, no statement obtained from the defendant can truly be the product of his free choice. . . .

Today, then, there can be no doubt that the Fifth Amendment privilege is available outside of criminal court proceedings and serves to protect persons in all settings in which their freedom of action is curtailed in any significant way from being compelled to incriminate themselves. We have concluded that without proper safeguards the process of in-custody interrogation of persons suspected or accused of crime contains inherently compelling pressures which work to undermine the individual's will to resist and to compel him to speak where he would not otherwise do so freely. In order to combat these pressures and to permit a full opportunity to exercise the privilege against self-incrimination, the accused must be adequately and effectively apprised of his rights and the exercise of those rights must be fully honored.

It is impossible for us to foresee the potential alternatives for protecting the privilege which might be devised by Congress or the States in the exercise of their creative rule-making capacities. Therefore we cannot say that the Constitution necessarily requires adherence to any particular solution for the inherent compulsions of the interrogation process as it is presently conducted. Our decision in no way creates a constitutional straitjacket which will handicap sound efforts at reform, nor is it intended to have this effect. We encourage Congress and the States to continue their laudable search for increasingly effective ways of protecting the rights of the individual while promoting efficient enforcement of our criminal laws. However, unless we are shown other procedures which are at least as effective in apprising accused persons of their right of silence and in assuring a continuous opportunity to exercise it, the following safeguards must be observed.

At the outset, if a person in custody is to be subjected to interrogation, he must first be informed in clear and unequivocal terms that he has the right to remain silent. For those unaware of the privilege, the warning is needed simply to make them aware of it—the threshold requirement for an intelligent decision as to its exercise. More important, such a warning is an absolute prerequisite in overcoming the inherent pressures of the interrogation atmosphere. It is not just the subnormal or woefully ignorant who succumb to an interrogator's imprecations, whether implied or expressly stated, that the interrogation will continue until a confession is obtained or that silence in the face of accusation is itself damning and will bode ill when presented to a jury. Further, the warning will show the individual that his interrogators are prepared to recognize his privilege should he choose to exercise it. . . .

The warning of the right to remain silent must be accompanied by the explanation that anything said can and will be used against the individual in court. This warning is needed in order to make him aware not only of the privilege, but also of the consequences of forgoing it. It is only through an awareness of these consequences that there can be any assurance of real understanding and intelligent exercise of the privilege. Moreover, this warning may serve to make the individual more acutely aware that he is faced with a phase of the adversary system—that he is not in the presence of persons acting solely in his interest.

The circumstances surrounding in-custody interrogation can operate very quickly to overbear the will of one merely made aware of his privilege by his interrogators. Therefore, the right to have counsel present at the interrogation is indispensable to the protection of the Fifth Amendment privilege under the system we delineate today. Our aim is to assure that the individual's right to choose between silence and speech remains unfettered throughout the interrogation process. A once-stated warning, delivered by those who will conduct the interrogation, cannot itself suffice to that end among those who most require knowledge of their rights. A mere warning given by the interrogators is not alone sufficient to accomplish that end. . . . Even preliminary advice given to the accused by his own attorney can be swiftly overcome by the secret interrogation process. Thus, the need for counsel to protect the Fifth Amendment privilege comprehends not merely a right to consult with counsel prior to questioning, but also to have counsel present during any questioning if the defendant so desires. . . .

If an individual indicates that he wishes the assistance of counsel before any interrogation occurs, the authorities cannot rationally ignore or deny his request on the basis that the individual does not have or cannot afford a retained attorney. The financial ability of the individual has no relationship to the scope of the rights involved here. The privilege against self-incrimination secured by the Constitution applies to all individuals. The need for counsel in order to protect the privilege exists for the indigent as well as the affluent. In fact, were we to limit these constitutional rights to those who can retain an attorney, our decisions today would be of little significance. The cases before us as well as the vast majority of confession cases with which we have dealt in the past involve those unable to retain counsel. While authorities are not required to relieve the accused of his poverty, they have the obligation not to take advantage of indigence in the administration of justice. Denial of counsel to the indigent at the time of interrogation while allowing an attorney to those who can afford one would be no more supportable by reason or logic than the similar situation at trial and on appeal struck down in *Gideon v. Wainwright*, 372 U.S. 335 (1963), and *Douglas v. California*, 372 U.S. 353 (1963).[10] . . .

Once warnings have been given, the subsequent procedure is clear. If the individual indicates in any manner, at any time prior to or during questioning, that he wishes to remain silent, the interrogation must cease. At this point he has shown that he intends to exercise his Fifth Amendment privilege; any statement taken after the person invokes his privilege cannot be other than the product of compulsion, subtle or otherwise. Without the right to cut off questioning, the setting of in-custody interrogation operates on the individual to overcome free choice in producing a statement after the privilege has been once invoked. If the individual states that he wants an attorney, the interrogation must cease until an attorney is present. At that time, the individual must have an opportunity to confer with the attorney and to have him present during any subsequent questioning. If the individual cannot obtain an attorney and he indicates that he wants one before speaking to police, they must respect his decision to remain silent. . . .

If the interrogation continues without the presence of an attorney and a statement is taken, a heavy burden rests on the government to demonstrate that the defendant knowingly and intelligently waived his privilege against self-incrimination and his right to retained or appointed counsel. This Court has always set high standards of proof for the waiver of constitutional rights, and we re-assert these standards as applied to in-custody interrogation. Since the State is responsible for establishing the isolated circumstances under which the interrogation takes place and has the only means of making available corroborated evidence of warnings given during incommunicado interrogation, the burden is rightly on its shoulders. . . .

In announcing these principles, we are not unmindful of the burdens which law enforcement officials must bear, often under trying circumstances. We also fully recognize the obligation of all citizens to aid in enforcing the criminal laws. This Court, while protecting individual rights, has always given ample latitude to law enforcement agencies in the legitimate exercise of their duties. The limits we have placed on the interrogation process should not constitute an undue interference with a proper system of law enforcement. As we have noted, our decision does not in any way preclude police from carrying out their traditional investigatory functions. Although confessions may play an important role in some convictions, the cases before us present graphic examples of the overstatement of the "need" for confessions. In each case authorities conducted interrogations ranging up to five days in duration despite the presence, through standard investigating practices, of considerable evidence against each defendant. . . .

MR. JUSTICE CLARK, dissenting in [three of the cases, including Miranda's case], and concurring in the result in [one of the cases].

. . . Such a strict constitutional specific inserted at the nerve center of crime detection may well kill the patient. Since there is at this time a paucity of information and an almost total lack of empirical knowledge on the practical operation of requirements truly comparable to those announced by the majority, I would be more restrained lest we go too far too fast. . . .

MR. JUSTICE HARLAN, with whom MR. JUSTICE STEWART and MR. JUSTICE WHITE join, dissenting [in all four cases]. . . .

What the Court largely ignores is that its rules impair, if they will not eventually serve wholly to frustrate, an instrument of law enforcement that has long and quite reasonably been thought worth the price paid for it. There can be little doubt that the Court's new code would markedly decrease the number of confessions. . . .

While passing over the costs and risks of its experiment, the Court portrays the evils of normal police questioning in terms which I think are exaggerated. Albeit stringently confined by the due process standards interrogation is no doubt often inconvenient and unpleasant for the suspect. However, it is no less so for a man to be arrested and jailed, to have his house searched, or to stand trial in court, yet all this may properly happen to the most innocent given probable cause, a warrant, or an indictment. Society has always paid a stiff price for law and order, and peaceful interrogation is not one of the dark moments of the law. . . .

MR. JUSTICE WHITE, with whom MR. JUSTICE HARLAN and MR. JUSTICE STEWART join, dissenting [in all four cases]. . . .

Although in the Court's view in-custody interrogation is inherently coercive, the Court says that the spontaneous product of the coercion of arrest and detention is still to be deemed voluntary. An accused, arrested on probable cause, may blurt out a confession which will be admissible despite the fact that he is alone and in custody, without any showing that he had any notion of his right to remain silent or of the consequences of his admission. Yet, under the Court's rule, if the police ask him a single question such as "Do you have anything to say?" or "Did you kill your wife?" his response, if there is one, has somehow been compelled, even if the accused has been clearly warned of his right to remain silent. Common sense informs us to the contrary. While one may say that the response was "involuntary" in the sense the question provoked or was the occasion for the response and thus the defendant was induced to speak out when he might have remained silent if not arrested and not questioned, it is patently unsound to say the response is compelled. . . .

On the other hand, even if one assumed that there was an adequate factual basis for the conclusion that all confessions obtained during in-custody interrogation are the product of compulsion, the rule propounded by the Court would still be irrational, for, apparently, it is only if the accused is also warned of his right to counsel and waives both that right and the right against self-incrimination that the inherent compulsiveness of interrogation disappears. But if the defendant may not answer without a warning a question such as "Where were you last night?" without having his answer be a compelled one, how can the Court ever accept his negative answer to the question of whether he wants to consult his retained counsel or counsel whom the court will appoint? And why if counsel is present and the accused nevertheless confesses, or counsel tells the accused to tell the truth, and that is what the accused does, is the situation any less coercive insofar as the accused is concerned? . . .

The most basic function of any government is to provide for the security of the individual and of his property. These ends of society are served by the criminal laws which for the most part are aimed at the prevention of crime. Without the reasonably effective performance of the task of preventing private violence and retaliation, it is idle to talk about human dignity and civilized values. . . .

In some unknown number of cases the Court's rule will return a killer, a rapist or other criminal to the streets and to the environment which produced him, to repeat his crime whenever it pleases him. As a consequence, there will not be a gain, but a loss, in human dignity. The real concern is not the unfortunate consequences of this new decision on the criminal law as an abstract, disembodied series of authoritative proscriptions, but the impact on those who rely on the public authority for protection and who without it can only engage in violent self-help with guns, knives and the help of their neighbors similarly inclined. There is, of course, a saving factor: the next victims are uncertain, unnamed and unrepresented in this case. . . .

NOTES

1. H. Richard Uviller, *Evidence from the Mind of the Criminal Suspect: A Reconsideration of the Current Rules of Access and Restraint*, 87 Colum. L. Rev. 1137, 1168 (1987).

2. Fred Graham, *Miranda*: The Self-Inflicted Wound 192 (1970).

3. Charles O'Hara and Gregory L. O'Hara, Fundamentals of Criminal Investigation 99 (1956).

4. *Id.* at 112.

5. Fred E. Inbau & John E. Reid, Criminal Interrogation and Confessions 40 (1962).

6. *Id.*

7. O'Hara, *supra* note 3, at 105–6.

8. *Id.* at 106.

9. Fred E. Inbau & John E. Reid, Lie Detection and Criminal Interrogation 185 (3d ed. 1953).

10. [The Court in *Douglas* held impermissible a state system that permitted defendants who could afford them to have lawyers on appeal but that made no provision for indigent defendants to have lawyers on their appeal. *Gideon* is discussed in Chapter 1 at page 17; it held that the Sixth Amendment right to counsel requires the state to provide counsel for indigent felony defendants.—Eds.]

4

Homicide:
A Year
on the
Killing
Streets
(1991)

•

DAVID SIMON

You are a citizen of a free nation, having lived your adult life in a land of guaranteed civil liberties, and you commit a crime of violence, whereupon you are jacked up, hauled down to a police station, and deposited in a claustrophobic anteroom with three chairs, a table, and no windows. There you sit for a half hour or so until a police detective—a man you have never met before, a man who can in no way be mistaken for a friend—enters the room with a thin stack of lined notepaper and a ballpoint pen.

The detective offers a cigarette, not your brand, and begins an uninterrupted monologue that wanders back and forth for a half hour more, eventually coming to rest in a familiar place: *"You have the absolute right to remain silent."*

Of course you do. You're a criminal. Criminals always have the right to remain silent. A least once in your miserable life, you spent an hour in front of a television set, listening to this book-'em-Danno routine. You think Joe Friday was lying to you? You think Kojak was making this horseshit up? No way, bunk, we're talking sacred freedoms here, notably your Fifth Fucking Amendment protection against self-incrimination, and hey, it was good enough for Ollie North, so who are you to go incriminating yourself at the first opportunity? Get it straight: A police detective, a man who gets paid government money to put you in prison, is explaining your absolute right to shut up before you say something stupid.

"Anything you say or write may be used against you in a court of law."

Yo, bunky, wake the fuck up. You're now being told that talking to a police detective in an interrogation room can only hurt you. If it could help you, they would probably be pretty quick to say that, wouldn't they? They'd stand up and say you have the right not to worry because what you say or write in this godforsaken cubicle is gonna be used to your benefit in a court of law. No, your best bet is to shut up. Shut up now.

"You have the right to talk with a lawyer at any time—before any questioning, before answering any questions, or during any questions."

Talk about helpful. Now the man who wants to arrest you for violating the peace and dignity of the state is saying you can talk to a trained professional, an attorney who has read the relevant portions of the Maryland Annotated Code or can at least get his hands on some Cliffs Notes. And let's face it, pal, you just carved up a drunk in a Dundalk Avenue bar, but that don't make you a neurosurgeon. Take whatever help you can get.

"If you want a lawyer and cannot afford to hire one, you will not be asked any questions, and the court will be requested to appoint a lawyer for you."

Translation: You're a derelict. No charge for derelicts.

At this point, if all lobes are working, you ought to have seen enough of this Double Jeopardy category to know that it ain't where you want to be. How about a little something from Criminal Lawyers and Their Clients for $50, Alex?

Whoa, bunk, not so fast.

"Before we get started, lemme just get through the paperwork," says the detective, who now produces an Explanation of Rights sheet, BPD Form 69, and passes it across the table.

"EXPLANATION OF RIGHTS," declares the top line in bold block letters. The detective asks you to fill in your name, address, age, and education, then the date and time. That much accomplished, he asks you to read the next section. It begins, "YOU ARE HEREBY ADVISED THAT:"

Read number one, the detective says. Do you understand number one?

"You have the absolute right to remain silent."

Yeah, you understand. We did this already.

"Then write your initials next to number one. Now read number two."

And so forth, until you have initialed each component of the *Miranda* warning. That done, the detective tells you to write your signature on the next line, the one just below the sentence that says, "I HAVE READ THE ABOVE EXPLANATION OF MY RIGHTS AND FULLY UNDERSTAND IT."

You sign your name and the monologue resumes. The detective assures you that he has informed you of these rights because he wants you to be protected, because there is nothing that concerns him more than giving you every possible assistance in this very confusing and stressful moment in your life. If you don't want to talk, he tells you, that's fine. And if you want a lawyer, that's fine, too, because first of all, he's no relation to the guy you cut up, and second, he's gonna get six hours overtime no matter what you do. But he wants you to know—and he's been doing this a lot longer than you, so take his word for it—that your rights to remain silent and obtain qualified counsel aren't all they're cracked up to be.

Look at it this way, he says, leaning back in his chair. Once you up and call for that lawyer, son, we can't do a damn thing for you. No sir, your friends in the city homicide unit are going to have to leave you locked in this room all alone and the next authority figure to scan your case will be a tie-wearing, three-piece bloodsucker—a no-nonsense prosecutor from the Violent Crimes Unit with the official title of assistant state's attorney for the city of Baltimore. And God help you then, son, because a ruthless fucker like that will have an O'Donnell Heights motorhead like yourself halfway to the gas chamber before you get three words out. Now's the time to speak up, right now when I got my pen and paper here on the table, because once I walk out of this room any chance you have of telling your side of the story is gone and I gotta write it up the way it looks. And the way it looks right now is first-fucking-degree murder. Felony murder, mister, which when shoved up a man's asshole is a helluva lot more painful than second-degree or maybe even manslaughter. What you say right here and now could make the difference, bunk. Did I mention that Maryland has a gas chamber? Big, ugly sumbitch at the penitentiary on Eager Street, not twenty blocks from here. You don't wanna get too close to that bad boy, lemme tell you.

A small, wavering sound of protest passes your lips and the detective leans back in his chair, shaking his head sadly.

What the hell is wrong with you, son? You think I'm fucking with you? Hey, I don't even need to bother with your weak shit. I got three witnesses in three other rooms who say you're my man. I got a knife from the scene that's going downstairs to the lab for latent prints. I got blood spatter on them Air Jordans we took off you ten minutes ago. Why the fuck do you think we took 'em? Do I look like I wear high-top tennis? Fuck no. You got spatter all over 'em, and I think we both know whose blood type it's gonna be. Hey, bunk, I'm only in here to make sure that there ain't nothing you can say for yourself before I write it all up.

You hesitate.

Oh, says the detective. You want to think about it. Hey, you think about it all you want, pal. My captain's right outside in the hallway, and he already told me to charge your ass in the first fuckin' degree. For once in your beshitted little life someone is giving you a chance and you're too fucking dumb to take it. What the fuck, you go ahead and think about it and I'll tell my captain to cool his heels for ten minutes. I can do that much for you. How 'bout some coffee? Another cigarette?

The detective leaves you alone in that cramped, windowless room. Just you and the blank notepaper and the Form 69 and . . . first-degree murder. First-degree murder with witnesses and fingerprints and blood on your Air Jordans. Christ, you didn't even notice the blood on your own fucking shoes. Felony murder, mister. First-fucking-degree. How many years, you begin to wonder, how many years do I get for involuntary manslaughter?

Whereupon the man who wants to put you in prison, the man who is not your friend, comes back in the room, asking if the coffee's okay.

Yeah, you say, the coffee's fine, but what happens if I want a lawyer?

The detective shrugs. Then we get you a lawyer, he says. And I walk out of the room and type up the charging documents for first-degree murder and you can't say a fucking thing about it. Look, bunk, I'm giving you a chance. He came at you, right? You were scared. It was self-defense.

Your mouth opens to speak.

He came at you, didn't he?

"Yeah," you venture cautiously, "he came at me."

Whoa, says the detective, holding up his hands. Wait a minute. If we're gonna do this, I gotta find your rights form. Where's the fucking form? Damn things are like cops, never around when you need 'em. Here it is, he says, pushing the explanation-of-rights sheet across the table and pointing to the bottom. Read that, he says.

"I am willing to answer questions and I do not want any attorney at this time. My decision to answer questions without having an attorney present is free and voluntary on my part."

As you read, he leaves the room and returns a moment later with a second detective as a witness. You sign the bottom of the form, as do both detectives.

The first detective looks up from the form, his eyes soaked with innocence. "He came at you, huh?"

"Yeah, he came at me."

Get used to small rooms, bunk, because you are about to be drop-kicked into the lost land of pretrial detention. Because it's one thing to be a murdering little asshole from Southeast Baltimore, and it's another to be stupid about it, and with five little words you have just elevated yourself to the ranks of the truly witless.

End of the road, pal. It's over. It's history. And if that police detective wasn't so busy committing your weak bullshit to paper, he'd probably look you in the eye and tell you so. He'd give you another cigarette and say, son, you are ignorance personified and you just put yourself in for the fatal stabbing of a human being. He might even tell you that the other witnesses in the other rooms are too drunk to identify their own reflections, much less the kid who had the knife, or that it's always a long shot for the lab to pull a latent off a knife hilt, or that your $95 sneakers are as clean as the day you bought them. If he was feeling particularly expansive, he might tell you that everyone who leaves the homicide unit in handcuffs does so charged with first-degree murder, that it's for the lawyers to decide what kind of deal will be cut. He might go on to say that even after all these years working homicides, there is still a small part of him that finds it completely mystifying that anyone ever utters a single word in a police interrogation. To illustrate the point, he could hold up your Form 69, on which you waived away every last one of your rights, and say, "Lookit here, pistonhead, I told you twice that you were deep in the shit and that whatever you said could put you in deeper." And if his message was still somehow beyond your understanding, he could drag your carcass back down the sixth-floor hallway, back toward the sign that says Homicide Unit in white block letters, the sign you saw when you walked off the elevator.

Now think hard: Who lives in a homicide unit? Yeah, right. And what do homicide detectives do for a living? Yeah, you got it, bunk. And what did you do tonight? You murdered someone.

So when you opened that mouth of yours, what the fuck were you thinking?

Homicide detectives in Baltimore like to imagine a small, open window at the top of the long wall in the large interrogation room. More to the point, they like to imagine their suspects imagining a small, open window at the top of the long wall. The open window is the escape hatch, the Out. It is the perfect representation of what every suspect believes when he opens his mouth during an interrogation. Every last one envisions himself parrying questions with the right combination of alibi and excuse; every last one sees himself coming up with the right words, then crawling out the window to go home and sleep in his own bed. More often than not, a guilty man is looking for the Out from his first moments in the interrogation room; in that sense, the window is as much the suspect's fantasy as the detective's mirage.

The effect of the illusion is profound, distorting as it does the natural hostility between hunter and hunted, transforming it until it resembles a relationship more symbiotic than adversarial. That is the lie, and when the roles are perfectly performed, deceit surpasses itself, becoming manipulation on a grand scale and ultimately an act of betrayal. Because what occurs in an interrogation room is indeed little more than a carefully staged drama, a choreographed performance that allows a detective and his suspect to find common ground where none exists. There, in a carefully controlled purgatory, the guilty proclaim their malefactions, though rarely in any form that allows for contrition or resembles an unequivocal admission.

In truth, catharsis in the interrogation room occurs for only a few rare suspects, usually those in domestic murders or child abuse cases wherein the leaden mass of genuine remorse can crush anyone who is not hardened to his crime. But the greater share of men and women brought downtown take no interest in absolution. Ralph Waldo Emerson rightly noted that for those responsible, the act of murder "is no such ruinous thought as poets and romancers will have it; it does not unsettle him, or frighten him from his ordinary notice of trifles." And while West Baltimore is a universe or two from Emerson's nineteenth-century Massachusetts hamlet, the observation is still useful. Murder often doesn't unsettle a man. In Baltimore, it usually doesn't even ruin his day.

As a result, the majority of those who acknowledge their complicity in a killing must be baited by detectives with something more tempting than penitence. They must be made to believe that their crime is not really murder, that their excuse is both accepted and unique, that they will, with the help of the detective, be judged less evil than they truly are.

Some are brought to that unreasoned conclusion by the suggestion that they acted in self-defense or were provoked to violence. Others fall prey to the notion that they are less culpable than their colleagues—I only drove the car or backed up the robbery, I wasn't the triggerman; or yeah, I raped her, but I stayed out of it when them other guys started strangling her—unaware that Maryland law allows every member of the conspiracy to be charged as a principal. Still others succumb to the belief that they will get a better shake by cooperating with detectives and acknowledging a limited amount of guilt. And many of those who cannot be lured over the precipice of self-incrimination can still be manipulated into providing alibis, denials, and explanations—statements that can be checked and rechecked until a suspect's lies are the greatest evidentiary threat to his freedom.

For that reason, the professionals say nothing. No alibis. No explanations. No expressions of polite dismay or blanket denials. In the late 1970s, when men by the names of Dennis Wise and Vernon Collins were matching each other body for body as Baltimore's premier contract killers and no witness could be found to testify against either, things got to the point where both the detectives and their suspects knew the drill:

Enter room.

Miranda.

Anything to say this time, Dennis?

No, sir. Just want to call my lawyer.

Fine, Dennis.

Exit room.

For anyone with experience in the criminal justice machine, the point is driven home by every lawyer worth his fee. Repetition and familiarity with the process soon place the professionals beyond the reach of a police interrogation. Yet more than two decades after the landmark *Escobedo* and *Miranda* decisions, the rest of the world remains strangely willing to place itself at risk. As a result, the same law enforcement community that once regarded the 1966 *Miranda* decision as a death blow to criminal investigation has now come to see the explanation of rights as a routine part of the process—simply a piece of station house furniture, if not a civilizing influence on police work itself.

In an era when beatings and physical intimidation were common tools of an interrogation, the *Escobedo* and *Miranda* decisions were sent down by the nation's highest court to ensure that criminal confessions and statements were purely voluntary. The resulting *Miranda* warning was "a protective device to dispel the compelling atmosphere of the interrogation," as Chief Justice Earl Warren wrote in the majority opinion. Investigators would be required to assure citizens of their rights to silence and counsel, not only at the moment of arrest, but at the moment that they could reasonably be considered suspects under interrogation.

In answer to *Miranda*, the nation's police officials responded with a veritable jeremiad, wailing in unison that the required warnings would virtually assure that confessions would be impossible to obtain and conviction rates would plummet. Yet the prediction was soon proved false for the simple reason that those law enforcement leaders—and, for that matter, the Supreme Court itself—underestimated a police detective's ingenuity.

Miranda is, on paper, a noble gesture which declares that constitutional rights extend not only to the public forum of the courts, but to the private confines of the police station as well. *Miranda* and its accompanying decisions established a uniform concept of a criminal defendant's rights and effectively ended the use of violence and the most blatant kind of physical intimidation in interrogations. That, of course, was a blessing. But if the further intent of the *Miranda* decision was, in fact, an attempt to "dispel the compelling atmosphere" of an interrogation, then it failed miserably.

And thank God. Because by any standards of human discourse, a criminal confession can never truly be called voluntary. With rare exception, a confession is compelled, provoked, and manipulated from a suspect by a detective who has been trained in a genuinely deceitful art. That is the essence of interrogation, and those who believe that a straightforward conversation between a cop and a criminal—devoid of any treachery—is going to solve a crime are somewhere beyond naive. If the interrogation process is, from a moral standpoint, contemptible, it is nonetheless essential. Deprived of the ability to question and confront suspects and witnesses, a detective is left with physical evidence and in many cases, precious little of that. Without a chance for a detective to manipulate a suspect's mind, a lot of bad people would simply go free.

Yet every defense attorney knows that there can be no good reason for a guilty man to say anything whatsoever to a police officer, and any suspect who calls an attorney will be told as much, bringing the interrogation to an end. A court opinion that therefore requires a detective—the same detective working hard to dupe a suspect—to stop abruptly and guarantee the man his right to end the process can only be called an act of institutional schizophrenia. The *Miranda* warning is a little like a referee introducing a barroom brawl: The stern warnings to hit above the waist and take no cheap shots have nothing to do with the mayhem that follows.

Yet how could it be otherwise? It would be easy enough for our judiciary to ensure that no criminal suspect relinquished his rights inside a police station: The courts could simply require the presence of a lawyer at all times. But such a blanket guarantee of individual rights would effectively end the use of interrogation as an investigative weapon, leaving many more crimes unsolved and many more guilty men and women unpunished. Instead, the ideals have been carefully compromised at little cost other than to the integrity of the police investigator.

After all, it's the lawyers, the Great Compromisers of our age, who have struck this bargain, who still manage to keep cuffs clean in the public courts, where rights and process are worshipped faithfully. It is left for the detective to fire this warning shot across a suspect's bow, granting rights to a man who will then be tricked into relinquishing them. In that sense, *Miranda* is a symbol and little more, a salve for a collective conscience that cannot reconcile libertarian ideals with what must necessarily occur in a police interrogation room. Our judges, our courts, our society as a whole, demand in the same breath that rights be maintained even as crimes are punished. And all of us are bent and determined to preserve the illusion that both can be achieved in the same, small room. It's mournful to think that this hypocrisy is the necessary creation of our best legal minds, who seem to view the interrogation process as the rest of us look upon breakfast sausage: We want it on a plate with eggs and toast; we don't want to know too much about how it comes to be.

Trapped in that contradiction, a detective does his job in the only possible way. He follows the requirements of the law to the letter—or close enough so as not to jeopardize his case. Just as carefully, he ignores that law's spirit and intent. He becomes a salesman, a huckster as thieving and silver-tongued as any man who ever moved used cars or aluminum siding—more so, in fact, when you consider that he's selling long prison terms to customers who have no genuine need for the product.

The fraud that claims it is somehow in a suspect's interest to talk with police will forever be the catalyst in any criminal interrogation. It is a fiction propped up against the greater weight of logic itself, sustained for hours on end through nothing more or less than a detective's ability to control the interrogation room.

A good interrogator controls the physical environment from the moment a suspect or reluctant witness is dumped in the small cubicle, left alone to stew in soundproof isolation. The law says that a man can't be held against his will unless he's to be charged with a crime, yet the men and women tossed into the interrogation room rarely ponder their legal status. They light cigarettes and wait, staring abstractedly at four yellow cinderblock walls, a dirty tin ashtray on a plain table, a small mirrored window, and a series of stained acoustic tiles on the ceiling. Those few with heart enough to ask whether they are under arrest are often answered with a question:

"Why? Do you want to be?"

"No."

"Then sit the fuck down."

Control is the reason a suspect is seated farthest from the interrogation room door, and the reason the room's light switch can only be operated with a key that remains in possession of the detectives. Every time a suspect has to ask for or be offered a cigarette, water, coffee, or a trip to the bathroom, he's being reminded that he's lost control.

When the detective arrives with pen and notepaper and begins the initial monologue to which a potential suspect or witness is invariably subjected, he has two goals in mind: first, to emphasize his complete control of the process; second, to stop the suspect from opening his mouth. Because if a suspect or witness manages to blurt out his desire for a lawyer—if he asks for counsel definitively and declines to answer questions until he gets one—it's over.

To prevent that, a detective allows no interruption of his soliloquy. Typically, the speech begins with the detective identifying himself and confiding that this is some serious shit that the two of you have to sort out. In your favor, however, is the fact that he, the detective, is a fair and reasonable man. A great guy, in fact—just ask anyone he works with.

If, at this moment, you try to speak, the detective will cut you off, saying your chance will come in a little while. Right now, he will invariably say, you need to know where I'm coming from. Then he'll inform you that he happens to be very good at what he does, that he's had very few open cases in his long, storied career, and a whole busload of people who lied to him in this very room are now on Death Row.

Control. To keep it, you say whatever you have to. Then you say it over and over until it's safe to stop, because if your suspect thinks for one moment that he can influence events, he may just demand an attorney.

As a result, the *Miranda* warning becomes a psychological hurdle, a pregnant moment that must be slipped carefully into the back-and-forth of the interrogation. For witnesses, the warning is not required and a detective can question those knowledgeable about a crime for hours without ever advising them of their rights. But should a witness suddenly say something that indicates involvement in a criminal act, he becomes—by the Supreme Court's definition—a suspect, at which point he must be advised of his rights. In practice, the line between a potential suspect and a suspect can be thin, and a common sight in any American homicide unit is a handful of detectives standing outside an interrogation room, debating whether or not a *Miranda* warning is yet necessary.

The Baltimore department, like many others, uses a written form to confirm a suspect's acknowledgment of *Miranda*. In a city where nine out of ten suspects would otherwise claim they were never informed of their rights, the forms have proven essential. Moreover, the detectives have found that rather than drawing attention to *Miranda*, the written form diffuses the impact of the warning. Even as it alerts a suspect to the dangers of an interrogation, the form co-opts the suspect, making him part of the process. It is the suspect who wields the pen, initialing each component of the warning and then signing the form; it is the suspect who is being asked to help with the paperwork. With witnesses, the detectives achieve the same effect with an information sheet that asks three dozen questions in rapid-fire succession. Not only does the form include information of value to the investigators—name, nickname, height, weight, complexion, employer, description of clothing at time of interview, relatives living in Baltimore, names of parents, spouse, boy-friend or girlfriend—but it acclimates the witness to the idea of answering questions before the direct interview begins.

Even if a suspect does indeed ask for a lawyer, he must—at least according to the most aggressive interpretation of *Miranda*—ask definitively: "I want to talk to a lawyer and I don't want to answer questions until I do."

Anything less leaves room for a good detective to maneuver. The distinctions are subtle and semantic:

"Maybe I should get a lawyer."

"Maybe you should. But why would you need a lawyer if you don't have anything to do with this?"

Or: "I think I should talk to a lawyer."

"You better be sure. Because if you want a lawyer then I'm not going to be able to do anything for you."

Likewise, if a suspect calls a lawyer and continues to answer questions until the lawyer arrives, his rights have not been violated. If the lawyer arrives, the suspect must be told that an attorney is in the building, but if he still wishes to continue the interrogation, nothing requires that the police allow the attorney to speak with his client. In short, the suspect can demand an attorney; a lawyer can't demand a suspect.

Once the minefield that is *Miranda* has been successfully negotiated, the detective must let the suspect know that his guilt is certain and easily established by the existing evidence. He must then offer the Out.

This, too, is role playing, and it requires a seasoned actor. If a witness or suspect is belligerent, you wear him down with greater belligerence. If the man shows fear, you offer calm and comfort. When he looks weak, you appear strong. When he wants a friend, you crack a joke and offer to buy him a soda. If he's confident, you are more so, assuring him that you are certain of his guilt and are curious only about a few select details of the crime. And if he's arrogant, if he wants nothing to do with the process, you intimidate him, threaten him, make him believe that making you happy may be the only thing between his ass and the Baltimore City Jail.

Kill your woman and a good detective will come to real tears as he touches your shoulder and tells you how he knows that you must have loved her, that it wouldn't be so hard for you to talk about if you didn't. Beat your child to death and a police detective will wrap his arm around you in the interrogation room, telling you about how he beats his own children all the time, how it wasn't your fault if the kid up and died on you. Shoot a friend over a poker hand and that same detective will lie about your dead buddy's condition, telling you that the victim is in stable condition at Hopkins and probably won't press charges, which wouldn't amount to more than assault with intent even if he does. Murder a man with an accomplice and the detective will walk your co-conspirator past the open door of your interrogation room, then say your bunky's going home tonight because he gave a statement making you the triggerman. And if that same detective thinks you can be bluffed, he might tell you that they've got your prints on the weapon, or that there are two eyewitnesses who have picked your photo from an array, or that the victim made a dying declaration in which he named you as his assailant.

All of which is street legal. Reasonable deception, the courts call it. After all, what could be more reasonable than deceiving someone who has taken a human life and is now lying about it?

The deception sometimes goes too far, or at least it sometimes seems that way to those unfamiliar with the process. Not long ago, several veteran homicide detectives in Detroit were publicly upbraided and disciplined by their superiors for using the office Xerox machine as a polygraph device. It seems that the detectives, when confronted with a statement of dubious veracity, would sometimes adjourn to the Xerox room and load three sheets of paper into the feeder.

"Truth," said the first.

"Truth," said the second.

"Lie," said the third.

Then the suspect would be led into the room and told to put his hand against the side of the machine. The detectives would ask the man's name, listen to the answer, then hit the copy button.

Truth.

And where do you live?

Truth again.

And did you or did you not kill Tater, shooting him down like a dog in the 1200 block of North Durham Street?

Lie. Well, well: You lying motherfucker.

In Baltimore, the homicide detectives read newspaper accounts of the Detroit controversy and wondered why anyone had a problem. Polygraph by copier was an old trick; it had been attempted on more than one occasion in the sixth-floor Xerox room. Gene Constantine, a veteran of Stanton's shift, once gave a mindless wonder the coordination test for drunk drivers ("Follow my finger with your eyes, but don't move your head. . . . Now stand on one foot"), then loudly declared that the man's performance indicated obvious deception.

"You flunked," Constantine told him. "You're lying."

Convinced, the suspect confessed.

Variations on the theme are limited only by a detective's imagination and his ability to sustain the fraud. But every bluff carries a corresponding risk, and a detective who tells a suspect his fingerprints are all over a crime scene loses all hope if the man knows he was wearing gloves. An interrogation room fraud is only as good as the material from which it was constructed—or, for that matter, as good as the suspect is witless—and a detective who underestimates his prey or overestimates his knowledge of the crime will lose precious credibility. Once a detective claims knowledge of a fact that the suspect knows to be untrue, the veil has been lifted, and the investigator is instead revealed as the liar.

Only when everything else in the repertoire fails does a detective resort to rage. It might be a spasm limited to a well-chosen sentence or two, or an extended tantrum punctuated by the slamming of a metal door or the drop kick of a chair, perhaps even a rant delivered as part of a good-cop, bad-cop melodrama, although that particular routine has worn thin with the years. Ideally, the shouting should be loud enough to suggest the threat of violence but restrained enough to avoid any action that could jeopardize the statement: Tell the court why you felt threatened. Did the detective hit you? Did he attempt to hit you? Did he threaten to hit you? No, but he slammed his hand down on the table, real loud.

Oh my. Motion to suppress denied.

What a good detective will not do in this more enlightened age is beat his suspect, at least not for the purpose of obtaining a statement. A suspect who swings on a homicide detective, who raves and kicks furniture, who tries to fight off a pair of handcuffs, will receive as comprehensive an ass-kicking as he would out on the street, but as a function of interrogation, physical assault is not part of the arsenal. In Baltimore, that has been true for at least fifteen years.

Simply put, the violence isn't worth the risk—not only the risk that the statement obtained will later be ruled inadmissible, but the risk to a detective's career and pension. It would be another thing entirely in those instances in which an officer or an officer's family member is the victim. In those cases, a good detective will anticipate the accusation by photographing a suspect after interrogation, to show an absence of injuries and to prove that any beating received prior to the suspect's arrival at the city jail had nothing to do with what occurred in the homicide unit.

But those are rare cases and, for the vast majority of murders, there is little for a detective to take personally. He doesn't know the dead man, he just met the suspect, and he doesn't live anywhere near the street where the violence occurred. From that perspective, what civil servant in his right mind is going to risk his entire career to prove that on the night of March 7, 1988, in some godforsaken tract of West Baltimore, a drug dealer, Stinky, shot a dope fiend, Pee Wee, over a $35 debt?

Still, circuit court juries often prefer to think in conspiratorial terms about back rooms and hot lights and rabbit punches to a suspect's kidneys. A Baltimore detective once lost a case because the defendant testified that his confession was obtained only after he had been mauled by two detectives who beat him with a phone book. The detective was sequestered and did not hear that testimony, but when he took the stand, the defense attorney asked what items were in the room during the interrogation.

"The table. Chairs. Some papers. An ashtray."

"Was there a phone book in the room?"

The detective thought about it and remembered that yes, they had used a phone book to look up an address. "Yeah," he acknowledged. "A yellow pages phone book."

Only when the defense attorney looked approvingly at the jury did the cop realize that something was wrong. After the not-guilty verdict, the detective swore he would never again begin an interview until he had cleared the room of every unnecessary item.

The passage of time can also damage the credibility of a confession. In the privacy of the interrogation room, it requires hours of prolonged effort to break a man to a point where he's willing to admit a criminal act, yet at some point those hours begin to cast doubt on the statement itself. Even under the best conditions, four to six hours of interrogation are required to break a suspect down, and eight or ten or twelve hours can be justified as long as the man is fed and allowed the use of a bathroom. But after a suspect has spent more than twelve hours in an isolated chamber without benefit of counsel, even a sympathetic judge will have qualms about calling a confession or statement truly voluntary.

And how does a detective know he has the right man? Nervousness, fear, confusion, hostility, a story that changes or contradicts itself—all are signs that the man in an interrogation room is lying, particularly in the eyes of someone as naturally suspicious as a detective. Unfortunately, these are also signs of a human being in a state of high stress, which is pretty much where people find themselves after being accused of a capital crime. Terry McLarney once mused that the best way to unsettle a suspect would be to post in all three interrogation rooms a written list of those behavior patterns that indicate deception:

Uncooperative.

Too cooperative.

Talks too much.

Talks too little.

Gets his story perfectly straight.

Fucks his story up.

Blinks too much, avoids eye contact.

Doesn't blink. Stares.

And yet if the signs along the way are ambiguous, there can be no mistaking that critical moment, that light that shines from the other end of the tunnel when a guilty man is about to give it up. Later, after he's initialed each page and is alone again in the cubicle, there will be only exhaustion and, in some cases, depression. If he gets to brooding, there might even be a suicide attempt.

But that is epilogue. The emotive crest of a guilty man's performance comes in those cold moments before he opens his mouth and reaches for the Out. Just before a man gives up life and liberty in an interrogation room, his body acknowledges the defeat: His eyes are glazed, his jaw is slack, his body lists against the nearest wall or table edge. Some put their heads against the tabletop to steady themselves. Some become physically sick, holding their stomachs as if the problem were digestive: A few actually vomit.

At that critical moment, the detectives tell their suspects that they really are sick—sick of lying, sick of hiding. They tell them it's time to turn over a new leaf, that they'll only begin to feel better when they start to tell the truth. Amazingly enough, many of them actually believe it. As they reach for the ledge of that high window, they believe every last word of it.

"He came at you, right?"

"Yeah, he came at me."

The Out leads in.

5

From Coercion to Deception: The Changing Nature of Police Interrogation in America (1992)

•

RICHARD A. LEO

Our police, with no legal sanction whatever, employ duress, threat,
bullying, a vast amount of moderate physical abuse and a certain degree
of outright torture; and their inquisitions customarily begin
with the demand: "If you know what's good for you, you'll confess."

—Ernest Jerome Hopkins (1931)[1]

Today, Ness said, interrogation is not a matter of forcing suspects to confess
but of "conning" them. "Really, what we do is just to bullshit them."

—William Hart (1981)[2]

. . . [D]uring the last fifty to sixty years there has been a profound transformation in the methods, strategies, and consciousness of police interrogators. Psychological deception has replaced physical coercion as one
of the most salient, defining features of contemporary police interrogation. Where once custodial interrogation routinely involved physical violence and duress, police questioning now consists of subtle and
sophisticated psychological ploys, tricks, stratagems, techniques, and
methods that rely on manipulation, persuasion, and deception for their
efficacy. Not only do police now openly and strongly condemn the use of
physical force during interrogation, they also believe that psychological
tactics are far more effective at eliciting confessions.[3] The use of deception has, in effect, become a functional alternative to the use of coercion.
With this change, police power in the context of interrogation has ac-

quired new meaning: It has become more subtle, more invasive, and more total, effectuated through psychological manipulation rather than physical violence.

*

. . . Although one occasionally reads or hears about abuses during custodial questioning,[4] police critics agree that use of the third degree during interrogation is now relatively infrequent.

*

The first rule of modern police interrogation is that the officer must project a sympathetic, friendly, and compassionate personality image. The officer maneuvers to show the suspect that he respects his dignity and will not condemn his behavior. By winning the suspect's trust the officer thus creates a conversational rapport with him. At the same time, however, the interrogating official exudes an "air of confidence" in the suspect's guilt. The interrogator firmly, relentlessly, and systematically implores the suspect to confess. The interrogator will try to sell the merits of confessing to the suspect, a kind of salesmanship that may crescendo into a fervent campaign of wheedling, coaxing, and cajoling. . . . In this process, the interrogator relies on psychological techniques and appeals involving manipulation, persuasion, and deception.[5] The goal of the interrogation is to create a psychological atmosphere that will facilitate the act of confessing.

Contemporary interrogation is shot through with deceptive techniques, tactics, and stratagems. By "deception" I mean any act, role, or statement that misleads a suspect or misrepresents the true nature of questioning, however subtly. As Fred Inbau and John Reid succinctly stated in the 1962 edition of their well-known interrogation training manual, Criminal Interrogation and Confessions: "Deceit is inherent in every question asked of the suspect, and in every statement made by the interrogator."[6] . . . We can identify eight general types of deceptive interrogation.

Misrepresenting the Nature or Purpose of Questioning

One of the most fundamental and overlooked deceptive stratagems police employ is questioning the suspect in a "noncustodial" setting so as to circumvent any legal necessity of rendering *Miranda* warnings. The Court in *Miranda* posited that warnings must be given *only* to a suspect who is in custody or whose freedom has otherwise been significantly deprived. Somewhat paradoxically, subsequent courts have ruled that police questioning outside of the station may be custodial,[7] just as police questioning inside the station may be noncustodial.[8] Although the (sometimes very fine) line between the two is legally defined as the "objective" restriction on a suspect's freedom, it may in fact have more to do with a suspect's state of mind than with the location of the questioning.[9] By informing the suspect that he is free to leave at any time, and by having him acknowledge that he is voluntarily answering their questions, police will transform what otherwise would be considered an interrogation into an interview. Although recasting the interrogation as an interview is more a legal than a factual deception, it has the effect of virtually removing police questioning from the realm of judicial control.

Miranda Warnings

If the form of questioning qualifies as custodial, however, police must recite the familiar warnings. The Court declared in Miranda that police cannot trick or deceive a suspect into waiving his Miranda rights.[10] The California Supreme Court has additionally ruled that police cannot "soften up" a suspect prior to administering the warnings.[11] However, police routinely deliver the Miranda warnings in a perfunctory tone of voice and ritualistic behavioral manner, effectively conveying that these warnings are little more than a bureaucratic triviality. To the extent that police undermine the import of Miranda, or negate the potential significance of the warnings, these verbal and behavioral mannerisms are deceptive. While it may be inevitable that police will deliver Miranda warnings less than enthusiastically, some investigators very consciously recite the warnings in a trivializing manner so as to maximize the likelihood of eliciting a waiver. It is thus not too surprising that police are so generally successful in obtaining waivers.[12]

Misrepresenting the Nature or Seriousness of the Offense

Another kind of deceptive stratagem police employ is misrepresenting the nature or seriousness of the offense for which the suspect is under questioning. Police typically accomplish this ploy by either withholding or exaggerating the information they present to the suspect. They may, for example, tell a suspect that the murder victim is still alive, hoping that this knowledge will compel the suspect to talk. Or police may exaggerate the seriousness of the offense—overstating, for example, the amount of money embezzled—so that the suspect feels compelled to confess to his smaller role in the offense. Or the police may suggest that they are only interested in obtaining admissions to a minor crime, when in fact they are really investigating a separate serious crime. For example, in a recent case, federal agents interrogated an individual on firearms charges and parlayed his confession into an additional, seemingly unrelated and unimportant, admission of first-degree murder.[13] Despite their pretense to the contrary, the offense federal agents were in fact investigating was the murder, not the firearms charge.

Role Playing: Manipulative Appeals to Conscience

Police are taught that effective psychological interrogation often demands the ability to convincingly feign different personality traits or to act out a variety of roles. As police trainers Robert Royal and Steven Schutt have written: "To be truly proficient . . . the interviewer/interrogator requires greater histrionic skill than the average actor."[14] Interrogators routinely project sympathy, understanding, and compassion in order to play the role of the suspect's friend, a brother or father figure, or even to act as a therapeutic or religious counselor. The most well-known role interrogators may feign is, of course, the good cop/bad cop routine, an act which may be contrived by a single officer. While playing one or more of these various roles, the investigator importunes—sometimes relentlessly—the suspect to confess for the good of his case, for the good of his family, for the good of society, or for the good of his conscience. These tactics are deceptive insofar as they create the illusion of intimacy between the suspect and the officer and misrepresent the adversarial nature of custodial interrogation. The purpose of emulating a primary or intimate role is to exploit the trust inherent in these relationships. In such a context, appeals to conscience become a powerful means of persuasion.

Misrepresenting the Moral Seriousness of the Offense

Another widely used deceptive stratagem police employ is to misrepresent the moral seriousness of an offense.[15] Interrogating officials offer suspects psychological excuses or moral justifications for their actions in order to psychologically facilitate the act of confession. Such excuses and justifications are intended to provide the suspect with an external attribution of blame that will allow him to save face while confessing. Police may, for example, attempt to convince an alleged rapist that he was only trying to show the victim love or that she was really asking for it; or they may persuade an alleged embezzler that low pay or poor working conditions are to blame for his actions. By allowing suspects to attribute moral culpability to external sources, these tactics are deceptive insofar as they create the appearance that the suspect is neither responsible, nor will be punished, for his actions.

The Use of Promises

The systematic persuasion—the wheedling, cajoling, coaxing, and importuning—that officers employ to induce conversation and elicit admissions may rest on convincing the suspect to confess for the good of his conscience, for the good of his family, for the good of society, or for the good of his case. Such invocations often involve, if only implicitly or indirectly, the use of promises. Although promises of leniency have been presumed coercive since 1897,[16] courts continue to permit vague and indefinite promises. The admissibility of a promise thus seems to turn on its specificity. For example, in one recent case, the suspect was repeatedly told that he had mental problems and thus needed psychological treatment rather than punishment.[17] Although this approach implicitly suggested a promise of leniency, the court upheld the validity of the resulting confession. Courts have also permitted officers to tell a suspect that his conscience will be relieved only if he confesses; that they will inform the court of the suspect's cooperation; that "a showing of remorse" will be a mitigating factor; or that they will help the suspect out in every way they can if he confesses.[18] Such promises are deceptive insofar as they create expectations that will not be met.

Misrepresentations of Identity

Police officials sometimes conceal their identity or pretend to be someone else while interrogating a suspect. This deceptive tactic goes beyond mere role playing, for the interrogator is not simply misrepresenting the circumstances surrounding the interrogation, but rather is misrepresenting the very act of interrogation itself. This type of interrogatory deception becomes co-terminous with undercover policing. As Gary Marx notes, police officials have posed as priests, newspaper reporters, lawyers, psychologists, meter readers, and students.[19] In other areas of

American law this deceptive technique qualifies as fraud.[20] Nevertheless, it is legally permissible for the police to misrepresent their identity so long as no constitutionally protected rights or constitutionally recognized norms of fairness are violated. While courts have traditionally not allowed officers to pose as lawyers or priests, they have permitted undercover police to pose as prison cell mates for the purposes of obtaining a confession through the pretense of friendly questioning.[21] Thus, the profession or social group with which an undercover officer or agent identifies during the actual questioning may be more significant to the resulting legal judgment than the deceptive act itself.[22]

Fabricated Evidence

As viewers of the television program *Columbo* are aware, police may confront a suspect with false evidence of his guilt. This stratagem consists of five particular physical evidence ploys. One is to falsely inform the suspect that an accomplice has identified him. Another is to falsely state that existing physical evidence—such as fingerprints, blood stains, or hair samples—confirm the suspect's guilt. Yet another is to assert that an eyewitness or the actual victim has identified and implicated the suspect. Perhaps the most dramatic physical evidence ploy is to stage a lineup, in which a coached witness falsely identifies the suspect. Finally, one of the most common physical evidence ploys is to have the suspect take a lie detector test and regardless of the results—which are scientifically unreliable and invalid in any event[23]—inform the suspect that the polygraph confirms his guilt. All of these tactics are legally permissible. Although one lower court has ruled that manufactured documentation violates due process, the law uniformly permits false verbal assertions, artifices, or subterfuges. The Supreme Court has yet to lay down any clear rules about interrogatory deception, effectively allowing police to define the outer limits of permissible trickery and deceit.[24]

*

The development of court-driven legal doctrine has played an important role in the movement from coercive to deceptive styles of interrogation. In the last sixty years the courts have elaborated and enforced constitutional rights and due process norms in order to restrict the discretionary authority that police may exercise during custodial questioning. The use of force, threats of harm, promises of leniency, denial of food and/or sleep, prolonged detention, and relay questioning are no longer condoned by legal officials. By excluding confessions that are the product of physically or psychologically coercive methods, the courts have reformed police interrogation practices. By inculcating higher normative and professional standards of conduct, the courts have oriented police to the rule of law. As a result, the courts have largely succeeded in policing the third degree out of existence. From a comparative perspective it seems remarkable, perhaps even revolutionary, that such dramatic changes have occurred in the American legal system in so brief a period of time.[25]

Prior to 1936, no single standard governed the law of confessions in state cases. In that year, the Supreme Court held in *Brown v. Mississippi* that confession evidence obtained through physically coercive interrogation must, as a matter of federal constitutional due process, be excluded in all state cases.[26] *Brown* set in motion a revolution in the constitutional jurisprudence of criminal procedure that culminated in the *Miranda* decision thirty years later.[27] Although *Miranda* is the most famous confession case, it was *Brown* that exercised the greatest influence on coercive interrogation practices: *Brown* set the standard for all comparable state and federal cases, effectively disallowing any court in America to uphold confession evidence that was explicitly coerced. Four years later the Supreme Court ruled that psychologically coerced confessions were equally inadmissible.[28] During the 1940s and 1950s, the interrogation cases coming before the high court virtually all involved psychological forms of coercion, as the high court began to exclude coerced confessions not only because of their inherent unreliability, but also if they were obtained by police methods that "shocked the conscience of the community."[29] In its watershed *Miranda* decision, the Supreme Court ruled that interrogating officers must recite to suspects the now familiar fourfold warnings before custodial questioning could legally commence. The declared purpose of these newfound constitutional requirements was to dispel the compulsion that, *no longer explicit*, had become "inherent" in American police interrogation. By 1966, the Warren Court argued, custodial interrogation in America consisted of manipulative psychological ploys that were designed to overbear the will of criminal suspects.[30]

Ironically, perhaps, the case law of criminal procedure has functioned not only to restrain coercive interrogation practices, but also to sanction the use of deceptive methods. Historically, the law of confessions has been almost exclusively concerned with the use of coercion—not deception—during interrogation. Although American courts have strongly condemned coercive tactics, they have rarely, and often only indirectly, addressed the issue of trickery and deceit.[31] By failing to lay down many bright lines, the courts have indirectly encouraged the police to engage in deceptive practices. One reason police trick and deceive suspects is to circumvent the legal restrictions placed on them by court rulings. Another reason is that deceptive tactics are perceived to be highly effective in eliciting admissions and confessions. As with undercover police work, once courts restrict the use of coercion, police deception seems, inevitably, to increase.

*

. . . [D]eceptive interrogation techniques may be a necessary evil in modern society. Despite the high-minded reasoning of the *Miranda* Court, confessions are often the only incriminating evidence against a guilty suspect.[32] Moreover, in a democratic society that values community participation in the legal determination of guilt, it is significant that confessions are generally regarded by jurors as the most conclusive form of inculpatory evidence.[33] To the extent that we view the appropriate function of the police as one of enforcing laws and combating crime, interrogatory deception becomes legitimate so long as it remains both fair and legal. Indeed, the movement from coercion to deception represents a triumph in the rule of law: As police have become oriented to the abstract and universal legal norms of due process, they no longer resort to physical violence or other extralegal interrogatory practices. Nevertheless, although crime control imperatives may justify its use, and although it may be legally permissible in virtually all of its forms, interrogatory deception inevitably entails morally troubling social costs. The effect of permitting trickery and deceit during interrogation may be (1) to officially sanction the manipulation and exploitation of human relationships, (2) to authoritatively encourage police to lie in other contexts,[34] (3) to undermine public confidence and social trust,[35] and, in some instances, (4) to provoke false confessions.[36] Whether or not we wish to accept these trade-offs, they compel us to think more carefully about the nature and consequences of psychologically deceptive interrogation. For we are, indeed, caught on the horns of a moral dilemma.

NOTES

1. Ernest Jerome Hopkins, Our Lawless Police: A Study of the Unlawful Enforcement of the Law 200 (1931).

2. William Hart, *The Subtle Art of Persuasion*, Police Chief, Jan. 1981, at 15–16.

3. See Albert D. Biderman, *Social Psychological Needs and "Involuntary" Behavior as Illustrated by Compliance in Interrogation*, 23 Sociometry 120–47 (1960).

4. See, e.g., *20/20: Confession at Gunpoint?* (ABC television broadcast, Mar. 29, 1991). See also Welsh White, *Defending* Miranda: *A Reply to Professor Caplan*, 39 Vand. L. Rev. 1, 22 n.73 (1986).

5. See Edwin Driver, *Confessions and the Social Psychology of Coercion*, 82 Harv. L. Rev. 42–61 (1970); Philip Zimbardo, *Coercion and Compliance: The Psychology of Police Confessions*, in C. Perucci & M. Pilisuk, The Triple Revolution 492–508 (1971); Gisli H. Gudjonsson, *Suggestibility in Police Interrogation: A Social Psychological Model*, 1 Soc. Behav. 83–104 (1986); and Richard J. Ofshe, *Coerced Confessions: The Logic of Seemingly Irrational Action*, 6 Cultic Stud. J. 6–15 (1989).

6. *Cited in* Gerald Caplan, *Questioning* Miranda, 38 Vand. L. Rev. 1417, 1458, n.201 (1985).

7. Orozco v. Texas, 394 U.S. 324 (1969).

8. See Beckwith v. United States, 425 U.S. 341 (1976); Oregon v. Mathiason, 429 U.S. 492 (1977); California v. Beheler, 463 U.S. 1121 (1983).

9. The Supreme Court has ruled that an incarcerated individual was not in custody for purposes of *Miranda*. Illinois v. Perkins, 496 U.S. 292 (1990).

10. However, police may deceive an attorney who attempts to invoke a suspect's constitutional rights, as to whether the suspect will be interrogated, and the police do not have to inform a suspect that a third party has hired an attorney on his behalf. See Moran v. Burbine, 475 U.S. 412 (1986).

11. People v. Honeycutt, 570 P.2d 1050 (1970).

12. See Otis H. Stephens, Jr., The Supreme Court and Confessions of Guilt 165–200 (1973).

13. Colorado v. Spring, 494 U.S. 564 (1987).

14. Robert F. Royal & Steven R. Schutt, The Gentle Art of Interviewing and Interrogation: A Professional Manual and Guide 65 (1976).

15. This method lies at the heart of the interrogation methods propounded in the leading interrogation training manual in the United States. See Fred E. Inbau, John E. Reid & Joseph P. Buckley, Criminal Interrogation and Confessions (3d ed. 1986).

16. Bram v. United States, 168 U.S. 532 (1897).

17. Miller v. Fenton, 796 F.2d 598 (1986).

18. Judy Hails Kaci & George E. Rush, *At What Price Will We Obtain Confessions*, 71 Judicature 254, 256–57 (Feb.–Mar. 1988).

19. Gary Marx, Undercover: Police Surveillance in America 2, 62 (1988).

20. The distinction I have drawn in this paper between role playing and misrepresentations of identity corresponds to the difference in the law of rape between "fraud in the inducement" (misrepresentation as to the inducement for submitting) and "fraud in the factum" (misrepresentation of the nature of the act). While the latter may be grounds for prosecution in rape cases, the former may not be.

21. Illinois v. Perkins, 496 U.S. 292 (1990).

22. See Fred Cohen, Miranda *and Police Deception in Interrogation: A Comment on* Illinois v. Perkins, Crim. L. Bull. 534–46 (1990).

23. See David Lykken, A Tremor in the Blood: Uses and Abuses of the Lie-Detector (1981).

24. Welsh S. White, *Police Trickery in Inducing Confessions*, 127 U. Pa. L. Rev. 581 (1979).

25. Caplan, *supra* note 6.

26. Brown v. Mississippi, 297 U.S. 278 (1936).

27. Miranda v. Arizona, 384 U.S. 436 (1966).

28. Chambers v. Florida, 309 U.S. 227 (1940).

29. Rochin v. California, 342 U.S. 165 (1952).

30. *Miranda*, *supra* note 27.

31. See Daniel W. Sasaki, *Guarding the Guardians: Police Trickery and Confessions*, 40 Stan. L. Rev. 1593 (1989).

32. The Law of Confessions v (David M. Nissman & Ed Hagen eds., 1985); Fred E. Inbau, *Police Interrogation—A Practical Necessity*, 52 J. Crim. L., Criminology & Police Science (1961); Zimbardo, *supra* note 5.

33. S. M. Kassin & L. S. Wrightsman, *Confession Evidence*, *in* The Psychology of Evidence and Trial Procedure 67–94, (S. M. Kassin & L. S. Wrightsman eds., 1985).

34. Jerome Skolnick, *Deception by Police*, *in* Criminal Justice Ethics 40–54 (1982).

35. Sissela Bok, Lying: Moral Choice in Public and Private Life (1978).

36. Kassin & Wrightsman, *supra* note 33; Gudjonsson, *supra* note 5; Ofshe, *supra* note 5; Zimbardo, *supra* note 5.

6

"You Have
the Right
to Remain Silent":
Miranda
after
Twenty Years
(1986)

•

PATRICK A. MALONE

Miranda v. Arizona is the only ruling of the U.S. Supreme Court to add a new verb to the language—to *Mirandize* the suspect. When issued [in 1966], it quickly became—and remains to this day—the most reviled decision ever issued by the Supreme Court in a criminal case. Congressmen called for Chief Justice Earl Warren's impeachment. Constitutional amendments were introduced. Police chiefs predicted chaos. Richard Nixon won the presidency in part by holding up *Miranda* as Exhibit One in the indictment against the excesses of the Warren Court for "coddling criminals" and "handcuffing the police."

All this controversy was over a decision that required police departments to do what many law enforcement agencies already practiced: inform a suspect before interrogation of his right not to talk to police and his right to a lawyer—appointed at no cost if he could not afford one—and warn him that, if he did talk, what he said could be used as evidence against him.

Everyone assumed that, once warned of these rights, few suspects would agree to talk to police without a lawyer. The Warren Court's many detractors feared this would paralyze criminal investigations, which relied heavily on obtaining confessions. The Court's few supporters hoped the *Miranda* warnings would reduce the widespread use of trickery and psychologically coercive tactics during police interrogation of suspects. This seemed clearly to be the goal of the majority opinion written by Chief Justice Warren, one that catalogued in damning detail the deceptive practices advocated by leading police procedure manuals and practiced across the country.

Miranda has met neither side's expectations. The creation of a suspect's right to be told his rights has not appreciably affected the confession rate. Nor has *Miranda* curbed the use by police interrogators of such tactics as showing the suspect fake evidence, putting the suspect to a phony lie detector test that he is guaranteed to flunk, and making fraudulent offers of sympathy and help.

Miranda never was as radical as critics have painted it. The Court in *Miranda* did not ban outright, as it could have, all use of questionable interrogation tactics. Nor did the high court require, as courts in other countries have, that any questioning of a suspect be conducted before a neutral magistrate. Instead, the court formulated what amounted to a warning label as an effort to accommodate ideals of fair play to the perceived necessities of police work.

Attorney General Edwin Meese . . . called *Miranda* "a wrong decision," "an infamous decision." But none of the major police and prosecutor lobbying groups, such as the International Association of Chiefs of Police or the National District Attorneys Association . . . joined in Meese's call to overrule *Miranda*.

That is because, on closer examination, *Miranda* turns out to be the police officer's friend. The *Miranda* warning has become, in the main, a benediction at the outset of every interrogation, sanctifying the very practices it was meant to end. Studies—in New Haven, Connecticut; Washington, D.C.; Pittsburgh, Pennsylvania; Denver, Colorado; and elsewhere—have found that *Miranda* warnings have little or no effect on a suspect's propensity to talk. Most suspects routinely waive their *Miranda* rights and submit to police questioning. Next to the warning label on cigarette packs, *Miranda* is the most widely ignored piece of official advice in our society. Even when *Miranda* is violated, it is rare that a confession will be ruled inadmissible or that a suspect will go free. Ernest Miranda himself was retried and reconvicted. A recent federally funded study in Illinois, Michigan, and Pennsylvania found that convictions were lost as a result of judges throwing out confessions in only 5 out of the 7,035 cases studied, or 0.07 percent.

Most people not closely related to a criminal defendant or a criminal defense lawyer will applaud this news, at least at first blush. The rights of defendants, most of whom richly deserve a spell behind bars, have never been a popular cause, and police tactics have never excited much public curiosity. As the constitutional law scholar Yale Kamisar once observed, the typical police suspect and his interrogator are generally viewed "as garbage and garbage collector, respectively."

But the debate, then and now, is not simply over ritual niceties in police questioning of criminal suspects. It is a debate over what kind of criminal justice system we will have.

The U.S. Constitution states that an accused shall not "be compelled to be a witness against himself" and shall enjoy the rights to "due process of law" and the "assistance of counsel." In a 1949 Supreme Court case, Justice Felix Frankfurter capsulized the criminal justice system envisioned by the Constitution when he wrote:

> Ours is the accusatorial as opposed to the inquisitorial system. Such has been the characteristic of Anglo-American criminal justice since it freed itself from practices borrowed by the Star Chamber from the Continent whereby an accused was interrogated in secret for hours on end. Under our system society carries the burden of proving its charge against the accused not out of his own mouth. It must establish its case, not by interrogation of the accused even under judicial safeguards, but by evidence independently secured through skillful investigation. [Watts v. Indiana, 338 U.S. 49, 54 (1949).—Eds.]

The American criminal justice system has in fact been far closer to the inquisitorial than Justice Frankfurter's ringing words would suggest. The reason for this is because we have not one system of criminal justice but two: One is conducted in the courthouse in the open, with phalanxes of lawyers and judges protecting the defendant's rights; the other is conducted in the police station, in private, with no one standing between the accused and the accusers.

Police interrogation, which is perhaps the most striking instance of this bifurcated system, presents two fundamental issues: Does it work? Is it fair? The answer to both questions is vigorously disputed.

It is beyond doubt that the time-honed and sophisticated methods taught by interrogation manuals and police academies are extremely effective in getting suspects to reveal incriminating information—a fact appreciated by few suspects when they sign *Miranda* waiver cards. What is far more uncertain is the frequency with which those statements by suspects are true or false or somewhere in between.

Cases of convincing but false confessions are by their nature difficult to ferret out. Yet they are regularly documented. An eighteen-year-old named Peter Reilly confessed to killing his mother in Canaan, Connecticut. Another young man in Great Britain confessed to raping an eleven-year-old girl. In each case, the confession seemed credible because it contained facts known only to the police and the real perpetrator. Reilly was freed only after an intense two-year campaign by friends and neighbors that enlisted the sympathy of playwright Arthur Miller and other celebrities. The British youth was exonerated when it was shown that his blood type was different from that of the attacker. In neither case was the defendant mentally disturbed or otherwise abnormal. Yet the police, using only standard interrogation techniques without any physical threats or violence, persuaded both young men to confess that they were guilty of crimes someone else had committed. . . .

The full-blown, fantastic confession is only the tip of the problem. Far more common is the confession that is false only in particular details— but twisted enough to turn excusable behavior into a crime or to convict a defendant of a crime far more serious than the one he in fact committed. In a . . . Wisconsin case, Gerald Larson confessed to killing a friend after the friend had assaulted him with a metal pipe. In a statement to police, Larson said his friend had turned away when he shot him, but on the witness stand, Larson repudiated his confession and said the friend was coming at him when he fired. The pathologist's findings supported either version. The jury chose to believe the initial confession, understandably but perhaps mistakenly discounting the possibility that out of shock, confusion, or suggestion (Larson said he was drunk when questioned), Larson's initial statement was wrong. As with the hundreds of other confessions that are recanted every year, the truth or falsity of Larson's confession will never be known.

Then there is the even more common variant of the false confession— the alibi statement, later proven to be a lie, which damns the defendant because of the logical but often untrue inference that he would not have lied if he had been innocent of the crime for which he was questioned.

Why would anyone overstate or falsely state his guilt, especially when the *Miranda* warnings instruct him that anything said will be used against him? The answer requires an exploration of why people confess and how they are led to do so, whether they are guilty or innocent.

From toddler years on, we are taught that confession is both social duty and its own reward. In Christian theology, confession is a key to salvation. The law itself encourages the private expiation of guilt by refusing to require the testimony of those most likely to have heard a criminal defendant's confession—spouse, minister, psychiatrist.

Beyond the ubiquitous social pressure to confess, psychological factors make silence virtually impossible for many people when they are interrogated. A universal rule of polite social discourse is to speak when spoken to. Silence conveys arrogance, hostility, rudeness, and, most of all, guilt. Police interrogators are taught to be careful not to provide an excuse for silence by violating the rules of etiquette. At the same time, they are taught to orchestrate environmental cues with stratagems designed both to lull and to intimidate the suspect into talking.

Training courses advise the interrogator in the style of his or her dress (conservative business suit stripped of any badges or other police identification), the location and decor of the interrogation room (quiet, remote, and bare, with neither reminders that it is in a police station nor with any tension-relieving small objects for the suspect to fiddle with), the seating arrangement (close to the suspect and at eye level), even the desirability of breath mints to avoid losing the psychological advantage of getting physically "next to" the suspect. Taking notes is strictly forbidden. As Fred Inbau and John Reid advise in their classic manual *Criminal Interrogations and Confessions*, "Avoid creating the impression that you are an investigator seeking a confession or conviction."

The orchestration of environmental cues cannot fully erase the suspect's awareness that the interrogator is who he is. But, after the interrogation begins in earnest, a series of techniques completes the transformation. The foremost is the interrogator's attitude. "The consistently successful interrogator," write Arthur Aubry and Rudolph Caputo in *Criminal Interrogation*, "is the one who can project himself to the suspect as a person in whom the suspect can place his confidence, and as a person whom he can trust."

The watchwords of the interrogation are sympathy, understanding, respect, flattery. Interrogators are thus cautioned to avoid any display of disgust or anger toward the suspect, except as part of a calculated "good guy, bad guy" approach designed to heighten the appearance of sympathy by occasionally showing mock impatience or anger.

Skillfully presented, the *Miranda* warnings themselves sound chords of fairness and sympathy at the outset of the interrogation. The interrogator who advises, who cautions, who offers the suspect the gift of a free lawyer, becomes all the more persuasive by dint of his apparent candor and reasonableness. "Interrogators change reality," notes the Stanford psychologist Philip Zimbardo, who teaches a course in mind control. "It's not a cop—it's your Dutch uncle, your friend, the father you never had. They can change reality very quickly."

Intelligence provides no immunity to the process. Researchers found that FBI agents investigating draft resistance in the mid-1960s had no trouble getting Yale faculty and staff members to incriminate themselves. The major factor prodding them to talk was, as the study put it, the "engaging, middle-class manner" of the FBI agents.

This transformation of the interrogator from adversary to older brother affects those on both sides of the table. Alvin A. Dewey, the famed Kansas Bureau of Investigation special agent, once told a Senate subcommittee in defense of police interrogation practices: "As to the description of an interrogation room, I wish to define it as a room where people can talk in privacy, which is nothing more than an attorney desires in talking to his client or a doctor in talking to his patient." The basic principle, Zimbardo maintains, is also employed by groups as exotic as religious cults and as commonplace as door-to-door salesmen: determine the subject's dominant need (be it flattery, respect, sympathy), stimulate and exaggerate the need, then offer to satisfy it in return for the subject's statement (or devotion or money).

Tips from Inbau and Reid's manual:

> Sympathize with the subject by telling him that anyone else under similar conditions or circumstances might have done the same thing.
>
> Reduce the subject's guilt feeling by minimizing the moral seriousness of the offense.
>
> Suggest a less revolting and more morally acceptable motivation or reason for the offense than that which is known or presumed.

Here are excerpts from an interrogation:

> *Interrogator 1*: David, you, look at you—you are on the verge of crying right now.
>
> *Interrogator 2*: 1 believe you cared for that little girl.
>
> *No. 1*: It's tearing you up inside.
>
> *No. 2*: 1 don't believe you're that kind of guy.
>
> *No. 1*: You can help yourself by telling the truth.
>
> *No. 2*: If you was drinking and you made a mistake, son. . . . If you was drunk—
>
> *Suspect David Miller*: If I was drunk, if I was sober, I've still got the rest of my life to look at behind bars.
>
> *No. 1*: . . . Son, you can only help yourself. No matter what happens, you're going to have to have peace of mind sooner or later.

At the same time, the interrogator is taught to display an air of unwavering confidence in the suspect's guilt and to bolster this by reciting the evidence against the suspect. A number of interrogation manuals, including that used by the National Association of State Directors of Law Enforcement Training, specifically endorse the use, if necessary, of falsified evidence.

Recent reports of criminal appeals show that police interrogators used, among other things, fabricated reports of physical evidence, statements from nonexistent eyewitnesses, and phony lie detector results. In one recent case, a Raleigh, North Carolina, police detective put his own bloody fingerprint on a knife and told the suspect the print had been conclusively shown to be that of the suspect. In each of these cases of falsified evidence, the appeals courts upheld the use of confessions so obtained.

Fake evidence is consistent with the entire milieu of the interrogation. As Inbau and Reid candidly state: "Whenever the police interrogate a person whom they believe to be guilty of a crime they are not doing so for *his* benefit. Deceit, therefore, is inherent in every question asked of the suspect, and in every statement made by the interrogator."

Excerpts from another interrogation:

Interrogator: I don't think you're a criminal, Frank.

Suspect Frank Miller: No, but you're trying to make me one.

Interrogator: No I'm not, no I'm not, but I want you to talk to me so we can get this thing worked out. . . . Frank, look, you want, you want help, don't you, Frank? . . .

Interrogator: Let it come out, Frank. I'm here, I'm here with you now. I'm on your side, I'm on your side, Frank. I'm your brother, you and I are brothers, Frank. We are brothers, and I want to help my brother. . . .

Interrogator: You killed this girl, didn't you?

Miller: No, I didn't.

Interrogator: Honest, Frank? It's got to come out. You can't leave it in. It's hard for you, I realize that, but you've got to help yourself before anybody else can help you. And we're going to see to it that you get the proper help. This is our job, Frank. This is our job. This is what I want to do.

Miller: By sending me back down there [to prison].

Interrogator: Wait a second now, don't talk about going back down there. First thing we have to do is let it all come out. Don't fight it because it's worse, Frank, it's worse. It's hurting me because I feel it. I feel it wanting to come out, but it's hurting me, Frank. You're my brother, I mean we're brothers. All men on this, all men on the face of this earth are brothers, Frank, but you got to be completely honest with me.

Advocates of these techniques, such as Fred Inbau, an emeritus professor of law at Northwestern University, draw a line between these psychological tactics and the use of physical threats or actual violence. Only the latter, they maintain, can produce confessions from the innocent. Evidence from the Korean prisoner of war studies and elsewhere, however, refutes this distinction. Indeed, social scientists have learned that physical coercion is often the least effective way of getting confessions. Psychological coercion produces more true confessions—and more false ones as well.

One classic experiment with college students documented how completely normal individuals, even without being placed in a stress-inducing setting, can be persuaded that their view of reality is wrong. Eight students were shown a set of lines of clearly identical length. Seven had been coached ahead of time to state that the lines were of different lengths. Of fifty students cast in the role of the eighth unwitting person in the group, only thirteen succeeded in consistently rejecting the majority's clearly erroneous judgment.

Studies by psychologist Elizabeth F. Loftus, author of *Eyewitness Testimony*, and others have consistently found that memory is extraordinarily malleable—particularly in the face of persistent and suggestive questioning. In the Peter Reilly case in Connecticut [*supra* at page 77], police repeatedly insisted that they knew he had killed his mother. Reilly finally adopted the police version (asking his chief interrogator during the same interview if he could come and live with the officer and his family). Later evidence was discovered that proved his innocence.

But in the two Miller cases (unrelated) whose interrogations were excerpted earlier, substantial circumstantial evidence linked the defendants to the respective murders—brutal stabbings of teenage girls. David Miller was sentenced to death for killing his girlfriend in Knoxville, Tennessee. Frank Miller was sentenced to life in prison for murdering a farm girl in East Amwell Township, New Jersey. In both cases, however, the interrogators repeatedly lied and made promises of help that never came to pass. Moreover, in the Frank Miller case, New Jersey state police detective Charles Boyce made up eyewitness accounts and physical evidence linking Miller to the crime.

These cases thus raise questions far more problematic than sending innocent persons to prison, which is unquestionably something everyone opposes. Should the police be allowed to commit fraud in the pursuit of justice? Even if the guilty do not deserve protection from such tactics, is it necessary to shield the guilty in order to prevent police from using the same methods on those eventually shown to be innocent?

Largely by default, it has been left to the courts to wrestle with these issues and to set standards of acceptable police conduct. Thus, the questions have been approached at an oblique angle, not by asking what is the wisest public policy, but by divining the pronouncements of the United States Constitution, which states that an accused shall not "be compelled to be a witness against himself " (Fifth Amendment) and shall enjoy the rights to "due process of law" (Fifth and Fourteenth Amendments) and "assistance of counsel" (Sixth Amendment).

Torture itself was a common and accepted tool of police procedure not many years before Justice Felix Frankfurter asserted that ours was an accusatorial, not an inquisitorial, system. Even after widespread police brutality was documented by a presidential commission in 1931, the "third degree" had many defenders. They pointed to its undeniable effectiveness in winning convictions and argued that criminals with no respect for the law deserved no special rights once they were caught. . . .

Subsequent cases exposed more subtle forms of police terror: removing the defendant late at night from his cell and driving him to a dark and remote location for questioning, depriving the defendant of food and sleep, engaging in long hours of secret grilling by relay teams of interrogators.

But the Court's unanimity in condemning torture quickly dissolved when confronted with more subtle forms of coercion. The Supreme Court shied away from policing the police with any kind of direct prohibitions on certain tactics. The Court perceived its job as protecting the voluntariness of the confessions of individual defendants. So it embarked on the psychoanalytic task of weighing the defendant's maturity and intelligence against the interrogator's tactics to determine, as the Court often put it, "whether the defendant's will was overborne"—all this by paging through trial transcripts without benefit of training in psychology or any personal acquaintance with the interrogators or the defendants.

On one level, of course, the search for voluntariness was both inevitable and correct. No system of justice is so solicitous of defendants that it bars them from volunteering evidence of their guilt to the authorities. . . .

Lurking beneath this language of free will has been another issue. Most judges have perceived, correctly or not, that interrogation of suspects is essential to the effective solution of crimes—regardless of any high rhetoric from Justice Frankfurter about the Star Chamber and the Fifth Amendment. As a result, the debate about voluntariness has been shadowed by a mostly unspoken struggle about how to strike the balance between the conflicting goals of effective law enforcement and fairness to the accused. Justice Frankfurter himself signaled the hidden agenda when he wrote, somewhat opaquely: "A statement to be voluntary of course need not be volunteered."

*

[*Miranda* held "that police questioning of suspects in private inherently coerces defendants to incriminate themselves." Thus,] the Court could have ruled flatly that such interrogation violates the Fifth Amendment right against self-incrimination. That would have required that any interrogation at a police station be conducted in the presence of the suspect's lawyer or a neutral magistrate. It would have effectively ended the two-tier system of criminal justice—one private, one public. Instead, the Court allowed tactics that it found violative of the right against self-incrimination to continue as long as suspects agreed to submit to them. The Court assumed that a recital of warnings could adequately educate a suspect to decide intelligently whether to undergo questioning unaided by counsel.

The justices who dissented from the *Miranda* opinion assumed—as did everyone else after the opinion was released on Monday, June 13, 1966—that the new *Miranda* warnings were tantamount to a ban on station house interrogation. Everyone recognized that, from the suspect's point of view, nothing can be gained and everything can be lost by talking to the authorities without one's lawyer—and everyone assumed that the *Miranda* warnings would effectively communicate this message to most suspects.

That confession rates have remained largely unchanged since *Miranda* is testimony both to psychological realities that no court could alter and to the flawed logic of the *Miranda* majority ruling. The compulsion to talk when one is accused of wrongdoing arises in part from the belief that silence is an admission of guilt. What most people do not understand, and what the *Miranda* warnings fail to explain, is that, under the Fifth Amendment, silence after arrest and *Miranda* warnings cannot be used against the defendant. . . .

These are but quibbles compared to the root problem of *Miranda*: It asks police to solve crime but to protect suspects from police investigations, and it assumes that these suspects can receive adequate advice and counseling about their constitutional rights from adversaries who would like nothing more than to see those rights surrendered.

While *Miranda* has done little to change the dynamics of the interrogation process or the techniques used by police, it has affected the *ex post facto* analysis by courts about whether a particular confession should be admitted into evidence. *Miranda* has shifted the legal inquiry from whether the confession was voluntarily given to whether the *Miranda* rights were voluntarily waived.

There are occasional—and well-publicized—cases where the defendant has won a ruling that his confession cannot be used against him because of such a *Miranda* violation. Generally, however, the shift in focus has proven to be a boon to police. For one thing, the issue is tidier. Staccato *Miranda* conversations, with their uniform statements and check-the-box answers, are easier for courts to evaluate than sprawling hours-long interrogations. When a suspect says yes, he understands his *Miranda* rights, and yes, he waives them, he is generally taken at his word no matter how ignorant his hapless lawyer may later try to prove him. (One study of 7,000 felony cases found that defendants tried to get confessions suppressed in only 6.6 percent of the cases and succeeded in only 0.17 percent of the cases.) . . .

Miranda has persisted this long because it allows us to celebrate our values of individualism without paying any real price. As a cultural symbol, *Miranda* stands for the enshrinement of individual rights over the need of the state for efficiency, equal justice for rich and poor before the law, the right to be presumed innocent, and the demand that the police follow the law while enforcing it. That it has managed to fail in any real sense to reform police conduct, that it serves interests opposite to those intended by its authors—this shows only that *Miranda* in [its first twenty years] has been transformed from a tool of law into an icon for our conflicting ideals.

II

The
Ethical
and Policy
Debate
Regarding
Miranda

Part I raised general questions about the law of confessions and *Miranda*. Part II sharpens the focus on the ethical and political dimensions of this question, which essentially breaks down into three issues. First, can *Miranda*'s approach to regulating the interrogation process be justified as a reading of the Fifth Amendment, on either constitutional or policy grounds? Second, what would replace *Miranda* if it were overruled? Third, if *Miranda* is not overruled, can it be improved and, if so, in what ways?

First, we continue the story of Ernest Miranda, begun in Chapter 1. Despite the fears of the dissenting Justices in *Miranda*, the new rules for interrogation did not permit at least one defendant to escape justice for his crime: Miranda himself. Courts rarely reverse a conviction and order a defendant released. Instead, a new trial is usually one of the options open to the prosecutor after a reversal on appeal. In Ernest Miranda's case, the new trial could not include the confessions he made to the police (this was the real-life effect of the Supreme Court's holding in *Miranda*). But the second trial ended again in a conviction, based largely on a confession Miranda made to his girlfriend when she visited him in jail a few days after he had confessed to the police.[1]

Miranda's second conviction was affirmed on appeal, and the U.S. Supreme Court refused to hear the second *Miranda* case. Thus, Ernest Miranda served a prison term for the very rape that led to the most controversial ruling in favor of a criminal defendant in the history of the Supreme Court. Few people know, or at least mention, this fact about Ernest Miranda. Critics of expanded rights for criminal suspects also rarely mention the self-adjusting quality of the criminal justice system manifested in Miranda's conviction. The Warren Court sought in *Miranda* to vindicate the right to fairness and equality in the interrogation room, but the system managed to convict a guilty defendant despite a benefit from the new rights.

During Ronald Reagan's presidency, Attorney General Edwin Meese headed a very conservative Department of Justice. In 1986, the Department released a report that called for the abolition of *Miranda*, thereby generating significant news coverage and controversy. Excerpted in Chapter 7, the Report chronicled the first twenty years after *Miranda*. Its perspective is exactly opposite that of Patrick Malone in Chapter 6. Instead of focusing on the power imbalance in the interrogation room, the Justice Department Report focused on the likelihood that guilty suspects avoid the police questioning that would establish their guilt.

The Report argues, moreover, that *Miranda* is not even based on the Constitution, citing later cases in which the Court talks about *Miranda* as a mechanism to protect the Fifth Amendment privilege not to answer questions—a presumption about when the Fifth Amendment is violated—rather than a part of the Fifth Amendment itself. Law often uses presumptions to help decide difficult issues. For example, criminal defendants are presumed innocent but sane. This means that the state must prove guilt, but a defendant who claims insanity has the burden of proving insanity. If *Miranda* is only a presumption about the Fifth Amendment, rather than being *part* of the Fifth Amendment, the *Miranda* rule can (in theory, at least) be ignored when a greater benefit results from not applying it. In this view, the *Miranda* requirements can be eliminated or reduced whenever the Court (or perhaps the Congress) comes up with a better means to protect the Fifth Amendment interests of suspects. The Justice Department Report proposed a series of new rules to govern police interrogation that, it claimed, would better protect suspects from police manipulation and trickery while permitting more legitimate pressure on suspects to tell the truth.

In Chapter 8, Stephen Schulhofer defends *Miranda's* interpretation of the Fifth Amendment. Keeping the focus on constitutional doctrine and policy, Schulhofer notes that the *Miranda* Court relied on three "conceptually distinct steps" to reach its decision. First, the Court held that informal pressure to speak—that which lacks a formal sanction such as contempt of court—can constitute Fifth Amendment compulsion. Schulhofer relies on two pre-*Miranda* Fifth Amendment cases to defend the notion that compulsion is not limited to situations in which the law requires an answer. Thus, police interrogation *can* constitute compulsion.

The second step is to conclude that police interrogation of a suspect in custody *always* constitutes compulsion. Admitting that this issue is "much more problematic than the first," Schulhofer nonetheless defends the Court's conclusion here. He rejects the equivalence that scholars and a few earlier cases had drawn between "involuntariness" under the due process clause and "compulsion" under the Fifth Amendment. Relying on cases applying the Fifth Amendment outside the context of police interrogation, Schulhofer concludes that compulsion was never limited to the kind of pressure that "broke" the will, as the voluntariness doctrine has usually been understood. For Schulhofer, the policy served by the privilege against self-incrimination "extends to all governmental efforts intended to pressure an unwilling individual to assist as a witness in his own prosecution." This, of course, encompasses police interrogation. The third part of the *Miranda* holding, which Schulhofer also defends, is that the required warnings are necessary to dispel the inherent compulsion found to exist in custodial police interrogation.

Gerald Caplan attacks *Miranda* in Chapter 9 not so much for its constitutional interpretation as for its underlying "fairness" premise. If "fairness" means not subjecting a suspect to humiliating, coercive interrogation, then *Miranda* is overinclusive in its insistence that every suspect has the right to terminate questioning at any time. If "fairness" means that a suspect must be given a "sporting chance" to win the battle of wits with police and avoid confessing, then *Miranda* is the right solution because it provides information that should put suspects on more equal footing with the police.

But why would we want to give suspects a sporting chance? We want to treat them with decency and humanity; we do not want police to beat or threaten them. But why would we cheer when guilty suspects resist police interrogation and refuse to testify? Not all suspects are guilty, of course, but police are required to have probable cause before they arrest and hold a suspect. So the question may be put this way: *why* should we give a sporting chance to a suspect when we have probable cause to believe he has committed a crime and all we want to know is the truth about that crime? For purposes of ethical discussion, we can leave to one side the constitutional text; almost all scholars, including

Yale Kamisar (in Chapter 2) and Stephen Schulhofer in (Chapter 8), agree that *Miranda*'s interpretation of the Fifth Amendment is but one permissible reading. If we are to choose among permissible readings, our choice should be informed by ethics. One can begin an ethical evaluation of a "right to silence" by noting that we do not provide a right to silence for students questioned by teachers, or one spouse questioned by the other, or one friend questioned by another, or even a citizen who has been asked his name and address by a police officer.

Caplan argues that maintaining silence in the face of evidence of guilt can be viewed as a virtue only if the government was wrong to ask. But how can it be wrong for the government to ask whether a suspect committed a crime? If the reply is that it is wrong because some, but not all, suspects know they do not have to answer, Caplan replies that guilt is personal. That one clever murderer avoids conviction "does not make the more vulnerable murderer less guilty. To hold otherwise is to confuse justice with equality." We should, instead, find it right and proper for police to encourage guilty suspects to admit their guilt. Caplan concludes: "There is no neutral position. One must lean toward the government or subversion."

Even if Caplan and the Justice Department Report are correct about the ethical and constitutional problems of *Miranda*, a pragmatic defense still exists. The *Miranda* "bright line" of warnings and waiver has eased the task of judges in deciding which confessions are admissible. Moreover, even if *Miranda* lacked judicial legitimacy when it was decided, it has been the law for more than thirty years and has been endorsed by many police and prosecutors.[2] What would it be like to overturn the only rules on interrogation that an entire generation of police have known?

Lawrence Herman provides an answer in Chapter 10 that should give pause to those who want to return to the "good old days of police interrogation." The most likely successor to *Miranda* is the traditional test of voluntariness—whether the confession was the product of the suspect's essentially unconstrained choice or instead resulted from an overbearing of his will. Herman provides examples of how courts manipulate the voluntariness test—both to exclude and admit confessions—in cases where the opposite result seems more defensible. He summarizes the results of the Supreme Court's voluntariness doctrine. In a thirty-year period, the Court granted review in more than thirty-five cases in which the lower courts had held the confessions voluntary, and the Court reversed most of those convictions. He concludes that the Court "failed" to make the doctrine "intelligible" and to give "illustrative examples." Herman also concludes that "failure was preordained."

Herman's point is fundamentally pragmatic. As he puts it,

> I am not saying that *Miranda* was correctly decided. . . . The point is that the dissenters in *Miranda* in 1966 and the Attorney General in 1985 were simply wrong in their claim that we got along well with the law that antedated *Miranda*. We did not, and we are not getting along well with its vestiges today, and recognition of these simple facts should inform any reasonable debate about whether *Miranda* should be overruled.

Whatever the failings of *Miranda*, in Herman's view, it is a better control on police and prosecutors, and easier for courts to apply, than the voluntariness doctrine.

But the simplicity of *Miranda*'s application—its "bright line" of warnings and waiver—has also made the lives of police and prosecutors easier. No longer do police and prosecutors have to guess about which of the voluntariness standards a court might choose to apply in a particular case. The police now have a set of relatively clear rules to follow, and if they follow them, the prosecutor can expect to have the confession admitted with little or no difficulty. The primary effect of *Miranda*, therefore, could be to ease the task of obtaining and admitting confessions. It seems clear that police have adapted to *Miranda* and have found ways to create the preference to answer questions despite the warning of the right to remain silent. In Part III, we will take up this issue in more detail.

If the *Miranda* warnings have been rendered largely ineffective by changes in police interrogation or methods of giving the warnings, and if *Miranda*'s original goal is still worth pursuing, perhaps more radical measures are required. As Chapter 11 makes plain, Irene Merker Rosenberg and Yale L. Rosenberg do not believe that the Supreme Court still has goals even remotely like the original *Miranda* Court. They argue that the Court has undermined *Miranda* in the last twenty years while appearing to affirm it. Moreover, lower courts are all too willing to find waiver of the *Miranda* rights.

Holding to the goals of the *Miranda* Court, the Rosenbergs propose a bold stroke: replace *Miranda* with a rule that makes all custodial statements inadmissible. If *Miranda* was right to find inherent coercion poisoning the station atmosphere, the only certain way to prevent the use of coerced statements is simply to bar all custodial statements.

This proposal solves what is a difficult problem for *Miranda* supporters: how can the decision to waive the *Miranda* rights be kept free from the police-dominated coercive atmosphere of the station house interrogation room? If the inherent coercion of police interrogation taints the answer to even the most innocuous question posed without warnings having been given, this coercion seems likely to taint the decision to give up the right to counsel and the right to remain silent. Adopting the Rosenbergs' solution would solve this theoretical problem.

The Rosenbergs' proposal would also solve an intensely practical problem that remains after thirty years of *Miranda*: judging the voluntariness of the *Miranda* waiver. Though the *Miranda* opinion stated that the prosecution would have a "heavy burden" to show waiver in the absence of counsel, there was no way to give substantive content to this "heavy burden" short of outlawing waivers. If a suspect who has been given *Miranda* warnings is found to have voluntarily decided to waive the warnings and answer questions, what theoretical doctrine would forbid those answers in court? The Court ultimately agreed that voluntariness is the measure of *Miranda* waivers. But this puts us, in a way, back where we started—having to determine whether the suspect voluntarily gave up something. In the pre-*Miranda* world, the question was whether the suspect voluntarily confessed. As Patrick Malone pointed out in Chapter 6, the question today is whether the suspect voluntarily gave up his *Miranda* rights. Both questions require a metaphysical inquiry into the suspect's "will." With the Rosenbergs' solution in place, this difficult inquiry would be a problem of the past.

But the Rosenbergs' solution—even *Miranda* itself—is quite a departure from the historical understanding of the Fifth Amendment prohibition of compelled self-incrimination. Albert W. Alschuler shows in Chapter 12 that for centuries of English common law and American law under the Fifth Amendment, there has existed a right not to be compelled to give testimony. But the Fifth Amendment does not confer on defendants a right not to be questioned. This is clear from the early debates about whether American magistrates could question defendants in the same way as English magistrates; though the issue was debated hotly, no one raised the argument that judicial questioning of defendants would violate the Fifth Amendment. If the Fifth Amendment permitted magistrates to question defendants, it would, of course, permit police to question defendants.

So how did a "right to silence" come into being? Alschuler speculates that it evolved through the "tyranny of slogans" that took on lives of their own. The phrase "no one shall be compelled in any criminal case to be a witness against himself" sounds like a "privilege against self-incrimination," which, in turn, sounds like a "right to remain silent." As Alschuler notes, "Much of the history of the privilege has been a story of slippage from one doctrine to another without awareness of the change." Officials "drifted" from one limitation on state power to a different, and greater, limitation, and we wound up with *Miranda* telling us that the Fifth Amendment provides a general right to remain silent.

Alschuler offers his own bold proposal at the end of Chapter 12: a statute that would require suspects arrested on probable cause to appear before a magistrate and face questions from the magistrate. A refusal to answer these questions would, under Alschuler's statute, be admissible at trial. Similarly, "a defendant should be expected to speak at trial—perhaps under oath but exempted from penalties for perjury—and if she declined, the judge or jury should be permitted to draw appropriate inferences." This is a bold stroke indeed. Imagine a post-*Miranda* world in which suspects are expected to answer questions posed by magistrates and prosecutors, and then penalized if they refuse!

On balance, as Part II will show in more detail, *Miranda* has created at least as many puzzles as it solved when it replaced the due process voluntariness test with a more precise requirement of warnings and waiver. As Fred Graham wrote, "[T]he ultimate judgment of the Warren Court's involvement in the question of confessions is likely to be not whether suspects should be warned of their rights, but whether *Miranda v. Arizona* was worth the price."[3]

NOTES

1. Liva Baker, *Miranda*: Crime, Law and Politics 291 (1983).

2. In 1992, four national police organizations and fifty former prosecutors filed a "friend of the Court" brief to ask the Supreme Court not to restrict the availablity of *Miranda* in certain appeals. See Brief Amici Curiae of the Police Foundation et al. in Support of the Respondent, Withrow v. Williams, 507 U.S. 680 (1993).

3. Fred Graham, *The Self-Inflicted Wound* 192 (1970).

Report to the Attorney General on the Law of Pretrial Interrogation (February 12, 1986, with addendum of January 20, 1987)

•

U.S. DEPARTMENT OF JUSTICE,

OFFICE OF LEGAL POLICY

Executive Summary

. . . The Court in *Miranda* promulgated a new, code-like set of rules for custodial questioning, including the creation of a right to counsel in connection with custodial questioning, a requirement of warnings, a prohibition of questioning unless the suspect affirmatively waives the rights set out in the warnings, and a prohibition of questioning if the suspect asks for a lawyer or indicates in any manner that he is unwilling to talk. These admittedly nonconstitutional standards impede the search for truth by conditioning inquiry, no matter how brief and restrained, on a suspect's consent to be questioned, and by excluding a suspect's statements at trial, though fully voluntary and reliable, if obtained in violation of *Miranda*'s "prophylactic" procedures. Beyond their costs to the truth-finding process, the *Miranda* rules can also validly be criticized as inept and ineffective means of promoting fair treatment of suspects. Their imposition by judicial fiat has effectively precluded the development of superior alternative procedures.

*

II

In general character, the *Miranda* decision stood somewhere between a code of procedure with commentary and a judicial decision in the conventional sense. Chief Justice Warren, who devised the detailed set of rules announced in the decision, initially drafted the opinion of the Court so as to make these rules constitutional requirements. However, he was forced to accommodate Justice Brennan, who insisted that the federal government and the states should have the option of developing alternative rules counteracting the pressures of custodial interrogation. The final version of the opinion took the position that compelled self-incrimination would necessarily occur if statements were obtained from a suspect without special safeguards, but acknowledged that the specific procedures prescribed by *Miranda* were dispensable if it could be shown that other rules were equally effective. . . .

Congress quickly repudiated the *Miranda* decision, and somewhat later the Supreme Court rejected its underlying rationale, following a change in the Court's membership. The legislative response was a statute (18 U.S.C. §3501) enacted in 1968 to overturn the *Miranda* decision and restore the pre-*Miranda* voluntariness standard for the admission of confessions in federal prosecutions. The Department of Justice attempted to establish the validity of this statute in litigation for several years with inconclusive results, but ultimately terminated this litigative effort after an initial appellate decision[1] which upheld the statute.

[The statute, 18 U.S.C. §3501, provides: "In any criminal prosecution brought by the United States or by the District of Columbia, a confession . . . shall be admissible in evidence if it is voluntarily given. . . .[2]

[In an omitted part, the Report argues that *Miranda* is no longer viewed by the Court as part of the Fifth Amendment but, rather, as a presumption that is broader than the Fifth Amendment, and thus serves the Fifth Amendment by ensuring that no compelled statements are introduced at trial. But this necessarily means that some clearly voluntary statements may not be introduced just because they run afoul of the overbroad presumption. See *Oregon v. Elstad*.[3] The Justice Department throughout the Report consistently points to this presumptive quality of *Miranda* as evidence that it is no longer a constitutional rule.—Eds.]

IV. Recommendations for Reform

*

A. Reasons for Abrogating Miranda

There are several considerations supporting the recommendation that we should seek to have *Miranda* overruled:

First, the continued application of *Miranda* violates the constitutional separation of powers and basic principles of federalism. *Miranda's* promulgation of a code of procedure for interrogations constituted a usurpation of legislative and administrative powers, thinly disguised as an exercise in constitutional exegesis which rested on fictions and specious arguments. The current Court has repudiated the premises on which *Miranda* was based, but has drawn back from recognizing the full implications of its decisions. We are left with admittedly nonconstitutional rules that continue to be applied in both federal and state proceedings, despite a contrary Act of Congress at the federal level and an admitted lack of supervisory authority to enforce such rules against the state courts. Fidelity to the Constitution's plan of government requires that this situation be corrected.

Second, *Miranda*, by impeding the prosecution of crime, impairs the ability of government to protect the public. Compliance with *Miranda* markedly reduces the willingness of suspects to respond to questioning by the police. In a substantial proportion of criminal cases, confessions and other statements from the defendant are indispensable to a successful prosecution. When statements are not obtained in such cases through the operation of *Miranda's* system, criminals go free. Other damage to the operation of the criminal justice system includes the need to expend limited investigative resources in developing cases that might easily have been made had the suspect cooperated; the need to accept pleas that are not commensurate with the seriousness of the actual offense, where a case has been weakened through the unavailability of the defendant's statements; and the need to expend prosecutorial and judicial resources in litigating questions of compliance with *Miranda's* formalities.

Third, *Miranda's* system is a poorly conceived means of protecting suspects from coercion and overreaching in police interrogations. Its consequences are to divide suspects into two classes: those who "stand on their rights," and those who waive their rights and submit to questioning. The effect of *Miranda* on suspects in the former class is not to protect them from abusive questioning, but to enable them to insulate themselves from any sort of questioning. In cases in which suspects do waive their rights, interrogations can be carried out much as they were before *Miranda*. In such instances *Miranda* is, in particular, virtually worthless as a safeguard against the specific interrogation practices that were characterized as abusive in the *Miranda* decision and cited as the empirical justification for *Miranda*'s reforms:

> The last laugh in the *Miranda* episode was not had by its author, Earl Warren . . . but by Fred E. Inbau and John E. Reid, the authors of the interrogation manual that he quoted frequently and with disapproval in the *Miranda* decision. To show that secret interrogation was inherently coercive, even without the rubber hose or third degree, Warren exposed the techniques taught in that manual and others, which enable the police to bring psychological pressures to bear on the suspect to "persuade, trick, or cajole him out of exercising his constitutional rights." With this to recommend it, the manual became a best seller among police and a second edition had to be printed. "All but a few of the interrogation tactics and techniques presented in our earlier publication are still valid," the authors purred in their post-*Miranda* edition, adding that all that is required is to give the warnings, get a waiver, and proceed.[4]

The judgment concerning *Miranda*'s inadequacies on this score is not limited to critics of any particular ideological stripe. Rather, there has been broad agreement among writers on the subject that *Miranda* is an inept means of protecting the rights of suspects and a failure in relation to its own premises and objectives.

Fourth, *Miranda* is damaging to public confidence in the law, and can result in gross injustices to crime victims. *Miranda*'s rules are completely rigid and formal, in the sense that no showing, however strong, that a suspect's statements were freely given and truthful is deemed sufficient to excuse noncompliance. Cases accordingly arise in which perpetrators of the most serious crimes secure the exclusion of their admissions or the reversal of their convictions on the basis of technical violations of *Miranda* or related decisions that do not cast the slightest doubt on their guilt. This can result in the freeing of known criminals or the prolongation of the anguish of crime victims through years of additional litigation. The perception of such cases by members of the public must be that the system has become deranged, treating their lives, their security, and their deepest sensibilities as pawns in an inscrutable game.

Fifth, the *Miranda* decision has petrified the law of pretrial interrogation for the past twenty years, foreclosing the possibility of developing and implementing alternatives that would be of greater effectiveness both in protecting the public from crime and in ensuring fair treatment of persons suspected of crime. The decision immediately stifled the active ferment in the law of pretrial interrogation that was underway at the time it was handed down, and nothing much has changed since then. Nothing is likely to change in the future as long as *Miranda* remains in effect and perpetuates a perceived risk of invalidation for any alternative system that departs from it.

On the other side, we see no substantial reasons for retaining *Miranda*'s system. The argument that it is necessary to guard against abusive interrogations requires no lengthy discussion. *Miranda* is not rationally designed to further that end, and it has precluded the development of other approaches that would avoid its shortcomings in that regard.

A second argument advanced in support of *Miranda* is that it serves to promote equity among defendants who might otherwise have disparate chances of avoiding conviction on account of differences in their personal circumstances. . . . In the controversy that followed the *Miranda* decision, apologists for *Miranda* also frequently relied on this point in supporting its warning rules. In the absence of such warnings, the argument ran, suspects who happened to know of the rights covered by the warnings would enjoy an unfair advantage in comparison with those who did not.

However, so long as interrogations are conducted so as to ensure that innocent suspects are not coerced into making false admissions, this argument is without force. It is not unfair to obtain and use a suspect's statements to convict him for a crime that he has in fact committed, just because more knowledgeable criminals are better able to exploit the rules of law to defeat justice. As Attorney General Nicholas Katzenbach observed: "I have never understood why the gangster should be made the model and all others raised, in the name of equality, to his level of success in suppressing evidence. This is simply the proposition that if some can beat the rap, all must beat the rap."[5] If disparities among defendants are to be addressed, the sensible way to do so is by devising rules of pretrial interrogation that minimize the potential for obstruction and manipulation by all defendants.

A third argument offered in support of *Miranda* is that it provides "bright line" rules which were not provided by the due process voluntariness standard. This argument may be taken in two ways.

First, it may amount to the contention that there is an unacceptable risk that unlawful coercion will take place if the relatively diffuse strictures of the voluntariness standard are not supplemented by rules providing more definite guidance concerning permissible interrogation practices. It may also involve the contention that the voluntariness standard is too permissive, and leaves room for practices that are inhumane or unworthy, even if not literally unlawful.

We agree that law enforcement officers should be provided with interrogation rules that are more definite than "thou shalt not engage in coercion." However, we do not see any merit in the particular rules that *Miranda* promulgated for this purpose, and do not believe that the courts are the appropriate agencies for developing and enacting such rules.

Second, the "bright line" argument may refer to the concern that the absence of more definite prophylactic rules would lead to increased litigation over the occurrence of actual coercion. The force of this point is limited to some degree by the fact that *Miranda* did not supplant the traditional voluntariness standard, but supplemented it. Defendants who have received the full *Miranda* treatment remain free to claim that they were coerced anyway, and do so frequently. This point also affords no reason for preferring *Miranda*'s rules over various other possible systems of prophylactic rules whose observance would make it difficult for a defendant to make a credible claim of coercion.

Moreover, *Miranda*'s requirements have given rise to an enormous volume of litigation of a wholly novel character. This includes litigation relating to the delivery and formulation of the warnings; the existence of a "custodial" situation requiring warnings prior to questioning; the adequacy of a defendant's waiver; compliance with the rules against questioning a defendant who has expressed an unwillingness to talk or requested counsel; compliance with the rule that a defendant's silence following the receipt of *Miranda* warnings must be concealed from the jury at trial; and various other matters. Given *Miranda*'s status as a major source of litigable issues in its own right, there is no reason to believe that it has had any effect of reducing the volume of litigation relating to the admission of pretrial statements by defendants.

A fourth argument is that the *Miranda* decision has become institutionalized in police practice to the point where it no longer exacts any unacceptable costs in terms of lost statements or evidence. Police training in *Miranda*'s rules and the use of such props as *Miranda* cards and printed waiver forms reduce the likelihood of errors by the police that would jeopardize the admissibility of a defendant's statements in subsequent proceedings.

This argument, however, basically misapprehends the nature of the costs associated with *Miranda*. While cases continue to occur in which police officers are tripped up by *Miranda*'s technicalities and statements are later excluded as a result, the main cost is the loss of statements which are never obtained to begin with because compliance with *Miranda* has enabled suspects to insulate themselves from inquiry, or has inhibited them from responding. Since the purpose and effect of *Miranda*'s rules are to enlarge the opportunities for suspects to remain silent, perfection in the machinery of compliance can only increase this cost.

Some final points that have been offered in support of *Miranda* are that it is somehow questionable or undesirable to use a person's own statements to convict him; that a system which relies frequently on such statements is likely to be less reliable and effective overall than one that does not; and that restrictive interrogation rules improve the quality of police work by requiring the development of greater facility in obtaining other sorts of evidence.

We see no merit in these arguments. There is nothing wrong with using a defendant's own statements to convict him, so long as the Constitution's prohibition of compulsion is not transgressed:

> The Constitution is not at all offended when a guilty man stubs his toe. On the contrary, it is decent to hope that he will. . . . Thus the Fifth Amendment does not say that a man shall not be permitted to incriminate himself, or that he shall not be persuaded to do so. It says no more than that a man shall not be "compelled" to give evidence against himself.[6]

The points relating to the overall effectiveness or reliability of the criminal justice system are also unpersuasive. So long as coercion is avoided, a suspect's incriminating statements are highly probative evidence, since innocent people are not prone to make false admissions that will send them to prison. While restrictions on obtaining evidence from suspects obviously will result in increased emphasis on obtaining evidence from other sources, it is difficult to see how this could be regarded as supporting the adoption of such restrictions. If any other important type of evidence were excluded or arbitrarily restricted—for example, fingerprint evidence, or documentary evidence, or eyewitness testimony—that would also result in an increased need to develop other types of evidence for use in criminal cases. No one regards this as an affirmative reason for adopting rules which would exclude evidence of these types in cases in which it is reliable and probative. A system that aims at justice will obtain and use every type of reliable evidence that can be secured by means that are legally and morally acceptable.

In sum, we see compelling reasons for attempting to secure an abrogation of *Miranda*, and no substantial arguments to the contrary. The interesting question is not whether *Miranda* should go, but how we should facilitate its demise, and what we should replace it with.

*

C. Administrative Rules for Interrogations by the Department's Agencies

Our second general recommendation is that the Department [of Justice] promptly develop a set of rules or guidelines for the components that carry out interrogations, and implement these rules concurrently with our renewal of a litigation challenge to *Miranda*. Issues that could appropriately be considered in the development of an interrogation policy for the Department would include the desirability of requiring that interrogations, where feasible, be videotaped or recorded; the desirability of rules providing additional guidance concerning the permissible duration and frequency of interrogations; and the desirability of rules restricting or prohibiting specific deceptive or manipulative practices that were characterized as abusive in the *Miranda* decision. The principal reasons for this recommendation are:

First, we consider such standards to be desirable as a matter of institutional responsibility. Currently, the basic rules for custodial interrogation are set by the *Miranda* decision, and enforced by courts through the exclusion of evidence. If this form of oversight is to be removed we should adopt other measures which ensure that interrogations are carried out in a manner that is fair to suspects, and that does not jeopardize the admissibility or credibility of confessions or other statements in subsequent judicial proceedings. . . .

Second, the existence of an administrative policy of this sort should be of substantial value in persuading the courts to abandon *Miranda*. The courts are now accustomed to setting the rules for custodial interrogations, and to enforcing the rules that they have created in particular cases. It should be easier for them to relinquish this role if they know that in doing so they are acceding to a responsible alternative system, rather than writing a blank check for individual officers or agencies.

Third, the adoption of such rules would provide us with two additional arguments for abrogating *Miranda*. The first of these arguments would be based on the *Miranda* decision's assertion that its rules are not the only acceptable means of ensuring compliance with the Fifth Amendment, and its invitation to develop "equally effective" alternatives. In light of this invitation, a reasonably designed administrative policy would provide an argument for dispensing with *Miranda*'s system even under the terms of the decision that created it. [The second argument draws an analogy to a Fourth Amendment case giving deference to a self-developed administrative system "for preventing and punishing" Fourth Amendment violations.—Eds.]

A final point in support of an administrative policy is that it would enable us to show that replacing the *Miranda* system with superior alternative rules offers major advantages in relation to the legitimate interests of suspects and defendants, as well as major gains in promoting effective law enforcement. Adopting publicly articulated standards which avoid the *Miranda* rules' manifest shortcomings as a means of ensuring fair treatment of suspects would be the most effective way of making this point.

D. *After* Miranda

The abrogation of *Miranda* would open the way for a comprehensive reconsideration of pretrial interrogation and related areas of self-incrimination law. The issues that would merit examination in this connection include (i) the desirability of dispensing with warnings, or including material in warnings which provides an affirmative incentive to suspects to respond to inquiry, (ii) whether any right to counsel should be recognized in connection with police interrogation, prior to a suspect's initial appearance in court, (iii) the propriety of continuing to question a suspect after he has expressed an unwillingness to talk, and (iv) the general admissibility of a defendant's pretrial silence at trial, both for impeachment and for other purposes. . . .

Conclusion

Miranda v. Arizona was a decision without a past. Its rules had no basis in history or precedent but reflected, rather, a willful disregard of the authoritative sources of law. In frank terms, it stood on nothing more substantial than Chief Justice Warren's belief that general use of the FBI warnings and other rules he had devised would be socially beneficial, and on his ability to persuade four other Justices to go along with him.

Miranda v. Arizona is a decision without a future. The current [1986] majority of the Supreme Court has rejected the doctrinal basis of *Miranda* and has no personal stake in perpetuating its particular system of rules. The persistence of *Miranda* appears to rest on nothing more than the current Court's reluctance to unsettle the law and the fact that it has not yet encountered a case that has forced the issue of *Miranda*'s validity. While a reluctance to rock the boat is, up to a point, understandable, it cannot be accorded controlling weight in supporting a decision that not only flies in the face of the principles of constitutional government, but also impairs the ability of government to safeguard "the first right of the individual, the right to be protected from criminal attack in his home, in his work, and in the streets."[7] The tragedy of *Miranda* is compounded by its shortcomings in relation to its own objective of ensuring fair treatment of persons suspected of crime. It is difficult to conceive of a legislature enacting so peculiar a set of rules, or keeping them in effect after their deficiencies have been discerned and their rationale discredited. Yet despite the repudiation of its underlying premises by the Supreme Court, *Miranda* drifts on twenty years later, a derelict on the waters of the law.

There is every reason to believe that an effort to correct this situation would be successful. We have at our disposal a uniquely favorable set of circumstances—several recent decisions by the Supreme Court holding, in effect, that *Miranda* is unsound in principle, and a statute 18 U.S.C. §3501, that is specifically designed to overrule it. It is difficult to see how we could fail in making our case.

The potential benefits from success in this effort are very great. A wide range of fundamental issues that have been foreclosed by *Miranda* would once again become amenable to study, debate, negotiation, and resolution through the democratic process, restoring "the initiative in criminal law reform to those forums where it truly belongs."[8] Beyond the correction of specific evils that have resulted from *Miranda*'s system, an abrogation of *Miranda* would be of broader import because of its symbolic status as the epitome of Warren Court activism in the criminal law area. We accordingly regard a challenge of *Miranda* as essential, not only in overcoming the detrimental impact caused directly by this decision, but also as a critical step in moving to repudiate a discredited criminal jurisprudence. Overturning *Miranda* would, accordingly, be among the most important achievement of this [Reagan] administration—indeed, of any administration—in restoring the power of self-government to the people of the United States in the suppression of crime.

N O T E S

1. United States v. Crocker, 510 F.2d 1129 (10th Cir. 1975).
2. Enacted by the Omnibus Crime Control and Safe Streets Act of 1968.
3. Fred Graham, The Self-Inflicted Wound 315–16 (1970).
4. *Id.*
5. *Quoted in* William Buckley, Four Reforms—A Guide for the Seventies 103 (1973).
6. State v. McKnight, 243 A.2d 240, 250 (N.J. 1968).
7. *Id.*
8. Miranda v. Arizona, 384 U.S. 436, 524 (1966) (Harlan, J., dissenting).

8

Reconsidering
Miranda
(1987)

•

STEPHEN J. SCHULHOFER

Talk about "overruling" *Miranda* usually obscures the fact that *Miranda* contains not one holding but a complex series of holdings. They can be subdivided in various ways, but three conceptually distinct steps were involved in the Court's decision. First, the Court held that informal pressure to speak—that is, pressure not backed by legal process or any formal sanction—can constitute "compulsion" within the meaning of the Fifth Amendment. Second, it held that this element of informal compulsion is present in *any* questioning of a suspect in custody, no matter how short the period of questioning may be. Third, the Court held that precisely specified warnings are required to dispel the compelling pressure of custodial interrogation. The third step, the series of particularized warnings, raises the concerns about judicial legislation that usually preoccupy *Miranda*'s critics. But the core of *Miranda* is located in the first two steps. To assess the soundness of the Justice Department's case [see Chapter 7—Eds.], we need to begin by considering these first two holdings in depth.

I. Informal Compulsion

The Court's first holding was that compulsion, within the meaning of the Fifth Amendment, can include informal pressure to speak. Note first that there is not the slightest doubt about the legitimacy of settling this question by adjudication. The Fifth Amendment says that no person shall be "compelled" to be a witness against himself. According to one view, this word referred only to formal legal compulsion. But it is a normal act of interpretation for a court to consider whether "compulsion" was intended to cover informal pressures as well.

A more important problem is to determine whether the Court's decision on this point was correct on the merits. In *Bram v. United States*,[1] decided in 1897, the Court had relied on the Fifth Amendment to suppress a statement made during a brief custodial interrogation, but *Bram* was promptly forgotten, and for the next sixty years the Court consistently held that the Fifth Amendment privilege was inapplicable to police interrogation. Because the suspect had no *legal* obligation to speak, the argument ran, there was no compulsion in the Fifth Amendment sense. Under the due process clause, which was conceived as a different and more flexible standard, confessions were held inadmissible only when involuntary, and this "voluntariness" requirement was violated only when police employed tactics that were sufficiently extreme to "break the will" of the suspect.

In 1936, in its first confessions ruling in a state case, the Court held inadmissible a statement obtained by beating the suspect with a leather strap.[2] Subsequent decisions restricted interrogation techniques, but gradually and only partially. Physical violence was ruled out, but psychological pressure was not. Although decisions throughout the 1950s and early 1960s seemed to reduce the degree of permissible pressure, the admissibility of a confession still turned only on whether, under all the circumstances, the suspect's will had been "overborne." Marathon, all-night interrogation sessions, persistent cross-questioning, and use of numerous interrogators in relays were permissible under some circumstances.

Any witness who has faced thirty minutes of cross-examination by an aggressive defense attorney can easily imagine the pressures that were brought to bear and the potential for confusion and mistake that arose when a suspect without counsel was questioned for hours on end in the secrecy of the police station.

Members of the Court began to recognize that interrogation of an isolated suspect in custody was difficult to reconcile with the Fifth Amendment. At trial, at legislative hearings, and at any other formal proceeding, the criminal suspect had a constitutional right to remain silent. Even under the watchful eye of a judge, with his own attorney at his side, the suspect could not be pressured to speak. Many members of the Court found it difficult to justify a constitutional interpretation that permitted pressuring the uncounseled suspect to submit to questioning in the isolated environment of the station house.

In holding the Fifth Amendment applicable to informal compulsion, *Miranda* rejected a long line of precedent. Nonetheless, this step in the *Miranda* analysis was not at odds with the original understanding of the

Fifth Amendment. The early history of the privilege is clouded and ambiguous, but it seems clear that the privilege was intended to bar pretrial examination by magistrates, the only form of pretrial interrogation known at the time. The reasons for concern about that form of interrogation under formal process apply with even greater force to questioning under compelling informal pressures. As Professor Edmund Morgan showed almost forty years ago:

> The function which the police have assumed in interrogating an accused is exactly that of the early committing magistrates, and the opportunities for imposition and abuse are fraught with much greater danger. . . . Investigation by the police is not judicial, but when it consists of an examination of the accused, it is quite as much an official proceeding as the early English preliminary examination before a magistrate, and it has none of the safeguards of a judicial proceeding.[3]

Although Morgan's view was not accepted by all leading experts on the law of evidence, the great majority concurred in his assessment. Indeed, the Justice Department, true to its originalist premises, concedes that the self-incrimination clause applies to the informal pressures of custodial interrogation.[4]

Not only do policy and history suggest the implausibility of restricting the Fifth Amendment's protection to purely formal pressures, but the principles applied in contexts other than police interrogation make clear that no tenable line can be drawn between formal and informal compulsion. In fact, *Miranda*'s first holding was strongly foreshadowed by *Griffin v. California*,[5] in which the Court held that prosecutorial comment upon a defendant's failure to testify at trial violated the privilege by making its assertion costly. The compulsion in *Griffin* did not flow from formal process or any legal obligation to speak. The problem was that the prosecutor's comment increased (indirectly) the chances of conviction. To be sure, the trial court lent its approval (indirectly) to that consequence, by declining to bar this kind of jury argument. But what mattered in *Griffin* were the real-world consequences of the prosecutorial behavior, not whether the state had brought to bear any formal process or official sanction. If a requirement of formal compulsion remained at all after *Griffin*, it surely had been stretched paper-thin.

Developments subsequent to *Griffin* have confirmed this evolution and made clear that compulsion can no longer be limited to the pressure of formal sanctions. Building on *Griffin*'s holding that the prosecution cannot comment on a defendant's silence at trial, the Court recently held that even in the absence of such comment, the judge must instruct the jury not to draw adverse inferences from silence; in effect, "compulsion" arises from the state's failure to take reasonable steps to eliminate pressure that is wholly informal and psychological.[6] Similarly, in an extension of decisions that bar the state from firing an employee who refuses to waive his Fifth Amendment privilege, the Court recently reasoned that to assess compulsion, "we must take into account potential economic benefits realistically likely of attainment. Prudent persons weigh heavily such *legally unenforceable prospects* in making decisions; to that extent, removal of those prospects constitutes economic coercion."[7]

Against this background, the pre-*Miranda* claim that the Fifth Amendment had no application to informal pressure seems an historical curiosity. Although *Miranda*'s rejection of this claim overruled numerous precedents, that step in its analysis no longer seems open to serious question.

II. Interrogation as Compulsion

Miranda's second major step was the holding that any custodial interrogation involves enough pressure to constitute "compulsion" within the meaning of the Fifth Amendment. Again, notice that there is no doubt about the legitimacy of settling this issue by judicial decision. The question of what pressures constitute "compulsion" unavoidably confronts the Court in cases involving loss of a job, a comment on silence, or the menacing look of a person in authority. There is nothing improper or even unusual about deciding such questions in the course of adjudication.

On the merits, is the Court's second holding sound? This issue is much more problematic than the first. One difficulty arises from the emphatically per se character of the Court's holding. But before addressing this problem, we must be clear about the standard that would apply, in the absence of a per se rule, to determine when interrogation is "compelling."

A. Confusion about Compulsion

The Fifth Amendment was no doubt intended to prohibit Star Chamber inquisition tactics such as the rack and the thumbscrew. But brutal torture is not the only method of interrogation that the amendment prohibits. Fifth Amendment compulsion perhaps can be identified more naturally with the requirement of voluntariness under the due process clause. Under this approach, a person is "compelled" for Fifth Amendment purposes when his will is overborne by pressure, whether physical or psychological. This conception of the Fifth Amendment test appears to be common, and it has been reinforced by loose language in numerous decisions. *Miranda* (and *Bram* before it) treated Fifth Amendment protection as distinct from the voluntariness requirement, but then drew on voluntariness concepts to explain "compulsion." Other Warren era decisions expanding Fifth Amendment protection again seemed to conflate the two concepts, even when no reading of the confession cases decided under the voluntariness concept could support the broad notion of "compulsion" that the Court applied. More recently, the Court has made explicit the connection between compulsion and the due process standard. In *Oregon v. Elstad*, for example, the Court said that an actual violation of the Fifth Amendment (as distinguished from a mere presumption of compulsion) occurs only when there is "physical violence or other deliberate means calculated to *break the suspect's will*."[8]

If this is what Fifth Amendment compulsion requires, then *Miranda's* second step involved a seemingly superfluous change in the wording of the governing test, followed by a glaring non sequitur in the application of that test to the facts. The Court replaced involuntariness (the due process touchstone) with compulsion (an identically defined Fifth Amendment criterion) but then found compulsion in circumstances that countless decisions had found consistent with voluntariness, circumstances that no stretch of the imagination could view as breaking the suspect's will. Thus, if compulsion is properly equated with the due process prohibition against breaking the will, *Miranda's* second holding not only departs from precedent but appears unjustified and even incomprehensible in terms of the applicable constitutional standard. . . .

The decisive question is whether Fifth Amendment compulsion should be equated with the due process rule against the use of "deliberate means to break the suspect's will." It is readily understandable that terms so similar in ordinary usage, "involuntary" and "compelled," can get confused with one another, even by lawyers. Nonetheless, this concept of compulsion involves a fundamental misunderstanding of uncontroversial Fifth Amendment principles and, if taken seriously, would make nonsense of the privilege against self-incrimination.

Consider, for example, the principle that a threat to discharge a public employee will render any resulting statement "compelled." No one would suggest that the threat "breaks the will" of the employee; he simply faces the unpleasant choice between silence and his job. Similarly, a comment on the defendant's silence at trial is impermissible because it makes exercise of the privilege costly; no one could suggest that the prospect of this disadvantage breaks the defendant's will. One might reconcile compulsion principles with the voluntariness standard by suggesting that language about "breaking the will" should not be taken literally, that due process prohibits even mild pressures that are perceived as unfair. *Miranda*'s critics cannot take this route, however, because mild interrogation pressures could then render a confession "involuntary." And no one trying to make sense of the law can take this route either, because it dilutes the voluntariness concept beyond recognition; a voluminous contemporary case law continues to find extended interrogation compatible with voluntariness in the due process sense.

There is an alternative route for reconciling current doctrine with the assumption that compulsion means involuntariness. Insisting that compulsion means *overbearing* pressure, one could question *Griffin* and the employment discharge cases. Indeed, if "breaking the will" or some similarly stringent test governs, then these decisions are wrong, and the Court must be prepared to overrule them. But apart from the fact that the Court has shown no inclination to do so, this way of thinking about "compulsion" cannot carry us very far. Consider a contempt statute subjecting a defendant to a fine or six months' imprisonment for refusal to testify. If the Fifth Amendment means anything, it means that a witness claiming a potential for self-incrimination cannot be punished under such a statute; modest fines and brief imprisonment constitute compulsion. Even a $100 fine for silence is improper. Yet no one would suggest that such a penalty "breaks the will," and without violating due process we regularly impose more severe sanctions upon recalcitrant witnesses not in a position to claim the privilege.

One may be tempted to say that imposing a direct penalty is especially offensive or unfair. But why? If we have to reinvent the distinction between formal and informal pressure, we are not on very attractive ground. Nor can we find refuge in the principle that bars punishment for the exercise of constitutional rights. If the Fifth Amendment grants only a right not to be "compelled" and if compulsion means overbearing the will, then the witness has no privilege to keep both his silence and his $100 in the first place.

The upshot is that compulsion for self-incrimination purposes and involuntariness for due process purposes cannot mean the same thing.

Much as one would like to resist the proliferation of terms, any attempt to get by with one concept, combining compulsion and involuntariness, creates more problems than it solves.

The need for distinct concepts of "involuntariness" and "compulsion" is confirmed by the law of waiver. When *Miranda*'s critics assume that self-incrimination and due process protections must be the same, they find waiver a mystery. Why would any sane person waive his right to be free of torture, physical abuse, or psychological pressure that breaks the will? Yet countless cases purport to deal with waiver of the Fifth Amendment privilege, in the interrogation context and elsewhere. Such waivers are not legally inconsequential, but neither do they give a green light for "breaking the will."

At trial, any penalty imposed on a witness for refusal to testify constitutes "compulsion" and is impermissible if there is potential self-incrimination. But once the witness freely chooses to testify, the state can subject the witness to "compulsion." This does not mean that the witness can be tortured, nor can he be subjected to thirty-six hours of continuous cross-examination by teams of attorneys in relay. Under no circumstances, with or without waiver, can the state break the witness's will. What waiver means is that the state can subject the witness to the more civilized but nonetheless "compelling" pressures that are prohibited only by the self-incrimination clause. Cross-examination is permissible (during business hours, with reasonable breaks, and with a defense attorney nearby), trick questions can be used to get at the facts, and if the witness balks, the state can deploy sanctions for the specific purpose of pressuring the witness to tell the truth. After waiver the state can "compel" answers, but it can never do so by overbearing tactics that render the answers "involuntary."

These examples make clear that Fifth Amendment compulsion cannot be identified with involuntariness and is never limited to breaking the will. At the other extreme, compulsion cannot be satisfied by any inconvenience resulting from failure to testify. Insisting on the latter point, opponents of *Miranda* argue that compulsion is a matter of degree and that the Court necessarily has discretion in determining *how much* pressure to permit. It follows, they suggest, that the line drawn by *Miranda* was no more logical than that drawn by the voluntariness cases and that law enforcement needs can be weighed in striking the constitutional "balance." But this kind of argument assumes that standards for "compulsion" in police interrogation can be independent of the benchmarks used to resolve this issue in other Fifth Amendment contexts. In self-incrimination analysis, the threshold of permissible pressure is low, and more importantly, the *amount* of pressure is less significant than the reason why pressures arise. Disabilities or pressures that have the effect of discouraging silence but are not created for that reason normally are permissible. But pressure imposed for the *purpose* of discouraging the silence of a criminal suspect constitutes prohibited compulsion whether or not it "breaks the will." This is the clear teaching of the Fifth Amendment's core applications to compulsion by legal process. The policy served by the amendment is not limited to preventing inhuman degradation or breaking the will, but extends to all governmental efforts intended to pressure an unwilling individual to assist as a witness in his own prosecution.

From this perspective, *Miranda* is not in conflict with the numerous voluntariness cases decided before 1966. *Miranda* overruled the implicit holding of these cases that the Fifth Amendment was inapplicable to *informal* compulsion, but on the question of *which* informal pressures constituted compulsion, these cases were silent. In holding that police had not "broken the will" of various suspects, these cases had not found an absence of state-created pressures to speak. Indeed, it was evident in every one of the voluntariness cases that police had employed significant pressure for the purpose of getting recalcitrant suspects to talk. Under the due process approach, such pressures were permissible if not so extreme as to "shock the conscience." Even express promises of benefit, designed to overcome silence, had been allowed when they did not break the suspect's will.

The one pre-*Miranda* precedent that is relevant to determining the degree of interrogation pressure permissible for Fifth Amendment purposes is *Bram*. There, in the course of a brief interview, the interrogator had suggested, "If you had an accomplice, you should say so, and not have the blame of this horrible crime on your own shoulders."[9] The Court found this statement sufficient by itself to establish a Fifth Amendment violation. The Court held that the statement

> might well have been understood as holding out an encouragement that by [naming an accomplice] he might at least obtain a mitigation of the punishment for the crime. . . . "[T]he law cannot measure the force of the influence used or decide upon its effect upon the mind of the prisoner, and, therefore, excludes the declaration *if any degree of influence has been exerted.*"[10]

It is this standard, never considered controversial when applied to judicial proceedings, that underlies *Miranda*'s second holding. Custodial interrogation brings psychological pressure to bear for the specific purpose of overcoming the suspect's unwillingness to talk, and it is therefore inherently compelling within the meaning of the Fifth Amendment.

B. The Conclusive Presumption of Compulsion

Even if the *Miranda* decision is supportable so far, difficulty arises from the per se character of the Court's holding. The Court found compulsion in a police officer's very first question. Defenders of *Miranda* would note that even one question can be compelling under some circumstances. The response of a naive young suspect, following just a few seconds of interrogation, can plausibly be seen as compelled by fear of mistreatment, by expectations of unrelenting interrogation, or more simply by the utterly natural assumption that he is obliged to answer—that when a person in authority asks a question, the official is legally entitled to a response.

But an argument of this kind cannot support *Miranda*'s crucial second step. The Court did not hold that a brief period of interrogation *can* involve compulsion. The Court held that the briefest period of interrogation necessarily *will* involve compulsion. To test this conclusion, we must consider whether a defendant's first answer always will be compelled.

In thinking realistically about this issue, one must recognize that even the sophisticated, knowledgeable suspect faces considerable state-created pressure to talk. The sophisticated suspect, precisely because he knows the law, will be aware that under the due process approach, the police can subject him to extended periods of interrogation, day and night. He will also know that if he does not talk, his silence can count against him. In fact, even after *Miranda*, it remains true that post-arrest silence can be used for impeachment purposes if the detained suspect has not received warnings. A sophisticated suspect would know that refusal to respond to questions would subject him to a penalty in the event of trial, and pre-*Miranda* interrogators were trained to get this point across to any suspect sufficiently knowledgeable to attempt to invoke his rights.

Beyond these problems lies a more basic difficulty. Even if our sophisticated suspect knows his rights and their ramifications, he needs to know whether the *police* know his rights. And he needs to know whether the police are prepared to *respect* those rights. If our sophisticated suspect knows anything about the law in action, he will know that custodial interrogation occurs outside the view of any disinterested observer. He will know that for perfectly understandable reasons, conscientious officers, intent on solving brutal crimes, sometimes lose their tempers and that instances of physical abuse, though not the norm, often surface in case reports and in the newspapers. Even the sophisticated law professor or professional investigator, if he found himself suspected of crime, would be under considerable pressure to cooperate with the police, to try to get them on his side by telling what he knew or what he thought he could safely disclose, rather than standing confidently on his right to remain silent. So it is by no means implausible for the Court to have said that any custodial questioning, even for a few seconds, is inherently compelling.

One might argue, however, that my examples do not go far enough, because they still depend on introducing elements of fear and anxiety. What justification is there for holding that such elements necessarily *must* be present in every custodial interrogation? Surely one can imagine a case in which a law professor-suspect knows his rights and is not in fear of abuses, in which he tells all in response to the first question, not because of any sense of pressure but simply because he wants the truth to come out. Because such a case is conceivable, and because the Court's per se rule would find a Fifth Amendment violation even in that case, some critics conclude that *Miranda*'s second holding is itself prophylactic, that the Court did not simply *interpret* the meaning of compulsion but rather replaced the no-compulsion rule with a much broader prohibition. Professor Joseph Grano develops this view in a particularly forceful article.[11] . . .

To put these problems in perspective, we must consider how often, after meticulous examination of the circumstances, a genuine absence of compulsion can be found. Police interviews are tension-filled matters under the best of circumstances. Interviews in the absence of counsel, in the police-dominated custodial environment, are filled with tension in spades. And the tensions are created for the very purpose of overcoming the suspect's unwillingness to talk. . . .

Under these circumstances, is it any wonder that the Court, exasperated after years of case-by-case adjudication, finally adopted a prophylactic rule? A conclusive presumption of compulsion is in fact a responsible reaction to the problems of the voluntariness test, to the rarity of cases in which compelling pressures are truly absent, and to the adjudicatory costs of case-by-case decisions in this area. Indeed, in any ranking of the issues that properly demand some form of prophylactic rule, the problem of determining compulsion in the context of custodial interrogation wins the prize hands down.

To summarize, then, one has to say that *Miranda*'s second step, like its first, not only was an unquestionably legitimate act of adjudication, but also was, on the merits, a sound and entirely justified interpretation of the Fifth Amendment. Indeed, the Court *cannot* overrule *Miranda*'s first or second holdings without tearing a wide hole in the fabric of Fifth Amendment doctrine and dismantling the foundations of numerous uncontroversial precedents outside the area of police interrogation.

III. The Warnings

This brings us to *Miranda*'s third step, its well-known panoply of "code-like rules,"[12] requiring that the suspect receive a complex, four-part warning of his rights. Here the complaints about judicial legislation seem at first glance to have some substance. But in weighing the force of those complaints, we should focus carefully on the *effect* of *Miranda*'s detailed rules. Do the warnings "handcuff" the police? We can now see that their function is precisely the opposite. If the Court was correct in the first two steps of its analysis, and I submit that it was, then far from handcuffing the police, the warnings work to *liberate* the police. *Miranda*'s much-maligned rules permit the officer to continue questioning his isolated suspect, the very process that the Court's first two holdings found to be a violation of the Fifth Amendment.

The Court's theory with respect to the warnings was that they could "dispel" the inherently compelling atmosphere of police interrogation. But there is great room for doubt about that theory. Indeed, the *Miranda* opinion itself suggests that such a theory is not especially realistic:

> The circumstances surrounding in-custody interrogation can operate very quickly to overbear the will of one merely made aware of his privilege by his interrogators. . . . A once-stated warning, delivered by those who will conduct the interrogation, cannot itself suffice to [ensure an unfettered choice between silence and speech] among those who most require knowledge of their rights. . . . Even preliminary advice given to the accused by his own attorney can be swiftly overcome by the secret interrogation process.[13]

The notion that police-initiated warnings can "dispel" the compulsion thus seems dubious at best. But whether or not they went far enough, *Miranda*'s warnings unquestionably serve—and from the outset were designed to serve—the function of permitting custodial interrogation to continue. Indeed, the Court would have incurred far more police criticism if it had remained within a narrow conception of the judicial role, pronounced interrogation "inherently compelling," and then left law enforcement officials to guess about what countermeasures would keep police on the safe side of the constitutional line. As Justice Rehnquist recognized, writing for the Court in *Michigan v. Tucker*, the purpose of the warnings is "to *help* police officers conduct interrogations without facing a continued risk that valuable evidence [will] be lost."[14]

Why do *Miranda*'s critics make such a fuss about the warnings? If the suspect already knows his rights, it hardly can hamper law enforcement for police to reiterate them. At the heart of the problem is the suspect who does not know his rights, who believes that the police are entitled to make him talk. But since such a suspect thinks he is *obliged* to respond, his answers are "compelled" in violation of the Fifth Amendment privilege.

The crux of the matter is that the Justice Department wants to use statements compelled by the suspect's belief that he is obliged to answer. But this objective contains the seeds of a dilemma. The Department's report asserts that statements can be induced by a mistaken sense of legal obligation without being "compelled." However, sensing that this is analytical double-talk, the report also recognizes that the absence of warnings will undermine the government's posture in litigation. So the report proposes an alternative: A substitute warning would state that the suspect need not make a statement, but that his refusal to do so could be used against him in court.

Will suspects who have difficulty grasping *Miranda*'s relatively straightforward warnings understand this convoluted message? Even sophisticated lawyers will need more time than a suspect has to decide whether or not this warning recognizes a right to silence. In either event, a warning like this, far from dispelling the interrogation pressures, can only increase them. That is, of course, precisely what the Justice Department wants to accomplish. But it is also precisely what the Fifth Amendment prohibits. . . .

NOTES

1. 168 U.S. 532 (1897).
2. Brown v. Mississippi, 297 U.S. 278 (1936).
3. Edmund Morgan, *The Privilege Against Self-Incrimination*, 34 Minn. L. Rev. 1, 27, 28 (1949).

4. See U.S. Department of Justice, Office of Legal Policy, Report to the Attorney General on the Law of Pretrial Interrogation 42 (February 12, 1986, with addendum of January 20, 1987). [Excerpted in Chapter 7.—Eds.]

5. 380 U.S. 609 (1965).

6. Carter v. Kentucky, 450 U.S. 288 (1981).

7. Lefkowitz v. Cunningham, 431 U.S. 801, 807 (1977) (Burger, J.) (emphasis added).

8. 470 U.S. 298, 312 (1985) (emphasis added).

9. *Bram*, 168 U.S. at 539.

10. *Id.* at 565 (emphasis added), *quoting* William O. Russell, Treatise on Crimes and Misdemeanors 479 (6th ed. 1896).

11. Joseph D. Grano, *Prophylactic Rules in Criminal Procedure: A Question of Article III Legitimacy*, 80 Nw. U. L. Rev. 100 (1985).

12. Edwin Meese III, *Square* Miranda *Rights with Reason*, Wall St. J., June 13, 1986, at 22.

13. 384 U.S. at 469–70.

14. 417 U.S. 433, 443 (1974) (emphasis added).

9

Questioning
Miranda
(1985)

·

GERALD M. CAPLAN

Erosion of the Voluntariness Test

In retrospect, it is easy to see *Gallegos v. Colorado*,[1] decided in 1962 by a 4–3 majority, as an ideological harbinger of both *Escobedo* and *Miranda*. Robert Gallegos, a "child of 14,"[2] and two companions followed an elderly man into his hotel and used a ruse to enter his room. Once in his room, they assaulted him and stole thirteen dollars. It was their second assault of the day, and, this time, the victim died. Later, a juvenile officer spotted Gallegos and his two younger brothers sitting on the curb in front of a local restaurant. Since the youths matched the description of the felons, the officer identified himself and invited the boys to come sit in his car. Gallegos did so and almost "immediately admitted the assault and robbery" (the victim had not yet died).[3] Gallegos repeated the confession the next day and once more five days later by signing a "formal" confession.

Although at times segregated during his confinement, Gallegos was allowed to eat and converse with the other youths. By his own account, he was not intensely questioned during this period or mistreated. Before making his "formal" confession, he had been advised of his right to remain silent, of the possibility that a murder charge might be placed against him, and of his right to be represented by counsel and to have his family present. Gallegos expressly indicated that he did not want an attorney and signed the confession.

In terms of the traditional criteria of the voluntariness test—length of questioning, denial of access to others, awareness of one's right to withhold incriminating information—there was little to commend the case for reversal,[4] unless as a matter of law a fourteen-year-old was held incapable of making a voluntary confession. The Court had refused to take this drastic course earlier . . . and it hesitated to do so here as well, resting its decision to reverse the conviction on the totality of the circumstances. Weight was accorded not only to Gallegos's youth but also to the authorities' failure to grant his parents immediate access to him and to present him promptly before the juvenile court. In addition, the Court focused on the superior status of the police officer investigating the case: "[W]e deal with a person [Gallegos] who is not equal to the police in knowledge and understanding of the consequences of the questions and answers being recorded and who is unable to know how to protect his own interests or how to get the benefits of his constitutional rights."[5]

The assertion that Gallegos was "not equal to the police," although surely correct, was nonetheless jarring. Why should this circumstance be relevant to whether an otherwise voluntary confession is admissible into evidence? The traditional inquiry was whether a particular suspect, however unequal in legal knowledge, emotional stability, and mature judgment, made a "voluntary" statement, not whether the government had the upper hand during interrogation. Although the absence of advice from his parents or a lawyer made it more likely that Gallegos would confess, this confession was in the public interest as long as the police acted with sufficient restraint. Gallegos's oral confession in the police car followed the officer's opening questions so quickly that the confession almost can be characterized as volunteered rather than voluntary. Nevertheless, the Court determined that the police showed "callous disregard" for Gallegos's "constitutional rights."[6]

The implications of *Gallegos* extended far beyond the special problems of juveniles. If it is true, as the Court concluded, that "[a]dult advice would have put [Gallegos] on a less unequal footing with his interrogators,"[7] then the same reasoning would apply to the adult suspect who was still not a match for the officer. . . . Of course, under the voluntariness test, the *Gallegos* Court focused on those characteristics of the defendant—his age, intelligence, mental stability, experience in life—that might make his statement unreliable or the interrogation itself unfair; but, prior to *Gallegos*, the Court had never conceptualized the problems of interrogation in terms of equality. . . .

Following the shooting of his brother-in-law, Danny Escobedo was questioned for several hours about the killing before his attorney secured his release. He made no statement. Ten days later, the police learned from another suspect, one DiGerlando, that Escobedo had been the trigger man. Escobedo was again arrested and questioned. During this second interrogation, Escobedo asked to see his attorney. At the same time, his attorney unsuccessfully sought admission to the homicide bureau where Escobedo was being held. This time the questioning was successful. When one of the detectives challenged Escobedo, who had been calling DiGerlando a liar, to repeat the accusation in front of DiGerlando, Escobedo agreed. DiGerlando was brought in, then Escobedo accused him of lying in these words: "I didn't shoot Manuel, you did it."[8] Thus Escobedo inadvertently implicated himself in the murder.

On its facts, *Escobedo* bore little resemblance to prior cases. The police had used no force, no intimidation, no questioning in relays, and no denials of food or sleep. Furthermore, Escobedo suffered no special handicap. He was not mentally disturbed, illiterate, the victim of discrimination, or inexperienced in the ways of the world. Perhaps most important, Escobedo had retained a lawyer, and in prior conversations with his lawyer, he had been told what he "should do in the event of interrogation."[9] Finally, during a chance encounter with his attorney during the interrogation—when the door to the homicide bureau was opened briefly, the attorney walked by—Escobedo took his attorney's passing gesture to mean that he should keep silent. Nonetheless, in a 5–4 decision, the Court reversed the conviction and held the statement inadmissible. . . .

In *Escobedo*, the balance was struck differently [from earlier cases]. Unlike earlier opinions such as *Gallegos*, in which the role of counsel was only vaguely specified as one factor in the "totality of the circumstances," the Court in *Escobedo* precisely identified how Escobedo had been injured by being denied access to his attorney: "Petitioner, a layman, was undoubtedly unaware that under Illinois law an admission of 'mere' complicity was legally as damaging as an admission of firing the fatal shots." The "guiding hand of counsel" was "essential" in this "delicate situation" to inform Escobedo of the applicable rules of law.[10] . . .

In making Escobedo's ignorance of a technical point of complicity law dispositive, the Court laid the foundation for an unrestricted right to counsel during custodial interrogation. Only a rare arrestee would know this subtlety of criminal law. Escobedo was just a layman on his own in the adversarial world of the law. In these strange waters, how could he, or any other suspect, navigate confidently? How could he know as much as his more experienced police opponents? The Court obviously was concerned that, without a lawyer, he would be at risk; he might incriminate himself. . . .

The "Sporting Theory" of Justice

The *Escobedo* majority opinion demonstrates a change in the Court's, and perhaps society's, perception of the accused. The opinion shows sympathy for Danny Escobedo because he was the underdog. One detects what Thurman Arnold referred to as "the humanitarian notion that the underdog is always entitled to a chance."[11]

Perhaps the impulse to allow even the unquestionably guilty some prospect of escaping detection or conviction is universal. Wigmore referred to this impulse as the "instinct of giving the game fair play."[12] Pound characterized it as "the sporting theory" of justice,[13] and Bentham derisively labeled it "the fox hunter's reason."[14] Under this view, fairness is given that special definition that sportsmen reserve for their games. Bentham elaborated on his analogy to the fox hunt: "The fox is to have a fair chance for his life: he must have . . . leave to run a certain length of way, for the express purpose of giving him a chance for escape."[15] Fairness, so defined, dictates that neither side should have an undue advantage; the police and the criminal should be on roughly equal footing and the rules of the game should be drawn to avoid favoring one side or the other. As Justice Fortas put it in a well-known article (written before he joined the Court), the accused and the accuser are "equals, meeting in battle."[16] The state was sovereign, but so was the individual. The individual possessed the "sovereign right . . . to meet the state on terms as equal as their respective strength would permit . . . strength against strength, resource against resource, argument against argument."[17]

In the context of police interrogation, this outlook translates as follows: Treating the accused fairly, as a worthy adversary, means encouraging him to view his right to silence as a weapon at his disposal, to be used when it offers the best chance of dismissal or acquittal. The suspect should be allowed to present his case in the time, place, and manner that, in accordance with his understanding or that of his attorney, will be most advantageous. And, of course, he must be told all the rules of the contest.

Danny Escobedo did not know the relevant rule relating to the liability of accomplices. As Chief Justice Warren subsequently noted in *Miranda*, Escobedo "fully intended his accusation of another [DiGerlando] . . . to be exculpatory as to himself."[18] Because the government took advantage of this unawareness in its interrogation, the Court penalized the government by denying it the use of Escobedo's confession as evidence in any subsequent trial. The government had failed to comport itself within the bounds of this new definition of fairness.

The sporting theory of justice, as Pound observed, has great attraction; but its appeal is easier to experience than to explain. In its origins, it may draw upon our childhood experiences with our parents, when justice was perceived largely in terms of equal treatment with our brothers and sisters. Beyond that, there seems to be something distinctly American in the subversive notion of beating the law, even though this feeling may be "only a survival of the days when a lawsuit was a fight between two clans" rather than a "fundamental right of jurisprudence." [19]

The weakness of the sporting theory in the context of *Escobedo* is not so much what Pound suggests, that by "its exaggerated contentious procedures . . . [it gives] the whole community a false notion of the purpose and the end of the law," [20] but rather that by arming the suspect with counsel at the station house the Court strikes the wrong balance—it gives the suspect too great an advantage. If the police are too formidable for the average offender, a lawyer will be too formidable for the average investigator. The lawyer will protect his client from injuring himself by confessing. Thus, even if one sees criminal law as a "mere game," to use Pound's expression, *Escobedo* may deprive the government of a fair chance at victory. By design, *Escobedo* was a significant step toward barring "from evidence all admissions obtained from an individual suspected of crime, whether involuntarily made or not." [21] . . .

The Impropriety of Warning the Suspect

Most of the controversy that followed *Miranda* centered on the right to counsel at the station. Scant attention was directed to the requirement that the police inform a suspect that he had a right to remain silent and that anything he said could be used against him as evidence in court. In part, this neglect arose from a general impression that these warnings would not have much consequence. Justice Harlan's dissent glossed over them as "minor obstructions." [22] Even the police offered no protest; moreover, many agencies, including the prestigious Federal Bureau of Investigation, already required its officers to administer a similar caution; the English police had done so since 1848. Finally, many believed that requiring the police to inform a suspect of his right to silence and of the consequences of his confession was only fair.

Nonetheless, the propriety of making the state responsible for informing the suspect of his rights is not evident. It is not easy to explain why fair play requires the police to warn a suspect of the danger in answering truthfully. As John Stuart Mill asked, "Whence all this dread of truth?"[23] Requiring an officer to tell a murder or rape suspect that he need not answer the officer's questions and that, if he does, he might suffer the consequences seems altogether too charitable. It suggests an ambivalence toward the suspect and his deed. Giving the warning is not a neutral act designed merely to place the suspect in an independent position to decide whether to take responsibility for his wrongdoing. A police warning provides information with a purpose. If delivered faithfully, it will encourage the suspect to withhold information.

One need not agree with J. F. Stephen that "the proper attitude of mind toward criminals is not long-suffering charity but open enmity"[24] to ask why such generosity is called for. If condemnation and punishment are appropriate responses to rape and murder, then paternalistic counseling is inappropriate. To expect truthful answers from a suspect is too much to ask; most persons would not perceive or honor an obligation to respond candidly. Nonetheless, the government has good reason to make the inquiry.

In related contexts we do not encourage persons to withhold information. Judge Friendly observed, "Every hour of the day people are being asked to explain their conduct to parents, employers, and teachers."[25] Sidney Hook similarly commented, "Let any sensible person ask himself whether he would hire a secretary, nurse, or even a babysitter for his children, if she refused to reply to a question bearing upon the proper execution of her duties with a response equivalent to the privilege against self-incrimination."[26] Professor Mayers offered this hypothetical:

> Suppose that evidence were laid before [a professor] warranting suspicion that one of his students, called upon to submit an essay to satisfy the requirements of the faculty, had employed another person to prepare the essay and had submitted it as his own. Would the [professor] regard it as an essential and inherent cruelty to demand of the student that he explain away the evidence? Would not the [professor] regard the student's refusal to offer an explanation as of itself sufficient ground for his expulsion from school—a fearful penalty?[27]

Of course, a man suspected of murder faces a greater penalty than a student risking expulsion, but does this factor support an argument for or against a warning of a right to remain silent? If the police were to issue a warning that reflected the common understanding of the implications of silence in the face of an accusation, the suspect would be told something like this: "We cannot compel you to answer our questions, but your failure to provide us with information concerning this matter may have a bad effect on your case in general." The exercise of the right to silence might not invariably lead to adverse inferences, but in many cases, perhaps most, a person could be expected to protest his innocence and give an account of himself rather than stand on his rights. The right that is being asserted, it must be recalled, is the right to withhold incriminating evidence, not evidence. However unpleasant it may be to testify, in the absence of privilege, a citizen ordinarily is required to do so. As Jeremy Bentham long ago wrote, "Evidence is the basis of justice: exclude evidence, you exclude justice." [28] A person may prefer not to respond to questions about a burglary or automobile accident he witnessed, but the law has never countenanced such reticence. Only the person who seeks to deny the state damaging material about himself is protected, and we provide protection not because we admire the man who stands silent, but because we do not wish to give the authorities the power to coerce testimony.

From the suspect's point of view, the privilege has undoubted appeal. It fosters self-preservation. But whether silence is a right, or something less worthy and more instinctive, there seems nothing admirable in standing silent in the face of a criminal accusation. The suspect who is told, "We are investigating the murder of your wife. What can you tell us about this matter?" and remains silent is not heroic; he is merely covering up. Only when viewed as a symbolic statement of the limits to truthseeking when the factfinding methods are demeaning does the right to silence justify the high praise that has been showered upon it. But when viewed from the perspective of the accused, it is difficult to see "just how the stature of the individual man gains in 'dignity and importance' by his maintaining silence in the face of grave evidence," [29] unless one takes the position that the government was wrong to ask.

All this is not to say that a suspect's knowledge of his right to silence should be ignored. Proof that the suspect knows his rights is relevant to a determination that his statements were not coerced. Knowledge that one is not compelled to answer may fortify the will; and the fact that the interrogator provided the suspect with the information about the suspect's rights evidence the government's awareness of the limitations on its inquiry. These considerations make sense in the determination of voluntariness, and the Court on several occasions has measured the suspect's awareness of his rights in deciding whether his statement was admissible. In the Fifth Amendment context, however, the automatic suppression of an incriminating statement solely because of a failure to advise a suspect who in fact knows his rights seems excessive. . . .

[T]he *Miranda* approach reflects a bias against self-accusation on principle. This bias has roots in the desire to treat suspects equally. Suspects who do not know their rights, or do not assert them, as a consequence of some handicap—poverty, lack of education, emotional instability—should not, it is felt, fare worse than more accomplished suspects who know and have the capacity to assert their rights. This "equal protection" appeal finds its way repeatedly into judicial opinions and legal commentary. In *Miranda* itself, Chief Justice Warren referred approvingly to the California Supreme Court's decision in *People v. Dorado*, which stressed that "the defendant who does not realize his rights under the law and who therefore does not request counsel is the very defendant who most needs counsel."[30] A few years earlier, Professor Beisel similarly argued that only the "frightened, the insecure, the weak, and untrained, the bewildered, the stupid, the naive, the credulous" confess.[31] More recently, Professor Kamisar asserted that the pre-*Miranda* voluntariness test favored the more sophisticated suspects because it probably did not permit greater-than-average pressures to be applied against stronger-than-average suspects.[32]

To the extent that these observations are true—and they seem true enough—they suggest two distinct remedies. One would be to make it more difficult to convict those who are most vulnerable; the other would be to develop ways to bring those hardier, more knowledgeable persons—the hired killer, the calculating embezzler, the experienced burglar—to justice. The critics—Kamisar, Beisel, and many others—have preferred the former. They do not see the lack of stamina and professionalism of the suspect as conferring a benefit on society by facilitating the identification of wrongdoers.

But guilt is personal. That another, equally guilty person got away with murder because of some fortuitous factor—he was more experienced in dealing with the police, he had a poorly developed sense of guilt, he had a smart lawyer, he knew his rights—or even because of discrimination, does not make the more vulnerable murderer less guilty. To hold otherwise is to confuse justice with equality. "Both are desirable. However, neither can replace the other."[33] Since sophisticated suspects ordinarily will choose not to confess (with or without knowledge of their rights), "[t]o strive for equality . . . is to strive to eliminate confessions."[34] Thus, the *Miranda* Court elected to let one person get away with murder because of the advantage possessed by another. . . .

Restoring the Balance

The crucial concern for criminal procedure is the appropriate bias to build into the rules. The rules can be constructed to favor either side. Historically, there has been a continual movement between the two sides, at one end showing "an extreme solicitude for the general security, leading to a minimum of regard for the individual accused," and at the other end showing an "extreme excessive solicitude for the social interest" in the individual, "leading to a minimum of regard for the general security and security of social institutions."[35] Because the rules function like a pendulum, at any given time they are likely to be out of balance. Every generation or so, they must be reset.

In evaluating the privilege against self-incrimination, we should start with the premise that the privilege shelters the guilty. As such, it exacts a costly price. This price is high not only because our society, more than others, is plagued by violent crime, but also because, as Sidney Hook reminds us, "justice in the individual case consists as much in not letting the guilty escape as in not letting the innocent suffer."[36] Although we are not prepared to adopt rules that allow many innocent persons to be convicted, it does not follow that there is merit in allowing individuals who have committed crimes to escape detection. Whenever a guilty person escapes detection as a result of the privilege against self-incrimination, justice, in an important sense, is denied. This is true even if we accept that we purposefully have adopted rules that are designed to allow many guilty persons to go unpunished. An adversary system will necessarily have some elements of chance to it, but to be just, the system must be reliable not only in screening out the innocent but in identifying the guilty. The rules must be fair, and the authorities must adhere to them, but such rules must be fashioned for the larger purpose of finding the truth without too much harshness. . . .

In retrospect, *Miranda* seems most understandable as an exaggerated response to the times rather than as an enunciation of a natural right mined at last from the Constitution. *Miranda* was a child of the racially troubled 1960s and our tragic legacy of slavery. It "was decided when blood was actually being spilled in the streets. There were civil rights protests in the South and civil disorders in urban areas elsewhere. On national television, black protesters [and their supporters] were bullied and beaten, black rioters beaten and shot."[37] *Miranda* itself was decided not only in the shadow of the police practices exposed in *Brown v. Mississippi*[38] and *Chambers v. Florida*[39] but also in the more recent past of the third-degree applied particularly to southern blacks. To many, the government itself seemed the cause of racism and poverty, and those apprehended by the police, armed robbers as well as civil rights protesters, were seen as victims rather than offenders. Crime was not understood as the offshoot of individual will but as a by-product of one's poverty or race or both. The goal was to attack "root causes" rather than root out individual felons. President Johnson proposed a "Great Society" that would bring "an end to poverty and racial injustice," in which both crime and police brutality would be banished. The country was ready to embark on a grand future that would make up for this troubled past.

In this setting, *Miranda* stood out like a crown jewel. It spoke to the disadvantaged and the discontented. It conferred status on the accused. As such, it infused vitality into larger social and political movements, and it contributed to a climate of greater respect for suspects. *Miranda* popularized the principle of warning one's adversary, of assisting him in defending himself, and of envisioning the criminal not as a foreigner but as a neighbor down on his luck. Criminals, *Miranda* suggested, were not wicked; they were unfortunate.

Given this orientation, a thorough evaluation of *Miranda* should look beyond the findings of empirical studies to what Thurman Arnold called the "symbols of government."[40] Values, beliefs, and emotions are implicated. Although some would alter their assessment of *Miranda* if research demonstrated that the decision has influenced the conviction rate greatly, as opposed to marginally, most of us, I suspect, would hold to our views. As a symbol, *Miranda* is too rooted in our attitudes toward authority to yield easily to statistics.

For its supporters, *Miranda* is a gesture of government's willingness to treat the lowliest antagonist as worthy of respect and consideration. They have a point. There is something attractive about a legal system that insists that suspects have a right to refuse to answer police inquiries, that imposes on the police an obligation to communicate that right, and that provides counsel to the indigent. The Fifth Amendment, as much as any constitutional provision, illustrates that ours is a limited government. It reflects an historic distrust of authority. It reveals an unwillingness to wage all-out war on crime, even heinous crime, lest other values be demeaned.

But the root idea of *Miranda* [and earlier cases] is quite different and more ominous. These decisions do more than suggest that the government must be restricted in the means it employs in criminal investigation. They impose a serious handicap on the government, which arises not merely from a desire to curb historic police abuses but also from an ambivalence about criminality itself and a confusion concerning the purpose behind the rules of criminal procedure. The result blurs the traditional and theoretical distinction between the police and the criminal: One is useful, the other noxious. . . .

When the existing order is widely considered unjust, offenders are encouraged to excuse their own misconduct and accuse their accusers. Confession then, far from providing relief from the pain of conscience or restoration to the community, becomes an "apparatus of personal and social degradation."[41]

When *Miranda* was decided in 1966, it was popular to see the criminal as a type of victim; he was caught in the role assigned to persons in his circumstances, a member of the underclass. One spoke not of volition but of status or condition. The idea of individual guilt and remorse for wrongful deeds was out of fashion. The causal factors of criminality were thought to lie outside the individual, in the deeper, corrupt foundations of the society—the so-called root causes.

*

. . . Certainly, the dangers of uncontrolled government rival or even exceed those of an uncontrolled populace. For this reason we properly build into criminal investigation and the criminal trial some elements of chance. It is fear of overzealous prosecution that, in part, causes us to provide the accused with counsel and to permit counsel a rather free hand in seeking an acquittal. But to go further, as the *Miranda* Court did, and posit rules designed to put the adversaries on equal terms in the investigative phase is "too great a concession to egalitarianism."[42]

It may be that at times the police and the criminal are adversaries "so well attuned to one another that they can and often do reverse roles with minor shifts in the historical climate,"[43] and it may be, as a defense counsel has recently suggested, that "many criminals think that the only difference between them and the police is that the police get health benefits and a pension."[44] But such should not be the case nor, as a matter of official policy, should both sides be treated as possessing equal moral worth.

There is no neutral position. One must lean toward the government or subversion. With respect to criminal investigations, we should not require the government to provide information that would discourage a suspect's participation when the lawful character of the interrogation can otherwise be guaranteed; the concern for accuracy runs too high and the public interest in identifying and segregating dangerous persons is too great. The ultimate issue is whether the government proceeded fairly, in a proper manner, not whether the suspect knew his rights. When the interrogation is noncoercive and the answers voluntary, the Constitution should be satisfied. The privilege against self-incrimination is best understood as a denial to the government of the power to extract confessions forcibly and indecently, not as a denial of the value of confession. "[P]eaceful interrogation," Justice Harlan wisely reminded us in his *Miranda* dissent, "is not one of the dark moments of the law."[45]

NOTES

1. 370 U.S. 49 (1962).
2. *Id.* at 49.
3. *Id.* at 50.
4. Perhaps the most troubling feature of the case was that Gallegos had been sentenced to life imprisonment.
5. 370 U.S. at 54.
6. *Id.*
7. *Id.*
8. [Escobedo v. Illinois} 378 U.S. 478, 483 (1964).
9. *Id.* at 485 n.5.
10. *Id.* at 486.
11. Thurman Arnold, Symbols of Government 135 (1935).
12. 1A John Henry Wigmore, Evidence in Trials at Common Law §57, at 1185 (3d ed. 1940).
13. Roscoe Pound, *The Causes of Popular Dissatisfaction with the Administration of Justice*, 29 A.B.A. Rep. 395, 404–5 (1906).
14. 5 Jeremy Bentham, Rationale of Judicial Evidence 238 (1827).
15. *Id.* at 238–39. . . .
16. Abe Fortas, *The Fifth Amendment: Nemo Tenetur Seipsum Prodere*, 25 J. Clev. B. Ass'n. 91, 98 (1954).
17. *Id.*
18. Miranda v. Arizona, 384 U.S. 436, 477 (1966).
19. Pound, *supra* note 13, at 405.
20. *Id.* at 406.
21. *Escobedo*, 378 U.S. at 495 (White, J., dissenting).
22. *Miranda*, 384 U.S. at 516.
23. *Quoted in* Sidney Hook, Common Sense and the Fifth Amendment 59 (1957).
24. 1 James Fitzjames Stephen, A History of the Criminal Law in England 432 (1883).

25. Henry Friendly, *The Fifth Amendment Tomorrow: The Case for Constitutional Change*, 37 U. Cin. L. Rev. 671, 680 (1968).

26. Hook, *supra* note 23, at 73.

27. Lewis Mayers, Shall We Amend the Fifth Amendment? 168 (1959).

28. Bentham, *supra* note 14, at 1.

29. Mayers, *supra* note 27, at 167.

30. 394 P.2d 952, 956 (1964).

31. Albert Beisel, Control Over Illegal Enforcement of the Criminal Law: Role of the Supreme Court 106 (1955).

32. [See Chapter 2.—Eds.]

33. Ernest van den Haag, *Comment on John Kaplan's "Administering Criminal Punishment,"* 36 U. Fla. L. Rev. 193, 199 (1984).

34. Joseph D. Grano, *Voluntariness, Free Will, and the Law of Confessions*, 65 Va. L. Rev. 859, 914 (1979).

35. Roscoe Pound, *Criminal Justice and the American City—A Summary*, in Roscoe Pound & Felix Frankfurter, Criminal Justice in Cleveland: Reports of the Cleveland Foundation Survey of the Administration of Criminal Justice in Cleveland, Ohio 576–77 (1922).

36. Hook, *supra* note 23, at 132.

37. Gerald M. Caplan, Miranda *Revisited*, 93 Yale L.J. 1375, 1382 (1984) (book review).

38. 297 U.S. 278 (1936).

39. 309 U.S. 227 (1940).

40. Arnold, *supra* note 11, at iv.

41. *Id.*

42. Friendly, *supra* note 25, at 711.

43. Kai Erikson, Wayward Puritans 20 (1966).

44. Wishman, *Evidence Illegally Obtained by Police*, N.Y. Times, Sept. 21, 1981, at A25, col. 2.

45. 384 U.S. at 517.

10

The Supreme Court, the Attorney General, and the Good Old Days of Police Interrogation (1987)

•

LAWRENCE HERMAN

What if *Miranda* were overruled—what test would courts use for determining the constitutional admissibility of confessions? How well would that test work? To these questions I want to add another. Is it true, as the *Miranda* dissenters and the Attorney General have said, that the law of confessions got along well for 175 years without *Miranda*? In order to answer these questions, it is necessary to consider what the law of interrogation was like in the good old days before *Miranda*. . . .

The Involuntary Confession Rule

a. Verbalization

It violates due process of law for the prosecution in a criminal case to use the defendant's involuntary confession against him. Whether a confession is involuntary must be determined by considering the totality of the circumstances—the characteristics of the defendant and the environment and techniques of interrogation. Under the "totality of the circumstances" approach, virtually everything is relevant and nothing is determinative. If you place a premium on clarity, this is not a good sign.

b. Origin

The involuntary confession rule originated as a part of the English common law of evidence. Its purpose was to exclude putatively unreliable evidence. The Supreme Court adopted the rule for federal cases in 1884. Prior to 1936, it was not clear whether the rule had any constitutional law dimension or was just a common law rule. In that year, however, the

Court for the first time held an involuntary confession inadmissible in a state criminal case.[1] Since the Court lacks the authority to prescribe mere rules of evidence for state proceedings, it had to base inadmissibility on the Constitution. It chose the due process clause of the Fourteenth Amendment.

c. The Meaning of "Voluntary" and "Involuntary"

Stating what the rule is and how it originated and developed leaves out the most important matter. If the words *voluntary* and *involuntary* describe admissible and inadmissible confessions, it is crucially important to define these terms. This definitional task can be approached from at least three directions: using the definition found in judicial opinions, extrapolating or inferring a definition from the facts and results of cases, and inferring a definition from the goals or objectives of the rule.

(1) Using the Definition Found in Judicial Opinions

The involuntary confession rule received its greatest development and direction between 1936 and 1963. In 1973, in the case of *Schneckloth v. Bustamonte*,[2] the Court surveyed what it had done. (I am tempted to say that it surveyed the wreckage, but that remains to be seen.) It began by acknowledging that "'[t]he notion of "voluntariness" . . . is itself an amphibian.'"[3] (If you will think about this statement for a moment, you will see that it is another bad sign.) Then it posed and rejected two diametrically different definitions of "voluntary." Under the first, any confession is voluntary if made during consciousness, even if made to avoid torture. This definition would result in the admissibility of virtually every confession. Under the second definition, a confession is voluntary only if volunteered, that is, only if made without any police inducement or effort such as interrogation. This definition would make most confessions inadmissible. Having rejected the extremes, the Court was forced toward the middle. It said, "[T]he ultimate test remains that which has been the only clearly established test in Anglo-American courts for two hundred years: the test of voluntariness. Is the confession the product of an essentially free and unconstrained choice?"[4] If you attend closely to this definition, you will immediately see how problematic it is. The words *free* and *unconstrained* are hardly terms of legal art. In nonlegal discourse, moreover, they have no clear meaning. Beyond that, however, the Court is not even using the words in an absolute sense. The question, according to the Court, is not whether the defendant's choice was free or unconstrained, but whether it was "essentially" free or unconstrained. Presumably, "some" constraint is permissible as long as it does not destroy the "essence" of freedom of choice. I am being picky about the words the Court used because I want you to see three related points. The first is that the Court's definition permits the police to interrogate a reluctant suspect—one who would rather not be interrogated—and to put some pressure on the suspect to get a confession. If the police get a confession, it will be admissible as long as the police did not go too far. The second point I want you to see is that the Court's definition gives us no clear criterion for determining whether the police did go too far in a particular case. The third point is that the involuntary confession rule is a compromise between the individual's interest in being free from any pressure to confess and society's interest in solving crimes. Indeed, the very fact that the involuntary confession rule is a compromise probably accounts for the vagueness of the Court's definition of voluntariness. Whatever the reason, however, it is perfectly plain that the Court's statement is not helpful and that we must look elsewhere for the definitions of "voluntary" and "involuntary."

(2) Extrapolating or Inferring a Definition from the Facts and Results of Cases

A second technique for ascertaining a definition is to look closely at the facts and results of a group of cases and ask, "What definition must the Court be using to get these results on these facts?" As a basis for using this technique, I have chosen four cases, one from each of the first four decades in which the involuntary confession rule has been applied to state cases.

The first of these cases is *Brown v. Mississippi*,[5] which is also the first state case in which the U.S. Supreme Court held a confession inadmissible. [The facts of *Brown* are set out in Chapter 1 at page 12. To summarize, three black defendants were brutally beaten, one of them over the course of several days, and threatened with more beatings unless they confessed in every detail given by the white deputy sheriffs.—Eds.] The repeated confessions were used against them at trial and they were convicted of murder and sentenced to death. The U.S. Supreme Court unanimously reversed the convictions, holding that the use of confessions obtained under "compulsion by torture" violated due process of law. Although the Court did not explicitly refer to the involuntary confession rule or cite any involuntary confession case, *Brown* is generally regarded as the beginning of the modern era of the involuntary confession rule.

The second case is *Ashcraft v. Tennessee*.[6] The defendant, a forty-five-year-old caucasian, had overcome a meager education to achieve a measure of financial success as a skilled construction worker. Suspected of complicity in the murder of his wife, he was arrested and interrogated for thirty-six consecutive hours by relays of interrogators. As each group of interrogators became exhausted, it was replaced by a new group. As Ashcraft became exhausted, he was not replaced by a surrogate suspect. Eventually he confessed, was convicted, and was sentenced to long-term imprisonment. In a 6–3 decision, the Supreme Court reversed, holding that the confession was involuntary. Using the language of presumptions in an apparent departure from the "totality of the circumstances" approach, the majority stated that thirty-six hours of relay interrogation was "inherently coercive."[7]

The third case is *Spano v. New York*.[8] Spano was a foreign-born, twenty-five-year-old man with a junior high school education. He had a history of emotional instability and had been found unfit for military service after failing an intelligence test. After being indicted for murder, Spano hired a lawyer and surrendered to the police. For the next eight hours, he was continuously interrogated by various persons in two different locations. He repeatedly asked to see his lawyer, but his requests were denied. Not having obtained a confession, the authorities enlisted the services of a probationary officer, Bruno, whom Spano had known since childhood and whom Spano had telephoned shortly before he surrendered. Bruno was instructed to pretend that Spano's telephone call had got him into trouble, that he might lose his job, and that he, his pregnant wife, and their three children would suffer unless Spano confessed. After the fourth entreaty by Bruno, Spano confessed. The Supreme Court held that Spano's will had been overborne and that his confession was involuntary and inadmissible.

The fourth case is *Haynes v. Washington*.[9] Haynes was a skilled sheet-metal worker, about thirty years old, "of at least average intelligence, who, in the eleven years preceding his trial, had been convicted of drunken driving, resisting arrest, being without a driver's license, breaking and entering, robbery, breaking jail, and taking a car." After a filling station robbery, Haynes was briefly interrogated on the street and then released. Seconds later, he returned to the police car, admitted his guilt, and identified the filling station. He was taken to the police station where he again admitted his guilt during a thirty-minute interrogation. The next morning, he made two more confessions, both of which were transcribed. He refused to sign the transcript of the later confession, but did sign the earlier transcript. Prior to signing, "he had been held incommunicado for about sixteen hours, contrary to state law, and, although he had requested permission to call his wife on the morning following the arrest, he was told that 'when I had made a statement and cooperated with them that they would see to it that as soon as I got booked I could call my wife.'"[10] Notwithstanding the fact that Haynes made no claim of physical abuse, lack of sleep or food, or prolonged interrogation, the Supreme Court in a 5–4 decision held that his will had been overborne by the "express threat of continued incommunicado detention,"[11] and that the signed confession was therefore inadmissible.

The four cases I have just mentioned are alike in one respect: The confession was held involuntary and inadmissible in each. In all other respects, they are dissimilar. They involved suspects with different personal characteristics and they ran a huge gamut of police interrogation tactics from the brutal beatings in *Brown* to "so mild a whip"[12] as the incommunicado detention in Haynes. These very differences make it hard for us to extrapolate or infer a definition of involuntariness from the facts and results of these cases. If a definition is to be found, we must look elsewhere.

(3) Inferring a Definition from Goals or Objectives

The third and final approach to the definitional problem is the functional approach: to try to infer a definition from the goals or objectives that the Court has attributed to the involuntary confession rule. A careful reading of the Court's more than forty involuntary confession cases discloses not one but five different objectives. I am not saying that every objective appears in every case. That is not so. But it is so that five objectives can be extracted from the entire body of Supreme Court cases. The objectives are: (1) to deter the police from engaging in conduct that may produce an unreliable confession; (2) to deter the police from engaging in conduct so offensive to the minimum standards of a civilized society that it shocks the conscience of the Court; (3) to deter the police from engaging in less-than-shocking misconduct; (4) to deter the police from using the techniques of an inquisitorial system and to encourage them to use the techniques of an accusatorial system; and (5) to deter the police from overbearing the suspect's will.

Your initial reaction may be that these objectives at last give us the definitional tool we need. Precisely the opposite is true, however. Each of the objectives is problematic in one or more ways, and the very number of them obfuscates rather than clarifies.

Look first at the unreliability and shocking misconduct objectives. Each is a traditional due process concern and each will explain a case such as *Brown* or perhaps *Ashcraft*. But neither objective will explain *Spano* or *Haynes*. It is highly unlikely that the confession in either case was false and also unlikely that the police tactics would produce false confessions in other cases. Moreover, whatever one may think of the tactics in *Spano* and *Haynes*, it is not easy to argue that they offend the minimum standards of a civilized society and therefore shock our conscience. Thus, these themes, although part of traditional due process analysis, are too narrow to explain the range of cases in which confessions have been held involuntary.

The remaining themes are even more troublesome. The Court has said in some cases that the police must obey the law while enforcing the law, thus suggesting that a purpose of the involuntary confession rule is deterring violations of law that fall short of being profoundly shocking. However, the Court has never made clear whether it was referring to state or federal law, to common, statutory, or constitutional law. In short, it has never identified the broken law and thus has given the police no guidance. It is true that many of the Court's involuntary confession cases probably involved a violation of statutes that require a prompt first appearance. However, it is hard to see why a statutory violation should necessarily be treated as offending due process. This objective, therefore, raises more questions than it answers.

The dichotomy between an accusatorial and an inquisitorial system is at least as problematic. In the first place, the line between the two systems is far from clear. Thus, it is of little help to be told that our system is accusatorial and that the police must adhere to its standards. Moreover, as actually administered by the Supreme Court, the standards of an accusatorial system apparently do not prohibit the police from arresting suspects who would rather not be arrested, from interrogating them although they would rather not be interrogated, and from subjecting them to some pressure to confess. Of course, the police cannot go too far, but the standards of an accusatorial system do not tell us how far that is. Thus, once again we find statements that are too imprecise to be useful.

The free will theme is similarly bereft of guidance. I explored this point earlier when I discussed the *Schneckloth* case [*supra* at page 133], and it is not necessary to repeat the discussion here.

A few minutes ago, I raised a question: Under the Supreme Court's involuntary confession rule, what is the meaning of the words *voluntary* and *involuntary*? In an effort to answer this question, I used three standard analytical tools—the Court's verbalization of a definition, extrapolating or inferring a definition from the facts and results of cases, and inferring a definition from the objectives of the involuntary confession rule. None of these approaches is very useful. One can say with some confidence that a confession is involuntary if obtained by a brutal beating, as in *Brown*, or by prolonged and uninterrupted interrogation, as in *Ashcraft*. But beyond these extreme situations, little can be said. Since the rule requires us to consider the totality of the circumstances, a slight change in the facts may change the result. Thus, today's decision is of limited utility in guiding tomorrow's practices and decisions.

Legal rules are addressed to audiences. If the rules are vague, the audiences suffer. The audiences for the involuntary confession rule are police officers who interrogate and obtain confessions, lawyers who try criminal cases, and judges who decide them. Of these three audiences, the lawyers suffer least. They have the advantage of being advocates. They know the result they want to reach and they will often try to match the facts of their case as closely as possible to the facts of some favorable precedent without paying too close attention to the subtleties of doctrine. The police and judges, on the other hand, are in a different situation. The police have to decide during the course of an interrogation what tactics to use and how far to go with them. Judges have to decide whether the police went too far. If the law governing these decision-making processes is vague, and it is, these processes will suffer. They will also suffer in another way. Police officers want to obtain confessions and are willing to go to the brink to get them. A few officers are willing to go beyond. Although even the most precise rules will not deter an officer who is strongly motivated to ignore them, vague rules encourage violation. If a rule is vague, the officer can always say with plausibility, "I thought I was permitted to do it." So also with judges. Trial judges do not want to exclude evidence that the prosecution needs for a conviction, particularly when they believe that the evidence is reliable, and appellate judges are reluctant to overturn convictions and order retrials with attendant expense and delay. The vaguer the standards, the easier it is for judges to act on their impulses in doubtful or marginal cases.

Lest you think I overstate the case, I want to share with you the words of a person who is well known for his expertise in criminal procedure and constitutional law—Professor Joseph Grano of Wayne State University. Professor Grano is no friend of *Miranda*; he believes it was wrongly decided. Nevertheless, in an article that urges the overruling of

Miranda, he refers to the "intolerable uncertainty that characterized the thirty-year reign of the due process voluntariness doctrine in the law of confessions."[13] Recent cases bear out this observation. Although *Miranda* has largely replaced the involuntary confession rule, the latter still exists; it was not overruled by *Miranda*. Cases do arise in which it is claimed that a confession, apart from *Miranda*, was involuntary, and courts, as they did in the pre-*Miranda* days, are still holding confessions admissible in doubtful or marginal cases. Let me give you five examples.

The first is *State v. Waugh*.[14] During an interrogation about a murder, Waugh claimed that the victim had died of a heart attack in Waugh's car and that in a panic he had dumped the deceased's body. Thereafter, Waugh asked at least three times to telephone his wife. The police denied all requests, thus keeping him incommunicado. Waugh then underwent a polygraph test. The examiner told him that he had truthfully admitted being an alcoholic but that he had falsely denied killing the deceased. The examiner then said that he wanted to help Waugh by getting him treatment for his alcoholism. After many such statements, Waugh finally confessed. Although this case bears remarkable resemblance to *Haynes v. Washington*,[15] the Kansas Supreme Court held that it was distinguishable. In *Haynes*, the police told the defendant that he would have to confess before he would be allowed to call his wife. In *Waugh*, however, no such statement was made; the police merely denied the suspect's requests. Thus, the confession was "voluntary."

The second case is *Vance v. Bordenkircher*,[16] in which the court held voluntary a confession made by a fifteen-year-old who had an IQ of sixty-two and a mental age of nine. The confession was made after nine hours of intermittent interrogation, without counsel or other support.

The third example is *United States ex rel. Cerda v. Greer*.[17] A sixteen-year-old suspect was arrested at 1:00 A.M. and was questioned at 4:00 A.M., 9:00 A.M., noon, and 6:00 P.M., for about thirty-five minutes per session. A police officer told him to tell the truth or he would "get his ass kicked." His confession was held voluntary and admissible.

The penultimate example is *Martin v. Wainwright*.[18] In this case, Martin was sentenced to death, based in part on his confession. He was interrogated for five hours after the police refused to honor his request that the interrogation be put off for a day. During the interrogation, one detective played the "bad guy," yelling and cursing at Martin. Another detective and an assistant prosecutor played the "good guys," feigning sympathy and promising to get psychiatric assistance for him. The assistant prosecutor told Martin that Florida had a bifurcated proceeding in capital cases, and that, although a confession would not help him in the guilt-determining phase, it would help him in the sentencing phase. The Florida courts and the federal courts held that the confession was voluntary and admissible.

The final case is *State v. Jenkins*,[19] also a death case. Approximately one-half hour before the police questioned him, Jenkins was taken to a hospital emergency room in deep shock from a gunshot wound in his chest and spinal cord which left him paralyzed. He was in pain, and a tube had been inserted into his chest to relieve pressure from fluid buildup. His blood pressure had been very erratic although it was apparently beginning to stabilize. He had a low IQ and had been in a class for slow learners. Although he was going nowhere, the police questioned him and obtained a confession. The Ohio Supreme Court held that the confession was voluntary and admissible and it affirmed the conviction and death sentence.

These cases, although all decided in recent years, are remarkably representative of the cases that were decided earlier—in the good old days of police interrogation before *Miranda*. Small wonder, then, that in a period of thirty years or so, the Supreme Court granted review in over thirty-five cases in which confessions had been held voluntary. Small wonder, too, that the Court reversed the convictions in most of these cases. And small wonder that the Court became disaffected from its own work product. All students of the Court recognize that it cannot police the application of doctrine by lower courts. All it can hope to do is make doctrine intelligible and give illustrative examples. The Court tried to do that in the confession cases, and it failed. Given the inherent vagueness of the crucial concepts and the many rationales underlying the rule, failure was foreordained. So also was the search for an alternative.

Please do not misunderstand what I am saying. I am not saying that *Miranda* was correctly decided. I happen to believe that it was, but that is beside the point. The point is that the dissenters in 1966 and the Attorney General in 1985 were simply wrong in their claim that we got along well with the law that antedated *Miranda*. We did not, we are not getting along well with its vestiges today, and recognition of these simple facts should inform any reasonable debate about whether *Miranda* should be overruled. . . .

. . . As Justice Frankfurter observed some years ago, "the history of liberty has largely been the history of observance of procedural safeguards,"[20] and "not the least significant test of the quality of a civilization is its treatment of those charged with crime."[21]

NOTES

1. Brown v. Mississippi, 297 U.S. 278 (1936).

2. 412 U.S. 218 (1973).

3. *Id.* at 224, *quoting* Culombe v. Connecticut, 367 U.S. 568, 604–5 (1961).

4. *Id.* at 225.

5. 297 U.S. 278 (1936).

6. 322 U.S. 143 (1944).

7. *Id.* at 154.

8. 360 U.S. 315 (1959).

9. 373 U.S. 503 (1963).

10. *Id.* at 509.

11. *Id.* at 514.

12. Malloy v. Hogan, 378 U.S. 1, 7 (1964).

13. Joseph D. Grano, *Voluntariness, Free Will, and the Law of Confessions*, 65 Va. L. Rev. 859, 863 (1979).

14. 238 Kan. 537 (1986).

15. 373 U.S. 503 (1963), discussed earlier.

16. 692 F.2d 978 (4th Cir. 1982).

17. 613 F. Supp. 1120 (N.D. Ill. 1985).

18. 770 F.2d 918 (11th Cir. 1985).

19. 15 Ohio St. 3d 164 (1984). I consulted with the attorney who represented the defendant in the Ohio appellate courts, so I am not merely a spectator as far as this case is concerned.

20. McNabb v. United States, 318 U.S. 332, 347 (1943).

21. Irvin v. Dowd, 366 U.S. 717, 729 (1961) (concurring opinion).

11

A Modest Proposal
for the Abolition of
Custodial
Confessions
(1989)

•

IRENE MERKER ROSENBERG & YALE L. ROSENBERG

The popular drumbeat against *Miranda*, which now is echoed by the U.S. Supreme Court, tends to obscure the factual and legal circumstances that led the Court to render *Miranda*'s per se ruling—widespread and unmonitored coercive police practices, uncontrolled by an ad hoc voluntariness test that gave no guidance to police or courts and resulted in lawlessness in the nation's police stations. *Miranda*'s solution was a warning and waiver requirement to be administered by the very individuals whose tactics had given rise to the problem of coerced confessions. Little wonder that some have viewed *Miranda* simply as *legerdemain*, offering the appearance but not the reality of an effective mechanism against police overreaching. According to this view, the decision's failing is not that it impedes the police, but that it does not impede them enough: *Miranda* is unable to protect suspects from improper police practices and the overwhelming pressures of custody. Instead, contrary to the popular belief, more rigorous safeguards, such as requiring counsel at interrogations, are essential to deter official misconduct and facilitate the knowledgeable exercise of free will.

Such voices favoring a stronger remedy are far less audible now, however, and it is not hard to discern why. The Supreme Court's general shift to the right on *Miranda* questions, as well as on other criminal procedure issues, almost necessarily has pulled the bounds of reasonable dialogue in the same direction. Furthermore, the executive department's most recent assault on *Miranda*, combined with escalating drug-related crimes, political calls for more stringent law enforcement, and a flurry of scholarly activity from those critical of the decision's per se approach, all appear to have helped create an atmosphere in which simply holding the line on *Miranda* would be a victory for the advocates of effective restraints on police. The question, though, is whether there is anything left to hold. While not overruled, *Miranda* has been so diluted that its main value today may be merely symbolic.

In the present political climate, it may appear quixotic to ask for something beyond an admittedly positive symbol—akin to ordering filet mignon during a famine. Nonetheless, the present Court's treatment of *Miranda* has so many negative aspects that the ruling itself basically has outlived its usefulness. The Justices' recent attempts to contain *Miranda* have led to mendacious jurisprudence in the confession area, which in turn has enabled the Court to avoid addressing the very real problem of involuntary and compelled confessions. Consequently, although *Miranda's* underlying premise that per se rules are the most effective means of overcoming the inherently coercive effects of custody is correct, its specific holding requiring police warnings fails to accomplish that result and should be abandoned.

In other words, *Miranda's* recognition that a per se remedy, rather than an ad hoc totality-of-the-circumstances test, is the best method of preserving the privilege against self-incrimination remains valid. Given the realities of police detention and human nature, however, it is not possible for custodial admissions to be the product of a suspect's free will. This [chapter], therefore, proposes a different per se rule—namely, that out-of-court statements made by defendants while in custody, whether or not the result of interrogation, cannot be used to establish guilt in criminal trials. Although appearing to be radical, this position is not too far removed from *Miranda's* original message. . . .

What Ever Happened to *Miranda*?

Despite calls to overrule *Miranda*, the Justices have declined to do so. Instead, the Burger and Rehnquist Courts have settled on a policy of chilling containment of the controversial ruling. In a variety of ways, the Court has undercut the decision, hollowing out its core while maintaining a pretext of viability. In particular, the Justices have diluted *Miranda* by denying its constitutional base;[1] by allowing statements obtained in violation of *Miranda* to be used derivatively and for impeachment;[2] by making the requirements for invocation of *Miranda* rights stricter and the requirements for waiver more lenient;[3] by interpreting terms such as *custody, interrogation,* and *criminal proceeding* in a narrow manner;[4] by carving a gaping hole in the decision in the form of an ill-defined public safety exception;[5] and by validating police deception and trading on the ignorance of suspects.[6] . . .

The Institutional Damage

Retention of a devitalized *Miranda* has many undesirable effects. The Supreme Court's post-*Miranda* decisions have impaired *Miranda's* original clarity, making it difficult for police and lower courts to determine the circumstances under which confessions may be obtained and admitted into evidence. The result is not merely confusion, but a tacit encouragement of police overreaching and judicial circumvention. Moreover, *Miranda's* seeming vitality effectively permits the Justices themselves to avoid devising meaningful remedies to deal with coercive police interrogation.

Even *Miranda's* detractors on the Court ultimately acknowledged that the decision had at least one virtue—the ruling created a bright line that made it relatively easy to separate admissible from inadmissible confessions. It was a line that gave fairly explicit guidance to both police and the lower courts. Law enforcement officers knew that unless they gave the warnings and secured a valid waiver, a suspect's statement could not be used to establish guilt. Even lower courts hostile to *Miranda* had little choice other than to abide by its clear-cut directives. As in the case of laws governing commercial transactions, there is a virtue in having a rule of criminal procedure that is well known and readily understood, even if its application in particular circumstances—such as when a confession concededly voluntary under traditional due process standards is excluded because of a defect in the police warning—may seem unfair or unreasonable.

Twenty years later, however, certainty and predictability are going, if not gone. Other than in cases of outright coercion, officers no longer can know what limits there are in securing confessions. At best, they realize that there is now considerable play in the joints. At worst, they believe that a skillful prosecutor can argue away successfully any deficiencies in eliciting a suspect's statement. Similarly, lower courts are asked to divine on a case-by-case basis whether *Miranda* governs a particular matter or if the matter instead falls within any of the numerous exceptions, conditions, and qualifications that have been engrafted over the years. . . .

The loss of *Miranda's* bright line also will have an adverse effect on lower court adjudication. Judges antagonistic to *Miranda* have been given numerous mechanisms for evading its reach. Even those who conscientiously attempt to apply the Supreme Court's decisions in this area must face a welter of rulings whose overall effect is to make it unclear under what circumstances a confession is admissible. This is not the usual Cardozian ebb and flow of the common law, with its inherent ambiguity and change that are the lifeblood of the judicial process. Rather, in many instances the *Miranda* progeny effectively obfuscate the operative principles governing the admissibility of confessions.

These post-*Miranda* rulings make it almost as difficult to determine the admissibility issue today as it was under the due process voluntariness test. Under that standard, lower court judges weighed and balanced a host of factors to determine admissibility, without any meaningful guidelines to assure that their assessments were correct. That same problem now exists to some extent in the *Miranda* context, for while the inferior courts are assured that, by and large, *Miranda* lives, they are also advised that its health is impaired in a variety of openended ways that must be taken into account. Reconciliation of these conflicting claims is at best problematic and is not unlike the ad hoc decisionmaking required prior to *Miranda*, except perhaps in one significant way. In the bad old days of the ad hoc voluntariness test, at least by the 1960s, Supreme Court reviews of coerced confession cases more often than not resulted in reversals of convictions. Thus, the Court was telling inferior tribunals that if they erred in determining what process was due, it was preferable to resolve mistakes in favor of the accused. Now, however, with the Court giving a different set of signals, mistakes are more likely to be made in a manner enhancing state power and constricting constitutional safeguards. . . .

The Modest Proposal

The *Miranda* decision itself recognized that warnings could be dispensed with if other equally effective remedies were used—remedies as effective as the *Miranda* majority apparently expected the warnings to be. The Court has not advanced any other such per se rules, and the few state proposals made in this area, as well as those of the Justice Department, are either unduly vague or are easily subject to circumvention.

Some of the more radical recommendations advanced over the years are meritorious. For example, having an attorney present at custodial interrogation certainly helps assure that any resulting confession will be a product of the defendant's free will.[7] The presence of counsel is often considered an ironclad guarantee against police elicitation of any confession, voluntary or coerced. Yet, like other warranties, it is only as good as its maker. To put not too fine a point on the matter, the question of ineffective assistance of counsel, even in the interrogation context, cannot be easily dismissed. While it may be true that "any lawyer worth his salt will tell the suspect . . . to make no statement to police under any circumstances,"[8] the problem is that some lawyers are not. Indeed, given the stress and time pressures of station house questioning, mistakes in judgment, such as erroneous advice to give an exonerating statement, are more likely to occur. Affording the right to counsel also would not obviate inquiries with respect to waiver once counsel has left the station house. Thus, such a proposal, while extremely helpful, does not assure that only voluntary confessions will be used at trial. It also does not eliminate litigation of issues, such as ineffective assistance of counsel, that may be peripheral to the question of coercion.

Similarly, proposals requiring police to bring suspects before magistrates without unnecessary delay and to advise them of their constitutional rights help encourage voluntariness, but do not guarantee it. Coercive tactics still can take place prior to presentation of the suspect to the magistrate. Moreover, this temporary respite from exclusive police custody ends when the suspect leaves the courtroom. Even if the defendant asserted his rights, the court still would face the question whether the police had honored defendant's invocation. Indeed, should the Court deem confessions admissible only when made to magistrates, voluntariness still would not be assured. In this context as well, the accused is in custody and in the presence of an authority who may appear to be soliciting if not demanding an admission of one sort or another.

In short, neither defense attorneys nor magistrates can assure the voluntariness of confessions. Whether suspects render self-inculpatory statements in the station house, the courtroom, or any other custodial context, the circumstances surrounding their elicitation are so intimidating that the exercise of free will is at best problematic. The voluntariness of admissions in such cases always will be debatable. Thus, to the extent that these proposals are meant to curb improper police questioning, they seem to finesse the real issue—whether any confession given by a suspect while in custody can be considered either voluntary within the meaning of due process or noncompelled under the Fifth Amendment. Our answers to those questions are maybe and no. The confession may or may not be voluntary, depending on various factors including the quality and quantity of police pressure, but it is, in any event, compelled. The Fifth Amendment prohibition against compulsion provides a separate and independent basis for assessing the admissibility of confessions, one that goes beyond preclusion of unreliable statements and of unlawful police overreaching, manipulation, deception, and the like, all of which are prohibited under the voluntariness standard of the due process clause—at least if the misconduct is sufficiently egregious. Professor Schulhofer has argued that the self-incrimination clause covers "more civilized but nonetheless compelling pressures."[9] While accepting his view that less blatant official pressure violates the self-incrimination privilege, one may also, at the same time, see compulsion as primarily situational in nature, at least if there is government involvement in creating the situation. Such a situational concept of compulsion would allow the courts to reject confessions when individuals are, as a result of state-created circumstances (such as being in custody), not fully able to exercise free will in determining whether to assist the state in securing their own convictions. . . .

The Bill of Rights incorporation process also lends credence to this concept of situational compulsion. Due process can be seen as a baseline, a lowest common denominator for determining constitutionally permissible governmental behavior. The criminal safeguards of the Bill of Rights, on the other hand, have their own individual and particular values. The entire painstaking process of incorporation assured that these concerns also would be relevant in assessing alleged state misconduct. Indeed, the Court has acknowledged that the assimilated provisions embody distinctive values by separately addressing particular Bill of Rights guarantees, on the one hand, and due process-fundamental fairness questions on the other. Thus, it seems unlikely that the long struggle culminating in incorporation of the Fifth Amendment prohibition against compelled testimony could have been simply an heroic effort to provide an official synonym for involuntariness. . . . Rather, it seems more probable that application of the Fifth Amendment privilege was meant to deal with something other than or in addition to active forms of police misconduct.

Just as the voluntariness concept has evolved, moving gradually from the prohibition against physical brutality and concern with reliability announced in *Brown v. Mississippi*[10] to the prohibition against deception and concern with police misconduct declared in *Spano v. New York*,[11] the compulsion doctrine is likewise susceptible of growth. The Court may have intended *Miranda* to be the equivalent of *Brown v. Mis-*

sissippi in this evolutionary process. Thus, *Miranda* required the conjunction of interrogation and custody as its baseline establishing compulsion. In time, had the Court permitted *Miranda* to be true to its teaching, the subsequent case law might have produced a more refined definition of compulsion and a more refined mechanism for its dissipation—from a system of warnings to a total bar against statements made in all circumstances viewed as compulsive. Thus, the Court might have viewed either custody or interrogation standing alone as sufficient to establish compulsion, and it might have reached even beyond to other circumstances that compel persons to incriminate themselves.

We would not go so far, at least at this time. It is our view, however, that suspects who are in custody cannot make truly voluntary or noncompelled confessions and that, therefore, any statements made by them, whether to police or to police agents, and whether the product of interrogation, should be inadmissible in evidence. We do recognize that everyone ultimately has free choice—of sorts. As the saying goes, even the condemned person awaiting execution can opt either to curse the hangman or pray to God. Admittedly, in the mundane, everyday world, there are also constraints on the exercise of free will that are simply endemic to the human condition—everyone's decisions are influenced by unconscious desires, time pressures, economic demands, cost-benefit analyses, and the like. In a very real sense, however, custody presents a difference in kind. Its circumstances are sui generis. The suspect is stripped of power, control, and dignity, and is subject, by and large, to the whims of jailers. If a purpose of the privilege is to create a parity of sorts between the individual and the state, it must be recognized that, in the confines of the station house or its functional equivalent, there is no equality, gross or otherwise.

Although *Miranda* focused on the inherent coerciveness of custodial *interrogation*, it is custody in and of itself that is coercive. Concededly, official interrogation heightens the tension, but even without questioning, custody tends to deprive persons of free choice. The lack of freedom simpliciter, therefore, requires a broader prophylactic rule than that set forth in *Miranda*. Given the nature of custody, advising suspects of their rights is unlikely to dissipate its oppressive effects, and waivers in such situations cannot be viewed realistically as noncompelled. Moreover, the case law interpreting the interrogation requirement suggests that drawing the line of protection at this point invites circumvention of the privilege. The police apparently have become adept at creating circumstances short of interrogation that nonetheless effectively compel a suspect to make ostensibly spontaneous utterances. . . .

Drawing the line at custody does deny protection in the atypical case of a confession by a previously unsuspected person who voluntarily appears at the police station, either with or without an attorney. Because this is not a state-initiated appearance, custody has not attached and under our proposal such a defendant's confession is presumptively voluntary. . . .

This [chapter] also does not advocate the arguably more radical position that *all* statements made by suspects to state officials or their agents during interrogation be inadmissible in evidence. As the *Miranda* majority acknowledged, custody is an appropriate dividing line, although that term should be defined in a considerably less grudging manner than the Burger and Rehnquist Courts have. At the same time, there is much merit in this more protective view, because the line between custodial and noncustodial interrogation may prove inadequate to deal with police questioning in noncustodial contexts, such as ostensibly nonthreatening but nonetheless inherently intimidating interrogation in the suspect's home. Indeed, if it became clear that our proposal was subject to circumvention through such techniques, we would not hesitate to propose a broader prophylactic rule.

A still more extreme position would prohibit even volunteered statements made outside custody without preceding interrogation. While we do not advocate it, there is merit to this position. We are simply uncertain whether any statements to government officials can be deemed noncompelled. . . .

Indeed, there is an even more drastic proposal that could be made—namely, that all confessions, whether voluntary or compelled, reliable or spontaneous, and whether made in custody, in court, or to government officials, be deemed inadmissible in evidence in criminal proceedings—that is, that confessions be considered of no evidentiary value. We have a philosophical predilection for such a position, which reflects the ancient Talmudic rule.[12] We recognize, however, that this position may be considered in tension with the Fifth Amendment prohibition, which is directed solely to compelled self-incriminating testimony.

Viewed in contrast to the foregoing alternatives, our proposition has much to recommend it, but is not such a sharp departure from the original understanding of *Miranda*. The proposal would not preclude admissibility of voluntary statements made in noncustodial situations, whether elicited or sua sponte, although we would define custody broadly. This compromise, however, at least would prevent the most abusive forms of police misconduct, for it is custody that permits the police to play havoc with the defendant's free will, and it is custody that invites the sort of official trickery effectively condoned by the Court in *Moran v. Burbine*.[13] At the same time, the proposal would respect the individual's decision to make incriminating statements in the noncustodial context. Furthermore, by generally precluding reliance on confessions, it would provide an incentive for improved police investigation. The proposal surely would discourage placement of suspects in custody absent sufficient evidence of guilt. It also would provide a brighter line to guide police, prosecutors, and judges with respect to the admissibility of confessions, and it would eliminate the need to litigate collateral issues other than the question of custody. Moreover, the proposal allows the Court to create a parity of sorts between indicted and unindicted defendants with respect to custodial confessions, without extending the Sixth Amendment right to counsel to the latter category of suspects, a step that the Court refuses to take. Finally, in comparison to the proposals requiring appearance before a magistrate or the presence of counsel during interrogation, this recommendation gives greater expression to a core value of the Fifth Amendment, namely, the protection of human dignity. To allow the state to prove a person's guilt based on a confession made in a government-created situation, that by its very nature psychologically induces people to disclose incriminating information, denigrates the concept of man as separate and apart from the state and entitled to the exercise of free will.

*

This proposal to eliminate the use of custodial confessions is not a Swiftian gesture. It is only the nature of the contemporary national debate concerning *Miranda* that may make it appear so. In the criminal law area at least, jurisprudence seems to be backing into the future. It is disheartening that, at this late date, serious scholars still contend that the appropriate means for resolution of the tension between state security and individual dignity is disincorporation of the Fifth Amendment to allow interrogation of suspects by magistrates or a return to a variant of the ad hoc, totality-of-the-circumstances test for determining the voluntariness of confessions. The former turns the accusatorial system on its head, even though it is designed to prevent de facto inquisitorial examinations by the police. The latter is a time-tested prescription for failure. While we do not denigrate government's need to deal effectively with criminal conduct, there is scant evidence that *Miranda* is either an impediment to effective law enforcement or, more specifically, a significant obstacle to conviction.

Even so, *Miranda* apparently has become a scapegoat for all the intractable criminal law problems facing this country. Crime abounds, and we do not know what to do about it. Why people commit crimes, how to stop them, how to sentence them, and how to control the scourge of drugs are all unanswered questions. On a gut level, at least, the problem of crime appears insoluble. Yet the public demands action. In the absence of meaningful solutions, critics seem to say, let us get rid of legal technicalities such as exclusionary rules that ostensibly allow criminals to evade justice. Let *Miranda*, not crack, serve as public enemy number one. Better yet, tie them together causally. There is more crack because of *Miranda*; therefore, *Miranda* must go. But if, after *Miranda* is gone, the same problems still persist, what constitutional guarantee will have to be sacrificed next?

If nothing else, we hope that this proposal can help to move the debate to a slightly more reasonable position on the ideological spectrum. After all, the evolving content of the due process clause in no small measure reflects this country's maturation as a civilized society. Surely the movement from the early decisions prohibiting physical brutality in the extraction of confessions to *Miranda*'s prophylactic rules bespeaks that truth. The trend has been to give more not less, to go forward not back, to refine rights rather than coarsen them. In this sense, the Warren Court was mainstream, and the Burger and Rehnquist Courts are aberrational. History dictates that we should examine how to strengthen Fifth Amendment protection rather than eviscerate it. . . .

NOTES

1. [For example, in Oregon v. Elstad, 470 U.S. 298 (1985), the Court stated that *Miranda* "serves" the Fifth Amendment by creating a presumption of compulsion that "sweeps more broadly than the Fifth Amendment itself." Because *Miranda* is broader than the Fifth Amendment, "unwarned statements that are otherwise voluntary within the meaning of the Fifth Amendment must nevertheless be excluded from evidence under *Miranda*. Thus, in the individual case, *Miranda*'s preventive medicine provides a remedy even to the defendant who has suffered no identifiable constitutional harm."—Eds.]

2. [If the state violates *Miranda* and secures a confession, that confession may be used to impeach different testimony that the defendant gives at trial. Harris v. New York, 401 U.S. 222 (1971). Though the judge will instruct the jury to con-

sider the confession only on the issue of the defendant's credibility, few scholars or lawyers believe that the jury can disregard the substance of the confession. Also, the Court has held that evidence learned from a confession taken in violation of *Miranda* can sometimes be used against the confessing defendant. Michigan v. Tucker, 417 U.S. 433 (1974).—Eds.]

3. [These cases are discussed at pages 86–90 of the Rosenbergs' original article.—Eds.]

4. [See pages 82–83 & 90 in the original article.—Eds.]

5. [New York v. Quarles, 467 U.S. 649 (1984).—Eds.]

6. [See pages 92–93 in the original article.—Eds.]

7. See Charles Ogletree, *Are Confessions Really Good for the Soul? A Proposal to Mirandize* Miranda, 100 Harv. L. Rev. 1826, 1842 (1987).

8. Watts v. Indiana, 338 U.S. 49, 59 (1949) (Jackson, J., concurring in part).

9. Stephen J. Schulhofer, Reconsidering *Miranda*, 54 U. Chi. L. Rev. 435, 444 (1987). [excerpted in Chapter 8.—Eds.].

10. 297 U.S. 278 (1936).

11. 360 U.S. 315 (1959).

12. See Irene Merker Rosenberg & Yale L.Rosenberg, *In the Beginning: The Talmudic Rule Against Self-Incrimination*, 63 N.Y.U. L. Rev. 955, 1048 (1988) ("The Talmudic rule [prohibiting the use of confessions in criminal cases] is simple; it is absolute; it is profound. We could do worse than look to it for guidance").

13. 479 U.S. 157, 164 (1986). [The Court found no constitutional violation in stating falsely to the suspect's lawyer that the suspect was not being interrogated.—Eds.]

12

A Peculiar
Privilege
in Historical
Perspective:
The Right
to Remain Silent
(1996)

•

ALBERT W. ALSCHULER

*

II. The Puzzling Ethics of the Right to Silence

In a classic article, *Silence as a Moral and Constitutional Right,* R. Kent Greenawalt discussed the ordinary morality of interrogating a person suspected of wrongdoing.[1] Greenawalt drew a contrast between questioning on slender suspicion and questioning on solidly grounded suspicion, and he offered a number of illustrations of the moral difference between these two practices.

When Ann has little basis for suspecting that Betty has stolen her property, Greenawalt suggested that it would be insulting and unfair for Ann to ask Betty to account for her activities at the time of the theft. Betty might properly respond, "That's none of your business." If, however, a friend had told Ann that he had seen Betty wearing a distinctive bracelet like the one that Ann had reported stolen, then Ann might appropriately describe the reason for her suspicion and ask Betty to explain. Ann's query would be less insulting and intrusive than most other means of confirming or dispelling her suspicion—surreptitiously watching Betty, searching her possessions, or interrogating her associates. In such circumstances, Betty would have powerful reasons for responding, and if she declined, Ann's suspicion could appropriately increase.

Although Greenawalt analyzed close personal relationships and less personal relationships separately, he concluded that the line between slight suspicion and well-grounded suspicion marked the boundary between proper and improper questioning in both. In Greenawalt's view of ordinary morality, a person interrogated on slender suspicion may appropriately remain silent; a person questioned on well-grounded suspicion may not.

If the U.S. Constitution had adhered to Greenawalt's view of morality, the Fifth Amendment might have provided a limited right to silence comparable to the limited freedom from governmental searches and seizures afforded by the Fourth Amendment. The Fourth Amendment provides only a qualified immunity from governmental intrusion—one that can be overcome by a showing of probable cause. The privilege afforded by the Fifth Amendment, however, is unqualified. The Framers of the Constitution apparently concluded that no amount of evidence could justify compelling a person to supply testimonial evidence against herself in a criminal case. The Fourth Amendment, which forbids only unreasonable searches and seizures, invites balancing. The Fifth Amendment does not. The Constitution says flatly that no person shall be compelled in any criminal case to be a witness against himself.

Like a police search, governmental interrogation invades a suspect's privacy and should not be permitted without antecedent justification. A limited right to silence—one that could be overcome by a showing of probable cause—could easily be justified. As many writers have observed, however, the rationales that the Supreme Court has offered for a more sweeping right to silence are unconvincing, and the more elaborate rationales offered by academic writers are similarly unpersuasive. . . .

Although the Supreme Court has said that the privilege is the "essential mainstay" of an accusatorial system[2] and that it "requir[es] the government in its contest with the individual to shoulder the entire load,"[3] our legal system is substantially less accusatorial than this rhetoric suggests. The Supreme Court has required defendants to shoulder much of the load by producing incriminating documents, giving pretrial notice of defenses and of the evidence to be used to support them, providing copies of defense investigative reports, and supplying all forms of nontestimonial evidence—blood samples, voice samples, and even, in one case, the body of a child whom a suspect was thought to have killed.[4]

The virtues of an "accusatorial" system in which defendants are privileged to remain passive are far from obvious. The person who knows the most about the guilt or innocence of a criminal defendant is ordinarily the defendant herself. Unless expecting her to respond to inquiry is immoral or inhuman—contrary to Greenawalt's view of ordinary morality—renouncing all claim to her evidence is costly and foolish.

Our legal system is in fact wise enough to reject in practice much of the accusatorial rhetoric it proclaims in theory. It actively seeks incriminating, testimonial evidence from the people it accuses of crime. Unfortunately, it often does so in troublesome ways. Every year, courts find that suspects in the back rooms of police stations have made multitudes of knowing and intelligent waivers of their Fifth Amendment rights. If these suspects had understood their situations in the slightest degree, most of them would have remained silent. In addition, 92 percent of all felony convictions in the United States are by guilty plea. Behind this figure lies the practice of plea bargaining. Prosecutors and other officials exert extraordinary pressure on defendants, not merely to obtain an answer, but to secure an unqualified admission of guilt. The Federal Sentencing Guidelines currently promise a substantially discounted sentence to a defendant who supplies "complete information to the government concerning his own involvement in the offense."[5] Few other nations are as dependent as ours on proving guilt from a defendant's own mouth.

No parent or schoolteacher feels guilty about asking questions of a child strongly suspected of misconduct. Similarly, no employer considers it improper to ask an employee accused of wrongdoing to give his side of the story. Criminal cases aside, there are apparently no investigative or factfinding proceedings in which asking questions and expecting answers is regarded as dirty business. Noting that "parents try hard to inculcate in their children the simple virtues of truth and responsibility," Justice Walter V. Schaefer once wrote that "the Fifth Amendment privilege against self-incrimination . . . runs counter to our ordinary standards of morality."[6]

People who regard criminal defendants as an appropriate source of evidence for resolving criminal disputes may wonder how the contrary position became, at least sometimes, a revered principle of American constitutional law. The common assumption that the privilege mandates an accusatorial system and forbids all efforts to induce a defendant to reveal what she knows explains much of the persistent criticism of the privilege. This criticism and much other discussion of the privilege, however, have rested on a historical misconception. The privilege in its inception was not intended to afford criminal defendants a right to refuse to respond to incriminating questions. Its purposes were far more limited.

III. A History of the Privilege in Three Acts

The history of the modern privilege against self-incrimination can be divided roughly into three stages, each of them captured by its own distinctive formulation of the doctrine. At the earliest stage, the privilege against self-incrimination was expressed in maxims like *Nemo tenetur seipsum accusare* ("No one shall be required to accuse himself") and *Nemo tenetur prodere seipsum* ("No one shall be required to produce himself" or "No one shall be required to betray himself"). At the second stage, the formulation was that of the United States Constitution: No person "shall be compelled in any criminal case to be a witness against himself." At the third stage (the modern stage), the warnings mandated by *Miranda v. Arizona* express the general although not universal understanding of the privilege: "You have a right to remain silent." These formulations often are treated as equivalent, but they are very different.

A. Nemo Tenetur Prodere Seipsum

As Richard Helmholz has demonstrated, the roots of the privilege in the early seventeenth century are to be found, not in the common law of England, but in the *ius commune*—the law applied throughout the European continent and in the English prerogative and ecclesiastical courts.[7] . . .

Several maxims of the *ius commune* expressed its most important limitation on interrogation. In addition to the familiar *nemo tenetur* maxim given above, the *ius commune* made use of two more: *Nemo punitur sine accusatore* ("No one is punished in the absence of an accuser") and *Nemo tenetur detegere turpitudinem suam* ("No one is bound to reveal his own shame").

The principle reflected in these maxims was unknown in classical Roman law, and when it entered the *ius commune* is uncertain. A plausible hypothesis is that the privilege began as a limitation upon the religious duty to confess. By the third century, penance for wrongdoing was an obligation of Christian faith, and the penance occurred in public. Whether this penance generally included a public confession, or whether, instead, private confession preceded public penance is a matter of dispute, but the Church ultimately demanded only private (auricular) confession. . . .

Far from reflecting the notion that wrongdoers have a right to remain silent, the privilege against self-incrimination originally may have reflected only a pragmatic judgment that a sinner's duty did not include a public disclosure that might lead to criminal proceedings. To demand either public disclosure or submission to criminal punishment would have diminished the willingness of wrongdoers to confess; and confession, not silence, was good for the soul.

By the seventeenth century, the privilege had grown into a right not to be interrogated under oath in the absence of well-grounded suspicion. All of the formulations of the *nemo tenetur* principle in the *ius commune* were consistent with the concepts of ordinary morality voiced by Kent Greenawalt. They concerned the initiation of criminal proceedings, declaring that a person could not be required to "accuse" or "produce" or "betray" himself. No person could be required to "reveal" his own wrongdoing. There must instead be an "accuser," someone other than the defendant who had revealed or asserted the defendant's crime. Officials must not commence prosecutions by interrogating at large, by conducting fishing expeditions, or by questioning on what Greenawalt would call slender suspicion. Officials in the seventeenth century and earlier were expected to have probable cause before asking suspects to respond under oath to incriminating questions.

Unlike the common law courts of the seventeenth century, which did not permit criminal defendants and other litigants to testify under oath, the High Commission [in investigating religious crimes,—Eds.] required parties to swear to answer truthfully all questions that the court might put to them. The High Commission often did so, moreover, without specification of the charges against a suspect or notification of the questions to be asked. . . .

The difference between the procedures of the High Commission and other ecclesiastical courts, in all of which defendants were sworn to tell the truth, and those of common law courts, in which defendants often spoke but were disqualified from testifying under oath, is important in understanding the history of the privilege against self-incrimination. The history of the privilege, from the struggles over the authority of the High Commission through at least the framing of the American Bill of Rights, is almost entirely a story of when and for what purposes people would be required to speak under oath. . . .

Under the *ius commune*, the propriety of inquisition before the High Commission thus turned upon the proper application of the principles of morality that Kent Greenawalt articulated more than 300 years later. Disputants considered what sort of antecedent justification the law required before the High Commission could administer the *ex officio* oath and ask questions. Once an appropriate preliminary showing had been made, suspects were required to submit to the oath and to answer. . . .

B. No Person Shall Be Compelled in Any Criminal Case to Be a Witness against Himself

The privilege against self-incrimination that the Framers included in the Bill of Rights of 1791 differed from the privilege that the English common law courts enforced against the High Commission. The Fifth Amendment, declaring that no person shall be compelled in any criminal case to be a witness against himself, plainly refers, not just to the initiation of criminal proceedings or to a first accusation, but to the conduct of the criminal trial.

By the time a felony defendant reaches trial, a strong basis for suspecting his guilt ought to be apparent, and a privilege afforded to defendants who have been placed on trial after a showing of probable cause goes beyond Greenawalt's principles of morality. Unlike the limited privilege of the *ius commune*, the Fifth Amendment's privilege was not designed merely to guarantee an adequate evidentiary basis for interrogation. The Constitution affords an absolute privilege, one that no evidentiary showing can overcome.

In assessing what this constitutional privilege meant to the people who enacted it, manuals used to instruct justices of the peace on the conduct of their offices offer a helpful starting point. For nearly 300 years, from 1584 through the mid-nineteenth century, these manuals declared that the *nemo tenetur* principle precluded the interrogation of suspects under oath. One of the most frequently used manuals in colonial America, Dalton's *Countrey Justice*, first published in England in 1618, declared, "The offender himself shall not be examined upon oath; for by the common law, *Nullus tenetur seipsum prodere*."[8]

A manual published in 1745 explained:

> The Law of *England* is a Law of Mercy, and does not use the Rack or Torture to compel Criminals to accuse themselves. . . . I take it to be for the same Reason, that it does not call upon the Criminal to answer upon Oath. For, this might serve instead of the Rack, to the Consciences of

some Men, although they have been guilty of Offences. . . . The Law has therefore wisely and mercifully laid down this Maxim, *Nemo tenetur seipsum prodere*.[9] . . .

In 1677 the Virginia House of Burgesses declared that forcing suspects to answer incriminating questions under oath was incompatible with their natural rights. In the aftermath of Bacon's Rebellion and its suppression, the House resolved "that a person summoned as a witnes against another, ought to answer upon oath, but noe law can compell a man to sweare against himselfe in any matter wherein he is lyable to corporall punishment."[10]

These sources and others discussed below support this judgment: The Fifth Amendment privilege prohibited (1) incriminating interrogation under oath, (2) torture, and (3) probably other forms of coercive interrogation such as threats of future punishment and promises of leniency. The Amendment prohibited nothing more, or at least the sources mention nothing more. The self-incrimination clause neither mandated an accusatorial system nor afforded defendants a right to remain silent. It focused upon improper methods of gaining information from criminal suspects.

If this understanding of the original understanding is correct, critics of the Fifth Amendment privilege have missed the mark. Although the intensity of the Framers' disapproval of sworn statements by suspects may seem foreign to us today, the policies that informed the privilege were coherent and compelling, and they were not in tension with ordinary morality. When Ann has a strong basis for suspecting that Betty has stolen her property, ordinary morality may permit Ann to interrogate Betty and to draw an adverse inference if she refuses to respond. Ordinary morality, however, does not permit Ann to place Betty on the rack or to insist that Betty swear upon threat of imprisonment for falsehood or silence that her explanation is true. When critics have spoken harshly of the privilege against self-incrimination, they have assumed that it afforded more than a right to be free of inhuman methods of interrogation. They have assumed that it afforded a right to silence—a right not to respond to incriminating questions at all. The evidence, however, is overwhelming that the privilege did not afford this right at the time that it appeared in the Bill of Rights.

What the Fifth Amendment privilege did not prohibit is in fact clearer than what it did. The privilege did not prohibit the forceful incriminating interrogation of suspects by judges and magistrates so long as the suspects remained unsworn. Unsworn suspects who refused to respond to the questions of English and American courts doubtless would have suffered no more severe sanction than the drawing of an adverse inference. The procedures of the pre-nineteenth-century trial, however, would have made that disadvantage substantial in every case and devastating in most. The privilege did not afford suspects a right to suffer no consequences for their refusal to speak.

John Langbein has distinguished between two historic models of the criminal trial: the "accused speaks" trial and the "testing the prosecution" trial.[11] He argues that the transformation of the "accused speaks" trial into the "testing the prosecution" trial began in the late eighteenth century when lawyers came to represent defendants in significant numbers. So long as defendants were unrepresented, no one could speak for them unless they spoke for themselves. In this situation, a right to remain silent would have been a right to commit suicide. Langbein notes that several other aspects of common law procedure also induced defendants to speak, and the evidence is clear that in the sixteenth, seventeenth, and eighteenth centuries virtually all English defendants did speak. One source described the criminal trial as an "altercation" between the defendant and his accusers.[12]

Trial, moreover, was not the only stage of the criminal process at which the accused was expected to speak. The Marian Committal Statute of 1555 required justices of the peace to interrogate suspects following their apprehension and to record anything "materiall to prove the felonie."[13] Until the mid-eighteenth century, the record of the defendant's pretrial examination was read routinely at her trial. Courts then began to express a preference for hearing the defendant's account from the defendant herself, but the record of her pretrial examination remained available for impeachment purposes. If the defendant said something different at trial from what she had told the magistrate, the jury heard about it. . . .

If someone had argued to judges of the founding generation that their "accused speaks" procedures violated the privilege against self-incrimination, they might have offered any or all of three responses. These responses would have denied each and every element of a violation of the privilege:

> First, far from compelling any defendant to be a *witness* against himself, we do not permit any defendant to be a witness against (or for) himself. The defendant is disqualified from giving evidence partly because we

are concerned that placing him on oath would be incompatible with his privilege.

Second, if our procedures compel defendants to do anything, it is not to *incriminate* themselves. We do not press defendants to admit their guilt. To the contrary, we want to hear anything that they may be able to say in their defense. When an occasional defendant attempts to plead guilty, we in fact discourage him. If there is any tilt to our procedures, we press defendants to *exculpate* rather than to incriminate themselves.

Third, our procedures do not in fact *compel* anyone to do anything. If a defendant were to refuse to respond to judicial questions or to the charges against him, we would impose no punishment for his refusal. We would merely permit the jury to draw whatever inference seemed appropriate in determining whether he was guilty of the offense with which he was charged. Permitting a jury to draw a fair inference is a far cry from torture, placing a defendant upon oath, or any other form of compulsion.

None of these judicial responses would have been plausible if defendants had been examined under oath. Then the defendant would have been a witness; he would have been subject to compulsion (the punishment for perjury) if he failed to speak the truth; and if the truth were incriminating, his oath would have pressed him to incriminate himself. . . .

The courts' unwillingness to receive sworn, self-incriminating testimony explains what otherwise would seem a paradox: that witnesses for the prosecution and witnesses in civil cases were much more likely to invoke the privilege—and to do so successfully—than criminal defendants. Unlike defendants, prosecution witnesses and witnesses in civil cases were sworn, and when they invoked the privilege, the courts forbade other trial participants from asking them incriminating questions. At least by 1700, both sworn defendants in religious courts and sworn witnesses in common law courts were permitted to decline to answer any questions that could lead to criminal punishment or forfeiture. Once a witness was sworn, he was subject to compulsion, and his only protection lay in the ability to decline to answer specific questions. The protection of common law defendants, by contrast, lay in not being sworn at all.

Eben Moglen offers persuasive evidence that American courts did not view the answers of unsworn defendants in the same light as those of sworn witnesses.[14] Following ratification of the Fifth Amendment, some American lawyers began to object on nonconstitutional grounds to the pretrial interrogation of defendants by justices of the peace. These lawyers noted that, although American law generally incorporated the common law of England, it did not, in the absence of legislative provision to the contrary, incorporate English statutory law. Because the pretrial examination of defendants was authorized by a statute, the Marian Committal Statute of 1555, the lawyers contended that American law did not allow this procedure.

Neither the lawyers nor the commentators who advanced this argument supplemented it with a claim that the pretrial examination of suspects violated either the Fifth Amendment privilege against self-incrimination or the similar provisions of state constitutions. If anyone had thought that the Constitution guaranteed a right to remain silent or that "accused speaks" procedures were inconsistent with the privilege, this would have been the occasion to say so. During three decades of debate over whether the Marian Committal Statute was a parliamentary innovation or merely declarative of the common law, however, no one did. Even the opponents of "accused speaks" procedures did not consider them inconsistent with the constitutional privilege against self-incrimination.

C. You Have a Right to Remain Silent

The transformation of the privilege into a right of criminal defendants to remain silent occurred only during the nineteenth century. Lawyerization of the trial contributed to a changed ideology of criminal procedure—one in which the dignity of defendants lay not in their ability to tell their stories fully, but rather in their ability to remain passive, to proclaim to the prosecutor "Thou sayest," and to force the state to shoulder the entire load. As defendants participated less in the proceedings that determined their fate, they were seen more as objects or as targets of the coercive forces of the state.

In parliamentary debates of the 1820s and 1830s, reformers complained that "accused speaks" procedures often worked unfairly. Many defendants were not sufficiently educated and articulate to tell their stories coherently. The remedy that the reformers sought, however, was not the declaration of a right to remain silent; instead, they proposed giving defense attorneys the power to argue on the defendants' behalf before juries. The expansion of the role of counsel which they secured in 1836 permitted defendants to take a still more passive role at trial and contributed to the rapidly changing ideology of English procedure.

An 1838 opinion declared that "[a] prisoner is not to be entrapped into making any statement" and that a magistrate should advise this suspect before taking his statement "that what he thinks fit to say will be taken down, and may be used against him on his trial."[15] A clearer doctrinal recognition of the right to remain silent came ten years later in Sir John Jervis's Act. This Act provided that, before the pretrial examination, the accused should be cautioned that he need not answer and that if he did answer, his answers could be used against him at trial. In New York City, magistrates began routinely to caution defendants in 1835, [and] the number of defendants who declined to submit to pretrial interrogation increased thereafter.[16]

A more significant doctrinal development than the magistrates' cautioning of suspects was the abolition of the testimonial disqualification of defendants. In 1864 Maine became the first American jurisdiction to allow defendants to offer sworn testimony in criminal cases, and other states quickly followed. The British Parliament, a latecomer to the movement, enacted its competency statute in 1898. By the end of the nineteenth century, Georgia was the only American state to retain the common law disqualification. It did not permit defendants to offer sworn testimony until 1962.[17]

The statutes that ended the testimonial disqualification of defendants were controversial, and the controversy centered on constitutional issues. Proponents maintained that defendants should have the same right as other witnesses to testify under oath and that the common law disqualification substituted a presumption of perjury for the presumption of innocence. Opponents contended, however, that the statutes threatened the privilege against self-incrimination. They argued that jurors would view the failure of a lawyer to call his client to the witness stand as a confession of the client's guilt and that the jurors would draw this inference regardless of whatever cautionary instructions they received. In practice, defendants would be pressed to take the oath; they would be subject to precisely the compulsion that state and federal constitutions condemned. . . .

In 1965 *Griffin v. California* held that prosecutorial or judicial comment on a defendant's failure to testify violated the Fifth Amendment privilege.[18] The Framers of the Fifth Amendment, who might not have approved of sworn testimony by defendants at all, probably would have agreed that a defendant's refusal to submit to the compulsion of an oath could not be the subject of adverse comment. *Griffin*, however, forbade comment not simply on the refusal of a defendant to submit to an oath, but "on the accused's silence." The Court offered no indication that refusal to submit to an oath might differ from any other form of silence, and one year after *Griffin*, the Court extended the right to remain silent to unsworn suspects in custody in *Miranda v. Arizona*. That the presence or absence of an oath might have made a difference seemed inconceivable in 1966. Because an unsworn statement made in response to police interrogation would be used against a suspect at trial, it was the "functional equivalent" of testimony. The distinction between sworn and unsworn statements, central to the Framers' understanding of what it meant to be compelled to testify, had disappeared. . . .

In the years since *Miranda*, Americans have seemed increasingly enamored of its accusatorial rhetoric, especially as they have learned that *Miranda*'s system for protecting the Fifth Amendment privilege has little practical effect. During the Reagan administration, the Justice Department proposed abandoning *Miranda* [see Chapter 7—Eds.], but its proposal generated considerable criticism even among police administrators.

England, by contrast, has reassessed the value of "testing the prosecution" trials. The Criminal Justice and Public Order Act of 1994 provides that, once an accused has been warned of the consequences of a failure to testify, "the court or jury . . . may draw such inferences as appear proper from the failure of the accused to give evidence."[19] In addition, the Act invites jurors and judges to draw inferences from the pretrial silence of defendants. The Act encourages suspects to cooperate with police investigations, to disclose defenses at the earliest opportunity, and to submit to cross-examination at trial, but its supporters contend that it is consistent with the privilege against self-incrimination because it does not treat a suspect's failure to speak as a crime or as contempt of court. . . .

[T]he history of the privilege against self-incrimination seems to reveal the tyranny of slogans. Shorthand phrases have taken on lives of their own. These phrases have eclipsed the goals of the doctrines that they purported to describe and even the texts that embodied these doctrines. The phrases and the images they evoked—what the phrases "sounded like"—shaped the law. Latin maxims declaring that "no one shall be compelled to betray himself" have sounded like the declaration that "no one shall be compelled in any criminal case to be a witness against himself." The latter declaration has been summarized as "the privilege against self-incrimination" (a description not generally in use before the twentieth century[20] and one that omits all reference to the constitutional concept of compulsion). The "privilege against self-incrimination," in turn, has sounded like the "right to remain silent." Much of the history of the privilege has been a story of slippage from one doctrine to another without awareness of the change. Officials appear to have drifted from limiting the burdens of the religious obligation to confess in the interest of obtaining more confessions to condemning incriminating interrogation under oath without adequate evidentiary justification. They have drifted from condemning interrogation under oath without evidentiary justification to condemning torture and *all* incriminating interrogation of suspects under oath. The officials then have drifted to a judgment that the framers of all of the earlier doctrines unquestionably would have disapproved—that it is unfair to expect defendants on trial and people arrested on probable cause to participate actively in the criminal process by telling what they know. . . .

The nearest analogue to police interrogation known to the Framers was interrogation before a magistrate under the Marian Committal Statute of 1555, and for decades, people whose names "read[ ] like an honor roll of the legal profession,"—Wigmore, Pound, Kauper, Friendly, Schaefer, Frankel, and others—have proposed a return to something like the Marian procedure.[21] Pretrial interrogation before a magistrate of the sort they envision might require the magistrate to find probable cause for a suspect's arrest before interrogation could begin. It might permit the suspect to be represented by counsel when her statement is taken. It might bow to the original understanding of the Fifth Amendment privilege by allowing the suspect to remain unsworn. It might permit the magistrate or, perhaps, a prosecutor to question the suspect, taking her statement in much the same manner that a lawyer engaged in a civil practice takes a deposition. The procedure might also afford the suspect a reciprocal opportunity to obtain the statements of prosecution witnesses. . . .

A suspect's answers to orderly questioning in a safeguarded courtroom environment should not be regarded as the product of compulsion. These answers might tend to prove the suspect's guilt because they were incriminating, seemed internally contradictory, rang untrue in certain details, or were inconsistent with the suspect's defense at trial. Equally, the answers might tend to prove the suspect's innocence by showing that she denied her guilt promptly, in a manner consistent with her trial defense, and in apparently forthcoming answers to specific questions. Interrogation before a judicial officer would be likely to promote accurate factfinding both when accurate factfinding would help the suspect and when it would hurt her. If the suspect refused to answer, her refusal should be admissible at trial both because it would have a rational bearing on her guilt and because its admission would express the judgment that, following a showing of probable cause, suspects can reasonably be expected to respond to orderly inquiry. For the same reason, a defendant should be expected to speak at trial—perhaps under oath but exempted from the penalties for perjury—and if she declined, the judge or jury should be permitted to draw appropriate inferences.

The history of the privilege against self-incrimination may raise as many questions for modern courts as it answers, but if a state legislature were to approve a procedure like this one, a court could take much of its guidance from the past. Because this procedure would require a showing of solidly grounded suspicion before interrogation could begin, it would be consistent with the maxim *Nemo tenetur prodere seipsum* as this maxim was understood in the *ius commune* and as it was enforced by the common law courts against the High Commission. The procedure also would be consistent with the original understanding of the Fifth Amendment privilege, for the Framers saw no tension between the privilege and their own interrogation practices—practices that differed from the proposal only in that they lacked some of its safeguards. Finally, the procedure would be consistent with the principles of ordinary morality articulated by Kent Greenawalt. When neither text, history, nor sensible policy condemns a practice, a court should find it constitutional; and if the practice seems inconsistent with the right to remain silent, courts should read the Constitution again. With the help of history and of ordinary morality, they should look at what the Fifth Amendment really says.

NOTES

1. See R. Kent Greenawalt, *Silence as a Moral and Constitutional Right*, 23 Wm. & Mary L. Rev. 15 (1981).

2. See Miranda v. Arizona, 384 U.S. 436, 460 (1966); Tehan v. Shott, 382 U.S. 406, 414 (1966); Malloy v. Hogan, 378 U.S. 1, 7 (1964).

3. Withrow v. Williams, 507 U.S. 680, 692 (1993) (citation omitted).

4. See Baltimore Dep't of Social Servs. v. Bouknight, 493 U.S. 549 (1990).

5. U.S. Sentencing Commission Federal Sentencing Guidelines Manual §3.E1.1(b)(1) (1995).

6. Walter V. Schaefer, The Suspect and Society 59 (1967).

7. Richard H. Helmholz, *Origins of the Privilege Against Self-Incrimination: The Role of the European* Ius Commune, 65 N.Y.U. L. Rev. 962 (1990).

8. Michael Dalton, The Countrey Justice 273 (Professional Books 1973) (1619).

9. Theodore Barlow, The Justice of Peace: A Treatise Containing the Power and Duty of That Magistrate 189 (Henry Lintot 1745), *quoted in* John H. Langbein, *The Historical Origins of the Privilege Against Self-Incrimination at Common Law*, 92 Mich. L. Rev. 1047, 1085 n.157 (1994).

10. 2 Statutes at Large: Being a Collection of All the Laws of Virginia 422 (William W. Hening ed., The Franklin Press 1820).

11. Langbein, *supra* note 9, at 1048.

12. See Langbein, *supra* note 9, at 1049 (*quoting* Thomas Smith, *De Republica Anglorum* bk. 2, ch. 23, at 114 (Mary Dewar ed., Cambridge University Press 1982) (1583, written circa 1565).

13. 2 & 3 Phil. & M., ch. 10 (Eng.).

14. Eben Moglen, *Taking the Fifth: Reconsidering the Constitutional Origins of the Privilege against Self-Incrimination*, 92 Mich. L. Rev. 1086, 1126–27 (1994).

15. R. v. Arnold, 173 Eng. Rep. 645, 645–46 (K.B. 1838).

16. See Mike McConville & Chester Mirsky, *The Rise of Guilty Pleas: New York, 1800–1865*, 22 J. Law & Soc'y 443, 452 (1995).

17. See Ga. Code Ann. §§24–9–20, 17–7–28 (Michie 1995).

18. 380 U.S. 609 (1965).

19. Criminal Justice and Public Order Act, 1994, §35 (Eng.).

20. Moglen, *supra* note 14, at 1090.

21. The quoted phrase comes from Lakeside v. Oregon, 435 U.S. 333, 345 n.5 (1978) (Stevens, J., dissenting), in which Justice Stevens commented in dissent that "the roster of scholars and judges with reservations about expanding the Fifth Amendment privilege reads like an honor roll of the legal profession." See Marvin E. Frankel, Partisan Justice 98–99 (1980); Schaefer, *supra* note 6, at 77–81; Henry J. Friendly, *The Fifth Amendment Tomorrow: The Case for Constitutional Change*, 37 U. Cin. L. Rev. 671 (1968); Paul G. Kauper, *Judicial Examination of the Accused—A Remedy for the Third Degree*, 30 Mich. L. Rev. 1224 (1932); Roscoe Pound, *Legal Interrogation of Persons Accused or Suspected of Crime*, 24 J. Crim. L. & Criminology 1014 (1934); John H. Wigmore, Nemo Tenetur Seipsum Prodere, 5 Harv. L. Rev. 71, 85–88 (1891); *see also* Donald A. Dripps, *Self-Incrimination and Self-Preservation: A Skeptical View*, 1991 U. Ill. L. Rev. 329; Yale Kamisar, *Kauper's "Judicial Examination of the Accused" Forty Years Later—Some Comments on a Remarkable Article*, 73 Mich. L. Rev. 15 (1974).

III

Miranda's Impact in the Station House: Participant Observations and Empirical Studies

As we have seen, the *Miranda* debate raises fundamental normative questions about the relationship between the state and the accused in a constitutional democracy: What are the proper ends of police interrogation? What constitutes fair interrogation procedures? What limits should be placed on police questioning of the accused in a system simultaneously committed to effective crime control and to the protection of individual rights? What is the proper role of testimonial evidence in an adversarial system of criminal justice? How should courts regulate custodial police questioning? What are the proper remedies when the police break the law or violate a suspect's constitutional rights? These are among the underlying ethical questions that continue to animate the *Miranda* controversy.

In addition to the normative issues it raises, *Miranda* also has an empirical dimension. In fact, the empirical effects of *Miranda* may be enormously important in evaluating the normative questions that drive the *Miranda* debate. While purely empirical knowledge cannot, by itself, provide answers to these normative questions—just as science cannot, by itself, provide answers to moral questions—it can deeply inform the basis for advancing or rejecting a particular ethical or policy position. In the case of *Miranda*, it makes a difference, for example, whether all suspects waive or invoke their rights, whether *Miranda* causes fewer guilty suspects to confess and to be convicted, and whether *Miranda* is responsible for guilty offenders' committing further violent crimes. To be sure, our normative precommitments—whether, for example, we believe that *Miranda* represented an illegitimate act of judicial policymaking or an important safeguard on police abuses—may determine the weight we place on any empirical evidence of *Miranda's* effects. But these effects are nevertheless important in evaluating how courts should regulate the relationship between the state and the accused and whether *Miranda* strikes the proper balance.

Whatever their policy and ethical implications, "impact" studies are also important for understanding the actual operation of law. Whether we support or reject *Miranda*, the empirical study of *Miranda* helps us better understand how it affects police practices, confession and conviction rates, and the criminal justice system generally. Judges, law professors, and practicing lawyers tend to make assumptions about the utility and impact of *Miranda*, but we can know whether such assumptions are correct only by studying how *Miranda* has been implemented, understood, and enforced in practice. Legal Realists have argued for some time that we can know the impact of law in society only by empirically studying how it is expressed in social action. Apart from its policy consequences, such knowledge has value for its own sake.

From 1966 to 1973 many scholars, lawyers, and policymakers studied *Miranda's* impact on police compliance and confession and conviction rates in a diverse array of geographical settings. After 1973, however, academic and policy interest in *Miranda's* impact lay dormant for almost two decades, even as the controversy over *Miranda's* doctrinal and ethical soundness continued seemingly unabated. Perhaps legal scholars and policymakers lost interest in *Miranda's* impact because all the early studies appeared to support the "conventional wisdom" that police, for the most part, complied with the letter of the *Miranda* ruling and that confession and conviction rates remained largely unaffected by the decision's code-like warning and waiver requirements. Perhaps those scholars and policymakers lost interest as it became clear that the Supreme Court was not about to overrule the *Miranda* decision. Or perhaps they lost interest in *Miranda's* impact as the law enforcement community appeared not only to accommodate itself to the *Miranda* rules but also to embrace its underlying professionalism.

Whatever the causes, the long academic silence on *Miranda's* impact has given way to a renewed focus on *Miranda's* empirical effects in the 1990s. Reanalyzing the early studies, Paul Cassell has recently challenged the conventional wisdom (see Chapter 13), while Stephen Schulhofer has also reanalyzed these studies only to defend it (see Chapter 14). Two new impact studies—one by Richard Leo (see Chapter 15), another by Paul Cassell and Bret Hayman (see Chapter 16)—have provided scholars and policymakers with data about *Miranda*'s impact not only on new generation of police but also on the present-day criminal justice system and society generally. At the same time there has been a great deal of criticism and debate among many of the authors of this section: Paul Cassell has critiqued the earlier impact studies and readjusted estimates of *Miranda*'s effect upward; Stephen Schulhofer has critiqued Paul Cassell's work and readjusted his estimates downward; Cassell and Hayman have readjusted Richard Leo's estimates upward; and George Thomas has readjusted Cassell and Hayman's estimates downward. Despite these disagreements, the empirical study of law in action is once again informing the larger debate about *Miranda*'s ongoing legitimacy and vitality.

Despite the enormous value of the *Miranda* impact studies, readers should be aware of their limitations. First, a study is only as good as its methodology. At its best, social science produces reliable and valid information that deepens our understanding, explains patterns and variation in human behavior, and allows conclusions to be generalized across settings. While few studies measure up to this ideal (if only because of the intrinsic problems of studying human behavior), the early *Miranda* studies are virtually all methodologically flawed and, by now, largely outdated.

Second, the empirical study of *Miranda* is fraught with deeper interpretive issues. When reading these chapters, readers should consider the following questions: How are we to measure *Miranda*'s costs, and what counts as a cost? What constitutes a serious impediment to effective law enforcement? How are we to measure *Miranda*'s benefits, and what counts as a benefit? What do *Miranda*'s supporters really want? Are *Miranda*'s empirical and normative costs and benefits commensurate? If so, at what point do the costs of *Miranda* begin to outweigh its benefits? If not, how are we to evaluate *Miranda*'s impact in light of the ongoing debate about its legitimacy and viability? In any event, to what extent is our normative evaluation of *Miranda* dependent on its observed empirical effects? Despite the valuable information they provide, the *Miranda* studies may ultimately raise far more questions than they answer.

This section begins with Paul Cassell's recent reassessment of *Miranda*'s empirical effect. Cassell argues that the conventional wisdom about *Miranda* is wrong and that, instead, *Miranda*—as a result of its warnings, waivers, and questioning cut-off rules—has significantly harmed law enforcement. Reanalyzing the early published and unpublished studies, Cassell attempts to quantify *Miranda*'s costs and then argues that these costs greatly outweigh its benefits. On the basis of his reanalysis, Cassell posits that *Miranda* reduces confessions in approximately 16 percent of all cases and that confessions are necessary for convictions in approximately 24 percent of all cases. Multiplying the two figures (.24 × .16), Cassell argues that *Miranda* is responsible for lost convictions in 3.8 percent of all serious criminal cases. Using the FBI's Uniform Crime Reports crime index for arrests (no figures are available for the number of individuals interrogated), Cassell concludes that approximately 28,000 violent crime and 79,000 property crime cases are lost each year. If one adds the crimes outside of the FBI crime index, even more cases are lost each year as a result of *Miranda*.

In Chapter 14 Stephen Schulhofer challenges Cassell's analysis, arguing that the *Miranda* warnings, waiver requirement, and cut-off rules have not impeded effective law enforcement in the last thirty years. Reanalyzing the same early studies, Schulhofer calculates that *Miranda* was initially responsible for at most a 0.78 percent (seventy-eight one-hundredths of 1 percent) decline in the conviction rate for serious criminal cases. Because this figure likely overestimates *Miranda*'s impact today, Schulhofer suggests that *Miranda*'s empirically detectable harm to law enforcement is, for all practical purposes, zero. Calling Cassell's analysis even further into question, Schulhofer points out that the studies on which Cassell relies suffer from significant methodological flaws and that we cannot so easily infer causation from correlation in any complex time-series analysis. Instead, Schulhofer suggests several competing alternative explanations for any decline in confession and conviction rates post-*Miranda*.[1] Whatever the correct figure, however, Schulhofer argues that the important question is whether *Miranda*'s constitutional mandate justifies any empirically detectable drop in conviction rates.

The Cassell-Schulhofer exchange touches on many of the questions that we raised above. Readers are invited to examine the early impact studies for themselves to determine whose figures are more likely correct. Once again, we run up against fundamental methodological and interpretive questions. The Cassell-Schulhofer exchange turns on the quality of their data and reasoning, on how they compare the so-called costs and benefits, and on their assessment of particular values (constitutional and otherwise) when making such comparisons. Readers should ask themselves: Whose arguments are most convincing and why? What kind of empirical findings would be necessary to persuade advocates on either side to change their position? Can even the best empirical data adequately resolve the larger normative issues at stake in the *Miranda* debate?

Richard Leo in Chapter 15 and Paul Cassell and Bret Hayman in Chapter 16 provide new data on *Miranda*'s impact in the 1990s. Based on participation-observation analysis, Leo quantitatively analyzes *Miranda*'s effects at several stages of the criminal process: police questioning, charging, conviction, and sentencing. In addition, Leo analyzes the strategies police detectives use to elicit *Miranda* warnings. Finally, Leo interprets the long-term impact of *Miranda* on police investigatory practices and culture. Based on prosecutorial screening sessions, Cassell and Hayman also provide quantitative data on *Miranda*'s impact in the criminal justice system. Their approach differs from Leo's, however. Arguing that the *Miranda* doctrine rests on a pragmatic foundation, Cassell and Hayman suggest that whether *Miranda* struck the proper balance between the interests of effective police interrogation and protecting the rights of those interrogated must be answered by reference to its empirical effects. Comparing their data with earlier studies, Cassell and Hayman argue that the rate of successful interrogation has declined since *Miranda* became law. *Miranda*, they argue, imposes costs on society by reducing the number of confessions and thus the number of successful criminal prosecutions. As a result, Cassell and Hayman conclude that *Miranda*'s costs outweigh its benefits.

In the final chapter of this section, George Thomas challenges the conclusions of Cassell and Hayman while positing his own, more conservative, "steady-state" hypothesis: *Miranda* simultaneously encourages suspects to speak to police while discouraging them from making admissions, thus producing off-setting effects that likely cancel each other out. Echoing some of Schulhofer's earlier criticisms of Cassell, Thomas challenges Cassell and Hayman's interpretation of the available evidence (arguing that their estimates of *Miranda*'s effect must be readjusted downward) and points out the difficulties of inferring cause from correlation across time and in light of other equally, if not more, plausible explanations. Thomas also questions Cassell and Hayman's premise that *Miranda* rests on a pragmatic foundation and thus stands in need of justification. Yet Thomas concedes that if there is good enough data to evaluate *Miranda*'s real-world costs and benefits, then we need to address the difficult ethical questions that Paul Cassell, Bret Hayman, and others have posed. In the absence of better data (and consistent with his own steady-state hypothesis), however, Thomas argues that for now we must accept the null hypothesis that *Miranda* has had no effect on the confession rate. As a result, Thomas urges scholars to undertake more empirical studies of police interrogation and confessions.

Readers should consider whether—and if so, how—the chapters in Part III influence their thinking about the *Miranda* debate. Based on the empirical studies and critiques presented here as a whole, readers may wish to revisit some of the fundamental questions raised earlier: Should *Miranda* be overruled? Should it be modified? If so, in which direction (i.e., weakened or strengthened)? If not, should *Miranda*—now in its fourth decade—simply be left alone?

NOTES

1. See also Stephen J. Schulhofer, Miranda *and Clearance Rates*, 91 Nw. U. L. Rev. 278–94 (1996).

13

Miranda's
Social Costs:
An Empirical
Reassessment
(1996)

•

PAUL G. CASSELL

Justice White argued in his dissenting opinion in *Miranda* that "[i]n some unknown number of cases the Court's rule will return a killer, a rapist or other criminal to the streets and to the environment which produced him, to repeat his crime whenever it pleases him."[1] Common sense suggests the same conclusion: Surely fewer persons will confess if police must warn them of their right to silence, obtain affirmative waivers from them, and end the interrogation if they ask for a lawyer or for questioning to stop. Yet today, with more than a quarter of a century of experience with the *Miranda* rules, legal academics generally take the opposite view—that *Miranda* has had only a "negligible" effect on law enforcement.[2] . . .

Given this wide agreement that *Miranda*'s effects are negligible, it is perhaps a little surprising that no one has quantified *Miranda*'s effects on the American criminal justice system. Legal scholars have assayed this type of "cost" (in terms of "lost arrests") for the Fourth Amendment search and seizure exclusionary rule. But for *Miranda*, no one has bothered to explain what a "negligible" effect is and how many dangerous criminals such an effect involves.

This [chapter] contends that the conventional academic wisdom about *Miranda*'s effects is simply wrong. As common sense suggests, *Miranda* has significantly harmed law enforcement efforts in this country. In defense of this thesis, this chapter makes the first (and admittedly preliminary) attempt to advance the *Miranda* debate beyond the prevailing qualitative level. Justice White was, of course, correct in concluding that we will never know exactly how many criminals have avoided conviction because of *Miranda*'s requirements. However, "[f]rom a policy perspec-

tive, what is needed is not precise numbers so much as a sound estimate of the general level of [*Miranda*'s] effects."[3]

*

One possible way of assessing *Miranda*'s costs is to look at how many
confessions are suppressed because of *Miranda* violations. In some
cases *Miranda* suppression motions have led to the release of dangerous criminals. . . .

While these cases are dramatic, defenders of *Miranda* respond—quite
correctly, according to the existing empirical data—that the suppression of confessions leading to the release of criminals, much less dangerous criminals, is quite rare. Peter Nardulli's detailed study of nine
medium-sized counties in Illinois, Michigan, and Pennsylvania in the
late 1970s found that, out of 7,035 cases studied, only five convictions
(.071 percent) were lost as the result of a successful Miranda suppression motion.[4] Nardulli's similar study in the city of Chicago in 1983
found that, out of 3,626 cases studied, only about one conviction
(.028 percent) was lost as the result of motions to exclude confessions.[5]
Similar conclusions came from a study conducted by Floyd Feeney,
Forrest Dill, and Adrianne Weir, who gathered data in Jacksonville,
Florida, and San Diego, California, and found that—at most—two of
619 cases (0.3 percent) could be said to have been dropped because of
Miranda problems with the confession.[6] Other studies suggest a similarly minimal impact of suppression motions on convictions.[7] To complete the picture, studies find that convictions are rarely reversed on appeal because of a motion to suppress under *Miranda.*[8]

Based on these small percentages, it has been argued that *Miranda*
has had only a minimal effect on law enforcement. . . .

These arguments fail to appreciate the true extent of the problems
Miranda creates for law enforcement. Analysis of numbers of suppressed confessions tells us only about what happens to cases *when police obtain confessions*. It tells us nothing about cases in which police
fail to obtain confessions because of the *Miranda* rules. . . . Suppression
motion analysis simply ignores these "lost cases." Indeed, whatever impact shows up in suppression motion analysis is not a substitute for the
costs of lost confessions; it is a cost that must be added on top. In any
event, proof that law enforcement is rarely harmed by suppressed confessions does not negate the contention that law enforcement is often
harmed by confessions never being obtained. . . .

To quantify *Miranda*'s costs from lost cases, we must examine whether *Miranda* has produced any lost confessions through its combination of warnings, waivers, and questioning cut-off rules. It now appears to be common ground that the *Miranda* litany dissuades at least *some* suspects from talking. That is why *Miranda*'s defenders carefully claim that *Miranda*'s costs are negligible rather than nonexistent.

A lost confession from *Miranda* does not necessarily translate into a social cost. Even when *Miranda* has resulted in a lost confession, prosecutors may have enough other evidence to obtain a conviction. In assessing *Miranda*'s costs, therefore, we need quantification not only of changes in the confession rate due to *Miranda* but also of the proportion of cases in which a confession is needed to convict. These two variables can then be multiplied together to determine *Miranda*'s costs. For example, if *Miranda* reduced confessions by 20 percent and confessions were needed in 20 percent of those cases to convict, then *Miranda*'s costs would be 4 percent of all cases (20 percent × 20 percent).

*

Quantifying *Miranda*'s effect on the confession rate is quite difficult because one cannot simply tote up the number of "lost confessions" by looking at a law enforcement bulletin or court docket. Instead, what is required is some comparison of the number of confessions[9] obtained outside of the *Miranda* regime with the number obtained under it. Two possible data sources suggest themselves. First, we can examine the "before-and-after" studies of custodial interrogation under *Miranda*. Second, we can compare the confession rate in the United States under *Miranda* with the confession rate in other countries that follow different approaches to regulating police interrogation.

1. Before-and-After Studies.   With regard to a change in the confession rate due to *Miranda*, the best evidence, if available, would probably be "before-and-after" assessments of changes in the confession rate in various American cities conducted after *Miranda*. Studies in a single jurisdiction automatically hold constant a variety of factors that might otherwise confound comparative analysis. Several such studies have been done, although they vary in quality. These studies allow preliminary estimates of the change in the confession rate due to *Miranda*.

*

(1) *Summary of the Before-and-After Studies.* All of the quantitative studies of changes in the custodial confession rate due to *Miranda* are summarized in Table 1, which follows. As can be seen, excluding the unreliable comparison made by extrapolating from two different Los Angeles surveys, all studies report a drop in the confession rate after the *Miranda* decision, most in double digits. This directly contradicts the prevailing myth in legal academe.[10] The change in rate ranges from 34.5 percent for New York County to 2.0 percent for Seaside City. The "reliable" studies—from Pittsburgh, New York County, Philadelphia, Sea-

---

Table 1. Estimates of Changes in the Confession Rate Due to Miranda.

City	Confession Rate Before	Confession Rate After	Change	Major Problems?
Pittsburgh	48.5%	29.9%	−18.6%	
N.Y. County	49.0%	14.5%	−34.5%	
Philadelphia	45.0% (est. /der.)	20.4% (der.)	−24.6%	
Seaside City	68.9%	66.9%	−2.0%	?
New Haven (1960–66)	58–63% (est.)	48.2%	−10–15%	Yes
New Haven (calculated)	?	?	−16.0%	
Washington, D.C.	21.5% (der.)	20.0% (der.)	−1.5%	Yes
Kansas City	?	?	−6.0% (der.)	?
Kings County	45.0% (est. /der.)	29.5% (der.)	−15.5%	
New Orleans	40.0% (est.)	28.2%	−11.8%	?
Chicago homicides	53.0% (der.)	26.5% (der.)	−26.5%	?
Los Angeles	40.4%	50.2%	+9.8%	Yes
Average of Studies without Major Problems			−16.1%*	

est. = estimated   der. = derived   *Excluding Chicago Homicide Study

---

side City, New Haven, Kansas City, Kings County, and New Orleans—show confession rate drops of 18.6 percent, 34.5 percent, 24.6 percent, 2.0 percent, 16.0 percent, 6 percent, 15.5 percent, and 11.8 percent, for an average reported drop of 16.1 percent. In other words, based on the comparative studies, the best estimate is that *Miranda* results in a lost confession in roughly one out of every six criminal cases in this country.

2. International Comparisons.   An alternative way of determining the change in the confession rate caused by *Miranda* is to compare confession rates in this country under *Miranda* with confession rates in other countries that do not follow *Miranda's* requirements.[11] Chief Justice Warren's decision in *Miranda* made something of an anticipatory comparison, arguing that "[t]he experience in some other countries also suggests that the danger to law enforcement in curbs on interrogation is overplayed."[12] He then examined the practices in England, Scotland, and other countries, described the restrictive features of the interrogation regimes there, and concluded that "[t]here appears to have been no marked detrimental effect on criminal law enforcement in these jurisdictions as a result of these rules."[13] While the accuracy of the Chief Justice's description of the practices in these countries has been powerfully challenged,[14] our concern here is whether the confession rates in these countries suggest anything about the validity of my estimate that *Miranda* reduced the American confession rate by about 16 percent.[15] I will examine data from the two obvious countries for comparison: Britain and Canada.

(a) Britain.   Britain is a good country for comparison. The historically prevailing English approach gave suspects the equivalent of the first two *Miranda* warnings, but did not employ the other features of the *Miranda* system—e.g., the right to counsel during questioning and waiver requirements.[16] The available studies suggest very high confession rates under this approach. A study conducted in Worcester found that suspects gave full confessions or made other incriminating statements in 86 percent of all cases.[17] A study of cases at the Old Bailey found an incriminating statement rate of 76 percent.[18] An observational study in Brighton found that 65 percent of observed interrogations produced incriminating statements.[19] An observational survey of four police stations in West Yorkshire, Nottinghamshire, Avon, and Somerset and of the Metropolitan Police District (London) found that police obtained in-

criminating statements in 61 percent of their interrogations.[20] A study of cases heard in the seven Crown Court centers in London found that a total 71.2 percent of defendants gave incriminating information.[21] Finally, interviews with a sample of defendants drawn randomly from Sheffield court records found that 94 percent admitted their guilt to police.[22] While recent (and highly publicized) examples of coerced confessions have been responsible for several miscarriages of justice in Britain,[23] it seems unlikely that the high overall British confession rate is attributable to such tactics.

Although varying definitions and methodologies make exact comparisons difficult, these reported English confession rates are substantially higher than the post-*Miranda* confession rate in the United States. . . . Comparing the reported British confession rates (ranging from 61 percent to 84.5 percent) with the American post-*Miranda* rates (generally in the range of 30 percent to 50 percent) suggests that the estimate made here of a 16 percent drop in the confession rate after *Miranda* is quite reasonable.

The British experience not only allows us to assess confession rates without *Miranda* rules, but also allows us to review what happens as a country moves to a *Miranda*-style regime. In the 1980s, Britain adopted a more heavily regulated structure for police interrogations, one that in many respects tracks *Miranda*. In 1984, Parliament adopted the Police and Criminal Evidence Act (PACE) to regulate, among other things, the process of custodial questioning of suspects. As required by PACE, the Home Office followed up with the Code of Practice for the Detention, Treatment and Questioning of Persons by Police Officers in 1985 and with the Code of Practice on Tape Recording in 1988.[24] These enactments provide a series of safeguards for suspects, including imposed access to counsel during questioning and recording of interrogations.

British confession rates have recently started to decline toward American levels as this *Miranda*-style interrogation regime has been put into effect. Summarizing the available studies in 1992, Gisli Gudjonsson noted that

> [t]he frequency with which suspects confess to crimes in England has fallen in recent years from over 60 percent to between 40 and 50 percent. This appears to have followed the implementation of PACE, which came into force in January 1986. The reasons for this decrease seem to be associated with the increased use of solicitors by detainees and changes in custodial interrogation and confinement procedures.[25]

Interestingly, the post-PACE drop in the British confession rate (from over 60 percent to between 40 percent and 50 percent) corresponds roughly with the post-*Miranda* confession rate drop suggested in this [chapter]. Because of law enforcement concerns, Parliament recently modified the warnings given to suspects and made other changes to encourage more confessions.[26]

(b) Canada. Another good country for comparison is our neighbor Canada. Until recently, the Canadian police gave *Miranda*-style warnings concerning the right to remain silent, but did not follow the rigid *Miranda* waiver requirements and questioning cut-off rules.[27] Since 1982, Canadian law on interrogation has moved toward the *Miranda* requirements because of the passage of Section 10(b) of the Canadian Charter of Rights and Freedoms.[28]

Canada apparently had confession rates substantially higher than the rates in this country. The only data on Canadian confession rates I have located come from a study in July 1985 of the Halton Regional Police Force in Ontario, Canada. The study reported the results of a two-year pilot project involving the videotaping of all interviews at the police station for crimes more serious than traffic and drunk driving offenses in Burlington compared with standard police interrogation in Oakville. Despite the presence of video cameras to prevent police misconduct, the Burlington officers obtained confessions or incriminating statements in 68 percent of their interviews.[29] The confession rate is even higher if one excludes the 4.8 percent of suspects who refused to be videotaped; of those agreeing to be videotaped, 71.6 percent made inculpatory statements.[30] In the "control" city of Oakville, police obtained incriminating information in 87.0 percent of the interviews.[31] These Canadian confession rates are substantially higher than any recently reported rate here, which suggests that *Miranda* may be inhibiting American suspects.

*

Of course if confessions were not needed for criminal convictions, the *Miranda* debate would be of little consequence. It appears to be common ground, however, that in at least some cases a confession is necessary for a successful prosecution. The debate focuses on how often a confession is necessary. As with allegations of changes in the confession rate, the dispute has often been conducted at the qualitative level. Critics of *Miranda* charge that confessions are often necessary; defenders claim they are only rarely needed. As with the confession rate issue, resort to the extant empirical data may be a more helpful approach.

*

The studies on the importance of confessions in obtaining convictions . . . report that confessions are needed in somewhere between 10.3 percent to 29.3 percent of all cases . . . and between 8.2 percent to 61.0 percent of cases involving confessions. Excluding my own recently completed study and examining the "reliable" estimates from Pittsburgh, New York County, Los Angeles (post-*Dorado*), and Seaside City produces an average estimate of confessions needed to convict in 23.8 percent of all cases and in 26.1 percent of confession cases.

*

The data reviewed in the preceding sections should allow us to make a general estimate of *Miranda*'s costs in terms of lost cases. To be sure, in view of the limited number of studies, one must approach this endeavor with some caution. Nonetheless, there is probably considerable heuristic value in making a rough calculation of *Miranda*'s impact on the criminal justice system. . . .

As explained [above], the appropriate method for assessing *Miranda*'s effects is to look at the number of cases that are "lost" due to *Miranda*. Expressed as a formula, the direct costs of *Miranda* in terms of the percent of lost convictions per year can be determined as follows:

(1) change in confession rate because of *Miranda* (in terms of suspects confessing/suspects questioned)

×

(2) cases in which confessions are needed to convict (in terms of confessions needed/suspects confessing)[32]

The absolute number of criminals who might escape conviction because of *Miranda* can be determined by multiplying that percentage figure by the absolute number of criminal suspects questioned.

The preceding sections provide some tentative estimates that allow a preliminary estimate of the costs of *Miranda*. For an estimate of the change in the confession rate, I will use the average of the reliable before-and-after Miranda studies, which report a mean 16 percent reduction in the confession rate; for an estimate of the importance of confessions, I will use the average of the reliable studies on the subject,

1 8 2

which report that confessions are needed in 24 percent of cases involving confessions. Combining these figures produces the following result:

$$16\% \times 24\% = 3.8\%$$

In other words, the existing empirical data support the tentative estimate that *Miranda* has led to lost cases against almost 4 percent of all criminal suspects in this country who are questioned.

. . . One definitional point should be emphasized. These "lost cases" are not necessarily the same as lost convictions. What these figures estimate is the additional number of cases in which, due to *Miranda*, a defendant did not confess and that confession was needed to convict. It may be that some viable criminal cases that are presented to prosecutors will be dismissed or pled down for reasons that have nothing to do with the *Miranda* decision. Nonetheless, most of the lost cases assessed here are probably cases that would "stick," that is, cases that would have ultimately resulted in a conviction.[33] While studies suggest that many cases are lost due to attrition as they work their way through the criminal justice system, the main reason for that attrition is evidentiary weakness in the case. A confession shores up a weak case unlike any other single piece of evidence, and prosecutors are probably particularly disinclined to plead down cases with confessions.

While defenders of *Miranda* may argue that a 3.8 percent "cost" is acceptable given *Miranda*'s benefits, critics will respond that the apparently small percentage figure multiplied across the run of criminal cases constitutes a large number of criminals. . . . To estimate such a number, it is necessary to multiply the percentage figure previously reported (3.8 percent) by the number of suspects interrogated. No national (and few if any local) statistics are available on the number of suspects interrogated. A surrogate number is the number of suspects arrested for particular crimes. Statistics on the number of "persons arrested" each year in this country are readily available in the Federal Bureau of Investigation's annual Uniform Crime Reports (UCR).[34] . . .

Using arrest figures, we can calculate total lost cases as follows. For 1993 (the most recent year for which statistics are available), the UCR's crime index reports 754,110 arrests for violent crimes and 2,094,300 arrests for property crimes.[35] Multiplying the *Miranda* cost figure (3.8 percent) by the UCR index arrest figures suggests that in 1993 *Miranda* produced roughly 28,000 lost cases against suspects for index violent crimes and 79,000 lost cases against suspects for index property crimes. The violent crime figure can be divided into specific crimes, specifically 880 murder and nonnegligent manslaughter cases, 1,400 forcible rape cases, 6,500 robbery cases, and 21,000 aggravated assault cases.

These lost numbers only reflect crimes counted in the FBI's crime index. The FBI also compiles an estimated total number of arrests for each year.[36] Using the same methods, additional lost cases in 1993 for crimes outside of the crime index were more than 500,000, including: 57,000 lost cases for driving under the influence; 44,000 lost cases for assaults (not including aggravated assault); 42,000 lost cases for drug offenses; 19,000 lost cases for forgery and fraud; 12,000 lost cases for vandalism; and 9,000 lost cases for weapons violations (carrying, possessing illegally, etc.). . . .

Based on the empirical evidence, we can calculate a rough estimate not only of *Miranda*'s direct costs (in terms of lost cases), but also indirect costs (changes in case disposition resulting from plea bargaining). Any assessment of the effects of *Miranda* on the criminal justice system would be incomplete if it did not consider plea bargaining. In the United States, the great majority of criminal cases are resolved by a guilty plea rather than a trial.[37] The literature suggests that in most jurisdictions, 70 percent to 90 percent of all felony cases are resolved by a plea of guilty or its functional equivalent.[38] Many, though not all,[39] of these guilty pleas will result from plea negotiations or plea "bargaining."

Plea bargaining depends on the strength of the government's case. Even where the government appears to have sufficient evidence to convict, an eccentric jury can always return a not guilty verdict. Prosecutors avoid this risk by taking "the bird in the hand" and allowing a plea to a lower charge. Because the risk of a not guilty verdict diminishes as the government's case becomes stronger, the incentives to allow pleas to reduced charges will become weaker.

The empirical research suggests that the strength of the government's case is an important factor in plea bargaining. . . .

A confession can strengthen the prosecution's case considerably. A confession is "direct" evidence of a defendant's guilt and thus is generally superior to indirect or circumstantial evidence.[40] Indeed, the Supreme Court has recognized that "a defendant's confession is probably the most probative and damaging evidence that can be admitted against him. The admissions of a defendant come from the actor himself, the most knowledgeable and unimpeachable source of information about his past conduct."[41] Accordingly, we can hypothesize that any reduction in the rate at which police obtain confessions would increase defendants' success in plea bargaining. This was a hypothesis advanced by Justice White in his *Miranda* dissent.[42]

*

Although the empirical data here are much more limited than those examined on confession rates, it is possible to provide some very rough quantitative estimate of *Miranda*'s effects on plea bargaining. To do this, assume that Neubauer's observed effects in Prairie City apply equally across the country. Specifically, we can generalize from his findings that in property cases approximately 19 percent fewer suspects who did not confess pled to the original charge; in violence cases, 6 percent fewer suspects who did not confess pled to the original charge and 13 percent fewer pled to reduced charges. Taking these percentages and taking the 16 percent reduction in the confession rate from *Miranda* discussed previously leads to the conclusion that, because of *Miranda*, roughly 3.0 percent fewer property offenders plead guilty to the original charge; 1.0 percent fewer violent offenders plead guilty to the original charge; and 2.1 percent fewer plead guilty to reduced charges (a total of 3.1 percent).[43] To come up with a general approximation of the total number of cases affected, we can use again the 1993 FBI arrest figures for index crimes of 754,110 arrests for violent crime and 2,094,300 arrests for property crimes. Multiplying the percentages derived here suggests that in 1993 there were 67,000 pleas to reduced charges in property cases and 24,000 pleas to reduced charges in violence cases attributable to *Miranda*.

*

One possible response to the costs of *Miranda* calculated in this [chapter] is that, all things considered, they are quite small. After all, it might be argued, "only" 3.8 percent of cases are lost due to *Miranda*. My reaction is quite different. We should be concerned about the total number of lost cases from such a percentage. Roughly 28,000 arrests for serious crimes of violence and 79,000 arrests for property crimes slip through the criminal justice system due to *Miranda*, and almost the same number of cases are disposed of on terms more favorable for defendants.

The Supreme Court has reached the same conclusion in modifying the Fourth Amendment exclusionary rule. In creating a good faith exception to the exclusionary rule, the Court cited statistics tending to show that the rule resulted in the release of between 0.6 percent and

2.35 percent of individuals arrested for felonies.[44] The Court concluded that these "small percentages . . . mask a large absolute number of felons who are released because the cases against them were based in part on illegal searches or seizures."[45] *Miranda*'s lost cases are 160 percent to 630 percent of those from the exclusionary rule. Moreover, while the costs of the exclusionary rule are sometimes said to be simply the price of complying with the constitutional prohibition of unreasonable searches, the costs of *Miranda* stem from restrictions that are not constitutionally required and for which reasonable alternatives exist. This suggests that reforming *Miranda* deserves a higher priority from court reformers than reforming the search and seizure exclusionary rule.

Another method of demonstrating that *Miranda*'s costs require a public policy response is to consider them in light of the recent debates in Congress over how to deal with the problem of crime. The various proposals ranged from midnight basketball leagues to placing more police officers on the streets. Each of these measures may be quite desirable on its own merits. Yet little empirical support was provided that any of these changes would have a quantifiable impact on the prevention of crime or conviction of criminals—certainly nothing suggesting that any individual measure could achieve a change in the handling of almost 4 percent of all criminal cases. Reducing *Miranda*'s costs thus is more important than any of these hotly debated proposals.

Still another suggestion of the seriousness of *Miranda*'s costs comes from taking the perspective of victims of crime. Concern for victims suggests that society is obligated to do its best to avoid the kinds of miscarriages of justice as when a confessed killer walks out of a courtroom with a "big smirky grin" on his face because of what can fairly be described as a *Miranda* technicality.[46] While cases in which confessions are suppressed under *Miranda* allow us to put a human face on *Miranda*'s costs, far more often *Miranda* means that a confession will not be obtained, with the result that a crime will go unsolved or unpunished. How do we tell the victims of these crimes that their suffering doesn't count?[47] Quantification of costs is important, but the calculus here stops well short of conveying the human toll involved in murders that go unpunished, rapists that remain at large, and treasured heirlooms and other stolen property that are never recovered. . . .

A final way of showing the significance of *Miranda*'s harms is the simple truism that an unnecessary cost is a cost that is too high. Given that *Miranda* is only one way of structuring custodial interrogation, even one inappropriately released defendant is one too many.[48] If *Miranda*'s costs can be reduced without sacrificing other values, they should be reduced—and as quickly and completely as possible. To argue against considering reform of *Miranda* on the grounds that its cost is small has always struck me as equivalent to arguing against curing diabetes because its toll is smaller than that from cancer. Yet surely no one in the medical profession is stopping a quest to cure a particular disease because the relative cost, compared to other human miseries, is small. Instead, the medical profession can tell the legal profession that it is moving forward on a broad range of fronts to solve all manner of medical problems. In contrast, in the area of the law governing confessions, we in the legal profession can report only that we are frozen in a 1960s conception of the optimal resolution of the issue. The fact that there has been no substantial change since *Miranda* is attributable either to *Miranda*'s foresight or our lack of progress—the costs documented in this [chapter] strongly suggest the latter. . . .

NOTES

1. Miranda v. Arizona, 384 U.S. 436, 542 (1966).

2. Welsh S. White, *Defending* Miranda: *A Reply to Professor Caplan*, 39 Vand. L. Rev. 1, 20 (1986).

3. Thomas Y. Davies, *A Hard Look at What We Know (and Still Need to Learn) About the "Costs" of the Exclusionary Rule: The NIJ Study and Other Studies of "Lost" Arrests*, 1983 Am. B. Found, Res. J. 611, 622.

4. Peter F. Nardulli, *The Societal Costs of the Exclusionary Rule: An Empirical Assessment*, 1983 Am. B. Found. Res. J. 585, 601 (table 12).

5. Peter F. Nardulli, *The Societal Costs of the Exclusionary Rule Revisited*, 1987 U. Ill. L. Rev. 223, 233 (table 8).

6. Floyd Feeney et al., Arrests Without Conviction: How Often They Occur and Why 144 (1983).

7. See Bureau of Justice Statistics, U.S. Dep't of Justice, Prosecutors in State Courts, 1992, at 6 (1993); Comptroller General of the U.S., Impact of the Exclusionary Rule on Federal Criminal Prosecutions 8 (1979); Floyd Feeney & Adrianne Weir, The Prevention and Control of Robbery: A Summary 56 (1974); Peter W. Greenwood et al., Prosecution of Adult Felony Defendants: A Policy Perspective 67 (table 44), 74 (table 49) (1976); see also Michael Zander & Paul Henderson, Royal Comm'n on Criminal Justice, Crown Court Study (1993).

8. See Thomas Y. Davies, *Affirmed: A Study of Criminal Appeals and Decision-Making Norms in a California Court of Appeal*, 1982 Am. B. Found. Res. J. 543, 616; Karen L. Guy & Robert G. Huckabee, *Going Free on a Technicality: Another Look at the Effect of the* Miranda *Decision on the Criminal Justice Process,* 4 Crim. J. Res. Bull. 1, 2 (1988).

9. This [chapter] will generally use "confession" as encompassing not only

outright admissions of guilt but also incriminating statements. See George C. Thomas III, *Is Miranda a Real-World Failure?: A Plea for More (and Better) Empirical Evidence*, 43 UCLA L. Rev. 821 (1996).

10. See, e.g., Charles J. Ogletree, *Are Confessions Really Good for the Soul?: A Proposal to Mirandize Miranda*, 100 Harv. L. Rev. 1826, 1827 (1987); White, *supra* note 2, at 18–19. But see Gerald M. Caplan, *Questioning* Miranda, 38 Vand. L. Rev. 1417, 1464–67 (1985).

11. See William T. Pizzi, Reflections on Confessions, Truth, and the Law (Jan. 23, 1995) (unpublished manuscript).

12. Miranda v. Arizona, 384 U.S. 436, 486 (1966).

13. *Id.* at 489.

14. See Office of Legal Policy, U.S. Dep't of Justice, Report to the Attorney General on the Law of Pre-Trial Interrogation 87–95 (1986) [excerpted in chapter 7—Eds.]; see also *Miranda*, 384 U.S. at 521–22; Ronald J. Allen et al., Constitutional Criminal Procedure: An Examination of the Fourth, Fifth, and Sixth Amendments and Related Areas 1222 (3d ed. 1995).

15. Cf. Craig M. Bradley, *The Emerging International Consensus as to Criminal Procedure Rules*, 14 Mich. J. Int'l L. 171, 175 (1993).

16. See generally Gordon Van Kessel, *The Suspect as a Source of Testimonial Evidence: A Comparison of the English and American Approaches*, 38 Hastings L.J. 35–72 (1986); see also OLP Pre-Trial Interrogation Report, *supra* note 14, at 88–89.

17. See Barry Mitchell, *Confessions and Police Interrogation of Suspects*, 1983 Crim. L. Rev. 596, 598.

18. See Michael Zander, *The Investigation of Crime: A Study of Cases Tried at the Old Bailey*, 1979 Crim. L. Rev. 203, 213.

19. Barrie Irving, Royal Comm'n on Crim. Proc., Police Interrogation: A Case Study of Current Practice 75, 149 (1980) (Research Study No. 2) (39 of 60 suspects).

20. Paul Softley, Royal Comm'n on Crim. Proc., Police Interrogation: An Observational Study in Four Police Stations 49, 85 (1980) (Research Study No. 4)

21. Michael McConville & John Baldwin, *The Role of Interrogation in Crime Discovery and Conviction*, 22 Brit. J. Criminology 165, 166 (1982).

22. A. E. Bottoms & J. D. McClean, Defendants in the Criminal Process 115–17 (1976).

23. See Royal Comm'n on Criminal Justice, Report 6 (1993).

24. See generally Michael Zander, The Police and Criminal Evidence Act 1984 (2d ed. 1990); Bradley, *supra* note 15, at 183–86.

25. Gisli H. Gudjonsson, The Psychology of Interrogations, Confessions and Testimony 324 (1992).

26. Criminal Justice and Public Order Act 1994, ch. 33 (Eng.).

27. See generally Mark Schrager, *Recent Developments in the Law Relating to Confessions: England, Canada and Australia*, 26 McGill L.J. 435, 437, 442–43 (1981); A. Kenneth Pye, *The Rights of Persons Accused of Crime Under the Canadian Constitution: A Comparative Perspective*, Law & Contemp. Probs. 221, 234–36 (Autumn 1982).

28. See Peter B. Michalyshyn, *The Charter Right to Counsel: Beyond Miranda*, 25 Alberta L. Rev. 190, 190 (1987); David M. Paciocco, *The Development of*

Miranda-*Like Doctrines Under the Charter*, 19 Ottawa L. Rev. 49 (1987). See generally Don Stuart, Charter Justice in Canadian Criminal Law 183–216 (1991).

29. See Alan Grant, The Audio-Visual Taping of Police Interviews with Suspects and Accused Persons by Halton Regional Police Force, Ontario, Canada—An Evaluation 28 (1987); Joyce Miller, Law Reform Comm'n of Can., The Audio-Visual Taping of Police Interviews with Suspects and Accused Persons by Halton Regional Police Force: An Evaluation 11 (1988).

30. Grant, *supra* note 29.

31. See *id.* at 32.

32. This multiplication assumes that the two variables are independent. This assumption may well underestimate the effect of *Miranda*, because it seems likely that those who do not confess are probably those against whom the prosecution has the weakest cases. . . . Put another way, the suspects deterred from confessing may disproportionately constitute those against whom confessions are needed.

33. Davies, *supra* note 8, at 621.

34. See Fed. Bureau of Investigation, U.S. Dep't of Justice, Uniform Crime Reports, Crime in the United States 1993, at 217 (1994).

35. See *id.* The crime index is composed of the violent crimes of murder and nonnegligent manslaughter, forcible rape, robbery, and aggravated assault and the property crimes of burglary, larceny-theft, motor vehicle theft, and arson. *Id.* at 5.

36. See *id.* at 217 (table 29).

37. See generally Herbert S. Miller et al., National Inst. of Law Enforcement and Criminal Justice, U.S. Dep't of Justice, Plea Bargaining in the United States (1978).

38. See Bureau of Justice Statistics, Sourcebook of Criminal Justice Statistics—1993, at 536 (1994); Barbara Boland et al., Prosecution of Felony Arrests, 1988, at 24–29 (1988); David A. Jones, Crime Without Punishment 192 (1979). But cf. Stephen J. Schulhofer, *Is Plea Bargaining Inevitable?*, 97 Harv. L. Rev. 1037, 1047–50 (1984).

39. See Peter F. Nardulli et al., The Tenor of Justice: Criminal Courts and the Guilty Plea Process 205 (1988).

40. David Jones, Crime Without Punishment 95–96 (1979); see David Neubauer, Criminal Justice in Middle America 199 (1974).

41. Arizona v. Fulminante, 111 S. Ct. 1246, 1257 (1991); see Saul M. Kassin & Lawrence S. Wrightman, *Confession Evidence, in* The Psychology of Evidence and Trial Procedure 67, 83–87 (Saul M. Kassin & Lawrence S. Wrightman eds., 1985); Gerald R. Miller & F. Joseph Boster, *Three Images of the Trial: Their Implications for Psychological Research, in* Psychology in the Legal Process 19, 21–22 (Bruce D. Sales ed., 1977); cf. David Simon, Homicide: A Year on the Killing Streets 454 (1991).

42. *Miranda*, 384 U.S. at 541 n.5.

43. These figures are derived by multiplying Miranda's confession rate reduction (16.1 percent) by the observed plea bargaining effects.

44. United States v. Leon, 468 U.S. 897, 908 n.6 (1984).

45. *Id.*

46. See OLP Pre-Trial Interrogation Report, supra note 14, at 125–27 (describing the case of Ronnie Gaspard) [excerpted in chapter 7—Eds.].

47. See David Clifton, *Unsolved Murders Reach 13 in 1994: Grief Goes On When Killers Go Unpunished*, Salt Lake Trib., Jan. 2, 1995, at D1.

48. Cf. Supplemental Brief for the United States as Amicus Curiae, Supporting Reversal [on reargument] at 3, Illinois v. Gates, 462 U.S. 213 (1983) (No. 81-430).

14

Miranda's
Practical Effect:
Substantial Benefits
and Vanishingly Small
Social Costs
(1996)

•

STEPHEN J. SCHULHOFER

This year marks the thirtieth anniversary of the Supreme Court's landmark decision in *Miranda v. Arizona.*[1] *Miranda* held that custodial police interrogation involves inherently compelling pressures and that, in the absence of safeguards sufficient to dispel that pressure, any statement given under custodial interrogation must be regarded as the product of compulsion, in violation of the Fifth Amendment.[2] Widely maligned at first, *Miranda* has gradually won acceptance across a broad spectrum. Among ordinary citizens and law enforcement professionals alike, a twofold perception is now pervasively shared. First, compliance with the *Miranda* safeguards is widely considered an elementary prerequisite of fair procedure and the decent restraint of police power.[3] Second, the *Miranda* safeguards do not pose any serious impediment to effective law enforcement.[4]

Professor Paul Cassell challenges the empirical strand of the current conventional wisdom.[5] Meticulously revisiting a series of before-and-after studies conducted at the time of the *Miranda* decision, he estimates that *Miranda* was (and still is) responsible for the loss of a conviction in 3.8 percent of all serious criminal cases. He also argues that this 3.8 percent attrition represents a substantial social cost and that we could avoid this cost by replacing the *Miranda* safeguards with a different set of standards.

Professor Cassell makes no effort to argue, as did early critics of *Miranda*, that the decision has had catastrophic effects on law enforcement. On the contrary, the 3.8 percent attrition figure that forms the centerpiece of Cassell's article stands as one of the many refutations of those apocalyptic claims. *Miranda's* supporters have long argued that the decision's effect on conviction rates was negligible.[6] Cassell's 3.8 percent figure could well be offered as evidence for the pro-*Miranda* side of this debate.

It is a surprise to discover, therefore, that even the scaled-down claim of a 3.8 percent impact quickly collapses. Professor Cassell's focus on old studies of the immediate post-*Miranda* period, before police had a chance to adapt to the new framework, carries a built-in risk of exaggerating *Miranda's* current impact on police effectiveness. But even if we accept Cassell's basic approach to the old before-and-after studies, a close look at the details shows that inconsistent and highly partisan procedures are necessary to bring *Miranda's* supposed attrition effect up to Cassell's 3.8 percent figure. Although Cassell is sometimes cautious and willing to forgo exaggerated claims, at critical points in his analysis, data are cited selectively, sources are quoted out of context, weak studies showing negative impacts are uncritically accepted, and small methodological problems are invoked to discredit a no-harm conclusion when the same difficulties are present—to an even greater extent—in the negative-impact studies that Cassell chooses to feature. If we accept Cassell's premise that the old studies are relevant, and reanalyze their data with all necessary qualifications in mind, we find that the properly adjusted attrition rate is not 3.8 percent but *at most* only 0.78 percent—a mere seventy-eight one-hundredths of 1 percent for the immediate post-*Miranda* period, and most likely even less today. For all practical purposes, *Miranda's* empirically detectable harm to law enforcement shrinks virtually to zero.

In a large country with a high crime rate, even 0.1 percent of all arrests represents a lot of cases. More to the point, the release of only one guilty murderer or rapist is one too many. A single case of that sort must be counted as a substantial social cost, if the rules requiring that disposition are unjustified and if the harm they cause is avoidable. Whether the right estimate for lost cases is 3.8 percent or (as I believe) only a small fraction of that figure, the key question is whether the rules leading to those results—the *Miranda* rules—are justified by their constitutional mandate.

✻

Shortly after the *Miranda* decision, a flurry of studies attempted to measure its impact on confession and conviction rates. Though some early, crudely designed studies did seem to show substantial effects, the weight of the evidence tended to suggest that any such effects were small and rapidly diminishing over time.[7] The informal impressions of law enforcement personnel and other criminal justice practitioners were—and continue to be—strongly in accord with this view.[8] By the time the Meese Justice Department launched its call for overruling *Miranda*,[9] that position had scant support in the law enforcement community. The conventional wisdom had turned to the view that the *Miranda* rules were playing a beneficial role in sustaining the professionalism of modern police[10] and that their impact on conviction rates was negligible.[11] As a blue-ribbon American Bar Association committee reported in 1988, after extensive hearings in three cities and a carefully randomized telephone survey of over 800 criminal justice officials, "[a] very strong majority of those surveyed—prosecutors, judges, and police officers—agree that compliance with *Miranda* does not present serious problems for law enforcement."[12]

Professor Cassell challenges this view through a reexamination of before-and-after studies conducted in the immediate aftermath of the *Miranda* decision.[13] He concludes that confessions were not obtained, when they would have been obtained before *Miranda*, in 16 percent of all interrogations.[14] He also estimates that such confessions were necessary for conviction in 24 percent of the cases.[15] The confessions not obtained in cases where they were necessary for conviction (.16 × .24) represent convictions lost because of *Miranda* in 3.8 percent of all serious criminal cases.

My review of the data suggests many essential qualifications that Cassell overlooks or decides to deemphasize. Some of these qualifications raise large doubts about the before-and-after studies in general; other caveats require only small changes in the magnitude of a particular estimate. But even the minor details are critical. We are attempting to tease out an impact that, on Professor Cassell's analysis, affects 3.8 percent of criminal cases. With small adjustments, the critical effects can quickly go to zero. My examination of the data suggests that several such adjustments are required. The cumulative effect of these adjustments radically alters Professor Cassell's bottom-line conclusion.

Professor Cassell wants to base his estimate of *Miranda's* current impact on a series of before-and-after studies conducted almost thirty years ago. There are two major problems here. First, *all* of the studies suffer from significant methodological flaws. Second, even if we can assume that the studies give a reliable picture of *Miranda*'s costs thirty years ago, there is strong reason to believe that such costs were transitory and that confession rates have since rebounded from any temporary decline.

1. Common Methodological Flaws. All the before-and-after studies were crudely designed attempts to capture *Miranda*'s immediate impact. Few, if any, included all necessary segments of the caseload, used proper sampling procedures, ensured strict equivalence of the groups compared, and controlled for relevant causal variables other than *Miranda*.[16] . . .

Because the studies are poorly designed, they cannot by themselves prove that *Miranda* does *not* damage law enforcement. The "conventional wisdom" about *Miranda*'s negligible costs is not based on such studies alone but on a distillation of numerous factors—the weak and inconsistent effects detected in the early studies, pervasive evidence that confession rates rebounded as police adjusted to *Miranda*, and the practical experience of officers in the field who, since the mid-1970s, have consistently reported their impressions that compliance with *Miranda* does not produce significant negative effects. All this evidence might be misleading or incorrect, but to raise substantial doubts about its validity requires more than speculation or admittedly flawed studies that are more than a quarter-century old. To build a refutation of "conventional wisdom" on the kinds of studies Cassell so meticulously tabulates is equivalent to building a modern computerized courthouse on a foundation of sand.

2. Adaptation to *Miranda*. Law enforcement professionals and academic researchers consistently report that police officers adjusted to *Miranda* over time and that any negative impacts quickly dissipated. Officers learned how to avoid mistakes that would create admissibility problems; they adapted interviewing methods so they could honor constitutional rights and still get confessions; and they altered investigatory practices so they could bolster the evidence in cases where no confession was obtained. Since the mid-1970s, the body of police testimony to this effect has been widespread and consistent. Against this background, *Miranda*'s current net cost (if any) is almost certainly *far lower* than the costs incurred in the immediate post-*Miranda* period.

Cassell cannot avoid acknowledging the importance of this accommodation or "rebound" effect.[17] His strategy is to dismiss it as a mere "hypothesis," no more plausible than the competing possibility that "as police have complied more strictly with the *Miranda* rules, confession rates [might] have dropped even further than shown in the early studies."[18] This is an imaginative but hollow speculation. The confession rates at issue, we must remember, are not those observed in cities where initial compliance with *Miranda* was sporadic, because Cassell decides (correctly) to exclude these cities altogether when constructing his estimate of *Miranda's* initial impact. Since the only cities included in the calculus of *Miranda's* initial impact are those in which compliance with *Miranda* was reasonably rapid and complete, the problem of inadequate compliance has already been taken into account.

Cassell offers no evidence—empirical, impressionistic, or otherwise—to support his conjecture that confession rates in the selected high-compliance cities might have declined after the initial post-*Miranda* period.[19] Instead he attempts to put the two competing hypotheses on an equal footing, by suggesting that there is no evidence to support the rebound hypothesis either. But that claim is simply untenable. As Cassell's own table of the empirical research makes clear, many post-1970 studies—including his own 1994 study of Salt Lake City—report confession rates that equal or even exceed those recorded prior to *Miranda*.[20] Moreover, "data" of this sort—though important when available—is not the only legitimate way to choose between plausible speculations. Another possibility is to find knowledgeable people and ask them. This has been done, and the answers are clear—a "very strong majority" of law enforcement professionals surveyed since the mid-1970s have reported satisfactory accommodation to *Miranda*; there are virtually no complaints (and Cassell cites none) that increasing compliance has aggravated *Miranda's* effects over time.

*

Comparing a situation before Event X to the situation after Event X can support valid inferences only if the variables measured before and after are truly comparable. Many of the before-and-after studies concerning *Miranda* are critically flawed because the kinds of cases examined or the kinds of statements counted as confessions were not identical in the before and after periods. Often it was not even clear that the first period studied was really a "before" or that the second period was really an "after": *Miranda's* requirements were anticipated in some jurisdictions before the decision was announced, and elsewhere those requirements were ignored long after they became the law. Professor Cassell pays close attention to these kinds of issues, and they will be a major concern when I turn to an examination of specific before-and-after studies.

Imagine, however, a carefully designed study that measured confession rates for the same kind of cases, investigated in the same way by the same police personnel, for a full year before any *Miranda* requirements were introduced and for a full year after *Miranda* was conscientiously implemented. The study reports a confession rate of 60 percent before and 45 percent after. Are we now justified in concluding (as Cassell would) that *Miranda* was responsible for losing confessions in 15 percent of the cases?

Not necessarily. Time-series analysis poses tricky issues in social science research, and even when studies are carefully designed to ensure comparable methods of measurement, there are a number of obstacles to drawing valid *causal* inferences.[21] If the confession rate really did drop by 15 percentage points, the conclusion that Event X (*Miranda*) caused the drop is only a hypothesis. Several competing hypotheses may be equally plausible. Three of these possibilities are especially relevant to before-and-after comparisons of *Miranda*: The observed change may be the result of a long-term trend unrelated to Event X; the change may be the result of other Events Y or Z that are close in time but unrelated to Event X; or the change may be the result of instability (random fluctuations) in the observed variable. In addition, we must be clear about the content of the "before-*Miranda*" baseline against which *Miranda* is being compared.

1. Long-term Trends. Considerable anecdotal and empirical evidence suggests that confession rates in the 1960s had started to drop well before *Miranda*.[22] Some of this drop may be attributable to anticipatory implementation of *Miranda*-like requirements, but that is clearly not the whole story. Other trends were at work. Police departments were becoming more professionalized, physical abuse was becoming less frequent, and courts applying the due-process voluntariness test were becoming less tolerant of extreme psychological pressure and marathon, all-night interrogation sessions.[23] Concurrently, the population (including the population of criminal suspects) was becoming better educated, better informed about constitutional rights, and less deferential to authority.[24]

These developments seem to have produced modestly declining confession rates prior to and independent of *Miranda*.[25] A well-designed comparison of Period A (*e.g.*, 1965) to Period B (1967) would probably show some drop in the confession rate, even if no *Miranda*-like requirements had been implemented in the second period.

How large was this trend-driven drop in the confession rate? A long-term trend could not account for a 25 percent drop over a few months before and after *Miranda*.[26] But small adjustments can affect Cassell's sensitive bottom-line figure, and some small adjustment for the long-term trend factor seems imperative here. The New Haven study, for example, found a 10–15 percent drop in the confession rate from 1960 to 1966.[27] Professor Cassell acknowledges that this 10–15 percent drop cannot be attributed to *Miranda*[28] and that it therefore seems to reflect a long-term trend.[29] We have no data sufficient for specifying the extent of this trend on a national basis, but in the absence of better data, the New Haven figure, a decline of 2 percent per year during the early and mid-1960s, can serve as a rough approximation. This long-term rate of decline must be subtracted from any total before-after change, in order to isolate the portion of the change that might be attributable to *Miranda*.

2. Competing Causal Events.   Analytically distinct from the hypothesis of a long-term trend is the hypothesis that observed changes might be caused by a discrete event, close in time to the event under study but not caused by it. Two important candidates for "competing event" status are *Mapp v. Ohio*[30] and *Gideon v. Wainwright*.[31] *Mapp*, decided in 1961, and *Gideon*, decided in 1963, were already on the books when "before-*Miranda*" measurements were taken, but these decisions (like *Miranda* itself) were implemented slowly and imperfectly in many jurisdictions. Since their effects would be felt more strongly in a post-*Miranda* period (e.g., 1967) than in a pre-*Miranda* period (*e.g.*, 1965), those effects must be subtracted in order to isolate the portion of any change that might be attributable to *Miranda* itself.

Mapp and *Gideon* could affect the confession rate in a number of ways. To the extent that *Mapp* reduced the frequency of illegal searches and seizures, police would be less likely to have physical evidence for use in confronting suspects under interrogation. *Gideon* increased access to counsel not only in states that had formally denied any right to appointed counsel but also in those states that theoretically recognized the right but had only haphazard methods of implementing it.[32] Although *Gideon* did not by itself afford a right to counsel at the interrogation phase, the right to appointed counsel meant that more suspects had some pre-interrogation contact with counsel, and if not, they learned later on, when they did meet with counsel, that they should have kept their mouths shut. This last effect of *Gideon* could generate declining confession rates among suspects who had previously been arrested, since "repeat players" interrogated post-*Miranda* would be more likely to have had some prior contact with counsel than would repeat players who were interrogated pre-*Miranda*.

The magnitude of these effects is a matter for speculation and might not be especially large. The declining confession rates in New Haven over the 1960–1966 period, previously discussed in connection with long-term trends, may also reflect, in part, the impact of discrete events such as *Mapp* and *Gideon*. As an approximation, we may take the 2 percent average annual decline as a rough estimate of the combined effect of long-term trends and discrete events independent of *Miranda*.

3. Instability.   Like crime rates, conviction rates, and automobile accident rates, confession rates in any police department no doubt vary from month to month and from year to year. A drop in any of these rates from year *A* to year *B* could be the result of an important intervening event (appointment of a new police chief, imposition of new interrogation rules), or it could be purely the result of random fluctuation. Changes that are very large (relative to the pattern of up-and-down movements in other years) are less likely to be due entirely to chance, but even then, the *size* of the change could be *partly* due to chance.[33]

In studies comparing two groups of known sizes, we can determine the exact probability that an observed difference between the groups is merely due to chance. By convention in the social sciences, a difference is considered "statistically significant" if there is less than a .05 (or .01) probability that the difference could have occurred by chance.

Statistical significance, in its conventional sense, is not a problem in most of the before-and-after studies of *Miranda*; if other methodological problems can be put aside, most of the observed differences are statistically significant.

But statistical significance does not avoid the instability problem. Statistical significance indicates that two populations (for example, those drawn from the "before" and "after" periods) are probably different in fact, but it cannot determine the *cause* of that difference, which may simply be the result of large year-to-year ups and downs, independent of any event intervening between the two years. And there is no agreed procedure in the social sciences for determining whether instability accounts for a difference between two years in a time-series analysis.[34]

4. Baselines.   A recurrent question in measuring *Miranda*'s impact is, "Compared to what?" In the "before-*Miranda*" world of the 1960s, many police departments used high-pressure tactics that might be questionable under today's voluntariness standards, other departments were more scrupulous but gave suspects no warnings of their rights, and still others did give some form of warnings. Whether we are attempting to measure *Miranda*'s impact as a matter of purely historical interest or as a question of current policy and reform, we must be clear about the kind of legal regime that serves as the before-*Miranda* or instead-of-*Miranda* point of comparison.

In legal scholarship, moreover, historical inquiry is seldom pursued purely for its own sake; policy and reform are the ultimate objectives. In that context, the implicit focus of interest, as a point of comparison to "after *Miranda*," is never really the "before-*Miranda*" period but instead the regime that would exist *after* the "after-*Miranda*" period. A before-and-after comparison will have limited relevance for current policy if the instead-of-*Miranda* regime for the 1990s differs significantly from the before-*Miranda* regime on which the historical research focuses.

The due-process voluntariness requirement, as interpreted in the 1960s, provides an especially tricky baseline. A comparison of *Miranda* to this regime is of legitimate historical interest, but of much less policy interest. Though we can speak loosely of "the" voluntariness requirement, voluntariness is in fact not a discrete test but a shifting set of numerous standards, which are not as permissive today as they were in the 1960s.[35] Thus a comparison of conviction rates under *Miranda* to conviction rates under the 1960s voluntariness test would probably exaggerate the gain, if any, to be expected from replacing *Miranda* with a voluntariness standard today.

For similar reasons, none of the voluntariness tests can provide an accurate baseline for policy purposes, if the instead-of-*Miranda* regime would require warnings or some other system of safeguards to supplement voluntariness standards. Though at least one prominent legal scholar advocates replacing *Miranda* with a traditional voluntariness approach,[36] warnings requirements of some sort have been a prominent feature of nearly all the replacement regimes proposed by *Miranda*'s critics, including the Meese Justice Department[37] and Professor Cassell himself.[38] For purposes of policy assessment and reform, therefore, the most relevant measure of *Miranda*'s impact is a comparison of conviction rates under *Miranda* to conviction rates under a regime that warns arrested suspects of their rights.

*

Table 1 below summarizes the results of [the author's] reanalysis [of the *Miranda* impact data], which modifies the average before-after change from a 16.1 percent drop (Professor Cassell's figure) to a confession-rate drop of only 9.7 percent in comparison to the 1960s voluntariness test and a drop of only 6.4 percent in comparison to a regime that warns arrested suspects of their rights. . . .

In addition to adjustments specific to studies at particular sites, sev-

---

Table 1. Confession-Rate Changes in Before-and-After Studies

	Change in Rate Used by Cassell	Corrected Comparison to Regime without Warnings	Corrected Comparison to Regime with Some Warnings
Pittsburgh	−18.6%	−16.2%	−16.2%
New York County	−34.5%	excluded	excluded
Philadelphia	−24.6%	−13.8%	−13.8%
Seaside City	−2.0%	0.0%	0.0%
New Haven	−16.0%	−12.3%	−12.3%
Washington, D.C.	excluded	excluded	excluded
New Orleans	−11.8%	excluded	excluded
Kansas City	−6.0%	−6.0%	−6.0%
Kings County	−15.5%	excluded	excluded
Chicago	excluded	excluded	excluded
Los Angeles	excluded	excluded	+9.8%
Average Change	−16.1%	−9.7%	−6.4%

eral other corrections must be considered. This subpart focuses on three particularly important concerns: *Miranda*'s initial negative effects may have been concentrated in the larger cities, confession rates were declining in the 1960s for reasons independent of *Miranda*, and declining confession rates overstate law enforcement damage because confessions are not always necessary for conviction.

1. Large City Effects.   Cassell points to a number of factors suggesting that "*Miranda* has a larger effect on major urban areas."[39] Although the data are not strong enough to permit confident conclusions, some of the evidence supports his view that in before-and-after comparisons from the 1960s, "*Miranda* has differential effects on the confession rate in cities of varying sizes."[40] For cities of over 250,000 population, the average confession-rate drop was 18.5 percent in the studies Cassell uses, and 6.6 percent in my reanalysis; in contrast, the two smaller cities (Seaside and New Haven) had a confession-rate drop of only 9 percent in Cassell's tabulation and 6.2 percent in my reanalysis.[41] . . .

2. Trends and Other Causes.   During the early- and mid-1960s, many developments independent of *Miranda* contributed to a declining trend in the confession rate. Though we cannot quantify those effects with certainty, the trend was clearly present, and the available evidence suggests that a reasonable approximation would be a confession-rate drop—independent of *Miranda*—on the order of 2 percent per year during this period. If we had a well-designed before-and-after study showing that the confession rate was 10 percent lower in January 1967 than it had been in January 1966, we would need to subtract the 2 percent trend factor to arrive at the part of the change (8 percent) that might be attributable to *Miranda*.

To make the proper trend adjustment, we need to know the time between the midpoints of the before and after periods, a detail that is not clear in some of the studies. As best I can reconstruct, this time interval averaged about sixteen months (*i.e.*, a 2.7 percent trend-related drop) for the eight studies Cassell uses and about thirteen months (*i.e.*, a 2.2 percent trend-related drop) for the six studies in the reanalysis. The average confession-rate drop, in comparison to a regime requiring some warnings, thus declines from 6.4 percent in the site-specific reanalysis to 6.3 percent after adjusting for large city effects and to 4.1 percent after adjusting for trends not related to *Miranda*. The final figure—4.1 percent—provides a measure of *Miranda*'s empirically detectable effect on the confession rate in the immediate post-*Miranda* period.

3. The Need for Confessions. We are not yet in a position to determine *Miranda*'s measurable impact on law enforcement. A confession is not always necessary for conviction, and thus a decline in the confession rate will not inevitably produce a decline in the conviction rate. Drawing on the various before-and-after studies and other empirical sources, Cassell estimates that confessions are needed for conviction in 24 percent of all cases. He thus calculates that his estimated 16.1 percent decline in the confession rate will lead to a loss of convictions in 3.8 percent of criminal cases. If his necessity figure is correct, but we apply it instead to the confession-rate changes demonstrated by this [chapter's] reanalysis of the data (4.1 percent after adjustments), *Miranda*'s impact on the conviction rate falls to 0.98 percent (4.1 × .24), i.e., less than 1 percent.

The estimates of necessity are almost invariably subjective. It is difficult to know whether the researchers Cassell cites made accurate judgments about the probability of conviction on the evidence at hand, much less about the possibilities of augmenting that evidence by other methods of investigation. Nonetheless, taking at face value the methods Cassell uses to estimate necessity, doubts remain about which studies are sufficiently sound to warrant consideration. My review of these data, though not worth extended discussion here, indicates that the best measure of necessity rates derivable from the empirical studies is not 24 percent (Cassell's figure) but 19 percent. If this is the better estimate, then *Miranda*'s measurable impact on the conviction rate falls to 0.78 percent (4.1 × .19), i.e., seventy-eight hundredths of one percent.

Cassell argues that the costs of *Miranda* include not only cases in which a confession is "necessary for conviction" but also cases in which lack of a confession will mean a less favorable plea bargain.[42] His point would be well taken *if* the first group of cases (those in which a confession is "necessary for conviction") is narrowly defined to include only cases in which, absent a confession, a conviction is unattainable in any manner. The necessity judgments in the empirical studies were not made in this manner, however. On the contrary, a confession was counted as necessary any time that the other evidence was insufficient to make conviction likely *at trial.*[43] With this trial-oriented focus, cases were counted as lost not only when the lack of a confession would produce a dismissal or acquittal at trial, but also when the prosecutor, facing the risk of defeat at trial, would have to negotiate a reduced sentence in order to get a guilty plea.

A "necessity" figure defined in this fashion already includes sentencing impacts, and in fact it inevitably *overstates Miranda*'s impact on the conviction rate. Plea bargaining dynamics tend to *offset* the numerically estimated loss of convictions (whether 24 percent or 19 percent), because prosecutors can use many sorts of leverage to obtain guilty pleas in some cases counted as "lost," *i.e.*, cases in which a confession would be necessary to make conviction likely at trial. The plea-bargained sentence may be lower in such a case than it would have been with a confession, but the case will not be lost altogether (as the empirically derived necessity figure implies). Serious offenders would be unlikely to "walk."[44] And the sentence might not be lower at all. Bargains for a specific sentence are rare in the federal courts and in many state systems;[45] absent such a bargain, the judge will be free to fit the sentence to her own conception of the "real" offense, and the defendant may get little credit for evidentiary weaknesses or even for a negotiated charge reduction.[46]

*

Professor Cassell concludes, in light of the before-and-after studies, that in the immediate post-*Miranda* period, *Miranda* caused a 16.1 percent drop in the confession rate, that confessions were necessary for conviction in 24 percent of the cases, and that *Miranda* accordingly caused a loss of convictions in 3.8 percent of serious cases. Even if we accept these conclusions at face value, *Miranda*'s estimated harm to law enforcement in the immediate post-*Miranda* period affected only a small minority of the cases.

With necessary adjustments, however, the losses estimated by Cassell disappear almost completely. . . . The estimated confession-rate change drops to 5.8 percent in comparison to the 1960s voluntariness test, and drops from 16 percent (Cassell's figure) to 4.1 percent in comparison to a regime with some warnings. Assuming (generously) that the absence of a confession meant a lost conviction in 19 percent of these cases, *Miranda* can be held responsible for harm to law enforcement in *at most* 0.78 percent, i.e., seventy-eight hundredths of 1 percent of the cases in the immediate post-*Miranda* period.

In a large country with a high crime rate, a 0.78 pecent attrition figure represents a large number of cases. Cassell wants to argue that his

3.8 percent estimate of *Miranda*'s impact (and even my 0.78 percent estimate) implies a shocking and unacceptable loss of cases. Applying his 3.8 percent figure to FBI arrest statistics for 1993, he calculates that *Miranda* causes the loss of 28,000 violent crime convictions per year.[47] Even if the correct figure is only 0.78 percent, Cassell would argue that the adjusted attrition figure—4,700 violent crime convictions per year—is still a serious cause for concern.

This sort of calculation presents a thoroughly misleading picture, however. Impact estimates in social science are notoriously subject to the fallacy of false precision. In rigorous experimental science, a 0.78 percent effect (implying, for example, the saving of 0.78 percent of affected lives in a cancer treatment) might be an important result. In contrast, crude before-and-after studies in social science generate "soft" estimates with a wide range of error. Under these circumstances, proportions are revealing, but absolute numbers can create a deceptive illusion of large benefits. Social science researchers cannot responsibly promise to produce 4,700 additional convictions with no risk of disrupting the remaining 749,300 cases.

Cassell himself is implicitly aware of these problems, because his own "compromise"—some warnings but no waiver and cut-off rules[48]—generates fewer convictions than would a regime of no warnings at all. Cassell repeatedly asserts that the number of convictions lost because of his proposed warnings would be small.[49] And undoubtedly he is right—since what he means is that the losses would be *relatively* small.[50] But how many cases would be affected? Based on the kind of before-and-after studies that Cassell considers reliable, *Miranda* produces an attrition rate of 0.78 percent compared to a regime with some warnings, and an attrition rate of 1.1 percent compared to a regime with no warnings. A regime like Cassell's (with some warnings) would thus lead to roughly 0.32 percent more attrition than a regime of no warnings at all. The 0.32 percent figure is a very low rate of attrition, but if Cassell is serious about his method of extrapolation, he must apply this figure to the FBI's estimate of arrests for violent crime, concluding that his recommendations would lead to the release of 1,930 violent criminals per year.[51] What would Cassell say to the families of all these victims, whose attackers would be released by his proposal? Cassell knows that his sort of extrapolation is simply rhetoric, not a serious foundation for assessing social policy. . . . To focus on a 0.78 percent estimate as a concrete, quantifiable gain—in the porous, rough-and-tumble world of criminal justice—is simply unreal.

. . . [T]he great weight of the evidence confirms that police have now adjusted to the *Miranda* requirements and overcome the limited difficulties experienced in the immediate post-*Miranda* period. Altogether, a realistic working estimate of *Miranda*'s impact on current law enforcement must be placed far lower than the 0.78 percent figure. For practical purposes, *Miranda*'s demonstrable impact on conviction rates today is virtually nil.

To be sure, there could be harmful net effects that did not show up in the studies under consideration. But Professor Cassell wants to use the empirical studies affirmatively, to refute the pervasively held view that *Miranda* has *not* caused significant harm. Nothing in the studies comes close to carrying that kind of burden. Indeed, the end result of the empirical exercise, with its vanishingly small evidence of harmful effects, serves only to reinforce the conventional view. If a harmful net impact exists, we will have to build the equivalent of the Superconducting Supercollider in order to find it. For all practical purposes, *Miranda*'s empirically detectable net damage to law enforcement is zero. . . .

NOTES

1. 384 U.S. 436 (1966).

2. *Id.* at 467, 478–79.

3. E.g., Tom Gibbons & Jim Casey, *Ed Meese's War on* Miranda *Draws Scant Support*, Chi. Sun-Times, Feb. 17, 1987, at 41. For a dissenting view, see Joseph D. Grano, Confessions, Truth, and the Law 27–58 (1993).

4. E.g., ABA Special Comm. on Criminal Justice in a Free Soc'y, Criminal Justice in Crisis 28 (1988); Eduardo Paz-Martinez, *Police Chiefs Defend* Miranda *Against Meese Threats*, Boston Globe, Feb. 5, 1987, at 25, 29.

5. Paul G. Cassell, Miranda'*s Social Costs: An Empirical Reassessment*, 90 Nw. U. L. Rev. 387 (1996) [excerpted in chap. 13—Eds.].

6. Welsh S. White, *Defending* Miranda: *A Reply to Professor Caplan*, 39 Vand. L. Rev. 1, 20 (1986); see also sources cited in Cassell, *supra* note 5, at 389 nn.4 & 5.

7. See Liva Baker, *Miranda*: Crime, Law and Politics 180–81, 403–5 (1983); Gerald N. Rosenberg, The Hollow Hope: Can Courts Bring About Social Change? 325–29 (1991); Otis H. Stephens, The Supreme Court and Confessions of Guilt 165–200 (1973); see also sources collected in Yale Kamisar, Police Interrogation and Confessions 47–49 & n.11 (1980).

8. See, e.g., ABA Special Comm., *supra* note 4; Gibbons & Casey, *supra* note 3; Wayne E. Green, *Police vs.* "Miranda": *Has the Supreme Court Really Hampered Law Enforcement?*, Wall. St. J., Dec. 15, 1966, at 16; Paz-Martinez, *supra* note 4; see also Rhode Island v. Innis, 446 U.S. 291, 304 (1980); Tom C. Clark, *Observations: Criminal Justice in America*, 46 Tex. L. Rev. 742, 745; Yale Kamisar, *Landmark Ruling's Had No Detrimental Effect*, Boston Globe, Feb. 1, 1987, at A27.

9. Office of Legal Policy, U.S. Dep't of Justice, Report to the Attorney General on the Law of Pre-trial Interrogation (1986) [excerpted in chap. 7—Eds.].

10. See, e.g., Gibbons & Casey, *supra* note 3; Paz-Martinez, *supra* note 4.

11. See sources collected in Cassell, *supra* note 5, at 389 nn.4 & 5.

12. ABA Special Comm., *supra* note 4, at 1–2, 28.

13. Cassell, *supra* note 5, at 395–437.

14. *Id.* at 416–17.

15. *Id.* at 433, 437–38.

16. See Richard Angelo Leo, *Police Interrogation in America: A Study of Violence, Civility and Social Change* 332–33 (1994) (unpublished Ph.D. dissertation, University of California, Berkeley).

17. Cassell, *supra* note 5, at 450–54.

18. *Id.* at 453–54.

19. See *id.* at 454 n.384.

20. See *id.* at 459.

21. See Donald T. Campbell, *Reforms as Experiments*, 24 Am. Psychol. 409, 411 (1969); H. Laurence Ross et al., *Determining the Social Effects of a Legal Reform*, 13 Am. Behav. Scientist 493, 494–95 (1970).

22. Project, Interrogations in New Haven: The Impact of *Miranda*, 76 Yale L.J. 1519, 1574 (1967).

23. See Developments in the Law: Confessions, 79 Harv. L. Rev. 938 (1966).

24. Project, *supra* note 22, at 1574.

25. *Id.* at 1573.

26. Cassell, *supra* note 5, at 450.

27. Project, *supra* note 22, at 1573.

28. Cassell, *supra* note 5, at 407–08.

29. *Id.*

30. 367 U.S. 643 (1961).

31. 372 U.S. 335 (1963).

32. See Stephen J. Schulhofer, *Is Plea Bargaining Inevitable?*, 97 Harv. L. Rev. 1037, 1098 n.200 (1984).

33. See Donald T. Campbell, *Measuring the Effects of Social Innovations by Means of Time Series*, *in* Statistics: A Guide to the Unknown 93, 95 (Judith M. Tanur et al. eds., 1989).

34. Campbell, supra note 33, at 97–99.

35. See Stephen J. Schulhofer, *Confessions and the Court*, 79 Mich. L. Rev. 865, 867–69 (1981).

36. Grano, *supra* note 3, at 218–22.

37. Pre-trial Interrogation Report, *supra* note 9, at 106 (1986).

38. Cassell, *supra* note 5, at 496–97.

39. *Id.* at 448.

40. *Id.* at 450.

41. See Table 1.

42. Cassell, *supra* note 5, at 440–46.

43. See, e.g., Richard H. Seeburger & R. Stanton Wettick, Miranda *in Pittsburgh—A Statistical Study*, 29 U. Pitt. L. Rev. 14 (1967).

44. It is disappointing in this connection to see Cassell repeat, as an example of *Miranda*'s cost, the Office of Legal Policy's emotionally inflammatory but misleading example of Ronnie Gaspard, a Texan accused of a brutal murder, who

was set free because of what Cassell calls "a *Miranda* technicality." Cassell, *supra* note 5, at 485. In fact, *Miranda* was irrelevant to Gaspard's release. Gaspard requested counsel at his arraignment, and counsel was formally appointed ten days later; the questioning that produced Gaspard's confession occurred three days afterward, i.e., thirteen days after the formal request for counsel at arraignment. See Stephen J. Schulhofer, *Reconsidering* Miranda, 54 U. Chi. L. Rev. 435, 458–59 n.60 (1987). Thus, Gaspard's release, though highly regrettable, was required by the violation of his Sixth Amendment right to counsel. See Brewer v. Williams, 430 U.S. 387 (1977). Cassell does not advocate repeal of the Sixth Amendment, and his own proposal expressly contemplates a right to appointed counsel as of the suspect's first judicial appearance. Cassell, *supra* note 5, at 496–97.

Equally misleading is Cassell's use of Edwards v. Arizona, 451 U.S. 477 (1981), as an example of a defendant who received a favorable plea bargain because of *Miranda*. See Cassell, *supra* note 5, at 442 n.322. Edwards's confession was suppressed on *Miranda* grounds, but Edwards was then convicted by a jury on retrial and sentenced to life imprisonment. See Schulhofer, *supra*, at 459–60. It was only when that subsequent conviction was reversed—for improper admission of hearsay—that Edwards pleaded guilty in return for a reduced (fifteen-year) sentence. *Id.* at 460 n.62. Since Cassell does not advocate repeal of the confrontation clause or the hearsay rule, his own approach would produce the identical result in *Edwards*.

45. See Stephen J. Schulhofer, *Due Process of Sentencing*, 128 U. Pa. L. Rev. 733 (1980).

46. *Id.* at 757; Kevin P. Reitz, *Sentencing Facts: Travesties of Real-Offense Sentencing*, 45 Stan. L. Rev. 523 (1993).

47. Cassell, *supra* note 5, at 440. Cassell's figure represents 3.8 percent of the 754,000 arrests for violent crime in 1993. But the 3.8 percent figure is an estimate of the confession rate for "suspects questioned," *id.* at 437, and roughly 20 percent of arrested suspects are never interrogated. See Paul Cassell & Bret Hayman, *Police Interrogation in the 1990s: An Empirical Study of the Effects of Miranda*, 43 UCLA L. Rev. 839 (1996) [excerpted in chap. 16—Eds.]. Thus, the population of violent offenders affected by Miranda consists of roughly 603,000 suspects (754,000 × 0.8), and Cassell's 3.8 percent figure implies an attrition of 23,000 cases.

48. Cassell, *supra* note 5, at 492–96.

49. *Id.* at 492–94.

50. *Id.* at 494.

51. Again, I assume that 80 percent of the arrested suspects would be interrogated, so that the number of lost convictions would be $(.8 \times 754,000) \times .0032 = 1,930$.

15

The Impact of
Miranda
Revisited
(1996)

•

RICHARD A. LEO

. . . In the last three decades, legal scholars have devoted tremendous
energy to ruminating over the implications of *Miranda*. Although virtually all of the scholarship on *Miranda* has been doctrinal and philosophical, several studies have examined the impact of *Miranda* on law
enforcement and whether it has been successful in achieving its declared goals.[1] Surprisingly, however, all of these impact studies were
undertaken within three, and published within eight, years of the
Miranda decision, and none have been subsequently replicated. Thus,
everything we know to date about the impact of *Miranda* comes from research that was undertaken when *Miranda* was still in its infancy. Since
the long-range impact of a court decision is far more important to scholars than its short-term effects, it is surprising that no scholar has studied the impact of *Miranda* in more than two decades.

*

. . . Although these studies posed a variety of questions and employed a
variety of methodologies to assess the impact of *Miranda* on custodial
interrogation, the criminal process, and the police organization, the
most important findings can be summarized as follows. First, in the
years 1966–1969, after an initial adjustment period, American police
began to comply regularly with the letter of the new *Miranda* requirements. Second, despite these warnings, suspects frequently waived
their constitutional rights and chose to speak to detectives. Third, once
a waiver of rights had been obtained, the tactics and techniques of
police interrogation did not change as a result of *Miranda*. Fourth, suspects continued to provide detectives with confessions and incriminating statements, though in some instances at a lower rate than prior to

Miranda. Fifth, the clearance and conviction rate did not appear to be significantly affected by the *Miranda* requirements, though in some instances it too dropped. Finally, although *Miranda* may have been responsible for a 20 percent decline in the confession rate in one study[2] and a 10 percent decline in the conviction rate in two of the studies,[3] *Miranda* did not appear to undermine the effectiveness of criminal investigation in the way that the law enforcement community had initially feared. Nevertheless, the interrogation rate appeared to drop, and *Miranda* may have been responsible for lessening the effectiveness of the collateral functions of interrogation such as identifying accomplices, clearing crimes, and recovering stolen property.

*

In this section, I will analyze *Miranda*'s impact on the detectives and cases in the three police departments in my sample of 182 cases at the "Laconia," "Northville," and "Southville" police departments [pseudonyms—Eds.] . . . .

[T]he detectives provided *Miranda* warnings to suspects in all the cases in which they were legally required to do so, approximately 96 percent of the cases in my sample. In seven (or almost 4 percent) of the cases I observed, the detective did not provide any *Miranda* warnings because the suspect technically was not "in custody" for the purpose of questioning. In other words, neither was the suspect under arrest nor was his freedom restrained "in any significant way" (in each case, the detective(s) informed the suspect that he did not have to answer their questions and that he was free to leave at any time). Therefore, in these seven cases the detectives were not legally required to issue *Miranda* warnings.[4] With the exception of these cases, the detective(s) read each of the fourfold *Miranda* warnings verbatim from a standard form prior to every interrogation I observed.[5] A suspect might respond in one of four ways: waiving his rights, invoking them, or changing his initial response either to a waiver or an invocation. As Table 1 indicates, 78 percent of my sample ultimately waived their *Miranda* rights, while 22 percent invoked one or more of their *Miranda* rights, thus indicating their refusal to cooperate with police questioning.

If a suspect chooses to waive his *Miranda* rights, the custodial interrogation formally begins. If a suspect chooses to invoke one or more of his *Miranda* rights, typically the detective terminates the interrogation and returns the suspect (if he is under arrest) to jail. However, in seven (4 percent) of the cases I observed, the detectives questioned suspects

Table 1. Frequency Distribution of Suspect's
Ultimate Response to *Miranda*

Whether Suspect Waived or Invoked	Freq.	Percent
Waived	137	78.29
Invoked	38	21.71
Total	175	100.00

even after receiving an invocation. In each of these cases, the detective(s) informed the suspect that any information the suspect provided to the detective could not and therefore would not be used against him in a court of law. The detective told the suspect that the sole purpose of questioning was to learn "what really happened." Of course, what the detectives knew and did not tell the suspect was that although the prosecution could not use such evidence as part of its case-in-chief, any information the suspect provided to the detective nevertheless could be used in a court of law to impeach the credibility of, and thus indirectly incriminate, the suspect if he chose to testify at trial.[6] In the remaining thirty-one cases in which the suspect invoked at some point during questioning (82 percent of all cases in which a suspect invoked a *Miranda* right), the detective(s) promptly terminated the interrogation.

As we have seen, the conventional wisdom in legal and political scholarship is that virtually all suspects waive their rights prior to interrogation and speak to the police. Almost one-fourth of my sample (22 percent) exercised their right to terminate police questioning, while over three-fourths (78 percent) chose to waive their *Miranda* rights. Nevertheless, one might expect that certain individuals are more likely to waive their rights than others. Indeed, the Warren Court in *Miranda* speculated that underprivileged suspects were less likely to be aware of their constitutional rights to silence and counsel than their more advantaged counterparts.[7] Though I tested for twelve social, legal, and case-specific variables, the only variable that exercised a statistically significant effect on the suspect's likelihood to waive or invoke his *Miranda* rights was whether a suspect had a prior criminal record (p<.006). As Table 2 indicates, while 89 percent of the suspects with a misdemeanor

Table 2. Suspect's Response to *Miranda* by Prior Criminal Record

Suspect's Prior Record	Whether Suspect Waived or Invoked		Total
	Waived	Invoked	
None	22	2	24
	91.67%	8.33%	100.00
Misdemeanor	42	5	47
	89.36%	10.64%	100.00
Felony	72	31	103
	69.90%	30.10%	100.00
Total	136	38	174
	78.16%	21.84%	100.00

Pearson chi2(2) = 10.1340 Pr = 0.006

record and 92 percent of the suspects without any record waived their *Miranda* rights, only 70 percent of the suspects with a felony record waived their *Miranda* rights. Put another way, a suspect with a felony record in my sample was almost four times as likely to invoke as a suspect with no prior record and almost three times as likely to invoke as a suspect with a misdemeanor record. This result confirms the findings of earlier studies,[8] as well as the conventional wisdom among the detectives I studied, who complained that ex-felons frequently refuse to talk to them as a matter of course. The more experience that a suspect has with the criminal justice system, the more likely he is to take advantage of his *Miranda* rights to terminate questioning and seek counsel.

At least as important as a suspect's response to the *Miranda* warnings is the effect that either a waiver or an invocation will exert on the processing of his case, the likelihood of conviction, and the final case resolution. Of course, a suspect's interrogation is less likely to be successful from the police perspective if a suspect invokes his *Miranda* rights (p<.000), yet this is neither necessarily nor obviously true. In my sample, the detectives acquired incriminating information against a suspect in six (approximately 16 percent) of the thirty-eight interrogations in which the suspect at some point invoked his *Miranda* rights.[9] Despite its effect on the outcome of an interrogation, a suspect's case was 4 percent less likely to be charged if he waived his *Miranda* rights than if he invoked his *Miranda* rights prior to or during interrogation (approximately 69 percent vs. 73 percent). While counter-intuitive, this difference, as Table 3 indicates, is not statistically significant and thus not significantly related to the prosecutor's decision to charge the suspect with a criminal offense.[10]

While the suspects in my sample who waived their *Miranda* rights were only 4 percent more likely to be charged by the prosecution, they were approximately 10 percent more likely to be convicted of an offense than those who invoked their *Miranda* rights (63 percent vs. 53 percent). This difference may seem large, but it is not statistically significant, as Table 4 indicates.

Although a suspect's response to *Miranda* is not significantly related to either the prosecutor's charging decision or the likelihood of conviction, it is significantly related to the process by which the suspect's case will be resolved ($p<.024$). For, as Table 5 indicates, a suspect who waived *Miranda* was twice as likely to have his case resolved through plea bargaining, and this difference is highly significant ($p<.009$). . . .

Table 3. Effect of Suspect's Response to *Miranda* on Prosecutor's Decision to Charge Case

Suspect's Response to Miranda Warnings	Whether Suspect Was Charged by Prosecutor		Total
	Not Charged	Charged	
Waived	42	95	137
	30.66%	69.34%	100.00
Invoked	10	27	37
	27.03%	72.97%	100.00
Total	52	122	174
	29.89%	70.11%	100.00

Pearson chi2(1) = 0.1832 Pr = 0.669

Table 4. Likelihood of Conviction by Response to *Miranda*

Suspect's Response to Miranda *Warnings*	Whether Suspect Was Convicted		Total
	Not Convicted	*Convicted*	*Total*
Waived	48	81	129
	37.21%	62.79%	100.00
Invoked	15	17	32
	46.88%	53.13%	100.00
Total	63	98	161
	39.13%	60.87%	100.00

Pearson chi2(1) = 1.0057 Pr = 0.316

That a suspect's decision to waive his *Miranda* rights significantly increases the likelihood that his case will be resolved by plea bargaining confirms Neubauer's earlier finding,[11] and may be the most notable effect of a suspect's response to the pre-interrogation *Miranda* warnings. Presumably, the greater evidence accumulated against suspects who elect to speak to their interrogators (and likely provide them with incriminating information) accounts for this statistically significant relationship. However, this relationship could also be an artifact of the selection bias created by *Miranda*: Those suspects who waive their constitutional rights and let police interrogate them may be more cooperative individuals and thus may be more predisposed toward less adversarial means of case resolution such as plea bargaining, while those suspects who invoke their *Miranda* rights may be more inclined to press their claims aggressively through the court system.

The final stage of the criminal process in which a suspect's response to the *Miranda* warnings may exert an effect is, of course, sentencing. In particular, one might reasonably expect that suspects who waived their *Miranda* rights during interrogation would be likely to receive more severe sentences than those suspects who had invoked. Although suspects who waive their *Miranda* rights are more likely to receive punish-

Table 5. The Relationship between *Miranda* and Plea Bargaining

| Suspect's Response to Miranda *Warnings* | Whether Suspect's Case Was Resolved by Plea Bargaining | | Total |
	No	Yes	
Waived	69	65	134
	51.49%	48.51%	100.00
Invoked	28	9	37
	75.68%	24.32%	100.00
Total	97	74	171
	56.73%	43.27	100.00

Pearson chi2(1) = 6.9076 Pr = 0.009

ment than their counterparts who invoke, the differences in the severity of punishment they receive are not statistically significant, as Table 6 indicates.

Even if we control for conviction (i.e., exclude from our analysis those suspects who were not convicted), the relationship between a suspect's response to the *Miranda* warnings and the severity of his sentence remains statistically insignificant (p<.349).

✱

[T]here is considerable variation in the way detectives read *Miranda* warnings to their suspects. . . . In the majority of cases I observed, detectives employed three kinds of subtle psychological strategies—what I will call "conditioning," "de-emphasizing," and "persuasive" strategies–to predispose a suspect to voluntarily waive his or her *Miranda* rights.

The Laconia Police are taught to employ conditioning strategies throughout interrogation, with the goal of structuring the environment so that the suspect is conditioned and positively reinforced to respond favorably to their questions. . . . In this strategy, the detective will walk down to the jail to meet the suspect, politely introduce himself to the suspect, sometimes apologize to the suspect for handcuffing him, in-

Table 6. Relationship between *Miranda* and Sentence Severity

Suspect's Response to Miranda Warnings	Severity of Suspect's Sentence				
	None	Low	Medium	High	Total
Waived	48	46	15	15	124
	38.71%	37.10%	12.10%	12.10%	100.00
Invoked	15	9	2	6	32
	46.88%	28.13%	6.25%	18.75%	100.00
Total	63	55	17	21	156
	40.38%	35.26%	10.90%	13.46%	100.00

Pearson chi2(3) = 2.6350 Pr = 0.451

quire about the suspect's physical condition, and then walk the suspect out of the jail and to the interrogation room of the Criminal Investigation Division. At this point, the detective provides the suspect with coffee and sometimes a newspaper, politely asking him if there is anything else he needs. Then the detective lets the suspect "stew" for fifteen to twenty minutes, a strategy thought to enhance the suspect's desire to talk to the police. When the detective returns, he makes pleasant small talk with the suspect, perhaps striking up a conversation about sports, the neighborhood in which the suspect lives, or some other point of common interest as he goes through the routine booking questions— full name, address, phone number, occupation, etc.—atop the standard advisement form. These background maneuvers are intended to disarm the suspect, to lower his anxiety levels, to improve his opinion of the detective, and to create a social psychological setting conducive both to a *Miranda* waiver as well as to subsequent admissions. Sometimes the detective may even subtly tease the suspect by prolonging the buildup to questioning so that the suspect eagerly waives the *Miranda* rights in his desire to speak to the police.

The defining feature of the conditioning strategy is that the police structure the environment and the interaction in a way to facilitate a waiver without explicitly stating so.

*

Another strategy detectives employ to maximize the likelihood of eliciting a waiver is to de-emphasize the potential importance of the *Miranda* rights. Following the standard booking questions and the detective's rapport-building small talk, the detective may attempt to de-emphasize *Miranda*'s potential significance in one of two ways: either by blending the *Miranda* warnings into the conversation as if to camouflage it, or by explicitly calling attention to the formality of the *Miranda* warnings so as to understate it. In the first approach, detectives try to blend *Miranda* into the ebb and flow of pre-interrogation conversation by not doing or saying anything unusual when reading the warnings so that the suspect pays no special attention to the admonition. Some detectives deliver the *Miranda* warnings in a perfunctory tone of voice and bureaucratic manner, implicitly suggesting that the warnings do not merit the suspect's concern. Other detectives read the *Miranda* warnings without pausing or looking up at the suspect, sometimes even a little quickly, before requesting the suspect's signature, all the while implying that the admonition is a formality that necessarily precedes any questioning.

In the second approach, the detectives de-emphasize the potential importance of the *Miranda* warnings by calling attention to their anomalous status, implicitly conveying that the *Miranda* warnings are unimportant or something to be ignored. For example, the detectives may tell the suspect that the *Miranda* warnings are a mere formality that they need to get through prior to questioning. Or the detective may refer to the dissemination of *Miranda* in popular American television shows and cinema, perhaps joking that the suspect is already well aware of his rights and probably can recite them from memory.

. . . [P]olice detectives may also attempt to persuade suspects to waive their *Miranda* rights. The defining feature of persuasion that distinguishes it from conditioning and de-emphasizing strategies is that the detective explicitly, if subtly, attempts to convince the suspect to waive his rights. Most commonly, detectives tell suspects that there are two sides to every story and that they will only be able to hear the suspect's side of the story if he waives his rights and chooses to speak to them. Detectives may emphasize that they already know the victim's side of the story, implying that the victim's allegations will become the official version of the event unless the suspect speaks. The detective might add that the prosecutor's charging decision will be influenced by what the detective tells the prosecutor, which in turn is based on what the detective knows about the suspect's side of the story.

Another persuasive strategy detectives employ is to tell the suspect that the purpose of interrogation is to inform the suspect of the existing evidence against him and what is going to happen to him, but that the detective can only do so if the suspect waives his rights. Detectives may also simply emphasize that they wish or need to speak to the suspect. And sometimes detectives modify the phrasing of "Having these rights in mind, do you wish to speak to me?" to "Having these rights in mind, do you want to hear what I have to say?" or "Having these rights in mind, do you want to tell me your side of the story?"

*

. . . Although no one has systematically analyzed the long-term effects of *Miranda* on police behavior, court cases, or popular consciousness, the issue of *Miranda*'s impact remains a source of controversy among scholars and policymakers. . . . Notwithstanding the ongoing debate between conservative and liberal critics of *Miranda*, the law enforcement community has successfully adapted itself to *Miranda*'s requirement of pre-interrogation constitutional warnings in the last three decades. Today's police officers and detectives—virtually all of whom have known no law other than *Miranda*—have also accepted *Miranda*'s legitimacy and recognized its value as a symbol of police professionalism. . . .

That the Supreme Court has progressively weakened the spirit of *Miranda* in the last thirty years and that detectives employ clever strategies with which to negotiate *Miranda* warnings and obtain waivers in a high percentage of cases may suggest that *Miranda* has become little more than an empty formality in the early stages of the criminal process. Such a view, however, is misguided. Whatever its symbolic value, *Miranda* has had practical consequences for police, suspects, and society—even if these consequences are not easily reducible to quantifiable measures.

I will argue that *Miranda* has had a profound [long-term] impact in at least four different ways. . . .

First, *Miranda* has exercised a civilizing influence on police behavior inside the interrogation room. . . .

Miranda has increased the level of professionalism among police officers and detectives. By laying down a formal rule that establishes regular procedures for interrogations, *Miranda* has created objective and written standards of accountability for custodial police behavior. Informally, *Miranda* has established the norm that patrolmen and detectives can no longer compel suspects to cooperate with them during custodial questioning. By setting limits on the manner in which they are permitted to question suspects, *Miranda* has fundamentally altered police perceptions of their proper relationship to custodial suspects inside the interrogation room. Although they may have devised clever strategies for successfully negotiating *Miranda* waivers and thereafter eliciting statements, American police in the last thirty years have, by necessity, become more solicitous of suspects' rights, more respectful of their dignity, and more concerned with their welfare inside the interrogation room. *Miranda* has also contributed to police professionalism by increasing the required level of training and education patrolmen and detectives receive in the law of evidence and criminal procedure, first in the academy and later in advanced and specialized courses on investigatory techniques. *Miranda* has increased police professionalism by rendering interrogation practices more visible and thus more subject to supervision and control by other actors within the criminal justice system—especially police managers, prosecutors, and judges. . . .

Second, the *Miranda* decision has transformed the culture—the shared norms, values, and attitudes—of police detecting in America by fundamentally reframing how police talk about and think about the process of custodial interrogation. In the last three decades, the language of *Miranda* has structured virtually every evaluation of interrogation practices in police work—whether these discussions occur in the academy, police stations, investigative training courses, court appearances, suppression hearings, or trials. Consequently, *Miranda* is at the forefront of every interrogator's consciousness, and over the years it has changed the sensibilities of police officers and detectives. "*Miranda* is the Bible as far as we're concerned," one detective informed me. . . .

In the world of modern policing, *Miranda* constitutes the moral and legal standard by which interrogators are judged and evaluated. Yet police officers and detectives no longer view the *Miranda* requirements as handcuffing their investigative abilities, but have come to accept *Miranda* as a legitimate and routine part of the criminal process, simply another aspect of the rules of the game. Indeed, virtually all police officers and detectives today have known no law other than *Miranda*. By redefining the moral and legal discourse of police interrogation in the last three decades, *Miranda* has forever changed how police in America think about, discuss, and understand the legal and moral meaning of custodial interrogation. . . .

Third, along with other Warren Court decisions, *Miranda* has increased public awareness of constitutional rights. The *Miranda* warnings may be the most famous words ever written by the U.S. Supreme Court. With the widespread dissemination of *Miranda* warnings in innumerable television shows as well as in the movies and contemporary fiction, the reading of the *Miranda* rights has become a familiar sight and sound to most Americans; *Miranda* has become a household word. As Samuel Walker writes, "every junior high school student knows that suspects are entitled to their '*Miranda* rights.' They often have the details wrong, but the principle that there are limits on police officer behavior, and penalties for breaking those rules, is firmly established." [12] A national poll in 1984 revealed that 93 percent of those surveyed knew that they had a right to an attorney if arrested, [13] and a national poll in 1991 found that 80 percent of those surveyed knew that they had a right to remain silent if arrested. [14] Perhaps it should not be surprising that, as many of my research subjects told me, some suspects assert their rights prior to the *Miranda* admonition or in situations where police warnings are not legally required. Indeed, in the last thirty years, the *Miranda* rights have been so entrenched in American popular folklore as to become an indelible part of our collective heritage and consciousness.

Fourth, *Miranda* has inspired police to develop more specialized, more sophisticated, and seemingly more effective interrogation techniques with which to elicit inculpatory statements from custodial suspects. The law enforcement community reacted to *Miranda* with bitter indignation, fearing that the Warren Court might issue even more expansive rulings (such as mandating attorneys in the station house) that would effectively put an end to police interrogation. After all, the Warren Court devoted more than six pages of the *Miranda* opinion to excoriating the interrogation methods advocated by the leading police training manuals of the time. [15] Yet although it sharply condemned "menacing police interrogation procedures," [16] the Warren Court did not specifically prohibit any tactic advocated in these manuals.

In response to the potential threat *Miranda* posed to interrogation practices, police have fashioned increasingly subtle and sophisticated interrogation techniques.

NOTES

1. See Neil A. Milner, The Court and Local Law Enforcement: The Impact of *Miranda* (1971); David W. Neubauer, Criminal Justice in Middle America (1974); John Griffiths & Richard Ayres, Faculty Note, *A Postscript to the* Miranda *Project, Interrogation of Draft Protesters,* 77 Yale L.J. 395 (1967); Lawrence S. Leiken, *Police Interrogation in Colorado: The Implementation of* Miranda, 47 Denv. L.J. 1 (1970); Richard Medalie et al., *Custodial Police Interrogation in Our Nation's Capital: The Attempt to Implement* Miranda, 66 Mich. L. Rev. 1347 (1968); Neil A. Milner, *Comparative Analysis of Patterns of Compliance,* 5 Law & Soc'y Rev. 119 (1970); David W. Neubauer, *Confessions in Prairie City: Some Causes and Effects,* 65 J. Crim. L. & Criminology 103 (1974); Cyril D. Robinson, *Police and Prosecutor Practices and Attitudes Relating to Interrogation as Revealed by Pre- and Post-*Miranda *Questionnaires: A Construct of Police Capacity to Comply,* 3 Duke L.J. 425 (1968); Roger C. Schaefer, *Patrolman Perspectives on* Miranda, 1971 Law & Soc. Ord. 81; Richard Seeburger & R. Stanton Wettick, Jr., Miranda *in Pittsburgh—A Statistical Study,* 29 U. Pitt. L. Rev. 1 (1967); Otis Stephens et al., *Law Enforcement and the Supreme Court: Police Perceptions of the* Miranda *Requirements,* 39 Tenn. L. Rev. 407 (1972); Michael Wald et al., *Interrogations in New Haven: The Impact of* Miranda, 76 Yale L.J. 1519 (1967); James W. Witt, *Non-Coercive Interrogation and the Administration of Criminal Justice: The Impact of* Miranda *on Police Effectuality,* 64 J. Crim. L. & Criminology 320 (1973); Evelle J. Younger, *Interrogation of Criminal Defendants—Some Views on Miranda v. Arizona,* 35 Fordham L. Rev. 255 (1966); Evelle J. Younger, *Results of a Survey Conducted in the District Attorney's Office of Los Angeles County Regarding the Effect of the* Miranda *Decision upon the Prosecution of Felony Cases,* Am. Crim. L. Q. 32 (1966).

2. See Seeburger & Wettick, *supra* note 1.

3. See Younger, *Results of a Survey, supra* note 1, at 38–39; Witt, *supra* note 1, at 328–30.

4. *Miranda* warnings are legally required only "after a person has been taken into custody or otherwise deprived of his freedom of action in any significant way." Miranda v. Arizona, 384 U.S. 436 (1966), at 444.

5. In two of the burglary interrogations I observed, one investigator recited the Miranda warnings verbatim from memory. One robbery interrogator had the habit of reading the Miranda warnings from a standard form but crossing out (and thus not reading) the words "and will" in the second of the four warnings.

6. Harris v. New York, 401 U.S. 222 (1971).

7. Miranda v. Arizona, *supra* note 4, at 471–73.

8. Wald, *supra* note 1; Neubauer, *supra* note 1.

9. In my sample, detectives questioned seven suspects after they had invoked their *Miranda* rights and two suspects who subsequently invoked their *Miranda* rights. Of these nine cases, six suspects provided incriminating information to detectives.

10. The same outcome remains even if we code probation and parole violations as not charged: Still, a suspect's case is approximately 4 percent more likely to be charged by the prosecutor if he waives, rather than invokes, his *Miranda* rights (61 percent vs. 57 percent), and once again this difference is not statistically significant (p<.674).

11. Neubauer, *supra* note 1.

12. See Samuel Walker, Taming the System: The Control of Discretion in Criminal Justice 52 (1993).

13. See Jeffrey Toobin, *Viva* Miranda, *New Republic*, Feb. 1987, at 11.

14. See Walker, *supra* note 12, at 51.

15. See Miranda v. Arizona, *supra* note 4, at 448–55.

16. See *id.* at 457.

16

Police Interrogation
in the 1990s:
An Empirical
Study of the
Effects of *Miranda*
(1996)

•

PAUL G. CASSELL & BRET S. HAYMAN

Miranda v. Arizona[1] is the Supreme Court's most famous criminal law decision,[2] spelling out the requirements for police interrogation of criminal suspects. Among other things, the decision required police officers to deliver warnings to suspects about their right to remain silent and to obtain a waiver of these rights before beginning any custodial interrogation. From the day the Court issued its decree in 1966, questions loomed about the new rules' effects on police questioning. In the immediate wake of the decision, a handful of researchers attempted to provide answers with empirical studies. But interest in the subject quickly waned, and research in the last couple of decades has been virtually nonexistent.

In this "empirical desert,"[3] we have little knowledge about what police interrogation looked like shortly after *Miranda*, much less what it looks like today. How many suspects waive their *Miranda* rights? How many confess? How important are confessions to the outcome of prosecutions? Even the most informed observers can offer little beyond speculation on these fundamental subjects. A few careful scholars have recognized the pressing need for more research in this area. . . .

This ignorance about police questioning has important public policy ramifications. The Supreme Court now characterizes the *Miranda* requirements not as a constitutional command but rather as a "prophylactic" rule.[4] Under this view, *Miranda* rests on a cost-benefit analysis in which its costs in reducing the effectiveness of police interrogation are assayed against its benefits in protecting suspects from abuses.[5] Given that the entire doctrine now rests on a pragmatic foundation, it is curious to discover that virtually nothing is known about the decision's real-world effects. Without practical information, how can the Court say whether the balance struck with the *Miranda* rules was (or remains) the right one?

To shed light on these important questions, we conducted a study in Salt Lake County, Utah, a large urban area. We gathered information on police questioning and suspects' confessions in a sample of more than 200 cases in the summer of 1994. This [chapter] presents our data on such subjects as the frequency of waivers of rights and confessions, police compliance with *Miranda*, and the role of confessions in the outcome of prosecutions.

*

We selected the Salt Lake County District Attorney's Office for the research because of its proximity [to the authors] and because of the willingness of the prosecutors in the office to allow the study. Salt Lake County has been the site of previous criminal justice research, which found that it was quite typical in its processing of criminal cases.[6] . . .

We collected the basic data for the study by attending 'screening' sessions held at the Salt Lake County District Attorney's Office during a six-week period in the summer of 1994. Prosecutors in the District Attorney's Office screen all felony cases for prosecutive merit. Our sample was drawn from the felony screening process.

Through the gracious consent of the District Attorney's Office, researchers were allowed to attend all screenings unless the case raised some special sensitivity. The screening session is a forty-five-minute interview by the prosecutor of the police officer concerning the evidence supporting the filing of charges. Screenings take place soon after the officer completes investigation of the case. For suspects in custody, the screening takes place on the next working day.

*

One important issue that has not been the subject of much empirical study is the frequency with which suspects are questioned. Not every person who is arrested will be questioned.[7] In our sample, police questioned 79.0 percent of the suspects. This means that a surprisingly large percentage (21.0 percent) were not questioned.

Our 1994 data that a significant proportion of suspects are never questioned, read in conjunction with older studies, support the hypothesis that questioning rates have declined somewhat since *Miranda*.[8] . . .

Of course, even if interrogation rates have declined over time, a remaining question would be whether this is due to *Miranda*. Here the data directly on point are quite limited. . . .

[W]e collected information on why police failed to interrogate suspects (as reported by the officer at screening). Our data are contained in Table 1. As can be seen, in two cases (4.9 percent of the nonquestioning cases), the reason for not questioning was a belief that the suspect would invoke *Miranda*. In two other cases (4.9 percent of the nonquestioning cases), the police cited the fact that a suspect had an attorney as the obstacle to questioning, a reason that has a possible connection with *Miranda*. Our data thus confirm what is suggested in the earlier studies: that some suspects will not be questioned due to *Miranda*.

One of the most important questions about the *Miranda* regime is how often suspects invoke their *Miranda* rights, preventing any police questioning. A suspect can claim *Miranda* rights in two ways. First, he can

Table 1. Reasons for Not Questioning Suspects

Reason	No.	%
Suspect's whereabouts unknown	14	34.1%
Overwhelming case	11	26.8%
Suspect intoxicated	7	17.1%
No opportunity given press of business	2	4.9%
Belief suspect would invoke *Miranda*	2	4.9%
Suspect already had an attorney	2	4.9%
Questioning thought unproductive	1	2.4%
Suspect in rehabilitation program	1	2.4%
Suspect injured	1	2.4%
TOTAL	41	100.0%

(N = 46; 5 unavailable)

refuse at the start of an interview to waive his rights (including the right to remain silent and the right to counsel), thus precluding any interview. Second, even if he initially waives his rights, he can assert them at any point in the interview.[9] If a suspect asserts *Miranda* rights, police questioning must stop. The effect of these questioning cutoff rules is important, because it appears that most of *Miranda*'s harms stem from the cutoff rules, not the more famous *Miranda* warnings.[10]

Surprisingly very little information is available on such a fundamental subject. The previously published evidence on invocations has been collected elsewhere.[11] The evidence, although generally quite dated, suggests that about 20 percent of all suspects invoke their *Miranda* rights.

We gathered data on how often and in what ways suspects asserted their *Miranda* rights. Table 2 shows that of suspects given their *Miranda* rights, 83.7 percent waived them. Reflecting the practices of the local law enforcement agencies, virtually all of these waivers were verbal rather than written. At the same time, 16.3 percent invoked their rights. Of the twenty-one suspects who invoked their rights, nine invoked their right to an attorney (two even before *Miranda* warnings could be read), six invoked their right not to make a statement, and six either refused to execute a waiver or otherwise invoked their rights. For these purposes, a suspect who partially waived his rights (that is, agreed to talk

---

Table 2.   Invocation of Rights

Suspect's Response to Miranda Rights	No.	%
Waived	108	83.7%
Throughout	103	79.8%
Changed Mind Later	5	3.9%
Invoked	21	16.3%
Asked for Attorney	9	7.0%
Invoked Right to Silence	6	4.7%
Refused to Waive/Other	6	4.7%
Total	129	100.0%

---

about some charges but not others), was classified as waiving his rights.[12] . . .

Finally, in none of our cases did the police continue questioning a suspect after an invocation of *Miranda* rights. This finding has considerable importance in the ongoing debate about *Miranda*'s scope. The Court crafted a limitation to the *Miranda* rule in 1971, holding that prosecutors could use statements obtained in violation of *Miranda* for impeachment.[13] Because of this exception, prestigious academic commentators have advanced the suggestion that police would deliberately flout *Miranda* to obtain impeaching statements.[14] We found no evidence that this was occurring.

Determining whether the frequency of invocation of rights we found is "high" or "low" is a matter of judgment that will not be pursued at length here. It bears noting, however, that a 12.1 percent invocation of rights figure [see Table 3] has substantial public policy implications. If our figure is typical of the nation as a whole, then each year approximately 300,000 criminal suspects for FBI index crimes invoke their rights before successful police questioning.[15] . . .

Perhaps *the* critical issue in the debate over *Miranda* is how often today suspects confess or otherwise make incriminating statements. Surprisingly little information is available on this subject, despite frequent definitive pronouncements that many suspects still confess.[16] . . .

We gathered detailed information on the frequency of confessions, incriminating statements, denials, and other results of police questioning. While categorizing statements is always difficult,[17] we divided the outcomes into "successful" and "unsuccessful" categories—looking at the results from law enforcement's point of view. The result of questioning was "successful" when the police: (1) obtained a written confession, (2) obtained a verbal confession, (3) obtained an incriminating statement, or (4) locked a suspect into a false alibi.

*

On the other side of the coin, an interrogation was "unsuccessful" when the police obtained from the suspect: (1) a "flat denial," (2) a "denial with explanation," or (3) "other," unincriminating statements.

A "flat denial" was the statement "I didn't do it" or "I don't know what you're talking about" and essentially nothing else.

A "denial with explanation" involved a suspect who denied the crime and provided "additional statements regarding circumstances surrounding the offense, an alibi, or mitigating version."

*

The catch-all category for "other" statements involved declarations that were not incriminatory and could not be otherwise categorized.

*

The number of incriminating statements and denials we found are shown in Table 3. Overall, 9.6 percent of the suspects invoked their rights, 33.3 percent were successfully questioned, 36.1 percent were questioned unsuccessfully, and 21.0 percent were not questioned. Because some might argue that only suspects who were in fact questioned should be included in determining a confession rate, we also report percentages for only those suspects who were questioned. As can also be seen in Table 3, of all police interviews, 12.1 percent produced an

---

Table 3.   Results

	No.	Questioned Only (%)	Overall (%)
Invoked rights	21	12.1%	9.6%
Successful	73	42.2%	33.3%
Written confession	5	2.9%	2.3%
Verbal confession	42	24.3%	19.2%
Incriminating statement	26	15.0%	11.9%
Locked into false alibi	0	0.0%	0.0%
Unsuccessful	79	45.7%	36.1%
Flat denial	34	19.7%	15.5%
Denial with explanation	40	23.1%	18.3%
Other	5	2.9%	2.3%
Not questioned	46	—	21.0%
Total	219	100.0%	100.0%

(N = 219 overall; 173 for those questioned)

---

immediate invocation of *Miranda* rights, 42.2 percent were successful, and 45.7 percent were unsuccessful.

*

Although our success rate is inflated, it is lower than success rates found in this country before *Miranda*, suggesting that *Miranda* has hampered law enforcement efforts to obtain incriminating statements. In an earlier article, one of the present authors collected the available pre- and post-*Miranda* information on confession rates in this country.[18] Although broad generalizations are hazardous, that evidence suggests that interrogations were successful, very roughly speaking, in about 55 percent to 60 percent of interrogations conducted before the *Miranda* decision. . . . Our 33.3 percent overall success rate (and even our 42.2 percent questioning success rate) is well below the 55–60 percent estimated pre-*Miranda* rate and, therefore, is consistent with the hypothesis that *Miranda* has harmed the confession rate.

*

One question that has not been the subject of any substantial empirical research is the extent to which police questioning falls inside or outside the *Miranda* regime and whether this makes any difference to ultimate outcomes. . . .

The *Miranda* rules cover only "custodial" interrogation.[19] Evidence suggests that police have adjusted to *Miranda* by shifting to noncustodial "interviews" to skirt *Miranda*'s requirements. In talking to police officers, the researchers found some anecdotal evidence supporting this view. In a few screenings, officers (mostly from one large department) referred to giving suspects a "*Beheler*" warning, as in "I gave him *Beheler*." This is a reference to the Supreme Court's decision in *California v. Beheler*,[20] which held that a suspect was not in custody when he "voluntarily agreed to accompany police to the station house [and] the police specifically told [him] that he was not under arrest."[21] Drawn from this case, the *Beheler* warning consists of telling a suspect that he is not under arrest and is free to leave during the "interview." This sophisticated approach suggests that at least some police forces know the difference between custodial and noncustodial interrogations and structure their investigations accordingly.

On the other hand, in a few cases in our sample it appeared that officers *Mirandized* when not required to do so. One department, the

Special Victims Unit (which handled primarily sex offenses), apparently had a policy of *Mirandizing* every noncustodial interviewee. . . .

To date, no one has quantified how often police interview in noncustodial settings. In our sample, 69.9 percent of the interviews were custodial while 30.1 percent were noncustodial. Of the noncustodial interviews, 40.3 percent were at the scene, 26.9 percent were field investigations, and 32.7 percent were arranged interviews (that is, interviews where police officers had previously contacted the suspects to set up an interview time).

Even if police are able to avoid *Miranda*'s requirements by conducting various noncustodial interviews, the question would remain whether such interviews are less effective in obtaining incriminating information. We found that police were less successful in noncustodial interviews, as noted in Table 4—a result that was statistically significant.[22] One hypothesis to account for this difference might be that police officers more frequently question suspects in custody for presumptively more dangerous crimes of violence and therefore might try harder to get a confession.[23] In our sample, however, property offenders were slightly more likely to be interviewed in custody: 72.5 percent of the interviews with property suspects were in custody as compared to 66.2 percent of the interviews with violent suspects. . . .

A conclusion that might be drawn from our data is that police have adapted to *Miranda* to some extent by shifting to noncustodial interviews. However, the value of that tactic appears to be mitigated by the lower success rates of noncustodial interviews. Also, the very fact that police have tried to shift suggests, contrary to the view of some defend-

Table 4. Questioning Result by Custodial Status

Kind of Questioning	Questioning Successful		Questioning Unsuccessful		Total	
	No.	%	No.	%	No.	%
Custodial	58	56.9%	44	43.1%	102	100.0%
Noncustodial	15	30.0%	35	70.0%	50	100.0%
Total	73	48.0%	79	52.0%	152	100.0%

ers of *Miranda*,[24] that interrogating police officers believe the *Miranda* rules are harmful to their efforts. . . .

In various decisions since 1966, the Supreme Court has created exceptions to the *Miranda* doctrine. Critics of these decisions have suggested that the exceptions dramatically scale back the *Miranda* regime.[25] For example, after the Court's 1984 decision recognizing a "public safety" exception to *Miranda*'s requirements,[26] articles proclaimed the "dissolution" of *Miranda*[27] because the exception "carv[ed] a gaping hole."[28]

We made an effort to determine the extent to which such exceptions play a part in everyday law enforcement. With respect to public safety questioning, only one of 173 suspects was even arguably questioned without *Miranda* warnings in such circumstances, and even that case probably did not fall under the *Miranda* requirements. The Court also recently held that "routine booking" questions were not subject to the *Miranda* requirements.[29] Our sample contained no instances of statements being obtained through such questioning. This finding that the *Miranda* exceptions are rarely used[30] supports the suggestion made elsewhere that *Miranda* has not been modified in ways likely to result in significantly more successful police questioning.[31] . . .

Another way in which police officers obtain statements outside the *Miranda* requirements is from suspects "volunteering" incriminating information. In *Miranda* itself, the Court held that "[v]olunteered statements of any kind are not barred by the Fifth Amendment. . . ."[32] Suspects who volunteer statements, even without the benefit of *Miranda* warnings or waivers, can find those statements used against them in court.[33]

In our study, 19 of 217 of suspects (8.8 percent) volunteered statements without any prompting or questioning by the officers. Thirteen of these suspects volunteered incriminating information (four verbal confessions and five incriminating statements), while an additional six volunteered denials of some type. Perhaps the most interesting aspect of these unbidden statements is that, for nine of the thirteen suspects, the volunteered statement was the only incriminating statement available to police.

*

A critical question about the *Miranda* rules is whether police obey them. The empirical evidence from the late 1960s suggests that, at least immediately following *Miranda*, police compliance varied widely.[34] Although little research has been conducted since then, the prevailing view now seems to be that police adhere to the *Miranda* requirements.[35] . . . [T]he evidence we gathered on this . . . issue supports the same conclusion.

Although the researchers were instructed to pay close attention to identifying possible *Miranda* violations, at most three arguable cases of noncompliance (out of a sample of 173 questionings) were discovered, with only one case of clear noncompliance. . . . Our data thus support the emerging consensus that police play by the *Miranda* rules. . . .

Because our study rests on information gathered at police-prosecutor screening sessions, one might argue that our methodology would automatically miss information about police misconduct. After all, cops and prosecutors are not likely to swiftly admit wrongdoing, particularly in the presence of an outside researcher. But our initial impression of police compliance was confirmed by the later paucity of motions to suppress the statements police obtained. Previous studies have found that motions to suppress under *Miranda* are rare and successful motions even rarer.[36]

In our sample, of cases in which police obtained incriminating statements and charges were filed, defendants filed suppression motions in 4.8 percent. All three of the suppression motions alleged only that police committed a technical *Miranda* violation, not that they coerced an "involuntary" confession under more general Fifth Amendment doctrine. The allegations involved disputes over when *Miranda* "custody" began, with one dispute also involving the validity of the waiver. All three motions were denied. Our data thus support earlier findings that successful *Miranda* suppression motions are rare.

*

While our study has . . . limitations, it may be useful to generalize from our findings (coupled with other available research) to more universal conclusions about the ongoing debate over *Miranda*'s real world effects. In recent cases, the Court has attempted to calibrate the *Miranda* rules by weighing costs and benefits.[37] Taken on these pragmatic terms,[38] it is fair to ask whether the Court's balance is the right one. To honestly answer that question requires empirical evidence of *Miranda*'s effects— evidence that our study begins to supply.

Turning first to society's interests, significant concern remains that *Miranda* has seriously hampered the prosecution and conviction of criminals. The frequency of confessions in our 1994 sample appears to be much lower than the frequencies in samples drawn before *Miranda*. Only 33.3 percent of all of the suspects in our sample gave incriminating statements; only 42.2 percent of the suspects who were questioned gave incriminating statements. Of suspects asked for waivers of *Miranda* rights, 16.3 percent declined to give them, thereby completely preventing any police questioning, no matter how restrained or reasonable. An indication that the possibility of invocations was a real concern to police was their shift in some cases to noncustodial interviews, which obviated the need to secure *Miranda* waivers but also appeared to reduce police success.

Our data also suggest that *Miranda*'s lost confessions would not have gilded already golden prosecution cases. Rather, the absence of confessions appears to make an important difference in the real-world processing of criminal cases. Our survey supports the conclusion that if police can obtain an incriminating statement from a suspect, that suspect is more likely to be convicted on more serious criminal charges. On the other side of the coin, if police are unsuccessful, it appears the suspect is more likely to "walk."

Further research on *Miranda*'s costs is undoubtedly warranted. Perhaps the most pressing area is the frequency of confessions. On this point, our study suffers from a lack of pre-*Miranda* data in Salt Lake County. We can only infer by looking to other jurisdictions, both domestic and foreign, that our 33.3 percent confession rate is lower than prevailed before *Miranda*. To shed light on this question, it might be interesting to return to a jurisdiction where pre-*Miranda* data are available and see what the confession rate looks like today. But the general thrust of our study, reviewed in light of other data, seems clear: *Miranda* imposes costs on society by reducing the number of confessions and, consequently, the success of criminal prosecutions.

*

In our view, then, the benefits of *Miranda* seem slim while the costs seem substantial. . . . But th[e] continuing need for research underscores a more general point. . . . The Court now tells us that *Miranda* is "a carefully crafted balance designed to fully protect *both* the defendant's and society's interests."[39] This is not a rhetorical device from a conservative Court designed to undercut the decision: As Professor Yale Kamisar reminds us, striking a balance "is the way *Miranda*'s defenders—not its critics—have talked about the case for the past twenty years."[40] Yet without an empirical foundation, the Court's balancing of interests is illusory.[41] If there is no empirical answer to the question of how many criminals the doctrine sets free, how can the Court blithely assert—as it has in various cases—that the benefits of the doctrine outweigh a cost of unknown magnitude?[42] From the start, the Court developed the *Miranda* rules without empirical support. . . . Justice Harlan exposed this deficiency in his *Miranda* dissent, explaining that the Court's precipitous imposition of the *Miranda* rules precluded other legislative action that "would have the vast advantage of empirical data and comprehensive study."[43] In applying the *Miranda* rules since then, the Court has had precious little information on what *Miranda* did *for* suspects, much less *to* law enforcement. Despite the Court's promise that it has "carefully" considered society's interests, in truth neither the Court nor *Miranda's* academic defenders have ever undertaken a substantial, empirically based cost-benefit assessment of the *Miranda* rules and possible alternatives to them. Indeed, it seems fair to number among *Miranda's* costs its preemptive effect, which has prevented research in different states on various ways of regulating police questioning. . . .

[T]hese deficiencies in the empirical underpinnings of *Miranda* must be regarded as extraordinary. The *Miranda* rules stem not from constitutional command, but rather from cost-benefit prophylaxis. Yet despite nearly three decades to make their case, *Miranda's* defenders have yet to provide research supporting the assertion that the decision's social costs are outweighed by its benefits. This failure leaves the entire *Miranda* doctrine apparently resting on nothing other than the personal intuitions or unarticulated assumptions of Supreme Court Justices about how the rules have operated in the real world. Perhaps *Miranda's* defenders are simply exercising their right to remain silent. But in the face of that silence, the rest of us will draw the reasonable inference— an empirical case for *Miranda* does not exist.

NOTES

1. 384 U.S. 436 (1966).

2. See Jethro K. Lieberman, Milestones! 200 Years of American Law: Milestones in Our Legal History vii (1976).

3. H. Richard Uviller, Tempered Zeal: A Columbia Law Professor's Year on the Streets with the New York City Police 198 (1988).

4. See, e.g., Davis v. United States, 114 S. Ct. 2350, 2355 (1994). See generally Joseph Grano, Confessions, Truth, and the Law 173–98 (1993).

5. See, e.g., New York v. Quarles, 467 U.S. 649, 657 (1984).

6. See, e.g., Kathleen B. Brosi, Institute for Law and Social Research, A Cross-City Comparison of Felony Case Processing 7, 9, 10, 12, 15, 24 (1979); see also John D. O'Connell & C. Dean Larsen, Note, *Detention, Arrest, and Salt Lake City Police Practices*, 1965 Utah L. Rev. 593.

7. See Uviller, *supra* note 3, at 199.

8. See Gordon Van Kessel, *The Suspect as a Source of Testimonial Evidence: A Comparison of the English and American Approaches*, 38 Hastings L.J. 1, 116–17 (1986). But see Stephen Schulhofer, Miranda's *Practical Effect: Substantial Benefits and Vanishingly Small Social Costs*, 90 Nw. U. L. Rev. 34 (1996) [excerpted in chap. 14—Eds.].

9. See generally Wayne R. LaFave & Jerold H. Israel, Criminal Procedure 479–83 (1984 & Supp. 1991). Cf. Davis v. United States, 114 S. Ct. 2350 (1994.)

10. See Paul Cassell, Miranda's *Social Costs: An Empirical Reassessment*, 90 Nw. U. L. Rev. 492–96 (1996) [excerpted in chap. 13—Eds.].

11. See *id.* at 495 n.623.

12. Cf. Roger Lend, The Right to Silence in Police Interrogation 16–17 (Royal Commission on Criminal Justice Research Study No. 10, 1993).

13. Harris v. New York, 401 U.S. 222 (1971).

14. See, e.g., Albert W. Alschuler, *Failed Pragmatism: Reflections on the Burger Court*, 100 Harv. L. Rev. 1436, 1442–43 (1987); Geoffrey R. Stone, *The Miranda Doctrine in the Burger Court*, 1977 Sup. Ct. Rev. 99, 113; Alan M. Dershowitz & John H. Ely, Comment, *Harris v. New York: Some Anxious Observations on the Candor and Logic of the Emerging Nixon Majority*, 80 Yale L.J. 1198, 1220 (1971); see also Harris v. New York, 401 U.S. 222, 232 (1971).

15. This figure is derived by multiplying 12.1% by the 2,800,000 arrests for FBI index crimes for 1993. See 1993 Uniform Crime Reports at 217, table 29. FBI index crimes are murder, rape, robbery, assault, burglary, larceny, and vehicle theft. Our sample includes all felonies, not just index crimes.

16. See, e.g., Yale Kamisar, *Edward L. Barrett, Jr.: The Critic with "That Quality of Judiciousness Demanded of the Court Itself,"* 20 U.C. Davis L. Rev. 191, 210 (1987).

17. See George C. Thomas III, *Is Miranda a Real-World Failure? A Plea for More (and Better) Empirical Evidence*, 43 UCLA L. Rev. 821 (1996). See also Thomas Grisso, Juveniles' Waiver of Rights: Legal and Psychological Competence 35 n.23 (1981); Mike McConville, Corroboration and Confessions: The Impact of a Rule Requiring that No Conviction Can Be Sustained on the Basis of Confession Evidence Alone 30 (1993).

18. See Cassell, *supra* note 10, at 458–59 & table 3.

19. See Stansbury v. California, 114 S. Ct. 1526 (1994).

20. 463 U.S. 1121, 1125 (1983).

21. *Id.* at 1122.

22. The chi-square is significant at the .01 level.

23. See Thomas, *supra* note 16, at 832–33.

24. See, e.g., Tamar Jacoby, *Fighting Crime by the Rules: Why Cops Like* Miranda, Newsweek, July 18, 1988, at 53; Schulhofer, *supra* note 8, at 12 n.32.

25. See, e.g., Mathew Lippman, *A Commentary on Inbau and Manak's "Miranda v. Arizona—Is It Worth the Costs?,"* The Prosecutor, Spring 1989, at 35, 37.

26. New York v. Quarles, 467 U.S. 649 (1984).

27. See, e.g., Mary M. Keating, Note, *New York v. Quarles: The Dissolution of Miranda*, 30 Vill. L. Rev. 441 (1985) [excerpted in chap. 11—Eds.].

28. Irene M. Rosenberg & Yale L. Rosenberg, *A Modest Proposal for the Aboli-*

tion of Custodial Confessions, 68 N.1C. L. Rev. 69, 82 (1989) [excerpted in chap. 11—Eds.].

29. Pennsylvania v. Muniz, 496 U.S. 582, 600–602 (1990).

30. Of course, even though the exceptions have a small quantitative impact, they might still be justified on their own merits. See, e.g., William T. Pizzi, *The Privilege Against Self-Incrimination in a Rescue Situation*, 76 J. Crim. L. & Criminology 567 (1985).

31. See Cassell, *supra* note 10, at 460–62.

32. Miranda v. Arizona, 384 U.S. 436, 478 (1966) [excerpted in chap. 3—Eds.].

33. See, e.g., United States v. Gonzalez, 875 F.2d 875, 881 (D.C. Cir. 1989).

34. Compare, e.g., Richard H. Seeburger & R. Stanton Wettick, Miranda *in Pittsburgh—A Statistical Study*, 29 U. Pitt. L. Rev. 8 (1967) with Richard Medalie et al., *Custodial Police Interrogations in Our Nation's Capital: The Attempt to Implement* Miranda, 66 U. Mich. L. Rev. 1362–70 (1968).

35. See, e.g., LaFave & Israel, *supra* note 9, §6.5, at 484; Stephen J. Schulhofer, *Reconsidering* Miranda, 54 U. Chi. L. Rev. 435, 456 & n.56 (1987).

36. See Comptroller Gen. of the U.S., Impact of the Exclusionary Rule on Federal Criminal Prosecutions 8 (1979); Peter F. Nardulli, *The Societal Cost of the Exclusionary Rule: An Empirical Assessment*, 1983 Am. B. Found. Res. J. 585, 595, 597, 598; Peter F. Nardulli, *The Societal Costs of the Exclusionary Rule Revisited*, 1987 U. Ill. L. Rev. 223, 228, 231, 232; see also Michael Zander & Paul Henderson, Royal Comm'n on Criminal Justice, Crown Court Study (1993).

37. See, e.g., Moran v. Burbine, 475 U.S. 412, 427 (1986); Oregon v. Elstad, 470 U.S. 298, 312 (1985).

38. Cf. Grano, *supra* note 4, at 202.

39. Moran v. Burbine, 475 U.S. 412, 433 n.4 (1986).

40. Yale Kamisar, *The "Police Practice" Phases of the Criminal Process and the Three Phases of the Burger Court, in* The Burger Years 143, 150 (Herman Schwartz ed., 1987).

41. Cf. Thomas Y. Davies, *A Hard Look at What We Know (and Still Need to Learn) About the "Costs" of the Exclusionary Rule: The NIJ Study and Other Studies of "Lost" Arrests*, 1983 Am. B. Found. Res. J. 611, 626; James B. White, *Forgotten Points in the "Exclusionary Rule" Debate*, 81 Mich. L. Rev. 1273, 1282 (1983).

42. See, e.g., Minnick v. Mississippi, 498 U.S. 146, 151 (1990).

43. Miranda v. Arizona, 384 U.S. 436, 524 (1966) [excerpted in chap. 3—Eds.].

17

Plain Talk
about the *Miranda*
Empirical Debate:
A "Steady-State"
Theory of Confessions
(1996)

·

GEORGE C. THOMAS III

Cassell and Hayman have performed a great service to the criminal justice community by gathering, categorizing, and presenting the Salt Lake County data. Though I interpret some of the data differently than Cassell and Hayman do, the debate is richer because of their data.

*

Despite the avowed empirical nature of the project, they occasionally engage in political advocacy. They are, of course, not alone in approaching an empirical issue with a predisposition about the outcome. *Miranda*'s supporters have at times either ignored the empirical question or assumed that we have enough good data to answer it.

*

For an example of our different approaches, Cassell and Hayman put the burden of proving *Miranda*'s value on its defenders: "Yet despite nearly three decades to make their case, *Miranda*'s defenders have yet to provide research supporting the assertion that the decision's social costs are outweighed by its benefits." [1] Once that burden is allocated to the defenders of *Miranda*, Cassell and Hayman find it not met; they then "draw the reasonable inference—an empirical case for *Miranda* does not exist." [2]

It is not clear to me why a constitutional interpretation that [is more than] thirty years old must justify itself with empirical evidence. Nor is it clear to me what the "clear social costs" of *Miranda* are. That, I thought, was the point to the empirical research. . . .

[M]y interpretation of their Salt Lake County data is that *Miranda* has had no effect on the overall confession rate, using "confession" to include all incriminating statements.[3] This is in line with the "steady-state" theory of confessions that I hypothesized [elsewhere].[4] On this steady-state theory, *Miranda* either has no effect at all, or it has effects in individual cases which cancel each other out. In either case, the confession rate will be the same now as in 1965.

*

In the Salt Lake County study, Cassell and Hayman conclude that "42.2 percent of the suspects who were questioned gave incriminating statements,"[5] a figure that is substantially lower than the 55–60 percent range they use for the pre-*Miranda* studies.[6] But I question the range. Using Paul Cassell's work from his earlier *Miranda* article, I think a range of 45–53 percent is a better estimate of the pre-*Miranda* confession rate. Moreover, . . . the Cassell-Hayman 42 percent figure is artificially depressed when compared to the pre-*Miranda* studies. Once adjustments are made to the Cassell-Hayman data to make them comparable to the pre-*Miranda* studies, as I will detail [shortly], the Salt Lake confession rate is 54 percent.

A 54 percent confession rate is closer to the range that Cassell and Hayman use for the pre-*Miranda* studies (55–60 percent) and slightly above my range (45–53 percent). . . .

Even without adjustments to their data, however, no *Miranda* effect appears when the Salt Lake County study is considered together with the other relevant studies. A single study is not sufficient grounds to find a *Miranda* effect. As Paul Cassell has shown in another article, the pre-*Miranda* confession rate varied wildly among jurisdictions. Comparing twenty-one cities, Cassell reported that the confession rates ranged from 31 percent to 88 percent, with nine below 50 percent.[7] The Salt Lake County rate without adjustments is 42 percent. That is low when compared to the pre-*Miranda* studies, but not an outlier. Indeed, of the twenty-one pre-*Miranda* rates, the unadjusted Salt Lake County rate would be higher than four cities and within 5 percent of five others.

Because of this wide variation among jurisdictions, the only approach to the long-term effect of *Miranda* that is fair and balanced is to average rates from several jurisdictions, beginning a few years after *Miranda*.

Once this is done, . . . the average is 52 percent, a rate that is within my range for the pre-*Miranda* rates and close to the Cassell-Hayman range.

A *Miranda* effect on the rate of confessions? There is still no evidence, meaning that the null hypothesis of a steady-state theory must be accepted until better evidence can be found. To do otherwise is to fall into the trap identified by Yale Kamisar: "[S]tatistics are especially potent when 'they give a sense of solid reality (usually false) to something people vaguely apprehend. . . .'"[8]

*

Proving that the *Miranda* warnings cause a change in confession rates is a complex task, which may explain why Cassell and Hayman use a burden-shifting procedural device. "Cause and effect" is an inherently treacherous concept. Events typically appear to have many causes. If we fully understood the relationship among these "causes," they might all be linked in a complex way that defies testing, or one could cause all the others, or an unidentified cause could explain the putative "causes" as well as the effect. It is also possible that the "effect" could cause the "cause." . . . In a world filled with many forces, isolating a cause-and-effect relationship is exceedingly difficult, and it requires compelling evidence.

Stephen J. Schulhofer has identified three reasons to be skeptical of evidence of a *Miranda* effect: (1) the possibility of independent long-term trends, (2) the likelihood of competing causal events, and (3) the instability in the confession rates.[9] If we had (*and we do not*) rigorous empirical evidence that the confession rate in Salt Lake County before *Miranda* was 60 percent and that the confession rate in Salt Lake County today is 42 percent, we would still have incomplete proof of a *Miranda* effect. A conservative researcher would consider alternative explanations (often called confounding variables).[10] Salt Lake County in 1994 may be very different from Salt Lake County in 1965 in terms of demographics, police characteristics, residential patterns, and many other social and cultural variables.

For example, there has been a halting but persistent effort since roughly the time of *Miranda* to empower the disempowered in our society; this trend might, all by itself, explain why fewer suspects today cooperate with the police. The police have been the object of more skepticism and distrust since the Rodney King case; perhaps this would cause more suspects in 1994 to refuse to cooperate with the police.

Instability in confession rates is less of a problem if more than one study is done, with results that replicate each other. I will argue [later] that the Cassell-Hayman rate should be adjusted upward to 54 percent, putting the Salt Lake County rate close to the average of the usable post-*Miranda* rates: 64 percent (San Francisco Bay Area), 62 percent (Jackonsville), 42 percent (San Diego). The unadjusted Cassell-Hayman rate of 42 percent gives two high rates and two low ones. A range from 64 percent to 42 percent suggests either differences in research methods, or some of Schulhofer's explanations, perhaps variations in subject populations or police departments.

The variation in rates and existence of other plausible explanations for differences over time suggest a conservative approach to evaluating claims that a *Miranda* effect has been isolated. . . . [T]he best reading of all the data supports the steady-state theory.

*

Miranda has been the law for [more than] thirty years. Researchers do not have to rush to judgment; we do not have to accept evidence simply because it is the best available. Cassell and Hayman concede that their conclusions are "tentative,"[11] but a research judgment on *Miranda* should not be based on studies conducted by prosecutors, studies based on estimates rather than hard data, or casual assumptions about the comparability of other countries.

Nonetheless, I will accept the Cassell-Hayman challenge to render a judgment on the available evidence. We differ on three major points. The most important difference is picking the relevant group of suspects from which to compute the confession rate. Cassell and Hayman sometimes seem to insist that the apt comparison is the group of all suspects, including those who are not interrogated. The net effect of making this comparison is to count any decline in the interrogation rate as a *Miranda* effect on the confession rate.

To take a hypothetical example, assume all suspects were interrogated before *Miranda*, and half of them confessed; also assume that in 1994, only half the suspects were interrogated, and half of them confessed. The confession rate based on all suspects would have declined from 50 percent to 25 percent, while the confession rate based only on interrogated suspects would have remained steady at 50 percent.

Comparing the confession rate among all suspects would make sense if *Miranda* were responsible for the decline in the rate of interrogating suspects, but the only evidence that exists suggests quite the contrary. This is a critical difference because all of my comparisons use the success rate among suspects who are interrogated. . . .

Our second major difference is whether to count noncustodial interrogations. Though the pre-*Miranda* studies are a little murky on this point, the best reading is that most of them included only custodial interrogations. . . .

[Third,] I would classify as incriminating more of the Salt Lake County statements than Cassell and Hayman apparently do. . . . [D]ifferences in classification may explain quite a bit of the variation in the rates found by different studies.

*

Miranda can, of course, have two very different effects: one on suspects, and the other on police. Police might assume that guilty suspects will behave rationally and refuse to talk once they are told they have a right to remain silent. This assumption could easily lead police to interrogate fewer suspects. In checking for this effect, there are two separate questions: (1) Has the rate of interrogation declined? (2) How much of this reduction can be fairly attributed to *Miranda*?

The evidence is far from clear on both questions. Indeed, the Cassell-Hayman claim is quite modest on this issue: that their 1994 data "read in conjunction with older studies, support the hypothesis that questioning rates have declined somewhat since *Miranda*."[12] They do not claim that *Miranda* itself caused this decline, conceding that the data on this point are "quite limited." Only one of the declines they cite is statistically significant, and it occurred immediately after *Miranda*, when the police were presumably still adjusting their perceptions and methodology.

Despite being unable to prove that *Miranda* caused a decline in the interrogation rate, Cassell and Hayman still insist that the apt comparison is the success rate for the total universe of suspects because some of the pre-*Miranda* studies included suspects who were not questioned. I strongly disagree. Whatever the early studies did, no comparison is acceptable if it arbitrarily assigns to *Miranda* the decline in interrogation rates since 1966. This is precisely what the Cassell-Hayman comparison does. It must be rejected.

Moreover, intuition suggests that *Miranda* should have little effect on the rate of interrogation. Police have nothing to lose by attempting interrogation. If the suspect invokes *Miranda*, the police are no worse off than if they did not interrogate. It also seems likely that the decline in interrogation rates can be explained in large part by increased reliance on forensic evidence and the increased workload of urban police departments.

The conjecture of no *Miranda* effect on interrogation rates is borne out by the follow-up questioning in the Salt Lake County study as to why the interrogators did not question a suspect. In only two cases (4.9 percent of the [suspects not interrogated]) did the interrogator cite a "belief suspect would invoke *Miranda*." This finding hardly suggests an ongoing *Miranda* effect of significance in the police decision not to question suspects. These data suggest that *Miranda* would cause police not to question 1 percent of all suspects [2 of a total of 219 suspects].

While a 1 percent rate is not de minimis if applied to the universe of FBI Index crimes (as Cassell is wont to do),[13] it overstates the true effect. An interrogator who believes a confession necessary to solving an important case is unlikely to be moved by the possibility that the suspect might invoke *Miranda*. Thus, the 4.9 percent *Miranda* effect in the Salt Lake County data is likely a proxy for another category: the belief that the case is overwhelming and a confession unnecessary, which is the largest category of reasons in the Cassell and Hayman data [for not interrogating] other than unknown whereabouts.[14]

*

Cassell and Hayman compute the rate of successful questioning as 42.2 percent of all interrogations,[15] which is well below the range Cassell and Hayman use for the pre-*Miranda* studies and a bit below the range I use. But I will argue that this figure is artificially depressed by two flaws in the Cassell-Hayman interpretation of the data. The first flaw is their inclusion of noncustodial interrogations in the data set that they compare to the pre-*Miranda* studies. Of the total Cassell-Hayman interrogations, 30.1 percent were in noncustodial settings, where one would naturally expect the police to be less successful.[16] The Salt Lake County data confirm that noncustodial settings produce fewer successful interrogations (30.0 percent) than the custodial interrogations (56.9 percent).[17]

Including noncustodial interrogations in the data set is a flaw because the best reading of the pre-*Miranda* studies is that they involved only custodial interrogations.[18] . . .

Nor is it necessary, as Cassell and Hayman claim, for me to prove that all the pre-*Miranda* studies included only custodial interrogations. Many of the pre-*Miranda* studies are of inferior quality and should, on my conservative view, be disregarded. Moreover, the Cassell-Hayman argument on this point is internally inconsistent. They argue (to make a different point) that *Miranda* has increased the rate of noncustodial interrogations.[19] So even if they are right that some pre-*Miranda* studies included some noncustodial interrogations, these studies would include fewer than the Salt Lake County study (on their own argument). Thus, it seems clear to me, despite their continued insistence otherwise, that Cassell and Hayman are comparing apples to oranges when they compare a rate that includes 30.1 percent noncustodial interrogations to the pre-*Miranda* rates.

I will therefore adjust their rate to include only custodial interrogations. The Cassell-Hayman rate of 56.9 percent [resulting from this adjustment] must be adjusted further, however, to be useful. It must be adjusted downward and then (I will argue) upward.

The Salt Lake County figure for custodial interrogations must be adjusted downward because Cassell and Hayman do not include the *Miranda* invocations in their universe for the purpose of this calculation.[20] It is not clear why they include invocations to compute the overall confession rate but not the custodial rate. In any event, if invocations are considered an unsuccessful interrogation (what else could they be?), the Salt Lake County custodial confession rate is 48 percent.

Another adjustment seems necessary, though I freely admit that it is more controversial than the adjustment to include only custodial interrogations. Because not every response is incriminating, researchers are forced to draw a distinction between incriminating and nonincriminating statements. Different researchers will classify borderline statements differently; this is a problem with all *Miranda* studies.[21]

Variability in classification is an example of why we should err on the side of being conservative in addressing the *Miranda* empirical issue. The potential difference in researcher judgment on classifying statements makes it difficult to compare any two studies on the issue of confession rates. We need several studies, from which an average can be obtained. One effect of averaging several studies is to minimize variations in how researchers classify statements.

The Cassell-Hayman study methodology here is more problematic than most. They use a category of unsuccessful outcomes called "denial with explanation." The test they use to decide whether a statement is "incriminating" (and thus more than merely an "explanation") is whether the statement had a "primary import" to "assist police in proving their case." I think that is the wrong test. It is not the test used by at least one of the pre-*Miranda* studies, and it is narrower than the *Miranda* Court's use of "self-incrimination."

The question the Court faced in *Miranda* was the coercive atmosphere of police-dominated interrogation that can operate to produce a wide range of responses in terms of "degrees of incrimination."[22] The Court refused to draw a distinction, for suppression purposes, between an inculpatory statement and one that was ostensibly exculpatory: "In fact, statements merely intended to be exculpatory by the defendant are often used to impeach his testimony at trial or to demonstrate untruths in the statement given under interrogation and thus to prove guilt by implication."[23]

The Court's focus is the right one: The question is not whether the statement proves immediately helpful to the police, but whether it potentially gives the prosecutor evidence to introduce if the case goes to trial. That is the right focus because the existence of the impeachment evidence will also be part of the calculus in the vast majority of cases that end in a plea bargain.

*

Thus, on my reading of the data, the Cassell-Hayman confession rate is artificially low when compared with the pre-*Miranda* studies. I do not know how many of the "denial with explanation" cases should be changed to "incriminating" statements. I found twelve candidates plus some number of stolen car suspects out of a universe of seventeen examples plus an [undisclosed] number of suspects charged with stealing vehicles and burglary/trespassing. This ratio suggests switching as many as two-thirds of the "denial with explanation" outcomes from unsuccessful to successful, but [to be conservative] I assume instead that one-third of the "denial with explanation" statements are incriminating by the standard of the pre-*Miranda* studies.

I would then apply my one-third adjustment to the number of unsuccessful custodial interrogations, reducing the number of unsuccessful outcomes and increasing the number of successful outcomes. Indulging

Table 1. Cassell-Hayman Salt Lake County Data as Reported and as Adjusted

Sample: 219 samples (46 not questioned—13 volunteered incriminating statements); 173 suspects questioned (custodial and noncustodial)

Successful	Unsuccessful	Success Rate
73	79 + 21 invocations = 100	42%

Adjustment 1: There were 52 noncustodial interrogations and 121 custodial interrogations. Removing the noncustodial interrogations from the sample leaves the following breakdown:

Successful	Unsuccessful	Success Rate
58	44 + 19 invocations = 63	48%

Adjustment 2: One-half of unsuccessful interrogations are classified as "denial with explanation." If one-third of these are incorrectly classified, then one-sixth of the unsuccessful interrogations (44) should be reclassified as successful (raw number 7).

Successful	Unsuccessful	Success Rate
65	37 + 19 invocations = 56	54%

this assumption produces a custodial confession rate of 54 percent. The Cassell-Hayman data and my adjustments can be displayed in tabular form, as follows:

Using the adjusted rate, the Salt Lake County data look remarkably like the pre-*Miranda* studies. . . . Cassell and Hayman offer a rough range for the pre-*Miranda* studies of 55–60 percent, while I would use a range of 45–53 percent. The adjusted Cassell-Hayman rate is close to the bottom of their pre-*Miranda* range and just over the top of mine.

If the adjustments in this section are reasonable, the Cassell-Hayman data require accepting the null hypothesis: *Miranda* has had no effect on confession rates. But even if my adjustments are rejected, Cassell and Hayman cannot rely on just their study. To avoid idiosyncracies in classifications, research methodology, and subject populations, we should average rates from as many jurisdictions as possible.

[In an omitted subpart, Thomas concludes that the average confession rate in the usable post-*Miranda* studes is 52–55 percent, depending on the best reading of the Salt Lake County data. This range is consistent with the pre-*Miranda* range.—Eds.]

*

The question of how often suspects invoke their *Miranda* rights is subsumed within the question of overall effect on confession rates. But I treat it separately as a way of bringing together my arguments. Cassell and Hayman conclude that 12.1 percent of felony suspects "who were questioned invoked their rights before police were successful in interrogation."[24] Two observations can be made about this figure. First, if the *Miranda* dissenters and the police in 1966 had been told that the effect of *Miranda* would be limited to 12.1 percent of felony suspects, they would have cheered in relief. Thus, while significant, 12.1 percent is hardly crippling to the law enforcement enterprise.

But another observation must be made: There is no way to credit *Miranda* with all of that 12.1 percent. Some suspects refused to cooperate with police prior to *Miranda*. The 12.1 percent who invoke their rights includes that category of suspects, now given an easier way to refuse to cooperate. On this point, though, Cassell and Hayman can find support among *Miranda*'s defenders. If *Miranda* is to have any of the effects envisioned by its supporters (reduce pressure in the interrogation room, level the playing field, increase equality among suspects), it simply must cause more invocations. Otherwise, *Miranda* is (as some cynics have charged) merely about symbolism and appearances. Thus, *Miranda* supporters should cheer an increase in invocations. . . .

The available data thus seem to demonstrate that more suspects invoke their right to remain silent, and the rate of confessions is roughly the same. This divergence supports my steady-state theory: *Miranda* encourages some suspects not to talk and encourages others to talk too much. It is possible that, in the pre-*Miranda* era, fewer suspects refused to talk but more suspects gave terse answers. Perhaps more suspects refuse to talk today, but those who do talk have a *Miranda*-created incentive to tell a fuller story. The *Miranda* warnings might make suspects believe they can avoid being prosecuted only if they tell a story close enough to the truth that the police will be fooled into letting them go. [Jacksonville and San Diego data show,] for example, more robbery suspects admitted being at the scene of the crime than gave an outright confession.[25]

. . . My best guess is still that *Miranda* has roughly offsetting effects; the new data are consistent with my conjecture. As I remain conservative in my research outlook, I make no claim that I have demonstrated the truth of my "steady-state" theory of confessions. But nothing in the old studies or the new ones provides sufficient evidence to accept the hypothesis that *Miranda* has depressed the rate of confessions.

*

Future studies might produce evidence that would persuade even a cautious researcher of a *Miranda* effect that reduces confession rates. We would then have to deal with the difficult ethical question posed by Fred Inbau, Joseph Grano, Paul Cassell, and Bret Hayman (among others): Is the cost of *Miranda* worth the benefits? . . .

[T]his is a more difficult ethical question than has been generally assumed in the last few years. But, with all respect to Cassell and Hayman, we are nowhere near the point where that question is relevant. We do not have enough evidence to accept the hypothesis that *Miranda* has an effect. Reaching any decision on the status of *Miranda* without better empirical evidence is roughly like having to decide whether you need surgery before knowing whether you are sick.

Indeed, I have argued in this response that the best reading of the new data is no net effect. . . .

I thus agree with Paul Cassell and Bret Hayman that we need more (and better) evidence. I disagree that the absence of evidence should be construed against the *Miranda* supporters.[26] We should understand how *Miranda* operates before we decide how to improve or whether to abandon it. It is not only supporters of *Miranda* who have an obligation to uncover this evidence.

I also mostly disagree with Cassell and Hayman when they claim that *Miranda* has made it impossible to obtain the kind of evidence we need to learn about confessions. The Leo study and the Cassell-Hayman study are rich sources of information.

*

[A]dditional studies could determine whether the Cassell-Hayman unadjusted 42 percent or my adjusted 54 percent is a better estimate of police success at interrogation throughout the nation. We would still be left without agreement as to the pre-*Miranda* rate. But some outcomes for the current rate would make the debate over the historical rate pointless. If the nationwide rate came in at 40 percent, it would seem quite likely that this is lower than the pre-*Miranda* rate. If the nationwide rate came in at 60 percent, the converse would seem likely.

Thus, we need good data from several jurisdictions as to the current rate. We also need to be as clear as possible about what constitutes an incriminating statement and how the pre-*Miranda* researchers classified statements. Hopefully, the Leo and Cassell-Hayman studies are just the first of a series of efforts to understand not only *Miranda*'s effects but also the process of police interrogation generally.

NOTES

1. Paul Cassell & Bret Hayman, *Police Interrogation in the 1990s: An Empirical Study of the Effects of* Miranda, 43 UCLA L. Rev. 839 (1996) [excerpted in chap. 16—Eds.].

2. *Id.*

3. *See* George C. Thomas III, *Is* Miranda *a Real World Failure? A Plea for More (and Better) Empirical Evidence*, 43 UCLA L. Rev. 825 (1996).

4. *Id.*

5. Cassell & Hayman, *supra* note 1, at 917.

6. *Id.* at 872–73.

7. Paul Cassell, Miranda's *Social Costs: An Empirical Reassessment*, 90 Nw. U. L. Rev. 459 (1996) [excerpted in chap. 13—Eds.].

8. Yale Kamisar, *How to Use, Abuse—and Fight Back with—Crime Statistics*, 25 Okla. L. Rev. 239, 239 (1972) (quoting criminologist Lloyd Ohlin).

9. Stephen J. Schulhofer, Miranda's *Practical Effect: Substantial Benefits and Vanishingly Small Social Costs*, 90 Nw. U. L. Rev. 500 (1996) [excerpted in chap. 14—Eds.].

10. See, e.g., Kamisar, *supra* note 8, at 242–50. For a discussion of confounding variables in the context of a legislative change designed to reduce the crime rate, see George C. Thomas III & David Edelman, *An Evaluation of Conservative Crime Control Theology*, 63 Notre Dame L. Rev. 123, 133–40 (1988).

11. Cassell & Hayman, *supra* Note 1, at 921.

12. *Id.* at 854.

13. Cassell, *supra* note 7, at 438–40.

14. Cassell & Hayman, *supra* note 1, at 858.

15. *Id.*

16. *Id.* at 882–83.

17. *Id.*

18. *See* Richard H. Seeburger & R. Stanton Wettick, Jr., Miranda *in Pittsburgh—A Statistical Study*, 29 U. Pitt. L. Rev. 1, 7 (1967); see also Richard Medalie et al., *Custodial Police Interrogation in Our Nation's Capital: The Attempt to Implement* Miranda, 66 Mich. L. Rev. 1351 (1968); James W. Witt, *Non-Coercive Interrogation and the Administration of Criminal Justice: The Impact of* Miranda *on Policy Effectuality*, 64 J. Crim. L. & Criminology 320, 323 (1973).

19. Cassell & Hayman, *supra* note 1, at 881.

20. *Id.* at 883 n.216.

21. See Thomas, *supra* note 3, at 831–32.

22. Miranda v. Arizona, 384 U.S. 436, 476 (1966) [excerpted in chap. 3—Eds.].

23. *Id.* at 477.

24. Cassell & Hayman, *supra* note 1, at 860.

25. Floyd Feeney et al., Arrests without Conviction: How Often They Occur and Why 142, Table 15-2 (1983).

26. Cassell & Hayman, *supra* note 1, at 922.

IV

The Future
of *Miranda*:
Dilemmas
and Prospects
for Change

The *Miranda* decision remains a source of controversy and spirited debate more than thirty years after it was decided. Of course, *Miranda* is in many ways a unique Supreme Court decision. To begin with, *Miranda* did not follow the pattern of the typical appellate court decision—i.e., the application of legal principles and precedents to a set of facts. Instead, the Court first reviewed the history of the privilege against self-incrimination, then criticized contemporary police interrogation training manuals, and finally announced a set of code-like warnings and waiver requirements—all before reviewing the specific facts of the cases at hand and applying the relevant law. Perhaps more significant than its "legislative quality"[1] is that *Miranda* broke with earlier doctrine and created a new set of rights based on the Fifth Amendment privilege against self-incrimination. Yet its own relationship to the Fifth Amendment remains strained. The Fifth Amendment incrimination clause appears to support neither an affirmative right to silence nor the assertion that police interrogation is inherently coercive. Even more curiously, the rights the *Miranda* Court so confidently announced later turned out merely to be prophylactic safeguards that protect the Fifth Amendment rights rather than constitutional rights themselves.[2] Yet regardless of its innovation or confusion, *Miranda* remains the most famous criminal law case the U.S. Supreme Court has ever decided,[3] and the *Mtranda* warnings may be the most famous words the Court has ever written.

As the earlier chapters have made clear, *Miranda* has come under attack primarily on two grounds: first, that it is doctrinally unsound or illegitimate, and second, that it has impeded law enforcement. Joseph Grano has argued persuasively that *Miranda*'s break with earlier precedent is not supported by the Fifth Amendment. The privilege against self-incrimination provides a suspect only with a right to refuse to answer questions, not with a right to terminate questioning or to obtain counsel during interrogation. In other words, the Fifth Amendment should not be interpreted to prevent police from questioning silent defendants nor should it prevent prosecutors at trial from drawing adverse inferences from a suspect's custodial silence. Moreover, argues Grano, if the *Miranda* warnings are merely prophylactic safeguards, rather than constitutional rights, then the Supreme Court does not have the authority to impose the *Miranda* warnings on the states.[4] As we saw in Chapter 13, Paul Cassell argues that because *Miranda* rests on a pragmatic foundation, its benefits must outweigh its costs for it to remain constitutionally justified. Yet according to Cassell, the truth is more nearly the opposite: *Miranda* has caused considerable harm (i.e., lost confessions and convictions) to law enforcement without providing any corresponding benefits.[5] Both Grano and Cassell believe that *Miranda* threatens the very institution of police interrogation and thus must be overruled.

Yet as it enters its fourth decade, *Miranda* seems more secure than ever. Despite *Miranda*'s doctrinal tensions and contradictions, a conservative Supreme Court appears reluctant to attack its foundations or significantly modify it. Instead, the current Court seems to have adopted the attitude former Chief Justice Warren Burger expressed more than fifteen years ago: "The meaning of *Miranda* has become reasonably clear and law enforcement practices have adjusted to its strictures; I would neither overrule *Miranda*, disparage it, nor extend it at this late date."[6] At the same time, the scholarly community—with the notable exceptions of Cassell and Grano—also seems largely to have complacently accepted *Miranda*. Despite the new and important empirical research by Cassell, Bret Hayman, and Richard Leo, the conventional wisdom of the earlier impact studies seems undisturbed: Most academics appear still to believe that police almost always comply with the letter of *Miranda* and that *Miranda*, for all its symbolism, still does not seriously undermine police apprehension and conviction of suspects. And, perhaps most significantly, police, prosecutors, and judges appear—from the best available empirical evidence—to have adapted to

Miranda and accepted its strictures.[7] Although Attorney General Edwin Meese in the mid-1980s called for overruling *Miranda*, no major police or prosecutor organizations joined his efforts; rather, many police chiefs hailed the virtues of *Miranda* and no longer question its legitimacy.[8] Indeed, the majority of police, prosecutors, and judges appear to support *Miranda* and believe that it does not significantly impede effective police investigation and prosecution of crime.[9]

Rather than focusing on *Miranda*'s past, this section invites readers to consider its future. Although they are inextricably connected, *Miranda*'s future may not be entirely dependent on its past. There is nothing final or absolute about *Miranda*; its doctrinal meaning and practical application—however settled they may appear at present—are always open to the possibility of change. Indeed, the Warren Court recognized in *Miranda* that there were other ways to regulate custodial questioning and encouraged states and the federal government to devise alternative schemes. But more fundamentally, as Albert Alschuler has pointed out, "no one really knows what *Miranda* means."[10] That is to say, although it may appear more secure than ever, *Miranda*'s ambiguities, tensions, and contradictions leave it vulnerable to doctrinal reinterpretation, while its decidedly liberal cast leaves it vulnerable to legislative reform— especially as crime control becomes increasingly politicized in America. The future of *Miranda* is as much a political question as a legal one.

If its meaning and future remain unclear as we approach the twenty-first century, we can at least identify and analyze *Miranda*'s future possibilities: It may be overruled, strengthened, weakened (but not eliminated) or retained more or less in its present form. Readers should consider the desirability and viability of each of these possibilities as they read the following chapters. Whatever its ultimate outcome, the *Miranda* debate will continue because it raises many of the most fundamental and controversial questions of criminal justice: What goals should the criminal justice system be designed to serve? How should we balance the interests of the state and of the accused to achieve such goals? More specifically, how should we prioritize our concerns for discovering truth, efficiently processing cases, maintaining fair procedures, preventing police misconduct, safeguarding constitutional rights, and protecting society from crime? At root, the *Miranda* debate turns on the answers we provide to these questions.

In Chapters 18 and 19, Joseph Grano and Yale Kamisar—conservative critic and liberal defender of *Miranda*, respectively—debate the Department of Justice's 1986 report recommending the abolition of

Miranda (excerpted in Chapter 7). This exchange is as much about *Miranda*'s past and present as about *Miranda*'s future. Grano argues that the old world of criminal procedure had more virtues than flaws and invites us to imagine a new world of criminal procedure without *Miranda*. Grano specifically asks us to evaluate the ends that criminal procedure should serve and, in particular, the importance of truth discovery relative to other goals. If this should be the primary goal of the criminal justice system, argues Grano, then *Miranda* "represents the wrong road taken" and should be overruled. Defending *Miranda*, Kamisar counterargues that the search for truth is not the only goal of criminal procedure and that sometimes it may reasonably be subordinated to other goals, such as the protection of constitutional rights. Kamisar also invites us to reconsider the old world of criminal procedure in light of Grano's criticisms, suggesting that the due process voluntariness test, like *Miranda*, was judicially created and may also impede the search for the truth. Kamisar concludes by praising *Miranda* and asking us to consider what overruling it would entail.

In Chapters 20–22, Richard Leo, Janet Ainsworth, and Phillip Johnson call attention to what they perceive—from very different vantage points—as *Miranda*'s ongoing failures.

In Chapter 20, Richard Leo begins by pointing out that psychologically induced false confessions—though they may seem counter-intuitive, irrational, and unlikely—are, in fact, not uncommon. Although he has pointed out the benefits of *Miranda* elsewhere,[12] here Leo chides *Miranda* for offering little or no protection against the eliciting of false confessions from innocent suspects or the admission of them into evidence. Perhaps *Miranda* has even worsened the problem by diverting attention away from the risk of wrongful convictions based on false confessions. Criticizing the constitutional law governing confessions more generally for placing too much importance on the procedural fairness of the interrogation process and too little importance on the substantive truthfulness of confession statements, Leo proposes that confessions should not be admissible into evidence at trial unless they meet a reasonable standard of reliability. Though he does not call for *Miranda*'s abolition, Leo's arguments here parallel Joseph Grano's emphasis on the importance of truth discovery in the criminal process.

In Chapter 21, Janet Ainsworth argues that the rule about how to invoke *Miranda* is couched in the language of the powerful in our society (the language of white males). The invocation rule requires direct, assertive speech on the part of the suspect—suspects must unambiguously request counsel before the police are required to cease interrogation.[11] As Ainsworth puts it, "From a feminist perspective, the characteristically masculine preference for assertive speech can be seen as simply one instance of a more generalized masculine preference for assertive behavior."

Ainsworth relies on linguistic research to show that women and minorities typically use less direct, more hedged forms of request when dealing with authority figures. For example, someone in an inferior position might say, "Maybe I need a lawyer," or ask the detective whether she should get one, even though she unambiguously wants one, thereby making it less likely that authority figures will be angered by her request. But hedged speech patterns make it less likely that requests for counsel will be honored when they come from the very groups the *Miranda* Court was seeking to assist—suspects who lack the ability to withstand the pressure of custodial interrogation.

This critique leads Ainsworth to question why the law should require unambiguous request for counsel. One alternative is to make a case-by-case determination of whether each suspect meant to request counsel. But Ainsworth proposes a more radical solution and one that is easier to administer. "Instead of requiring the suspect to confront police by asserting her rights, why not automatically provide arrested suspects with counsel to be consulted before interrogation begins?" At present, the Court is unlikely to adopt the Ainsworth global right to counsel. Thus, suspects must face police interrogation alone when deciding whether to waive *Miranda* rights and, more importantly, when answering questions after waiving.

As mentioned above, the *Miranda* Court acknowledged the possibility of regulating police interrogation through nonjudicial means and invited states and the federal government to devise legislative alternatives to *Miranda* so long as they protected the same underlying rights. Taking this invitation seriously, Phillip Johnson in Chapter 22 proposes a hypothetical statute to replace the *Miranda* doctrine. Before evaluating the content of Johnson's hypothetical legislation, readers should ponder whether (and how) comprehensive legislation might be superior to piecemeal judicial decisionmaking in criminal procedure. Johnson's hypothetical statute describes the *Miranda* decision as internally inconsistent and as creating a body of case law that has failed to curb police abuses just as it has failed to recognize the legitimate role of interrogation in criminal investigation. Johnson proposes a number of statutory provisions that seek to strike a more desirable balance between these competing imperatives. Readers should evaluate the extent to which this hypothetical statute succeeds at crafting such a balance. Readers should also notice that Johnson's hypothetical statute restricts the rights enumerated in *Miranda* by modifying the warning structure, withdrawing the right to the assistance of counsel until a suspect is arraigned on criminal charges, and calling for alternative remedies to the exclusionary rule. At the same time, Johnson's hypothetical statute creates specific rights not found in *Miranda* by setting explicit limits on the length of permissible interrogation, specifying permissible and impermissible interrogation techniques, and proposing recording requirements.

In Chapter 23, William Geller reports findings from his comprehensive study of the effects of videotaping on interrogation and confessions. Though various commentators have recommended electronic recording of interrogation over the years,[13] only recently has it received sustained attention from the legal and scholarly communities. In 1985, the Supreme Court of Alaska held that substantive due process requires police to record interrogations,[14] and in 1994 the Supreme Court of Minnesota (relying on its supervisory powers) ruled that police must electronically record custodial interrogations when feasible.[15] Yet many state appellate and supreme courts have declined to mandate recording requirements.[16] At the same time, however, an increasing number of police departments have voluntarily implemented their own recording policies. As Geller points out, a majority of police, prosecutors, defense attorneys, and judges all support the recording of interrogations. In addition, the scholarly community—from *Miranda*'s most vocal critics to its most ardent defenders—almost unanimously endorse taping requirements. Readers should consider, first, whether the benefits of videotaping outweigh its costs and, second, whether videotaping should be a supplement to,[17] or a replacement for,[18] *Miranda* warning and waiver requirements.

Finally, in Chapter 24 George Thomas asks us to consider the justifications for *Miranda* as we approach the twenty-first century. Whether *Miranda* is ethically supportable, argues Thomas, depends on its empirical consequences. Thomas identifies four possible outcomes: (1) that *Miranda* may cause fewer suspects to confess, (2) that *Miranda* may not change the behavior of suspects, (3) that *Miranda* may—as Thomas's "steady-state" hypothesis predicts (see Chapter 17)—have roughly offsetting effects that encourage some suspects to answer questions while discouraging others from cooperating with police, and (4) that *Miranda* may encourage more suspects to confess. By predicating *Miranda*'s justification on its empirical consequences, Thomas departs from the doctrinally oriented approaches of most legal scholars and judges. Just as Thomas identifies several possible empirical outcomes, there are several possible normative outcomes: (1) that *Miranda* may be justifiable whatever its empirical effect (on a theory of *stare decisis* or Fifth Amendment jurisprudence, for example), (2) that *Miranda* may be unjustifiable regardless of its empirical effect (because it is unprincipled or doctrinally illegitimate or because its empirical effect cannot be adequately measured, for example), and (3) that, depending on its empirical effects, *Miranda* may be ethically justifiable up to a point. Even if we accept Thomas's empirical framework, however, we still have no good theory to tell us how to weigh *Miranda*'s costs and benefits (assuming, for the moment, that they are commensurable). Yet if we reject Thomas's empirical framework, we are left merely with intuition and speculation. Neither outcome is ideal, but both remind us of *Miranda*'s inherent empirical and normative ambiguity. As Thomas concludes in Chapter 24, we do not know whether the twenty-first century will be "a world without *Miranda*." But the most fundamental questions animating *Miranda*'s past remain the most fundamental ones of its future. According to which values and considerations shall *Miranda*'s fate be decided?

NOTES

1. Joseph D. Grano, Confessions, Truth and the Law 173 (1993).

2. Michigan v. Tucker, 417 U.S. 433 (1974).

3. Jethro K. Lieberman, Milestones vii (1976).

4. See Grano, *supra* note 1.

5. Paul G. Cassell, *Miranda's Social Costs: An Empirical Reassessment*, 90 Nw. U. L. Rev. 387–499 (1996).

6. Rhode Island v. Innis, 446 U.S. 291 (1980).

7. See Richard A. Leo, *The Impact of* Miranda *Revisited*, 86 J. Crom. L. & Criminology, 621–92 (1996).

8. See Patrick Malone, *You Have the Right to Remain Silent*: Miranda *After Twenty Years*," American Scholar, 1986, at 367–80; Tamar Jacoby, *Fighting Crime by the Rules*, Newsweek, July 1988, at 53; Eduardo Paz-Martinez, *Police Chiefs Defend* Miranda *Decision against Meese Threats*, Boston Globe, Feb. 5, 1987.

9. American Bar Association, Criminal Justice in Crisis (1988).

10. Albert Alschuler, *A Peculiar Privilege in Historical Perspective: The Right to Remain Silent*, 94 Mich. L. Rev. 2629 (1996).

11. Davis v. United States, 512 U.S. 452 (1994). Though *Davis* had not been decided when Ainsworth published her article, the *Davis* "unambiguous" rule was the majority position of the lower courts.

12. See Leo *supra* note 7.

13. See, e.g., Roscoe Pound, *Legal Interrogation of Pesons Accused or Suspected of Crime*, 24 J. Crim. L., Criminology & Police Science 1014–18 (1934); Yale Kamisar, Police Interrogation and Confessions: Essays in Law and Policy (1980); Glanville Williams, *The Authentication of Statements to Police*, 1 Crim. L. Rev. 1–23 (1979).

14. Stephan v. State, 711 P.2d 1156 (Alaska 1985).

15. State v. Scales, 518 N.W.2d 587 (Minn. 1994).

16. See People v. Raibon, 843 P.2d 46 (Colo. Ct. App. 1992); Commonwealth v. Fryar, 414 Mass. 732 (1993); State v. Buzzell, 617 A.2d 1016 (Me. 1992); Williams v. State, 522 So. 2d 201 (Miss. 1988); Jimenez v. State, 105 Nev. 337 (1989); State v. James, 858 P.2d 1012 (Utah App. 1993); State v. Spurgeon, 63 Wash. App. 503 (1991); State v. Rhoades, 119 Idaho 594 (1991); State v. Gordon, 149 Vt. 602 (1988).

17. See Stephen Schulhofer, Miranda's *Practical Effect: Substantial Benefits and Vanishingly Small Social Costs*, 90 Nw. U. L. Rev. 556–60 (1996).

18. See Cassell, *supra* note 5, at 486–92.

18

The Changed
and Changing World
of Constitutional
Criminal Procedure:
The Contribution
of the Department
of Justice's Office
of Legal Policy
(1990)
•

JOSEPH D. GRANO

I. Remembering the Past of Criminal Procedure

It has been disturbing for me, as I am sure it has been for other law
teachers similarly situated, to realize that although I am only in my
forty-sixth year, the students I teach share in their consciousness few
of the historical experiences that helped to define my life. Whether it be
the election of the first Roman Catholic president, the political assassi-
nations of the sixties, the civil rights marches, the riots in the streets,
the Chicago-7 trial, the passage of the Civil Rights Act of 1964 and the
Voting Rights Act of 1965, the Cuban missile crisis, the Goldwater campaign, the first human landing on the moon, the Vietnam War, or increasingly even the Watergate crisis and the impeachment proceedings
against President Nixon, the events that are indelibly pressed in my consciousness—and that help put flesh on many of the cases I teach—are
little more than cold history to my students. So it is with criminal procedure. When I graduated from high school in 1961, the "old world" of
criminal procedure still existed, albeit in its waning days; when I graduated from law school in 1968, circa the time most of today's first-year
law students were arriving on the scene, the "new world" had fully dis-

lodged the old. Indeed, the force of the new world's revolutionary impetus already had crested.

Some of the change that the criminal procedure revolution effected was for the better, but much of it, at least as some of us see it, was decidedly for the worse. My students, however, cannot make the comparison; to them the old world has no flesh, and the new world is all they know. For those to whom a world without *Miranda* is as antiquarian as a world without satellites or videocassette recorders, the question of whether we made wrong choices, or of whether we should re-embrace some of what we so precipitously and often casually discarded, does not call for serious analysis.

Crooker v. California[1] and *Cicenia v. LaGay*,[2] decided together a mere thirty years ago, illustrate the old world. The Supreme Court upheld the admissibility of confessions in both of these cases even though the police had denied the suspects' requests to consult with counsel; indeed, in *Cicenia*, the police refused to permit the suspect's lawyer to consult with his client even though the lawyer was present at the station. Acknowledging that successful interrogation was likely to affect adversely the defendant's chances at trial, the *Crooker* Court nevertheless concluded that recognition of a right to counsel during police interrogation would have a "devastating effect on enforcement of criminal law, for it would effectively preclude police questioning—*fair as well as unfair.*"[3] Repeating much the same argument in *Cicenia*, the Court added that a right to counsel during police interrogation required an interpretation of the Fourteenth Amendment that was "foreign both to the spirit in which it was conceived and the way in which it has been implemented by this Court."[4] A different world.

I always assign my students the portion of the one page in the casebook devoted to the majority opinions in *Crooker* and *Cicenia*. I not only assign this page; I pause over it in class because it provides a glimpse, however inadequate, of the world that the students do not know and of its underlying thinking. When my students are incredulous to learn that I support removing counsel, both retained and appointed, from the interrogation room, I again refer to these cases to demonstrate that the criminal justice system not so long ago proceeded from quite different assumptions, that we did have choices along the way, and that today's way of thinking—the students' axiomatic way of thinking—was not predestined to prevail. . . .

II. The Contribution of the Office
of Legal Policy to the Effort to Achieve Reform

Contrary to any suggestion about a conservative trend in Supreme Court cases, criminal procedure, though once again changing, is not changing "fast." Indeed, it is noteworthy that most of the Warren Court's criminal procedure revolution has remained in place. . . . Much of the Supreme Court's change in direction during the past twenty years has involved no more than a refusal to extend Warren Court rulings. In fairness, a considerable amount of chipping away at existing doctrine also has occurred, but most of the primary precedent remains in place, waiting in repose for a Court with an inclination to repair the minor damage and reclaim the Warren Court's torch. Overruled cases are difficult, though by no means impossible, to disinter, but cases that merely distinguish previous cases, especially when done unconvincingly, are themselves easy to distinguish away. The Warren Court achieved revolutionary change in less than one decade; twenty years of supposedly "conservative" jurisprudence, the wails of the academy notwithstanding, have produced nothing even remotely comparable. . . .

The first step in any fundamental reexamination of the existing order should involve an evaluation of the importance of truth discovery relative to other goals the system might have. Proceeding from the premise that "the criminal justice system must be devoted to discovering the truth," the [Justice Department's Office of Legal Policy] Truth in Criminal Justice Series was prompted by "grave concern" that "[o]ver the past thirty years . . . a variety of new rules have emerged that impede the discovery of reliable evidence at the investigative stages of the criminal justice process and that require the concealment of relevant facts at trial."[5] This emphasis on truth as the primary goal of the criminal justice system recalls an earlier day when such a premise was virtually unassailable. Roscoe Pound, for example, did not risk ridicule when he stressed early in the century the primary importance of truth as a goal of procedural rules in general. . . .

To say that discovery of truth must be primary is not to say that it must be the only desideratum. As Professor Mirjan Damaska has indicated, even an "extreme inquisitorial" system must establish a balance between efficiency and other goals.[6] If discovery of truth is the primary goal, however, the rules of procedure will sacrifice truth only when necessary to accomplish other goals of overriding importance. Too often, though, the American system, with the endorsement of its lawyers, seems willing to sacrifice truth for ends that are not compelling and when the necessity of sacrificing truth to accomplish such ends is little more than speculative.

Moreover, many American lawyers seem willing to support the view that prosecution should be made difficult as an end in itself. I frequently have heard arguments, for example, that discovery from the defendant is "unfair," even if it is perfectly constitutional, because it facilitates the prosecutor's task of proving the defendant's guilt. I would have thought that proving the defendant's guilt was precisely the goal, at least absent a serious concern about convicting the innocent, condoning or encouraging official misconduct, countenancing violations of the defendant's dignity, or encouraging some other evil of comparable gravity. Apparently, however, a view has taken hold that facilitating the discovery of truth is itself an evil, even when these other concerns are not present. Purging the influence of such misguided thinking from our system is a necessary first step to accomplishing serious reform. By focusing our attention where it should be focused first, the Truth in Criminal Justice Series hopefully will increase the likelihood of expurgation.

The first [Department of Justice] Report in the Series—the one that has received the most attention—concerns the law of pretrial interrogation. [See Chapter 7.—Eds.] This Report elaborates upon the thesis that *Miranda*'s rules "impede the search for truth by conditioning inquiry, no matter how brief and restrained, on a suspect's consent to be questioned, and by excluding a suspect's statements at trial, though fully voluntary and reliable."[7] Of course, if the Constitution actually required either of these impediments, the sacrifice of truth would have to be accepted as necessary to further the compelling goal of constitutional compliance. The Report properly observes, however, that the Supreme Court consistently has taken the view that *Miranda*'s safeguards are only "prophylactic"—that the prosecution may violate *Miranda*'s rules without actually violating the Fifth Amendment. The Report weighs truth against the values that *Miranda*'s prophylactic rules purport to serve and argues, quite persuasively in my view, that *Miranda* represents the wrong road taken. . . .

[T]he Report views *Miranda* as a "decision without a past" and predicts, more controversially, that it also is a "decision without a future."[8] It is true, as the Report maintains, that the "Supreme Court has rejected the doctrinal basis of *Miranda*, and has no personal stake in perpetuating its particular system of rules."[9] Nevertheless, a philosophical tension exists in the Supreme Court's cases, and until this tension is conclusively resolved, it cannot be stated with certainty that *Miranda* does not reflect the wave of the future.

The tension can best be illustrated by juxtaposing passages from two quite dissimilar Supreme Court opinions. The first set of passages, taken from *Escobedo v. Illinois*, reflects the thinking that underlies *Miranda* and the Warren Court's approach to police interrogation in general: . . .

> The rule sought by the State . . . would make the trial no more than an appeal from the interrogation; and the "right to use counsel at the formal trial [would be] a very hollow thing [if], for all practical purposes, the conviction is already assured by pretrial examination." "One can imagine a cynical prosecutor saying: 'Let them have the most illustrious counsel, now. They can't escape the noose. There is nothing counsel can do for them at the trial.'"
>
> It is argued that if the right to counsel is afforded prior to indictment, the number of confessions obtained by the police will diminish significantly. . . . This argument, of course, cuts two ways. The fact that many confessions are obtained . . . points up its critical nature as a "stage when legal aid and advice" are surely needed. . . .
>
> We have learned the lesson of history . . . that a system of criminal law enforcement which comes to depend on the "confession" will, in the long run, be less reliable and more subject to abuses than a system which depends on extrinsic evidence independently secured through skillful investigation.[10]

The second set of passages, taken from *Moran v. Burbine*, reflect the thinking of the recent cases that have been chipping away at *Miranda*:

> No doubt the additional information [that a lawyer, obtained by the suspect's sister, had called the police station] would have been useful to respondent; perhaps even it might have affected his decision to confess. But we have never read the Constitution to require that the police supply a suspect with a flow of information to help him calibrate his self-interest in deciding whether to speak or stand by his rights.[11]

Later in the same opinion, the Court added:

> "[T]he need for police questioning as a tool for effective enforcement of criminal laws" cannot be doubted. Admissions of guilt are more than merely "desirable"; they are essential to society's compelling interest in finding, convicting, and punishing those who violate the law. . . . [A] rule requiring the police to inform the suspect of an attorney's efforts to con-

tact him would contribute to the protection of the Fifth Amendment privilege only incidentally, if at all. This minimal benefit, however, would come at a substantial cost to society's legitimate and substantial interest in securing admissions of guilt.[12]

The contradictory premises in these two cases are apparent. What deserves emphasis, however, is that *Miranda* and its progeny . . . are essentially dependent upon the thinking reflected in *Escobedo*, while the Court's recent limitations . . . in this area are essentially dependent upon the thinking reflected in *Burbine*. "[W]hat we really have is a Court that pays homage to cases that challenge the legitimacy of police interrogation but that protects police interrogation from those very same cases."[13] In Professor H. Richard Uviller's words, "[h]aving taken us to the very edge of a confessionless abyss . . . the Court swerved, unable in the crunch to renounce altogether the product of the station house 'inquisition.'"[14]

As long as these incompatible philosophical premises co-exist in the case law, albeit in an unstable equilibrium, the Court always will have a choice between the two. For this reason, the possibility cannot be dismissed that a future Court will resolve the conflict by swerving again, this time in the direction of taking *Miranda* seriously. It is precisely because of the possibility that *Miranda* may be a decision with a future—one far more frightening than its past—that the Office of Legal Policy's invitation to consider first principles is so vital.

*

III. Contemplating the Future of Criminal Procedure

The world of constitutional criminal procedure would be quite different were the reforms proposed by the Office of Legal Policy to be adopted. The new world would be one without *Miranda*. . . . It would be a world in which comment upon the defendant's failure to testify would be permissible and in which the rules of evidence would aim primarily at the discovery of truth.

Those who can see only the existing world are bound to decry the Office of Legal Policy proposals as frightening, extreme, and out of the mainstream. Others, however, may see in much of the proposed new world the good features, but not the bad, of the pre-1960s world, features that too hastily were discarded in the headlong pursuit of a vision that the Constitution did not impose and that the people did not, and still do not, share. For those who agree with the public that the American criminal justice system has gone seriously and fundamentally awry, the proposed reforms will seem not frightening or extreme but an overdue step along the road toward restoration.

The world of constitutional criminal procedure is changing slowly. Repudiating much of the thinking that led to the existing world, the changes are being driven by arguments that share common ground with those expressed in the Office of Legal Policy Reports. The unanswered question is whether tomorrow's changes will mirror the logical ramifications of this new way of thinking. What we cannot know today, as we ponder these Reports, is whether twenty years hence, as a new generation of law students begins to study our endeavors, the mistakes of the 1960s will be little more than "cold history." Whatever our society does in the years ahead . . . we do have a rather clear choice.

N O T E S

1. 357 U.S. 433 (1958).
2. 357 U.S. 504 (1958).
3. 357 U.S. at 441 (emphasis in original).
4. 357 U.S. at 510.
5. Prefatory Statement of Attorney General Edwin Meese III, U.S. Dep't of Justice, Office of Legal Policy, Report to the Attorney General on the Law of Pre-trial Interrogation (February 12, 1986, with addendum of January 20, 1987). [the Report is excerpted in Chapter 7.—Eds.]
6. Mirjan Damaska, *Evidentiary Barriers to Conviction and Two Models of Criminal Procedure: A Comparative Study*, 121 U. Pa. L. Rev. 506, 576 (1973).
7. Report, *supra* note 5, Executive Summary.
8. *Id.*, as reprinted in 22 U. Mich. J. L. Reform, at 564.
9. *Id.*
10. Escobedo v. Illinois, 378 U.S. 478, 486–89 (1964) (citations omitted).
11. Moran v. Burbine, 475 U.S. 412, 422 (1986). The passages from *Escobedo* seem to come close to requiring this.
12. *Id.* at 426–27 (citations omitted).
13. Joseph Grano, *Police Interrogation and the Constitution: Doctrinal Tension and an Uncertain Future*, 25 Crim. L. Bull. 5, 23 (1989); see also Joseph Grano, *Selling the Idea to Tell the Truth: The Professional Interrogator and Modern Confessions Law*, 84 Mich. L. Rev. 662, 665–75, 690 (1986) (contending that the institution of police interrogation is itself inconsistent with the philosophical premises of *Escobedo* and *Miranda*).
14. H. Richard Uviller, *Evidence from the Mind of the Criminal Suspect: A Reconsideration of the Current Rules of Access and Restraint*, 87 Colum. L. Rev. 1137, 1168 (1987) (footnote omitted).

19

Remembering the "Old World" of Criminal Procedure: A Reply to Professor Grano (1990)

•

YALE KAMISAR

Impeding the "Search for Truth"

In his . . . essay, Professor Grano looks back on the "old world" of criminal procedure, the pre–Warren Court era, with considerable fondness. I do not. Grano bemoans the fact that the Warren Court seemed to forget that the search for truth is the primary goal of American criminal procedure. I would put it somewhat differently—the Warren Court remembered that the ascertainment of truth is not the *only* goal of American criminal procedure.

Grano quotes with approval an observation by Roscoe Pound: "Legal procedure is a means, not an end; it must be made subsidiary to the substantive law as a means of making that law effective in action."[1] I would agree that criminal procedure is a means, not an end, but add: Therefore, it must be made subsidiary to the values and principles found in the Bill of Rights as a means of making *those constitutional provisions* effective in action.

There is nothing new or unusual about subordinating the search for truth to other values and policies. As Charles McCormick, one of our greatest commentators on the law of evidence, once observed, the privileges that shield confidential communications between attorney and client, husband and wife, physician and patient, and priest and penitent (and, one might add, the identity of the police informant)—

> do not in any wise aid the ascertainment of truth, but rather they shut out the light. Their sole warrant is the protection of interests and rela-

tionships which, rightly or wrongly, are regarded as of sufficient social importance to justify some incidental sacrifice of sources of facts needed in the administration of justice.[2]

. . . If the search for truth may be obstructed in the name of an attorney-client or marital relationship, what is so odd about doing so in the name of *constitutional guarantees*?

Professor Grano assails *Miranda* and its progeny for disregarding the value of truth in the confession context. He has considerably more affection for the due process "totality of the circumstances"–"voluntariness" test than he does for *Miranda*. But the pre-*Miranda* "voluntariness" test *also* "impede[d] the search for truth." . . . As the voluntariness test developed over the years, and it became increasingly clear that the Court was applying a "police methods" as well as a "trustworthiness" rationale, the concern that an "involuntary" or "coerced" confession was likely to be unreliable became less important. On the eve of *Miranda*, as Illinois Supreme Court Justice Walter Schaefer noted at the time, although the concern about unreliability "still exert[ed] some influence" in involuntary confession cases, it had "ceased to be the dominant consideration."[3] . . .

The courts that applied the "voluntariness" test in the decades preceding *Miranda* did believe that the Constitution *actually compelled* (a) the exclusion of "involuntary" confessions and (b) the reversal of convictions based on such confessions—but they thought that such results were compelled by what might be called "straight due process," not by the privilege against self-incrimination. These courts "appl[ied] the Due Process Clause to its historic function of assuring appropriate procedure before liberty is curtailed or life is taken"—without regard to how "relevant and credible" the evidence produced by unconstitutional police methods might be.

If a confession had been obtained by police methods that rendered it involuntary—and thus violated due process—it had to be excluded, however verifiable, and if the trial court had not done so the conviction could not stand. It was that simple. . . .

No doubt the many trial courts that excluded "involuntary" but reliable confessions and the many appellate courts that reversed convictions based on such confessions assumed that such consequences were self-evident or inescapable. But they are not. Such results are *not* "actually compelled" by the Constitution, if one means by that term *explicitly* or *necessarily* required by the Constitution.

The "voluntariness" test and its accompanying baggage is as much a "judge-made" or "judicially created" doctrine as is the search and seizure exclusionary rule. The Constitution does not specifically mention "confessions" or "admissions," neither "involuntary" nor any other kind. Nor does the document say explicitly that a conviction based on an "involuntary" confession cannot stand. It certainly does not say that a conviction resting in part on a coerced confession cannot stand regardless of how much untainted evidence remains to support the conviction.

If the confession it produces turns out to be a trustworthy one, coercion *does* advance the search for truth at trial. Why can't the criminal justice system make use of an "involuntary" confession if it is so impressively corroborated that there is no doubt about its trustworthiness? . . .

Those who balk at imposing the search and seizure exclusionary rule on the states remind us that it "is a remedy which *directly* serves only to protect those upon whose person or premises something incriminating has been found."[4] But the same may be said for the prohibition against the use of "involuntary" but reliable confessions. This rule, too, *directly* serves only to protect the victim of police lawlessness who actually confesses and (because I am discussing only "involuntary" confessions that are reliable) only the person whose confession "checks out." . . .

Suppose five suspects are "brought in for questioning." Suppose further that after each one is held incommunicado overnight and subjected to a long stretch of intensive questioning, two confess, but only one confession "checks out." Why not *admit* the verifiable confession and remand the defendant—together with those who were mistreated but never confessed and the one who confessed but was released when his confession did not check out—"to the remedies of private action and such protection as the internal discipline of the police, under the eyes of an alert public opinion, may afford"?[5]

Of course, the Court rejected, or never seriously considered, these "alternative approaches" to the "involuntary" confession problem. But why? So far as I am aware, the Court never really spelled out why. But if pressed to do so, I am confident that the Court would have offered one or more of the following reasons:

    (a) "The natural way" to respond to a constitutional violation is to "nullify" it;

(b) We are unwilling to give even tacit approval to official defiance of constitutional rights by permitting the use of evidence obtained in violation of those rights;

(c) We are unwilling to let the government profit from its own wrongdoing;

(d) The Court's aid should be denied in order to maintain respect for the Constitution and to preserve the judicial process from contamination by "partnership" in police lawlessness;

(e) To declare that in the administration of criminal justice the end justifies the means—to say that government officials may act lawlessly in order to secure the conviction of a private criminal—is a pernicious doctrine; and,

(f) The alternative remedies suggested are likely to be so infrequently or sporadically enforced that they must be deemed inadequate, if not largely illusory. . . .

Will (Should) the Court Overrule *Miranda*?

Professor Grano recalls that shortly after *Miranda* was handed down I reported that the decision had "'evoked much anger and spread much sorrow among judges, lawyers and professors.'"[6] Where, Grano wonders, have all those judges, lawyers, and professors gone?

A major reason *Miranda* caused much anger and sorrow *at first* is that many feared—as did the *Miranda* dissenters—that the landmark decision would strike law enforcement a grievous blow. Few press accounts of the case failed to quote from Justice White's bitter dissent, [which predicted that the Court's rule would return killers, rapists, and other criminals to the streets].[7]

No one could be sure what the effects of *Miranda* would be. No less staunch a supporter of the Warren Court's "revolution" in criminal procedure than A. Kenneth Pye warned at the time that "[i]f the fears of the dissenters prove justified, it may be necessary to reconsider whether society can afford the luxury of the values protected and implemented in [*Miranda*]."[8] As twenty-five years of life with *Miranda* have demonstrated, however, the *Miranda* dissenters' fears did not prove justified.

By the early 1970s, well before the Supreme Court began trimming *Miranda*, the view that *Miranda* posed no barrier to effective law enforcement had become widely accepted, not only by academics but also by such prominent law enforcement officials as Los Angeles District Attorney Evelle Younger and Kansas City police chief (later FBI director) Clarence Kelly. Justice Tom Clark, who filed an impassioned dissent in

> *Miranda*, later confessed "error" in his "appraisal of [its] effects upon the successful detection and prosecution of crime."[9]

Professor Grano does not attempt to refute Professor Stephen Schulhofer's assessment of *Miranda*'s impact on law enforcement. Nor does he challenge Professor Welsh White's view that "[t]he great weight of empirical evidence supports the conclusion that *Miranda*'s impact on the police's ability to obtain confessions has not been significant."[10] Indeed, Grano takes no notice of any of the empirical studies relied on by Schulhofer, White, and other commentators who have reached similar conclusions. . . .

Another reason that *Miranda* evoked more dismay in the 1960s than it does today is the confusion and uncertainty it generated in its early years. For example, did it extend to questioning "on the street"? Did it apply, or would the Court soon apply it, to a person interviewed in his own home or office by an IRS agent? That uncertainty has largely been dispelled. It is now fairly clear that absent special circumstances (such as arresting a suspect at gunpoint or forcibly subduing him), police questioning "on the street" or in a person's home or office or "roadside questioning" of a motorist detained pursuant to a traffic stop is not "custodial"; as a general matter the *Miranda* doctrine has been limited to the police station or an equivalent setting.

If, as seems to be the current state of affairs, *Miranda* is not adversely affecting law enforcement work to any significant degree; the police have learned to "live with" that *once* much-maligned and much-misunderstood case; the opinion has not, to put it mildly, been given an expansive reading; and the Court now views the decision as a serious effort to strike a proper balance between the need for police questioning and the importance of protecting a suspect against impermissible compulsion, why overrule it?

As sociologists are fond of telling us, the instrumental effects of governmental action may be slight compared to the response which it entails as a symbol. The authors of the Justice Department's Office of Legal Policy Report make no secret of the fact that they are bent on toppling *Miranda* "because of its symbolic status as the epitome of Warren Court activism in the criminal law area."[11]

Miranda is a symbol. But which way does that cut? As the author of a book-length account of the case and its aftermath has noted, "[I]t was perhaps as a symbol that *Miranda* had the most salutary impact."[12] Symbols are important, especially "the symbolic effects of criminal procedure guarantees"; "they underscore our societal commitment to restraint in an area in which emotions easily run uncontrolled."[13] Even one of *Miranda*'s harshest critics recognizes that the case may be seen as "a gesture of government's willingness to treat the lowliest antagonist as worthy of respect and consideration."[14]

Moreover, what does overruling *Miranda* entail? How could the public forget a doctrine that has been part of the popular culture for twenty-five years? How could the public forget that a custodial suspect has certain rights and that the police are supposed to advise him of those rights when that message has been so frequently repeated in mystery novels, television dramas, and comic strips?

How can we tell the many police officers who have spent their entire professional lives in the post-*Miranda* era to go about their business henceforth as if the most famous criminal procedure case in American history had never been decided? (And what kind of message would that send?) How, in a *Miranda*-less station house, would (should) the police respond if a suspect asks them whether she *has to answer* their questions?

Would overruling *Miranda*, as Professor White fears, "convey the message that restraints on police interrogation have been largely abandoned"?[15] Or would the police, as Professor Israel suggests, continue to advise people of their rights because "[e]ven without *Miranda*, an important factor in determining whether a confession was voluntary would be whether the warnings had been given?"[16] Even if the police would continue to give warnings in the event *Miranda* were overruled, would they be the same *Miranda* warnings or some abbreviated or diluted version? At this point in our history, would overruling *Miranda* cause more confusion and uncertainty than *Miranda* did in the first place?

Where, wonders Professor Grano, have *Miranda*'s critics of yesteryear gone? Maybe they haven't gone anywhere. Maybe they have just grown older and wiser.

NOTES

1. Joseph Grano, *Introduction, The Changed and Changing World of Constitutional Criminal Procedure: The Contribution of the Department of Justice's Office of Legal Policy*, 22 U. Mich. J. L. Reform, 395, 402–3 (quoting Pound, *The Canons of Procedural Reform*, 12 A.B.A. J. 541, 543 (1926)).

2. Charles McCormick, Evidence 152 (1st ed. 1954).

3. Walter Schaefer, The Suspect and Society 10 (1967) (based on a lecture delivered before *Miranda*).

4. Wolf v. Colorado, 338 U.S. 25, 31 (1949) (emphasis added).

5. *Id.*

6. Grano, *supra* note 1, at 399 (quoting Kamisar, *A Dissent from the Miranda Dissents*, 65 Mich. L. Rev. 59, 59 (1966), *reprinted in* Yale Kamisar, Police Interrogation and Confessions 41 (1980)).

7. [See chapter 3 at page 47—Eds.]

8. A. Kenneth Pye, *Interrogation of Criminal Defendants—Some Views on* Miranda v. Arizona, 35 Fordham L. Rev. 199, 219 (1966).

9. Stephen J. Schulhofer, *Reconsidering* Miranda, 54 U. Chi. L. Rev. 435, 456 (1987) [excerpted in chap. 8.—Eds.].

10. Welsh White, *Defending* Miranda: *A Reply to Professor Caplan*, 39 Vand. L. Rev. 1, 19 n.99 (1986).

11. Report to the Attorney General on the Law of Pre-trial Interrogation, *as reprinted in* 22 U. Mich. J. L. Reform, at 565 [excerpted in chap. 7.—Eds.].

12. Liva Baker, *Miranda*: Crime, Law and Politics 407 (1983).

13. Schulhofer, *supra* note 9, at 460.

14. Gerald M. Caplan, *Questioning* Miranda, 38 Vand. L. Rev. 1417, 1471 (1985) [excerpted in chap. 9.—Eds.].

15. White, *supra* note 10, at 22.

16. Jerold Israel, *Criminal Procedure, the Burger Court, and the Legacy of the Warren Court*, 75 Mich. L. Rev. 1320, 1386 n.283 (1977).

20

Miranda
and the Problem
of False Confessions
(1998)

·

RICHARD A. LEO

The purpose of *Miranda* is to protect the accused from the inherently compelling pressures of police-dominated custodial questioning. According to the Warren Court's logic in *Miranda*, these inherently compelling pressures are dispelled if (1) police inform suspects of their Fifth Amendment rights to remain silent and to appointed counsel, and (2) the suspect waives these rights knowingly and voluntarily. Absent properly issued warnings or a properly obtained waiver, the suspect's incriminating statements cannot be admitted into evidence at trial. These procedures (both the warnings and the exclusionary rule) are intended to protect the suspect's rational and voluntary decisionmaking ability within the interrogation environment and, by implication, the reliability of the suspect's statement. According to the Warren Court's logic, then, *Miranda* should offer some protection not only against the admission of involuntary confessions but against the admission of unreliable ones as well. Indeed, the Supreme Court has subsequently "referred to *Miranda* as a decision that is designed to enhance accurate fact-finding by excluding unreliable statements."[1]

The purpose of this chapter is to examine the relationship between *Miranda* and the largely neglected problem of false confessions to police. False confessions are admissions to a criminal act that are either partially or wholly untrue; I use the term, however, to refer only to those cases in which the confessor is entirely innocent. This chapter will proceed in three steps. First, I will argue that however unlikely or implausible it may seem, false confessions to police are not uncommon; instead, they appear to occur with troubling, if unquantifiable, frequency. Second, I will argue that despite its noble intentions—and whatever its practical effect on the guilty—*Miranda* does not dispel, or arguably even affect, the conditions of modern interrogation that lead to false confessions from the innocent. Third, I will argue that the law governing confessions places far too much importance on the procedural fairness of the interrogation process and far too little importance on the substantive truthfulness of confession statements. To remedy this, confessions should not be admissible into evidence at trial unless they meet a reasonable standard of reliability. More specifically, judges should use existing evidence law (Federal Rule 403 or the state law equivalent) to exclude unreliable confession evidence when its potential to cause "unfair prejudice" to the defendant "substantially outweighs" its probative value.[2]

False confessions have long been one of the leading causes of miscarriages of justice in the United States.[3] Viewed historically, this fact may not seem surprising: Through at least the early 1930s, police in the United States regularly relied on physical coercion and psychological duress to extract confessions from criminal suspects.[4] It is not difficult to understand how torture, physical assaults, threats of harm, or promises of leniency may cause innocent suspects to confess to crimes they did not commit. Since the 1930s, however, U.S. police interrogation practices have changed profoundly: Psychologically sophisticated interrogation methods have replaced third-degree tactics.[5] Police today no longer routinely employ force or duress to elicit confessions, but instead have developed and refined interrogation methods that are based on influence, manipulation, and deception. As a result, it is no longer obvious why innocent suspects falsely confess.[6] And while psychologically induced false confessions may seem unlikely to many, the research literature clearly documents that contemporary police interrogation techniques can and do lead to false confessions from entirely innocent suspects.[7]

Despite the reality of false confessions to police, it is currently not possible to determine—or even to reliably estimate—their actual incidence[8] or prevalence.[9] There are at least three reasons for this. First, for the most part custodial interrogation continues to be conducted in secrecy. Police virtually always question suspects privately, and typically they do not record the interrogation session in any form. Second, neither police nor any criminal justice agency keeps records or collects statistics on the number or frequency of police interrogations of criminal suspects. Therefore, we do not know how often suspects are interrogated or how often they confess, whether truthfully or falsely. Many, if not most, cases of false confession are therefore likely to go entirely unreported and unnoticed. Third, even in reported cases, it is frequently difficult to unequivocally establish the "ground truth" (i.e., what really happened) necessary to infer the likely truth or falsity of confessions to police, especially if—as appears likely in most cases involving both true and false confessions—the suspect is eventually convicted by a judge or jury.[10] In short, it is at present impossible for scholars either to determine or to quantitatively estimate the frequency of false confessions to police. It follows that it is also impossible to determine or to quantitatively estimate how often false confessions lead to wrongful convictions.

Even though precise estimates are not possible, false confessions do appear to occur with troubling frequency. In recent years American scholars, popular writers, and journalists have documented numerous cases of psychologically induced false confessions to police.[11] Because of the multiple selection biases that likely cause most false confessions to go entirely unnoticed, unreported, or unacknowledged, only the most egregious and high-profile cases involving clearly documented or demonstrably false confessions are likely to be written about in either the academic or popular literature. We may confidently conclude that the cases documented by popular and academic writers are therefore likely to represent only the proverbial tip of the false confession iceberg.

I am not suggesting that police intentionally set out to extract false confessions or that prosecutors intentionally set out to convict innocent suspects. I have seen little evidence to support either scenario. Rather, I begin with the elementary presumption that all human institutions are fallible, including police, prosecutors, and the criminal justice system generally. While some miscarriages of justice are caused by negligence, incompetence, or malicious intent, most error in the U.S. criminal justice system appears to be unintentional.[12] In addition, some degree of system error is, of course, inevitable. Regretably, however, police in the United States are trained neither to avoid eliciting false confessions nor to recognize their logic, variety, or distinguishing characteristics.[13] Instead, police trainers and interrogation manuals persist in the misguided belief that contemporary psychological methods are not apt to cause an innocent suspect to confess[14]—a fiction so thoroughly contradicted by all of the social scientific research on false confessions that it can only be described as myth.

A confession of guilt—whether true or false—is the most damaging evidence the government can present in a criminal trial.[15] As a result, police-induced false confessions are highly likely to lead to the wrongful conviction and incarceration of innocent individuals. Confessions (whether they are true or false) set in motion a virtually irrebuttable working presumption of guilt among legal officials, who, like most Americans, rarely question the veracity of incriminating statements to police. Not surprisingly, once a confession is introduced into evidence, any attempt to refute it will almost always be futile.[16]

A suspect who confesses to police, whether truthfully or falsely, will not only be presumed guilty from the start, but also be pressured to plead guilty and treated more harshly by every legal official and at every stage of the criminal process.[17] Police typically "clear" the case as solved once they elicit a confession—even if it is not supported by any independent evidence, is internally inconsistent, or was obtained under questionable conditions. Criminal justice officials typically will not believe a suspect's retractions, which they may interpret as further evidence of his deceitfulness. Suspects who confess—especially in serious cases—will experience greater difficulty making bail, a disadvantage that significantly reduces a criminal defendant's likelihood of acquittal.[18] Prosecutors will be more likely to charge suspects who confess[19] and charge them with more counts, while defense attorneys will pressure these suspects to concede guilt and accept a plea bargain. If the case goes to trial, the jury will treat the confession as more probative of the accused's guilt than any other type of evidence,[20] and the suspect is more likely to be convicted and more likely to be convicted of serious crimes.[21] And if convicted, a suspect who has falsely confessed is likely to be sentenced more harshly for failing to show remorse.

The Fifth, Sixth, and Fourteenth Amendments regulate the admissibility of confession evidence in American courts; if any one of these doctrines is violated, the confession statement should be excluded from evidence at trial. According to current interpretations of the Fourteenth Amendment due process clause, a confession is inadmissible if police interrogation methods overbear the suspect's will and thus cause him to make an "involuntary" confession. Under this standard, the voluntariness (and hence admissibility) of a confession is evaluated case by case, based on the totality of the circumstances (i.e., the facts of the case, the suspect's personality characteristics, and the specific police interrogation methods). The Fourteenth Amendment due process clause additionally permits courts to exclude as "involuntary" any confession obtained by fundamentally unfair police methods, regardless of the confession's voluntariness.[22] According to the Sixth Amendment, a confession may be excluded from evidence if *after a suspect has been indicted* he is questioned outside the presence of his lawyer.[23] And, of course, the

Fifth Amendment privilege against self-incrimination permits judges to exclude confessions from evidence if police did not properly recite the *Miranda* warnings or if they did not obtain a knowing and voluntary waiver.[24]

None of these doctrines currently provides much protection against the admission of unreliable or false confessions into evidence at trial. While the Fourteenth Amendment due process test may have once focused on the reliability of a confession in determining its voluntariness, the early nexus between reliability and voluntariness has long been severed.[25] The due process test no longer concerns itself in any meaningful way with the reliability of a suspect's confession, but instead is interpreted as protecting a suspect from coercive and/or fundamentally unfair police questioning methods. If an unreliable confession is excluded under the Fourteenth Amendment due process test, it is only because the confession was judged involuntary or because police pressures were so unfair as to shock the judicial conscience. To the extent that standard interrogation methods or procedures—which can and do cause confessions from the factually innocent—do not rise to the level of legal coerciveness or fundamental unfairness, the Fourteenth Amendment due process test does not prevent unreliable or false confessions from being admitted into evidence. The Sixth Amendment's entirely procedural concern with post-indictment questioning also offers little or no protection against the admission of false confessions, since virtually all police interrogations occur prior to indictment. Like the Fourteenth Amendment due process test, the Sixth Amendment is concerned entirely with the procedural fairness that occurs during *the process* of police interrogation, but not at all with the substantive reliability of the confession statement that is *the outcome* of police interrogation.

And so too it is with *Miranda*. For all its fanfare, *Miranda* is concerned only with the procedural fairness of the interrogation process—whether a suspect retains his rational and voluntary decisionmaking ability in the face of inherently compelling police pressures—not with the substantive truth of the interrogation outcome. While it may prevent some suspects from speaking to police, *Miranda* offers little or no protection against the elicitation of false confessions from innocent suspects or their admission into evidence. This is true for at least two reasons. First, the vast majority of suspects—ranging from 78 percent to 96 percent[26]—waive their *Miranda* rights and willingly submit to police interrogation. What is more important here, however, is understanding who chooses to speak to police. Those suspects least likely to give a false confession—individuals who have prior criminal records and have been hardened by their earlier exposure to police and the criminal justice system—are most likely to invoke their *Miranda* rights to terminate police questioning.[27] Conversely, those suspects who are most likely to give a false confession—individuals who do not have criminal records and are more vulnerable to suggestion—are least likely to invoke their *Miranda* rights to terminate police questioning.[28] Ironically, then, the minimal protection *Miranda* in theory offers against the possibility of false confessions is in practice entirely misdirected.

Second, once the interrogator recites the fourfold warnings and obtains a waiver, *Miranda* is irrelevant to both the process and the outcome of the subsequent interrogation. Any protection *Miranda* might have offered a suspect typically evaporates as soon as an accusatory interrogation begins—which is exactly when a suspect is most likely to feel the inherently compelling pressures of police-dominated custodial questioning. Once issued and waived, *Miranda* does not restrict deceptive or suggestive police tactics, manipulative interrogation strategies, hostile or overbearing questioning styles, lengthy confinement, or any of the inherently stressful conditions of modern accusatorial interrogation that may lead the innocent to confess.[29] In other words, once police issue warnings and obtain a waiver (and very few suspects subsequently invoke their *Miranda* rights after they have been waived[30]), *Miranda* is virtually irrelevant to the problem of false confessions.

It is even possible that *Miranda*—despite its high-minded intentions—has undermined any protection the law might have otherwise offered against the admission of false confessions into evidence. For *Miranda* has de facto displaced the due process voluntariness standard as the primary test of a confession's admissibility, shifting the court's analysis from the voluntariness of a confession to the voluntariness of the *Miranda* waiver. Though the *Miranda* holding is logically independent of the due process voluntariness standard, my own empirical observations suggest that trial judges will almost always declare a confession voluntary if the *Miranda* procedures appear to have been properly followed. To put it differently, by focusing on the proper reading and waiver of the simple *Miranda* formula, trial judges often appear to avoid the more difficult and elusive task of analyzing whether police pressures have overborne the suspect's decisionmaking capacity. Perhaps more importantly, by generating seemingly endless controversy (both popular and academic) about its symbolic messages and its allegedly disastrous effects on the confession and conviction rates of the guilty, *Miranda* has diverted attention away from the substantive reliability of interrogation outcomes and the very real risk of wrongful convictions based on false confessions. It seems that contemporary legal commentators have wished away the problem of false confessions, as if it somehow no longer exists or as if *Miranda's* civilizing, yet entirely procedural, influence on police interrogation somehow ensures the reliability of all confession statements.

I do not wish to be misunderstood here or cited out of context; I am not calling for *Miranda's* abolition. As I have argued elsewhere,[31] I think *Miranda* should be neither weakened nor strengthened. Rather, I wish merely to call attention to *Miranda's* utter irrelevance, as well as our own blindness, to the ongoing and tragic problem of false confessions. Regretably, neither the Fourteenth Amendment due process clause nor the Sixth Amendment right to a fair trial nor the Fifth Amendment privilege against self-incrimination nor the prophylactic *Miranda* rules offer any significant protection against the admission of false confessions. Oddly, the constitutional law of criminal procedure has no substantive safeguards in place to prevent them.[32]

The more general problem is that constitutional law seems concerned only with the procedural fairness of police questioning, so much so that it currently lacks any rules to guarantee the reliability of confession statements. Yet it is not uncommon for suspects—especially highly suggestible ones such as the mentally handicapped, juveniles, and individuals unusually trusting of authority—to give false confessions (after waiving their *Miranda* rights) in response to police inducements that do not legally qualify as coercive or fundamentally unfair. In other words, police pressures that do not rise to the level of legal definitions of coercion or fundamental unfairness (and that are exerted after a voluntary *Miranda* waiver) may nevertheless cause innocent suspects to falsely confess.

Richard Ofshe and I have recently identified two types of false confession that fall into this category: the *stress-compliant* false confession and the *noncoerced persuaded* false confession.[33] Some suspects knowingly give a *stress-compliant* false confession in order to escape the punishing experience caused by the aversive—but not legally coercive—stressors typically present in all accusatory interrogations. And some suspects give a *noncoerced persuaded* false confession after they have been persuaded (by legally noncoercive techniques) that it is more likely than not that they committed the offense despite no memory of having done so. Since neither type of false confession is elicited in response to legally coercive or fundamentally unfair police tactics or pressures, however, the law currently offers no protection against their admission.

To prevent the admission of false confessions and their potential to cause miscarriages of justice, courts should evaluate the substantive reliability of confession statements. I am not suggesting that the law should weaken its concern with the procedural fairness of the interrogation process or abandon its current procedural safeguards. This is not a zero-sum trade-off. Rather, the law must create new or enforce existing substantive safeguards to protect suspects against the admission of false confession evidence. Apart from its concern with the voluntariness of the confession or the adequacy of the *Miranda* warnings and waiver, trial courts should evaluate the truthfulness of every confession statement and declare inadmissible those that do not meet a reasonable standard of reliability. More specifically, judges should use Federal Rule 403 or its equivalent in state law cases to exclude unreliable confession evidence where "its probative value is substantially outweighed by the danger of unfair prejudice, confusion of the issues, or misleading the jury."[34] If, as I have argued above, a confession is almost certain to lead to conviction, it should not be admitted into evidence when it appears so unreliable that it will unfairly prejudice, confuse, or mislead a jury in its assessment of a suspect's culpability. Trial judges regularly use Federal Rule 403 or its state law equivalent to exclude evidence—such as brutal crime scene pictures, for example—when its effect is more prejudicial than probative.

As Richard Ofshe and I have recently argued,[35] the reliability of a confession statement can often be determined by evaluating the fit between the suspect's post-admission narrative (i.e., the account he or she offers after saying the words "I did it") and the facts of the crime. A guilty confessor will have personal knowledge of the crime, but an innocent confessor will be ignorant of many crime facts. Consequently, the guilty confessor will be able to verify information that only the police know, to provide additional information that only the true offender knows, to supply police with missing information or lead them to missing evidence, and to provide convincing explanations about any seemingly inexplicable or discrepant crime facts. The innocent confessor, however, will not personally know the crime facts, but instead will likely respond to police questions with guesses, infer proper answers from police suggestions, or simply repeat the information the police provide him. The post-admission narrative of a false confession is likely to be riddled with demonstrable factual errors and thus cast doubt on the confessor's guilt. By contrast, the post-admission narrative of a true confession should match and corroborate the crime facts and thus verify the confessor's guilt. Consequently, if the suspect's post-admission narrative fits poorly with the facts of the crime, the judge should rule the confession inadmissible because its prejudicial effect will vastly outweigh its probative value. By focusing on the substantive truthfulness of the confession statement rather than (or in addition to) the procedural fairness of interrogation process and by relying on the rules of evidence rather than (or in addition to) the constitutional law of criminal procedure,[36] judges can introduce a reasonable standard of reliability into the legal process that will safeguard suspects against the admission of false confessions.

In conclusion, I have argued in this chapter that demonstrably false confessions from entirely innocent suspects appear to occur with troubling, if unquantifiable, frequency in the United States. The *Miranda* decision, however, fails to protect suspects in any meaningful way against the elicitation and admission of unreliable confession statements. Like the constitutional law of criminal procedure more generally, *Miranda* places far too much emphasis on the procedural fairness of the interrogation process and far too little emphasis on the substantive outcome or truthfulness of confession statements. To remedy this substantive failure in the constitutional law, judges should admit confessions into evidence only after they have first met a reasonable standard of reliability based on Federal Rule 403 or its state law analogue. More specifically, judges should evaluate the fit of the suspect's post-admission narrative with the facts of the crime. If the post-admission narrative fits poorly with the crime facts, the judge should exclude the confession from evidence because its prejudicial effect will greatly outweigh its probative value. Only then will the law substantively safeguard the factually innocent from miscarriages of justice based on false confessions.

NOTES

1. Welsh S. White, *False Confessions and the Constitution: Safeguards to Prevent the Admission of Untrustworthy Confessions* 19 (1997) (unpublished paper), citing Withrow v. Williams, 507 U.S. 680, 692 (1993), and Schneckloth v. Bustamonte, 412 U.S. 218, 240 (1973).

2. Fed. R. Evid. 403; Cal. Evid. Code §352; Ballou v. Henri Studios, Inc., 656 F.2d 1147 (5th Cir. 1981). Richard Ofshe and I first made this point in an earlier article. See Richard J. Ofshe & Richard A. Leo, *The Social Psychology of Police*

Interrogation: The Theory and Classification of True and False Confessions, 16 Stud. L., Pol. & Soc'y 185–247 (1997).

3. See C. Ronald Huff, Arye Rattner, & Edward Sagarin, Convicted but Innocent: Wrongful Conviction and Public Policy (1996); Michael Radelet, Hugo Bedau, & Constance Putnam, In Spite of Innocence: Erroneous Convictions in Capital Cases (1992); Martin Yant, Presumed Guilty: When Innocent People Are Wrongly Convicted (1991); Jerome Frank & Barbara Frank, Not Guilty (1957); and Edward M. Borchard, Convicting the Innocent: Errors of Criminal Justice (1932).

4. See Wickersham Commission Report (1931), also known as National Commission on Law Observance and Law Enforcement, Report on Lawlessness in Law Enforcement, vol. 11.

5. Richard A. Leo, *From Coercion to Deception: The Changing Nature of Police Interrogation in America*, 18 Crime, Law and Social Change 35–59 (1992) [excerpted in chap. 5].

6. Mock jury research shows that people find it difficult to believe that anyone would confess to a crime that he or she did not commit. See Saul Kassin & Lawrence Wrightsman, *Coerced Confessions, Judicial Instructions, and Mock Juror Verdicts*, 11 J. Applied Soc. Psychol. 489–506 (1981); and Saul Kassin & Lawrence Wrightsman, *Prior Confessions and Mock Juror Verdicts*, 10 J. Applied Soc. Psychol. 133–46 (1980).

7. Ofshe & Leo, *supra* note 2; Lawrence Wrightsman & Saul Kassin, Confessions in the Courtroom (1993); Gisli H. Gudjonsson, The Psychology of Interrogations, Confessions and Testimony (1992); Richard J. Ofshe, *Coerced Confessions: The Logic of Seemingly Irrational Action*, 6 Cultic Stud. J. 6–15 (1989).

8. "Incidence" refers to the number of false confessions occurring in a specific time period.

9. "Prevalence" refers to the number of false confessions in the population accumulated across all time periods.

10. In addition, innocent individuals—even if they are convicted—do not always retract their false confessions. See Gudjonsson, *supra* note 7.

11. See, e.g., Ofshe & Leo, *supra* note 2; Edward Connors, Thomas Lundregan, Neal Miller, & Tom McEwen, Convicted by Juries, Exonerated by Science: Case Studies in the Use of DNA Evidence to Establish Innocence after Trial (1996); Donald Connery ed., Convicting the Innocent: The Story of a Murder, a False Confession, and the Struggle to Free a "Wrong Man" (1995); Roger Parloff, Triple Jeopardy: A Story of Law at Its Best—and Worst (1996); Huff, Rattner, & Sagarin, *supra* note 3; Mark Sauer, *Some Strange Cases Examined of Innocents Who Confess to Murder*, San Diego Union & Tribune, July 27, 1996, at B10; Paul Hourihan, *Earl Washington's Confession: Mental Retardation and the Law of Confessions*, 81 Va. L. Rev. 1471–1503 (1995); Paul Mones, Stalking Justice (1995); Mickey McMahon, *False Confessions and Police Deception: The Interrogation, Incarceration and Release of an Innocent Veteran*, 13 Am. J. Forensic Psychol. 5–43 (1995); T. N. Thomas, *Polygraphy and Coerced-Compliant False Confession: "Serviceman E" Redevivus*, 35 Sci. & Just. 133–39 (1995); Richard A. Leo, *False Memory, False Confession: When Police Interrogations Go Wrong*, presented at the Annual Meeting of the Law & Society Association (Toronto, June 1995); Allan Gray & Courtenay Edelhart, *Judge Rules Cruz Innocent; Finally "The Whole Case Fell Apart*," Chicago Tribune, Nov. 4, 1995, at 1; Robert Sigman, *The Tragedy of False*

Confessions, Kansas City Star, June 19, 1995, at B4; Lawrence Wright, Remembering Satan: A Case of Recovered Memory and the Shattering of an American Family (1994); Joseph Shapiro, *Innocent but Behind Bars: Another Man Confessed to Murder. Why Is This Retarded Man in Prison?*, U.S. News & World Report, Sept. 19, 1994, at 36; Wrightsman & Kassin, *supra* note 7; Russ Kimball & Laura Greenberg, *False Confessions*, Phoenix Magazine, Nov. 1993, at 85–95; David Rossmiller & Glen Creno, *City to Probe Police on False Confession; Mom's Other Sons Returned to Family*, Phoenix Gazette, Mar. 31, 1993, at B4; K. Davis & A. Friedberg, *Wrongly Convicted Man Enjoys Freedom from "Hell,"* Fort Lauderdale Sun-Sentinel, Jan. 16, 1993, at 1B; Radelet, Bedau, & Putnam, *supra* note 3; Ralph Underwager & Hollida Wakefield, *False Confessions and Police Deception*, 10 Am. J. Forensic Psychol. 49–66 (1992); Robert Perske, Unequal Justice: What Can Happen When Persons with Retardation or Other Developmental Disabilities Encounter the Criminal Justice System (1991); Yant, *supra* note 3; Anthony Pratkanis & Elliot Aronson, Age of Propaganda: The Everyday Use and Abuse of Persuasion (1991); Tom Demoretchky, *Detective in Murder Case Transferred; 3 Confessions to Crime*, Newsday, Oct. 24, 1991, at 7; Mark Paxton, *Nightmare of Confession Continues. Two Claimed Responsibility for Murders*, Tulsa World, Feb. 11, 1990, at C26; Ofshe, *supra* note 7; Philip Weiss, *Untrue Confessions*, Mother Jones, Sept. 1989, at 20–24, 55–57; Philip Coons, *Misuse of Forensic Hypnosis: A Hypnotically Elicited False Confession with the Apparent Creation of a Multiple Personality*, 36 Int'l. J. Clinical & Experimental Hypnosis 1–11 (1988); Patricia Derian, *"Confessions" of Embassy Guards Raise Many Questions*, St. Petersburg Times, Feb. 20, 1988, at 17A; David Lykken, A Tremor in the Blood: Uses and Abuses of the Lie Detector (1981); William Hart, *The Subtle Art of Persuasion*, Police Magazine, Mar. 1981, at 7–17; Donald S. Connery, Guilty until Proven Innocent (1977); Henry H. Foster, *Confessions and the Stationhouse Syndrome*, 18 De Paul L. Rev. 683–701 (1989).

12. See Huff, Rattner, & Sagarin, *supra* note 3.

13. See Richard A. Leo, Police Interrogation in America: A Study of Violence, Civility and Social Change (1994) (Ph.D. dissertation, University of California, Berkeley); Leo, *supra* note 11; Ofshe & Leo, *supra* note 2.

14. See Fred E. Inbau, John E. Reid, & Joseph P. Buckley, Criminal Interrogation and Confessions (1986).

15. See Richard A. Leo, *Inside the Interrogation Room*, 86 J. Crim. L. & Criminology 266–303 (1996); David Simon, Homicide: A Year on the Killing Streets (1991) [excerpted in chap. 4]; Saul Kassin & Katherine Kiechel, *The Social Psychology of False Confessions*, 7 Psychol. Sci. 125–28 (1996); G. R. Miller & F. J. Boster, *Three Images of the Trial: Their Implications for Psychological Research, in* Psychology in the Legal Process (B. Sales ed., 1977); John Wigmore, 3 Evidence (1970).

16. See Wrightsman & Kassin, *supra* note 7.

17. Richard A. Leo, *The Impact of Miranda Revisited*, 86 J. Crim. L. & Criminology 621–92 (1996) [excerpted in chap. 15].

18. Samuel Walker, Sense and Nonsense about Crime and Drugs: A Policy Guide (1994).

19. Paul G. Cassell & Bret S. Hayman, *Police Interrogation in the 1990s: An Empirical Study of the Effects of Miranda*, 43 UCLA L. Rev. 839–931 (1996) [excerpted in chap. 16].

20. See Miller & Boster, *supra* note 15. Jurors appear simultaneously to weigh confession evidence too heavily and to be generally unaware of the inability of many individuals to resist police pressures to confess. See Wrightsman & Kassin, *supra* note 7.

21. Cassell & Hayman, *supra* note 19, at 909, 912 Table 16.

22. Rogers v. Richmond, 365 U.S. 534 (1961). See also Yale Kamisar, *What Is an Involuntary Confession? Some Comments on Inbau and Reid's* Criminal Interrogations and Confessions, 17 Rutgers L. Rev. 728–59 (1963).

23. Massiah v. United States, 377 U.S. 201 (1964).

24. Miranda v. Arizona, 384 U.S. 436 (1966).

25. See Welsh White, *False Confessions and the Constitution: Safeguards against Untrustworthy Confessions*, 32 Harv. C.R.–C.L. L. Rev. 105–57 (1997).

26. See Leo, *supra* note 15; George C. Thomas III, *Plain Talk about the* Miranda *Empirical Debate: A "Steady-State" Theory of Confessions*, 43 UCLA L. Rev. 933–59 (1996) [excerpted in chap. 17].

27. See Leo, *supra* note 15; Gudjonsson, *supra* note 7.

28. See Leo, *supra* note 15.

29. For an analysis of the conditions of interrogation that lead to different types of false confession, see Ofshe & Leo, *supra* note 2.

30. See Leo, *supra* note 15; Cassell & Hayman, *supra* note 19.

31. See Leo, *supra* note 17.

32. The Supreme Court has recently stated that assessing a confession's lack of reliability "is a matter to be governed by the evidentiary law of the forum . . . and not by the Due Process Clause of the Fourteenth Amendment." See Colorado v. Connelly, 479 U.S. 157 (1986), at 167. More generally, see White, *supra* note 25.

33. For a discussion of the various types and logics of police-induced false confession, see Ofshe & Leo, *supra* note 2.

34. See *supra* note 2.

35. See Ofshe & Leo, *supra* note 2.

36. Although the constitutional law of criminal procedure currently offers no substantive safeguards against the use of false confession evidence at trial, the Fourteenth Amendment due process clause could be interpreted to forbid the admission of unreliable confession evidence independent of the interrogation procedures used to elicit confessions. For more general suggestions about possible constitutional safeguards against the admission of unreliable confession evidence, see White, *supra* note 25.

21

In a
Different Register:
The Pragmatics
of Powerlessness
in Police
Interrogation
(1993)

•

JANET E. AINSWORTH

I. Introduction

Imagine that you are in police custody, about to be interrogated concerning a crime. Before the questioning begins, the interrogating officer tells you that you have the right to remain silent and to have an attorney present during questioning. If you decide to invoke your right to the presence of an attorney, you must be very careful about how you phrase your request. Make your request in the wrong way, and you may lose legal protection for your constitutional rights.

The Supreme Court has yet to resolve the question of what legal effect, if any, should be accorded to an arrestee's use of equivocal or ambiguous language in invoking *Miranda* rights during police interrogation. Three different approaches have emerged in the state and lower federal courts. Some jurisdictions have adopted a rule requiring invocations of the right to counsel to be direct and unambiguous before they are given any legal effect. [The Supreme Court has now decided the question, adopting this first solution. Davis v. United States, 512 U.S. 452 (1994).—Eds.] Other jurisdictions allow the police to continue questioning a suspect whose invocation is ambiguous or equivocal, but only to determine the suspect's intent with respect to the exercise of the right to counsel. Still others treat any recognizable invocation as legally sufficient to bar any further police interrogation.

The first two doctrinal approaches, which are observed in the majority of jurisdictions, provide enhanced constitutional protection from further police interrogation for those who use direct and assertive modes of expression, and penalize those who adopt indirect or qualified ways of speaking. The legal distinctions in the degree of protection accorded to arrestees rest on implicit and unexamined norms about how people express themselves—namely, that people naturally do and should use direct and unqualified ways of speaking.

Invocation doctrines that favor direct speech operate to the detriment of certain groups within society. Sociolinguistic research has demonstrated that discrete segments of the population—particularly women and ethnic minorities—are far more likely than others to adopt indirect speech patterns. An indirect mode of expression is characteristic of the language used by powerless persons, both those who are members of certain groups that have historically been powerless within society as well as those who are powerless because of the particular situation in which they find themselves. Because criminal suspects confronted with police interrogation may feel powerless, they will often attempt to invoke their rights by using speech patterns that the law currently refuses to recognize. Ironically, invocation standards used in a majority of jurisdictions, although intended to protect the individual from abuses of power by the police, in practice provide systematically inferior protection to the least powerful in society.

The inadequacy of the majority legal approach to the invocation of *Miranda* rights is symptomatic of a more general phenomenon within the law: the incorporation of unconscious androcentric assumptions into legal doctrine. Feminist theory has exposed many of these assumptions and thus has had a powerful impact on many aspects of contemporary legal thought. It may not be immediately obvious what relevance feminist theory has for such areas of law as criminal procedure that are, or at least appear to be, gender-neutral. However, recent works in feminist jurisprudence have examined a variety of legal doctrines and practices that seem on the surface to be gender-neutral, and have discovered gender bias through the use of one of the primary methodological tools of feminist theory—asking the "woman question." As framed in feminist jurisprudence, the "woman question" asks, "What would law be like if women had been considered by the drafters and interpreters of the law?" Asking the "woman question" forces us to imagine a counterfactual world in which women's experiences, perspectives, and behavior were taken into account in constructing the legal order. By measuring the actual legal order against this imagined world, feminist methodology exposes assumptions that are deeply embedded within the law, assumptions that influence the shape of legal doctrine and the dynamics of legal practice.

In the case of *Miranda* rights, asking the "woman question" means asking whether a legal doctrine preferring direct and unqualified assertions of the right to counsel takes into account the speech patterns of women as well as other powerless groups. As I will detail, sociolinguistic research on typical male and female speech patterns indicates that men tend to use direct and assertive language, whereas women more often adopt indirect and deferential speech patterns. Because majority legal doctrine governing a person's rights during police interrogation favors linguistic behavior more typical of men than of women, asking the "woman question" reveals a hidden bias in this ostensibly gender-neutral doctrine.

The sociolinguistic evidence that women disproportionately adopt indirect speech patterns predicts that legal rules requiring the use of direct and unqualified language will adversely affect female defendants more often than male defendants. The real world consequences of such a bias are by no means trivial. If women are indeed disadvantaged by this doctrine, then the law has compromised the ability of millions of women arrestees to exercise their constitutional rights.

The detrimental consequences of interrogation law, however, are not limited to female defendants. Asking the "woman question" provokes related inquiry into whether legal doctrine may similarly fail to incorporate the experiences and perspectives of other marginalized groups. The fact that asking the "woman question" can prompt fruitful inquiry into other missing perspectives is what Katherine Bartlett calls "[c]onverting the [w]oman [q]uestion into the [q]uestion of the [e]xcluded."[1] Although the sociolinguistic research on speech patterns of various ethnic groups in the United States is less extensive than that detailing gender-linked differences in language use, the available evidence demonstrates that there are a number of ethnic speech communities whose members habitually adopt a speech register including indirect and qualified modes of expression very much like those observed in typical female language use.

Even within communities whose speech is not characterized by indirect modes of expression, individual speakers who are socially or situationally powerless frequently adopt an indirect speech register. In fact, several prominent researchers have concluded that the use of this characteristically "female" speech [hereinafter "female register"] style correlates better with powerlessness than with gender. The psychosocial dynamics of the police interrogation setting inherently involve an imbalance of power between the suspect, who is situationally powerless, and the interrogator, whose role entails the exercise of power. Such asymmetries of power in the interrogation session increase the likelihood that a particular suspect will adopt an indirect, and thus seemingly equivocal, mode of expression. This study, which begins by focusing on the disadvantages to women defendants of current invocation doctrine, ultimately has far-reaching implications for various other classes of speakers that do not share the linguistic norm of assertive and direct expression.

*

III. Gender and Language Usage: A Different Register

In 1975 the linguist Robin Lakoff first made the claim that there is a distinctive "women's language" that differs from typical male speech in both syntactic and paralinguistic features. She argued that women who use this mode of speech appear less assertive and confident than those who use male speech patterns.[2] Lakoff went on to assert that this "women's language" not only reflects women's subordinate position in society, but also reinforces that subordination. Her controversial thesis triggered an explosion of research designed to test her theory and sparked a renewed interest among anthropological linguists in studying gender as a variable within speech communities.

. . . Rather than say that women and men speak different languages or dialects, it is preferable to say that gender correlates with the use of different linguistic registers. By register, I mean a characteristic manner of speaking that is adopted by certain members of a speech community under specific circumstances. A speech community may possess multiple registers of the language shared by its members. Use of a particular linguistic register depends on the context of the speech occasion. It may be associated with certain settings or situations, or may be correlated with a social role or relationship.

Here I want to emphasize two important caveats. First, in proposing that gender is correlated with the use of a distinctive linguistic register, I am not claiming that all women share these speech characteristics or that no men do. Some women will never exhibit this register of speech, and some men may sometimes do so. . . .

Second, the use of this register is not exclusively a factor of gender but varies according to other factors as well. Women who exhibit these gender-linked characteristics in their language use will do so to a greater or lesser degree depending upon the context of the linguistic usage. Gender differences in language use are magnified in some contexts, particularly when there is a power disparity between the speaker and the hearer, and are minimized in others, particularly when the encounter is an impersonal, formulaic interaction such as making an inquiry at a public information booth. Use of this register may also be affected by such variables as race or class. Since most of the research in this area has been conducted with white middle-class subjects, it is risky to extrapolate from the results of this research to women who are members of groups whose language usage is known to vary from that of the dominant white social order. Nevertheless, the current state of research in this area justifies speaking of a characteristic female register of speech.

A. Characteristics of the Female Register

With these important qualifications in mind, we can examine the gender-linked syntactic and paralinguistic characteristics that together constitute a distinctive register of linguistic usage. Five main characteristics of this register have been identified: (1) use of hedges, (2) use of tag questions, (3) use of modal verbs, (4) avoidance of imperatives and the use of indirect interrogatives as a substitute for the imperative, and (5) rising intonation used in declarative statements. Collectively, the syntactic features of this gender-linked speech register contribute to a distinctive pragmatic effect that must be considered in interpreting the use of this register in social context.

1. Hedges

Hedges are lexical expressions that function to attenuate the emphasis of a statement, or to make it less precise. For example, "kind of," "sort of," and "to some extent" are hedges that soften an assertion by qualifying the applicability of the modified statements, undercutting their assertiveness. Similarly, such hedges as "about" or "around," when used before a numerical quantity, render the statements they modify less precise and thus less contestable. Other hedges, such as beginning statements with "I think," "I guess," or "I suppose," or using "maybe" or "perhaps," convey the sense either that the speaker is uncertain about the statement or that the speaker prefers not to confront the addressee with a bald assertion. Lakoff argues that women use lexical hedges more often than men do, and that frequent use of lexical hedges "arise[s] out of a fear of seeming too masculine by being assertive and saying things directly." . . .

2. Tag Questions

A second characteristic of this register is the use of tag questions. Tag questions are formed by the following syntactic transformation: Take a declarative statement, append to it a clause made by reversing the negativity of the tense-bearing verb, and add an appropriate anaphoric pronoun to match the subject. Here are two examples of tag questions:

> (1) (a) "Philadelphia is a large city."
> (b) "Philadelphia is a large city, isn't it?"
> (2) (a) "I should see a lawyer."
> (b) "I should see a lawyer, shouldn't I?"

Like hedges, the illocutionary force of tag questions varies substantially depending upon the context of the utterance. Robin Lakoff ascribed several slightly differing functions to the tag question. She noted that tag questions can be "used when the speaker is stating a claim, but lacks full confidence in the truth of that claim"; or when the speaker is seeking to solicit agreement, corroboration, or acquiescence from the addressee; or when the speaker wishes to avoid confronting the addressee with an unqualified assertion.[3] Each of these uses of the tag question reflects the speaker's intent to refrain from assertively imposing her opinions or desires upon the addressee. The speaker thus avoids conflict with the addressee by using a grammatical form that invites the addressee's response, but in doing so undercuts the directness and emphatic power of the original statement.

Tag questions can, however, have a radically different illocutionary force in certain circumstances. When used by a speaker seeking an advantage over an addressee, tag questions can serve to exert power over the addressee by suggesting that taking a position contrary to that of the speaker would be unreasonable. Tag questions used in this way are generally pronounced with a falling intonation, as if to emphasize that the speaker is in no way unsure of the claim being made. Tag questions with this assertive illocutionary power share the syntactic structure of tag questions used to attenuate the force of the discourse, but their pragmatic function differs completely. If, however, we confine our consideration to those tag questions whose pragmatic function is to atten-

uate the emphatic nature of the statement, the use of such tag questions has been demonstrated to correlate with the gender of the speaker.

3. Modal Verb Usage

A third gender-linked characteristic observed by sociolinguists is the
frequent use of modal verbs such as "may," "might," "could," "ought,"
"should," and "must." While it is easy to see that modals such as "may"
and "might" function similarly to hedges in their pragmatic impact, an
example will demonstrate that even strong, assertive-sounding modal
verbs can sometimes act to soften the emphasis of the statement, depending upon the context of their use. Consider, for example, the following sentences:

This may be the right house.

This might be the right house.

This could be the right house.

This ought to be the right house.

This should be the right house.

This must be the right house.

This is the right house.

None of the sentences using modal verbs has the same matter-of-fact
emphatic character as "This is the right house." Even the example sentences using strong modal verbs such as "should," "ought," or "must"
carry the implication that the statement is the product of surmise, de-
duction, or process of elimination rather that an unmediated statement
of fact. Like lexical hedges, modal verbs can undercut the emphatic
force of an utterance.

As [with] lexical hedges and tag questions, the pragmatic interpretation of modal verbs, too, varies considerably according to context. For
instance, the modal verb "must" has a very different meaning in the sentence "You must leave immediately" than in the sentence "You must be
Terry's friend; we've been expecting you." Only the second example is an
instance of the type of modality that Lakoff identifies as a characteristic
of women's language.

4. Absence of Imperatives

A fourth characteristic of the female register is that its users avoid using the imperative grammatical mood, substituting interrogative forms
for the syntactically indicated imperative form. As Lakoff put it: "An
overt order (as in an imperative) expresses the (often impolite) assumption of the speaker's superior position to the addressee, carrying with it

the right to enforce compliance, whereas with a request the decision on the face of it is left up to the addressee."[4]

Imperatives, the verbs of command, are the most starkly assertive of all grammatical forms. Phrasing an imperative as a question, however, softens the imperative's aggressive edge. Compare the nuances in the following sentences:

Tell me the time.

Could you tell me the time?

Sit down.

Won't you sit down?

Call my lawyer.

Would you call my lawyer?

Although each of these utterances makes a demand, those phrased in an interrogative form sound less presumptive and more tactfully deferential than the baldly stated imperatives. When a speaker combines such interrogative forms with other polite qualifiers, the assertiveness of the underlying imperative is further weakened:

If it isn't too much trouble, would you call my lawyer?

If you don't mind, could you call me a lawyer?

Because the exercise of power is considered "unfeminine," women are socialized from earliest childhood to avoid directly ordering other people to do things. Not surprisingly, then, studies of children's discourse have shown that young female children characteristically avoid direct imperatives just as adult women do.

5. Rising Intonation

The fifth major feature of the female register is a paralinguistic characteristic: Its speakers use rising inflection in making declarative statements. Ordinarily, English speakers use rising intonation to signal a question or for some other special effect. This is especially true for questions that are syntactically identical to declarative statements. For example, each of the following pairs of utterances typically would be distinguished in speech by the use of a high, rising intonation at the end of the second sentence in each pair.

Chris isn't here.

Chris isn't here? (expressing uncertainty and request for confirmation or explanation)

I need a lawyer.

I need a lawyer? (expressing incredulity)

The use of rising intonation in ordinary declaratives that are not intended to express uncertainty or incredulity is a gender-linked paralinguistic trait. In making declarative utterances, American men tend to pronounce their sentence endings, called terminals, at the lowest level of intonation that they customarily use, whereas women often adopt a rising terminal. In addition, women commonly exhibit a much greater dynamic range in their intonation patterns than men do. Whereas men seldom use more than three levels of intonation, women typically use four or more separate levels of intonation, and change levels more frequently and more dramatically than do men. Since changes in intonation level are paralinguistically associated with emotion, those who use a greater range of pitch in their intonations may have their speech interpreted as more highly emotional; others may dismiss these utterances as irrational, because such speech has a dynamic range which would indicate extreme emotion in normal male speech.

B. The Pragmatics of Powerlessness in the Female Register

. . . What all of the syntactic and paralinguistic characteristics of the female register have in common is that they attenuate the illocutionary force of the speech in which they occur. Speakers adopt this register to convey uncertainty, to soften the presumptiveness of a direct statement, or to forestall opposition from the addressee. Each of these pragmatic functions is a typical communicative strategy of the powerless:

> Men's language is the language of the powerful. It is meant to be direct, clear, succinct, as would be expected of those who need not fear giving offense, who need not worry about the risks of responsibility. . . . Women's language developed as a way of surviving and even flourishing without control over economic, physical, or social reality. Then it is necessary to listen more than speak, agree more than confront, be delicate, be indirect, say dangerous things in such a way that their impact will be felt after the speaker is out of range of the hearer's retaliation.[5]

Understanding the significance of the female register within its social context, then, is impossible without carefully considering the issues of power and domination underlying the choice of linguistic registers by speakers. It misses the point to ask whether a particular utterance is "really" equivocal or only just "apparently" equivocal, since the adoption of this register, whether conscious or unconscious, is a response by the speaker to contextual powerlessness. In a recent study of equivocal language use, several researchers concluded that individuals do not freely choose to express themselves in an equivocal manner; rather, equivocation is the product of the social context in which speakers find themselves, in which direct and assertive statements are seen as leading to negative consequences for the speakers. This analysis suggests that powerless people, who most often perceive themselves to be in such "no-win" situations, would tend to adopt more equivocal speech patterns.

Empirical research on the female register suggests that the greater the imbalance of power in the communicative relationship, the more likely the powerless speaker is to use features associated with the female register. . . .

The question of who uses this register and under what circumstances is multifactored, and consequently complex. Still, virtually all researchers note that this register tends to be adopted in situations in which the speaker is at a disadvantage in power, and most agree that women in our society more frequently find themselves in such situations than do men. In the context of this [chapter], it is particularly notable that the disparity in linguistic usage between men and women appears to be greatest among lower socioeconomic classes, the persons who are most likely to find themselves the subject of police interrogation.

C. Power Asymmetry in Police Interrogation

Whether any particular person undergoing police interrogation will adopt the mode of expression that I have called the female register is not a random matter. Rather, some distinct segments of the population— women, members of certain ethnic communities, and the socioeconomically powerless—are more likely than others to speak in this register. Thus, suspects who fall into any of these categories are less apt to use the mode of expression that will give them the highest degree of constitutional protection.

Gender, ethnicity, and socioeconomic class are not the only factors determining the likelihood that a speaker will use this register. Whether a speaker adopts one register of speech rather than another depends to some degree on the specific situation in which the speech occurs. Therefore, pragmatic analysis of any particular interaction must take into account the context of that interaction, including the power relations inherent in the situation. A communicative context in which the speaker is, or is made to feel, relatively powerless enhances that individual's tendency to adopt the mode of expression characteristic of the female register.

Police interrogation of a criminal suspect may be the paradigmatic context in which one participant, the questioned suspect, feels powerless before the other. Many features of the typical police interrogation reinforce the questioned suspect's sense of powerlessness. First, interrogation in and of itself creates a power disparity between the person asking the question and the person being questioned. The questioner has the right to control the subject matter, tempo, and progress of the questioning, to interrupt responses to questions, and to judge whether the responses are satisfactory. The person questioned, on the other hand, has no right to question the interrogator, or even to question the propriety of the questions the interrogator has posed.

The impact of these factors, present in any interview, is magnified in the highly adversarial context of a police interrogation of an arrested suspect, especially when the police officer consciously manipulates the interaction to enhance the perceived power of the interrogator and the suspect's feelings of vulnerability. Police interrogators are trained to conduct the questioning in a way calculated to increase the anxiety felt by the suspect and soften her resistance. For example, the interrogating officer ideally maintains complete control over the physical environment in which the questioning takes place, isolating the suspect, who remains in unfamiliar surroundings designed to keep her psychologically off balance. The interrogator decides how long the interrogation session will last; often the session is intentionally prolonged to achieve an advantage over the suspect. Similarly, the interrogator unilaterally determines the subject matter of the interrogation and the manner in which the questions are asked, and may employ a wide variety of tactics designed to control the interrogation and overcome the suspect's resistance, including confrontational accusations, trickery and deception, baiting questions designed to insult or humiliate, and appeals to the suspect's religious values. Even the suspect's ability to answer questions is constrained by the interrogator, who may repeatedly interrupt the suspect's denials and explanations to condition the suspect to accept complete domination by the interrogating officer. In short, the interrogating officer aims to exercise total control over every aspect of the interrogation session. When, as in police interrogation, the power asymmetry of the discourse is coupled with the actual physical power that the police have over the body of the individual in custody, the suspect feels a sense of powerlessness dramatically more acute than that felt in ordinary life. The criminal suspect in police interrogations will therefore be more likely to speak in the register of the powerless.

*

*V. Transcending the "Woman Question": Cultural Pluralism and the
Female Register*

In a majority of jurisdictions, the standard governing invocation of the
right to counsel affords greater protection to suspects who speak in a direct and assertive manner. Implicit in the majority doctrine is the assumption that direct and assertive speech—a mode of expression more
characteristic of men than women—is, or should be, the norm. This
kind of gender bias, which tacitly treats prototypically *male* behavior
and experience (confident, assertive, powerful) as a synonym for *human*
behavior and experience, is especially pernicious because it is generally
invisible and therefore immune to criticism. The androcentric nature of
such legal doctrines can easily be mistaken for true gender neutrality.
As this study demonstrates, the law's incorporation of a male normative
standard may be invisible but it is not inconsequential. Those whose behavior fails to conform to these presumed norms of behavior encoded
within legal doctrine are penalized.

The framers of the majority doctrine never asked the "woman question," and failed to shape legal standards to take into account the characteristic speech patterns of women. The insight derived from asking
the woman question—that the underpinnings of legal doctrine uncon-
sciously and unwittingly incorporate a bias favoring males—raises another question. If women were not considered in the framing and interpretation of legal doctrine, are there other groups whose perspective
may likewise be missing from the law?

Women are not the only group whose typical speech patterns put
them at a legal disadvantage. In light of the link established between the
use of the female speech register and powerlessness, one would expect
that speech patterns among those from historically disempowered communities would manifest similar characteristics. It is therefore unsur-
prising that at least one researcher has observed that indirect speech
patterns are common within African-American spoken language. In his
pragmatic analysis of Black English, Thurmon Garner described what
he termed a "strategy of indirection" by speakers as a linguistic mechanism to avoid conflict.[6] The speaker's "message is delivered as suggestions, innuendos, implications, insinuations, or inferences."[7] This use
of indirect speech patterns in order to avoid conflict is the hallmark of a
pragmatic usage by persons without power, and can be found both in

the female register and in the adaptive speech patterns of subordinated African Americans forced to deal with white authority figures. . . .

Other speech communities within the United States fail to share the legally privileged norm of a direct, assertive, unqualified speaking style. For example, many ethnic groups—whose native tongues include such languages as Arabic, Farsi, Yiddish, Japanese, Indonesian, and Greek— use indirect and hedged speech patterns more frequently than do speakers of standard English. Moreover, speakers of these languages often use these indirect speech patterns when speaking English. In fact, evidence suggests that ethnic communities perpetuate their indirect speech conventions over generations, and even third and fourth generation members who speak only English continue to use speech patterns typical of their ethnic groups.

Under the standards requiring clear and unambiguous invocation of the right to counsel, therefore, a speaker from an ethnic group that uses more indirect speech conventions is likely to be misunderstood as having declined to invoke that right. Further, the norms of behavior and expression typical of many of these ethnic groups, particularly those from the Middle East and Asia, require refusing an offer, with the expectation that the offerer should and will make the offer again. To accept an offering the first time it is offered is considered impolite and impertinent. Obviously, someone whose cultural conventions include this rule of first refusal would be unlikely to invoke her right to counsel directly and unambiguously upon being read the *Miranda* rights, even though she might well desire the assistance of counsel. Current legal doctrine, premised on the expectation that an invocation of rights should be direct and unequivocal in form, does not serve the interests of the many speech communities whose discourse patterns deviate from the implicit norms in standard, "male register" English. . . .

. . . From a feminist perspective, the characteristically masculine preference for assertive speech can be seen as simply one instance of a more generalized masculine preference for assertive behavior. Such a critique would lead one to ask why the law should obligate suspects in police custody affirmatively to invoke the right to counsel at all. Instead of requiring the suspect to confront police by asserting her rights, why not automatically provide arrested suspects with counsel to be consulted before interrogation begins? . . .

NOTES

1. Katharine T. Bartlett, *Feminist Legal Methods*, 103 Harv. L. Rev. 829, 847 (1990).

2. Robin T. Lakoff, Language and Woman's Place 9–19 (1975).

3. *Id.* at 15–18.

4. *Id.* at 18.

5. Robin Lakoff, Talking Power: The Politics of Language in Our Lives 206 (1990).

6. Thurmon Garner, *Cooperative Communication Strategies: Observations in a Black Community*, 14 J. Black Stud. 233, 234–48 (1983).

7. *Id.* at 235.

22

A Statutory
Replacement
for the
Miranda
Doctrine
(1986)

·

PHILLIP E. JOHNSON

The following hypothetical statute is offered to illustrate the justifications that might be offered for a statutory replacement for the *Miranda* doctrine and the form such a statute might take. The specific provisions are drafted to illustrate the issues that should be addressed. Readers are invited to propose amendments.

Preamble

Whereas, the Supreme Court in *Miranda v. Arizona*[1] imposed detailed regulations on the interrogation of criminal suspects in both state and federal criminal investigations; and

Whereas, the constitutional basis of the *Miranda* decision has been eroded by subsequent decisions of the Courts; and

Whereas, the majority opinion in *Miranda* invited a legislative solution to the problem of protection of Fifth Amendment rights in the police interrogation process; and

Whereas, the *Miranda* majority opinion was internally inconsistent in describing custodial interrogation as inherently coercive while permitting uncounseled defendants to waive their rights in this setting; and

Whereas, the initial incoherence in the *Miranda* opinion has led to a body of case law which does not either satisfactorily curb abuse in the interrogation process or recognize the legitimate role of custodial interrogation in identifying the perpetrators of criminal acts;

Now therefore, the Congress of the United States makes the following Findings and enacts the following statutory provisions:

Findings

1. Police interrogation of suspected persons is a necessary and legitimate practice in solving crimes and ensuring that guilty persons are brought to justice.

2. Law enforcement officers have no authority to require any person, whether suspected of a crime or not, to answer their questions. The fact that persons may not be *compelled* to answer does not mean, however, that they may not be *encouraged* to do so. "[F]ar from being prohibited by the Constitution, admissions of guilt by wrongdoers, if not coerced, are inherently desirable."[2]

3. The Sixth Amendment right to the assistance of counsel, applicable to the states through the Fourteenth Amendment, attaches at the initiation of adversary judicial proceedings, when the accused is in court for arraignment on a criminal charge. Prior to that time, a suspect in custody is protected by the Fifth Amendment prohibition of compulsory self-incrimination, and by the due process clause, but not by the right to counsel. No warning of a right to counsel is necessary or appropriate before that right attaches at the initiation of adversary judicial proceedings.

4. There is an inherent potential for coercion and inhumane treatment during the police interrogation process, particularly when the crime under investigation is one which arouses strong public revulsion. The law should prohibit interrogation techniques that are inhumane or likely to induce unreliable statements, while permitting reasonable methods of persuasion aimed at encouraging truthful admissions of guilt.

5. It is highly desirable for interrogation sessions to be recorded, so that reviewing courts and other agencies can have complete and accurate information regarding the content of any statements and the circumstances under which statements were obtained.

6. Constitutional principles require that coerced admissions not be used as evidence against the accused. However, excessive reliance on exclusion of evidence as the remedy for improper police conduct is costly to the public interest in accurate factual determinations in judicial proceedings. Excluding evidence is also often ineffective as a means of affecting police behavior. There is a need for clearer standards of con-

duct to guide police in questioning suspects. There is also a need to employ remedies other than (or in addition to) exclusion of evidence.

7. Federal legislation on this subject, governing both state and federal investigations and judicial investigations, is constitutionally appropriate. Congress has plenary power to legislate rules of investigative and judicial procedure for the federal system and power to ensure, by appropriate legislation, that no person shall be deprived of life, liberty, or property without due process of law.[3] In the *Miranda* opinion itself, the Supreme Court specifically invited legislatures to address the problem of custodial interrogation.[4] Legislative action is even more appropriate now that we have the benefit of more than twenty years of experience under the rules promulgated in *Miranda.*

Statutory Provisions

On the basis of these Findings, the Congress of the United States enacts this legislation, which shall be called the Interrogation and Confession Act of 19??.

Section 1. Subject to constitutional principles and the provisions of this Act, officers may question persons, whether in custody or not, while investigating crimes and for the purpose of obtaining evidence.

Section 2. (a) Before questioning a suspect in custody, an officer shall advise the suspect that he (she) is not required to answer questions and that any answers given may be used in evidence.

(b) An officer is not required to cease questioning merely because a suspect has initially refused to answer. When the suspect has communicated a firm and considered refusal to answer, however, the officers should respect that refusal and cease questioning.

Section 3. (a) In the custodial interrogation of a suspect, an officer shall not:
(1) Employ force or threats;
(2) Make any statement which is intended to imply or may reasonably be understood as implying that the suspect will not be prosecuted or punished;
(3) Intentionally misrepresent the amount of evidence available

against the suspect, or the nature or seriousness of the anticipated charges; or

(4) Intentionally misrepresent his identity or employ any other deceptive stratagem not authorized by this Act which, in the circumstances, is fundamentally unfair; or

(5) Deny the suspect reasonable opportunity for food and rest.

(b) It does not violate this Act for an officer to:

(1) Express sympathy of compassion for the offender, whether real or feigned;

(2) Suggest that the crime may be morally understandable or excusable, whether or not the suggestion is sincere;

(3) Appeal to the suspect's conscience or values, religious or otherwise;

(4) Appeal to the suspect's sympathy for the victim or other affected persons;

(5) Inform the suspect honestly about the state of the evidence; or

(6) Inform the suspect that a voluntary admission of guilt and sincere repentance may be given favorable consideration at the time of sentence.

Section 4. (a) A suspect in custody shall be taken without unreasonable delay before a magistrate for arraignment, appointment of counsel, and consideration of pretrial release.

(b) Any period of delay shall be presumed to be reasonable if the suspect is brought before a magistrate on the next court day following arrest.

Section 5. When a suspect has appeared for arraignment in a court in the locality in which charges are to be filed, the adversary stage of the process commences and the Sixth Amendment right to counsel attaches. Thereafter, statements obtained in violation of the right to counsel are not admissible against the interrogated defendant on the pending charges.

Section 6. (a) A confession, admission, or other statement shall be excluded from evidence on motion of the defendant if it was coerced by an officer, or if there is substantial doubt as to its reliability.

(b) A statement is presumed to have been coerced if it was obtained as a result of a violation of this Act.

(c) If any evidence of a violation of this Act is produced, the prosecution has the burden of establishing by clear and convincing evidence that the statement in question was not coerced.

(d) Evidence other than statements of the defendant shall be excluded only as required by the Constitution or to the extent necessary to effectuate the purposes of this Act.

(e) Nothing in this Act prevents a state from enacting or maintaining additional grounds for excluding statements or other evidence from proceedings in its own courts.

Section 7.   When a judicial officer excludes a statement pursuant to Section 6 on the ground that it was coerced by a substantial and willful violation of this Act, or admits a statement into evidence despite a substantial and willful violation of this Act, the judicial officer shall cause a report of the proceedings and the identities of the offending officer(s) to be transmitted to the appropriate United States Attorney for review for possible prosecution under 18 U.S.C. §§242,[5] or any other applicable provision of law.

Section 8.   It is the intent of the Congress that, to the greatest extent feasible, interrogations of suspects in custody shall be recorded so as to provide a complete and accurate record of the content of any statements and the circumstances under which statements were obtained. The Attorney General is directed to prepare regulations implementing this Section and to report to Congress on or before June 30, 19??.

Section 9.   It is the intent of Congress that the provisions of this Act shall be widely circulated to judicial officers and law enforcement officers throughout the nation, in order to obtain full compliance. Officers conducting interrogations shall be trained or retrained in compliance with this Act. The Attorney General is directed to prepare regulations implementing this Section and to report to Congress on or before June 30, 19??.

Section 10. *Definitions.* As used in this Act:

(a) "Officer" means a federal, state, or local law enforcement officer, or a person acting under the direction of such an officer;

(b) "Judicial Officer" means a judge or magistrate of a federal or state court or record;

(c) "Interrogation" and "Questioning" means saying or doing anything which is intended to elicit or reasonably calculated to elicit an incriminating statement from a suspect where the primary purpose is to obtain evidence for prosecution;

(d) "Custody" exists when a suspect is under the physical control of a officer under circumstances which objectively indicate that the suspect is not free to leave.

NOTES

1. 384 U.S. 436 (1966).
2. United States v. Washington, 431 U.S. 181 (1977).
3. U.S. Const. amend. XIV, §5.
4. 384 U.S. at 490.
5. 18 U.S.C. §242 (1982) provides:

Whoever, under color of any law, statute, regulation, or custom, wilfully subjects any inhabitant of any State, Territory, or District to the deprivation of any rights, privileges, or immunities secured or protected by the Constitution or laws of the United States or to different punishments, pains, or penalties, on account of such inhabitant being an alien, or by reason of his color, or race, than are prescribed for the punishment of citizens, shall be fined not more than $1,000 or imprisoned not more than one year, or both; and if death results he shall be subject to imprisonment for any term of year or for life.

23

Videotaping
Interrogations
and Confessions
(1992)

•

WILLIAM A. GELLER

The use of video technology in criminal interrogations is well known, but—at least in the United States—unexamined. It is estimated that in 1990, about one-sixth of all police and sheriffs' departments in the United States—almost 2,400 agencies—videotaped at least some interrogations or confessions.

*

The study consisted of three parts:

> A review of English-language literature (primarily from the United Kingdom, Australia, and Canada) on the subject to identify important issues; a nationwide survey in 1990 of police and sheriffs' departments to identify agencies that videotape interrogations or confessions, and a follow-up telephone survey of a sample of agencies that do and do not videotape; and interviews of local detectives, police supervisors, prosecutors, public and private defense attorneys, and judges in eleven diverse cities or counties where interrogations are videotaped . . .

The aim of this exploratory study was to identify issues and practices pertaining to videotaping interrogations as a possible prelude to evaluative research. This [chapter] describes a variety of videotaping policies and procedures in various locales and explores the perceptions of criminal justice practitioners about videotaping and its effects. . . .

On the basis of the survey and analysis of other data, researchers calculated that one-third of all American police and sheriffs' departments serving populations of 50,000 or larger are videotaping at least some interrogations. . . .

When surveyed in 1990, most departments had been videotaping in-

terrogations for at least three years; 41 percent had done so for at least
five years. Usually departments employ audiotapes (a technique raising
many of the same issues as videotapes) for at least four years after relying solely on written methods before they advance to video documentation. A few leapfrogged directly from paper to video. In the latter agencies, one might expect videotaping to present more of a culture shock to
criminal justice practitioners. Evidence from the study's interviews indicates that even when such culture shock occurred, its effects were not
necessarily negative.

In 1990 U.S. police and sheriffs' deputies (hereafter generally referred to simply as police) videotaped suspects' statements in an estimated 57,000 criminal cases.[1] They were most likely to use videotapes
in homicide cases. . . . Interrogation videotaping is used in investigating
many other crimes but as the severity of the felony decreases, so does
the likelihood of videotaping.

*

Agencies that videotape suspects' statements gave a variety of reasons for initiating the practice: avoiding defense attorneys' challenges
of the accuracy of audiotapes and the completeness of written confessions; helping reduce doubts about the voluntary nature of confessions; jogging detectives' memories when testifying; and countering
defense criticism of "nice guy" or "softening up" techniques for interrogating suspects.

Most police agencies use video technology in some way; it is not lack
of exposure that explains the reluctance of some in the profession to
videotape suspects' statements. Conversations with police officers and
prosecutors who do not videotape suspects' statements revealed strong
views against doing so. Some said that suspects would be afraid to start
talking with a video camera rolling since they knew everything they said
would be recorded and heard in court.

Cost was the explanation most police agencies around the country
gave for not videotaping interrogations. Financial concerns included the
cost of video equipment, remodeling interview rooms, storing tapes, and
maintaining the video and audio recording equipment. . . .

Officials in some departments had another concern: the fear of having to videotape *all* suspects' statements in most types of serious felony
cases. These criminal justice practitioners argued that failure to videotape when the capacity to do so exists would result in the court's sup-

pression of nonvideotaped statements offered by the prosecution, or adverse findings by judges and juries who would find a written confession unconvincing.

In fact, evidence was found both for and against the prediction that a police department that tapes *any* serious felony interrogations or confessions will have to tape *most* or *all.* In the national survey, 70 percent of responding agencies reported that after introducing videotaping they found it no harder to present in court suspects' confessions without video documentation. . . .

In most communities visited, defense attorneys had at times insinuated to judges that police failure to videotape a confession implied that the interrogation could not stand scrutiny. In most locales these arguments rarely proved helpful in motions to suppress. Nor did they normally seem to aid the defense much in raising judges' or jurors' doubts about a defendant's guilt.

Those interviewed who expressed concern about having to videotape all confessions generally turned out to be investigators who were *not* engaged in videotaping. In Houston, Texas, for example, homicide detectives who rarely videotape their interrogations cited this concern, while robbery investigators who videotape many confessions did not. In addition, it appears from the survey that most detective units that introduced videotaping avoid the possible consequences of selective videotaping because they find the practice sufficiently beneficial to do it uniformly.[2] . . .

The national survey found that nearly all agencies videotape openly, either telling suspects they are being taped or leaving the camera or a microphone visible during the session. Still, those agencies that tape covertly thought highly of the procedure and its apparent benefits.

The ethics of surreptitiously videotaping a suspect during an interrogation are hotly debated in this and in other countries. The police cannot force a suspect to submit to a videotaped interrogation; the suspect can foil the interview by exercising his or her *Miranda* right to refuse to talk. This is one reason that covert videotaping is sometimes done: to portray a suspect talking willingly, who might, if aware of it, object to a video record being made. Another reason is to avoid distracting the suspect—and interrogators—with the video camera, microphone, and equipment operator.

Concealing a camera using pinhole lenses or behind one-way mirrors and using subminiature microphones, however, may occur in overt as well as covert tapings. Police investigators who are committed to overt taping may also wish to keep distractions to a minimum during an interrogation. . . .

A department may decide against covert taping for several reasons. State or local law may bar surreptitious taping. Federal constitutional law should not be a bar, however, since a suspect would be hard-pressed to prove that he or she had a "reasonable expectation of privacy" while under police interrogation in a station house interview room. Indeed, the *Miranda* warning makes explicit that anything suspects say can and probably will be used against their interests. A department may realize that, as a practical matter, word spreads too rapidly in jail and on the streets to keep covert taping practices a secret long. Covert taping may not square with the image of fairness in handling criminal suspects that a department wants to present to the public.

*

Departments are sharply divided between taping the entire station house interrogation and a recapitulation, that is, a videotaped summary of highlights of information that the suspect is willing to repeat, after a previously untaped interrogation. A recap might include both incriminating and exculpatory statements or consist largely of a confession. A few of the visited departments also record recaps they expect to consist primarily of denials of guilt.

At agencies visited, fully videotaped interviews took an estimated average of two to four hours; the longest videotaped interview was approximately seven hours. Recaps were estimated to take an average of fifteen to forty-five minutes. The distinction has cost implications both for the purchase of blank videotapes and the creation of transcripts from recorded tapes.

As a rule, defense attorneys interviewed said they strongly prefer entire interviews to recapitulations. They objected to recaps full of "leading questions with 'yes' or 'no' answers" and spoke of "suspects who have been Pavlov-dogged into a reaction during rehearsals." One public defender suggested that taping entire interviews might make the police more respectful of a suspect's rights.

Another concern, expressed mainly by defense attorneys and judges, is that recaps minimize the apparent remorse of the defendant. He or she is apt to have repeated an account again and again before the recording begins, robbing a recap of an emotional edge. As a result he or she may seem atypically cold and callous in the recap.

Another objection to recaps is that a seemingly trivial comment by a suspect under interrogation might prove crucial at trial but be lost in a recap. For example, a suspect might say, "I was there but I didn't do anything." This may seem unimportant at the time, but capturing the "I was there . . ." admission on videotape would more than likely prevent an alibi defense at trial. . . .

Some detectives don't like taping an entire interview because they don't know what the suspect will say or where the interview is going. "You won't get the truth the first time around," said one police official, "and the defense attorneys will make use of the exculpatory statements." Yet others said that judges and jurors *expect* a suspect to begin an interrogation with denials, and their ability to watch the anticipated progression from protestations of innocence to admissions of guilt gives them even more confidence in the authenticity, sincerity, and voluntariness of the incriminating statements.

Some practitioners asserted that recaps can lead to accusations that interrogators used coercion. A judge acknowledged that a defense attorney could "make points" with a jury over a "rehearsal" interrogation that preceded the recap. "But the police could overcome that," he noted, "by recounting at the beginning of the taped interview what transpired before the videotaping began." A number of agencies visited do just that; they even ask the suspect to describe how he has been treated by the police to that point. Most of the criminal justice personnel interviewed believe that turning on the videocamera only for a recap still suffices to remind interrogators to use tactics during the pretape interview that will not impede placing any recorded confessions into evidence.

*

The vast majority of surveyed agencies that videotape interviews believed that videotaping has led to improvements in police interrogations. These include, according to agencies visited: better preparation for interviews by investigators; . . . [i]nterrogations without such traditional distractions as a typewriter, notebooks, or additional personnel, such as a court reporter; [s]upervisors' monitoring of the interrogation on closed-circuit television or by subsequent viewing to assess interrogators' performance; [u]se of old tapes to train both new and experienced detectives in interview techniques; and [a]bility to show an accomplice's taped confession to an uncooperative suspect and thus possibly stimulate a change in attitude.

Both the national survey and site visits produced information on how videotaping affects the interrogation process. The survey did not support the notion, advanced in some studies in other countries, that videotaping, because it is seen as fairer to suspects, makes them more willing to talk. Since their adoption of videotape procedures, for each agency that reported suspects more willing to talk, three others reported suspects *less* willing (8.6 percent versus 28.3 percent; 63.1 percent of the agencies reported no change in suspects' propensity to talk due to the adoption of videotaping). . . .

. . . The survey found that most of the suspects who appear on camera provide more incriminating information than suspects did previously. Sixty percent of responding agencies found they profited in this way, although 13 percent reported suspects provided less incriminating information. Yet most agencies visited during the study reported obtaining more of both incriminating *and* exculpatory information through videotaping. However, exculpatory statements generally were made in interviews in which the suspect offered an admission or confession. Most prosecutors said the added exculpatory information had not presented a problem for them. . . .

Detectives reverted to a more balanced approach once they became accustomed to being taped; they realized that they could maintain professionalism while using traditional tactics. For example, when interrogators use profanity, as long as they are following up on the suspect's choice of words to communicate clearly rather than gratuitously or in an intimidating manner, it does not seem to bother judges or juries. Indeed, an interrogator's fastidious politeness often backfires, suggesting to suspect, judge, and jury alike that the interrogator is either naive or disingenuous. . . .

The survey results, confirmed by many officers interviewed, indicated that because of videotaping fewer allegations of coercion or intimidation were made by defense attorneys. On-camera administrations of the *Miranda* warning by the police are one major reason for this result. Those officers interviewed also noted they felt less pressure in the courtroom and faced fewer defense assertions that police had fabricated confessions;[3] claims that were made typically were pro forma and were offered by defense attorneys primarily to avoid a client's claim of inadequate representation by counsel.

. . . Prosecutors visited could point to no substantial effect of videotaping on decisions to charge suspects, but they were in virtually unanimous agreement that videotaping helped them assess the state's case and prepare for trial. Said one district attorney: "You learn a lot from the videotape—how sophisticated the defendant is, how he answers questions, how you might cross-examine."

Prosecutors credited videotaping with providing details impossible to capture from written interview notes or a transcript and mostly lost in an audiotape as well: the suspect's and officer's physical condition, demeanor, attire, intonation in speaking, body language, and the situation on the night (or day) of the arrest. Such nonverbal cues can greatly add to—or subtract from—what the suspect is saying.

Although most prosecutors claimed that videotaping is an asset in negotiating acceptable pleas, one noted that it can cut both ways: Sometimes the video raises hopes among defense attorneys that they may be able to assert a defense (such as insanity or intoxication) that otherwise would not be credible. Even when videotaped statements produce unfavorable results for the state, they often help prosecutors prepare for either trial or plea bargaining. For example, one prosecutor noted that videotapes help her distinguish genuine remorse in a suspect from feigned remorse, an advantage in either situation.

Even if "the news is going to be bad," at least the prosecutor is warned about what lies in store. And should a tape reveal the state's case against a defendant to be weak, it may help the prosecution decide whether to charge the defendant with a less serious crime or to drop charges entirely.

. . . Defense attorneys' opinions of videotapes were much more mixed than those of prosecutors. Some were flatly opposed to videotaping, primarily because it generally gives the state a strategic edge. Written and, to a certain extent, audiotaped confessions are easier for the defense to attack as the product of coercion or fabrication; these types of documentation also permit the defense to explore more areas of ambiguity in courtroom interpretations than can be done with videotaped statements.

Others—particularly public defenders with daunting caseloads—appreciated the client-control benefits of videotaping. They also claimed the nonverbal information conveyed was useful; for example, torn clothing could corroborate a defendant's claim that he got into a fight with the homicide victim and the killing was not premeditated. Two of them separated their professional and personal reactions to videotaping. Said one private attorney who specializes in murder cases: "As a defense lawyer, I hate videotaping. As a citizen needing the protection of the police against criminals, I love it."

One public defender said that videotapes can help the defense by capturing meaningful pauses in an interview that would be lost in a written documentation. In another instance, a private attorney recalled a case in which his client was told that if he cooperated with the police he would not be charged; a co-defendant would be charged instead. Because the videotape of his client's response showed an eagerness to confess, the lawyer succeeded in his claim of improper promises. Another public defender pointed out that a defendant's behavior and speech on camera can help an attorney assess whether it would be useful to put him or her on the witness stand. . . .

Some attorneys also said videotapes help them achieve "client control" by cutting through lies clients try to tell attorneys about how they were interrogated or what incriminating remarks they made. Tapes can also help attorneys persuade clients they are better off pleading guilty to a reduced charge because a taped confession virtually assures conviction. Most defense attorneys agree that if their clients confess, they prefer they do so on videotape; the others who prefer written confessions say they are easier to attack as the product of improper promises, coercion, fabrication, or other forms of interrogator misconduct.

Videos can be useful to attorneys not only in getting the client to admit what he did, but also in helping a defendant's family accept the fact of his or her wrongdoing. And for defendants trying to be honest with their attorneys, videotapes can help jog memory about details that may help the defense.

*

In the literature review, the researchers found that some commentators estimated that videotaping would save the criminal justice system money because fewer officers would have to attend an interrogation. However, in three-quarters of the agencies surveyed, videotaping produced no change in the number of officers on hand.

*

The survey found high levels of satisfaction with videotaping equipment technically. Equipment malfunctions or operator errors were described as a major problem by only 7 percent of police agencies. More than one-half reported having no problems at all.

*

Departments that paid for audio-video equipment and renovated interview rooms with soundproofing and proper lighting spent between

$5,000 and $40,000. The Bronx district attorney's expert on videotaping, with more than twenty years of firsthand experience in setting up and running a video recording program for serious felony confessions, reported that it costs $25,000 to construct "one complete interview setup, including playback equipment and top-of-the-line editing equipment. This," he observed, "is slightly more than the cost of one police car and certainly less than a police officer's salary." He acknowledged that "multiple setups for larger departments will be more," and reported that the Bronx district attorney's office "replaced all [its] equipment— five field units, five playback setups, and editing—for $60,000. I doubt," he suggested, "anyone in the world really will need more than we have, so cost is very low."

. . . Police and prosecutorial officials in some jurisdictions worry that everyone involved in a case will, as a matter of routine, insist on verbatim transcripts of the audio of entire interrogation tapes, which can run five hours or longer. In many jurisdictions transcription has become the rule rather than the exception.

Making so many and such lengthy transcripts could be problematic for some criminal justice budgets. However, if agencies videotape only short recaps, transcriptions are more affordable.

*

Videotaping is thought to help win acceptance into evidence of incriminating statements by accused persons. This is primarily because it makes it easier to show the voluntary nature of a confession. Most judges interviewed saw such benefits in videotaping. One noted, "It makes police work credible." Another said, "Juries really like videotapes. This form of evidence holds the juror's interest." Judges believe decisions to admit confessions in evidence and to convict or acquit are more credible when the suspect is questioned on camera. Others interviewed substantiated that videotaping facilitates court admission of confessions, even if they are recapitulations of long statements.

. . . Prosecutors interviewed reported that videotaping was a factor in their negotiating more guilty pleas and higher sentences. Likewise, the vast majority of police departments surveyed reported that videotaping had helped secure guilty pleas. Tulsa police reported:

> As soon as the defense attorneys around here find out that their clients have given a videotaped confession, the cases are plea bargained out. With audiotape, we didn't get nearly so many pleas. The defendant could still claim the police held a gun to his head or had a foot on his throat.

3 1 1

As for securing convictions, an equally overwhelming proportion of agencies surveyed believed videotaping had helped to do this. Those interviewed generally agreed. . . . As to how videotaped confessions affected sentences, most but not all of those interviewed felt longer sentences resulted. . . .

Police tools and tactics must be employed in a way that balances several sometimes competing objectives. A balance must be struck between effectiveness, efficiency, and legitimacy. On the basis of this exploratory study, videotaping appears to be a distinctly useful tool, because it is seen as simultaneously furthering the criminal justice system's pursuit of disparate objectives:

Videos can help police accurately and efficiently assess a suspect's guilt or innocence. They foster humane treatment of suspects, fairness, and respect for civil rights and liberties. They can help to persuade other authorities and the public that police interrogations are conducted professionally and thereby reduce some of the stresses that impede excellence in police work.

In a national survey, a striking 97 percent of all departments that have ever videotaped suspects' statements continue to find such videotaping, on balance, to be useful. Likewise, agencies visited were asked, knowing what they know of videotaping now, if they would do it again. Every agency said yes.

In departments that have adopted video documentation of suspects' statements, early resistance by detectives has been transformed into active support among most. The survey found that 60 percent of agencies switching to videotape reported that their detectives at first disapproved of or had mixed feelings about the practice. By the time of the survey, however, after most of these agencies had several years of experience with videotaping, the disapproval and mixed review figure had fallen to 26 percent. Initial resistance, the interviews suggested, is primarily a general resistance to change. . . .

The weight of opinion among criminal justice practitioners who have firsthand knowledge of videotaping interrogations and confessions thus seems clearly positive. . . .

Future evaluations that build on this preliminary study of issues and practices in videotaping should provide more insight into the benefits and drawbacks of an increasingly popular investigative tool for U.S. police.

N O T E S

1. Site visits disclosed that many departments' records did not distinguish between the videotaping of statements by suspects and the videotaping of statements by *witnesses* or *victims*. As a result, the findings of this national survey—in which respondents, forewarned of researchers' telephone interviews, probably checked records to estimate how often their agencies videotape *suspects'* statements—must be taken as preliminary.

2. Even detectives who aim to videotape interrogations turn off the camera occasionally when suspects insist they will speak only if they are not taped.

3. Some of the advantages of videotaping suspects' interrogations or confessions are intangible but no less valuable. In an era where homicide tallies have set new records and staffing levels in police and sheriffs' departments are not growing, some wonder how departments consider adopting a time-consuming use of video technology. Many criminal justice practitioners, however, argue that videotaping could save time compared with other ways of documenting interrogations. Even if it does not, it seems to avoid something even more important—wear and tear on officers. Backed by a videotape clearly showing that a suspects' confession is voluntary, a detective on the witness stand who denies using coercion to win a confession is in a strong position. Whatever videotaping's costs in terms of time and money, it promises savings of officer stress and burnout, which may be among its most valuable advantages.

24

The
Twenty-first
Century:
A World
without *Miranda?*
(1998)

•

GEORGE C. THOMAS III

As we approach the twenty-first century, *Miranda*'s ethical problems are receiving renewed attention. Several chapters in this book question the way *Miranda* struck the balance between persuading guilty suspects to confess and preventing the inherent compulsion of police interrogation. What is wrong with persuading guilty suspects to confess? If the answer is "nothing," as is likely, the question becomes whether *Miranda* limits the ability of police to persuade suspects and, if so, whether *Miranda* achieves any ethical gains that compensate for the reduced persuasion.

Conducting an ethical analysis of *Miranda* is rife with difficulties. One problem can, however, be eliminated by definition. Much of the voluminous *Miranda* scholarship focuses on the distinct legal question of whether *Miranda* can be justified as a reading of the U.S. Constitution. This question has dimensions of its own. Albert Alschuler in Chapter 12 raises the question of whether the historical understanding of the privilege against self-incrimination can justify *Miranda*'s "right to silence." Many chapters in the book phrase the question of *Miranda*'s justifiability as a mixture of legal analysis and policy rationales: Once we understand what goes on in the police interrogation room, does it make sense to read the Constitution to create a right to silence?

The goal in this chapter is to isolate the policy and ethical questions from the overlapping question of how best to read the Constitution. Thus, I leave to one side the issue of constitutional interpretation, including the rule of *stare decisis* that weighs against overruling prior cases. The only question examined here is whether *Miranda* can be ethically justified if we consider the question afresh and without regard to what the Constitution might say (or might be interpreted to say).

Similarly, I will not consider the symbolic value of *Miranda* because I am persuaded by Gerald Caplan (Chapter 9) that *Miranda*'s symbolism is morally ambiguous. To be sure, *Miranda* can claim the high ground as a symbol of government's appreciation for the dignity of the individual suspect, even when the police have probable cause to believe that he has committed a serious crime. But what about the symbolism of allowing suspects, some or most of whom are guilty, to cut off questioning designed to solve crimes? The symbolic message implicit here is that we care more about suspects than we do about the victims of crime.[1]

To be sure, as Yale Kamisar has pointed out, the problem continues to defy simplification because the rules of interrogation interlock with the rules of arrest. If the Fourth Amendment had a meaningful probable cause standard that was vigilantly enforced by courts, we would all worry less about vigorous interrogation because the chances of the suspect's being innocent would be drastically reduced. But Kamisar argues, and I agree, that the Fourth Amendment does not pose a significant barrier to arrest based on whim, caprice, or prejudice.[2] Nonetheless, for purposes of this chapter's theoretical exercise, I will assume that police are interrogating only suspects whom they have meaningful probable cause to believe are guilty of a particular crime.

Indeed, many of my assumptions are highly artificial. Lacking relevant data, however, there is no other way to isolate the ethical question. Plenty of problems remain even after these simplifying assumptions. What does it mean to ask whether *Miranda* achieves ethical gains that compensate for any loss in the persuasion of guilty suspects to answer questions? How can we measure either side of the ethical equation? Are the two sides commensurable? We can begin by thinking in general terms about the harm and benefit that *Miranda* might produce. On the harm side, we can place the failure to solve an undetermined number of crimes and the use of more police trickery to get around the effect of the warnings. On the benefit side, we can place a reduction in police compulsion, an increase in police professionalism, a greater assurance that answering questions was what the suspect wanted to do, and an increased ability for police, prosecutors, and judges to know which confessions will be admissible and which will not.

One of the problems in conducting the ethical balance is that there is much we do not know about the effect of *Miranda*. For example, we do not know whether *Miranda* gives assurance that answering questions is what the suspect really wanted to do, or whether *Miranda* acts in subtle ways to compel suspects to answer questions they would not otherwise have answered.[3] So we do not know whether to count changes in the suspect's attitude toward the interrogation as a benefit or harm.

More fundamentally, we do not know how to compare the variables. How much should we count one lost conviction? To what extent does *Miranda* prevent false confessions and thus unjust convictions? How does a lost conviction of a guilty person compare to the reduction in interrogation pressures provided by *Miranda*? One way to attempt to compare the two variables is to consider whether, on balance, the world is a better place if we have reduced pressure in a particular case instead of gaining a conviction in that very case. We can imagine this as counterfactual possibilities. In one world, the police comply with *Miranda*, the suspect does not answer questions, the crime is not solved, and the suspect goes free. In the other world, the police do not give *Miranda* warnings, the suspect answers questions, and is convicted. Let us further assume that in both worlds the police did not use Fifth Amendment compulsion but engaged in vigorous questioning to produce a response that would be considered noncompelled if a court examined the facts of the interrogation. Finally, let us assume that the suspect is guilty of the crime for which the police are questioning him. Which world do we prefer: world #1, in which the guilty suspect goes free but escapes vigorous questioning, or world #2 in which vigorous questioning produces an incriminating admission, solves a crime, and likely results in incarceration for the guilty party?

Before tentatively suggesting answers to these questions, we must defend an assumption underlying the counterfactual hypothetical—that *Miranda* provides a broader protection against compulsion than the Constitution requires. This is a key assumption. If *Miranda* is precisely co-extensive with the Fifth Amendment, then any ethical concerns about the effect of police persuasion on suspects must be directed at the Fifth Amendment rather than *Miranda*. In the aftermath of *Miranda*, little controversy has attended the limitations on government that are at the core of the Fifth Amendment right against compelled self-incrimination, such as the right of defendants not to be compelled to testify and perhaps even the right of witnesses at grand jury hearings and congressional committees to refuse to answer incriminating questions. That more people are unwilling to accept *Miranda* probably indicates that *Miranda* is at the margin of the Fifth Amendment protection, and thus perhaps over-inclusive.

That *Miranda* is over-inclusive is now firmly established in the Supreme Court's jurisprudence. Whatever the *Miranda* Court may have thought on this issue, and whatever scholars may still think, the Court has been clear for the last twenty years: *Miranda* is a presumption that "serves" the Fifth Amendment's prohibition of compelled self-incrimination. Thus, the Court has told us, *Miranda* "sweeps more broadly than the Fifth Amendment itself."[4] The over-inclusive nature of the *Miranda* presumption necessarily means that, in the Court's words, "unwarned statements that are otherwise voluntary within the meaning of the Fifth Amendment must nevertheless be excluded from evidence under *Miranda*. In the individual case, *Miranda*'s preventive medicine provides a remedy even to the defendant who has suffered no identifiable constitutional harm."[5]

On this understanding, *Miranda* bars some incriminating statements that would be admitted if the Court had a better test of Fifth Amendment compulsion. Some defendants go free because *Miranda* prohibits questioning even when it does not constitute compulsion. Whether *Miranda* is ethically supportable as an over-inclusive presumption depends, at least in part, on the empirical consequences of the presumption. The empirical effect of *Miranda* remains open to question, as we saw in the debate between Cassell and Schulhofer (Chapters 13 and 14), and between Cassell/Hayman and me (Chapters 16 and 17). The relevant outcomes may be grouped into four categories. In each category, I will use *confession* to identify any incriminating statement produced by police interrogation, realizing that not all answers to police questions are incriminating. First, *Miranda* might cause a substantial reduction in the incidence of confessions. Second, *Miranda* might not cause any change in the behavior of individual suspects—at least not any change we can measure. Third, *Miranda* might have two overlapping and largely self-canceling effects: While it might persuade some suspects to answer questions, it might persuade roughly an equal number not to cooperate. This is the "steady-state" theory of confessions sketched in Chapter 17—an overall confession rate that is not measurably different from what it would be without *Miranda*—though, to be sure, the "steady state" acts to mask measurable changes in the behavior of subgroups of suspects. Fourth, *Miranda* might persuade suspects to incriminate themselves without deterring an equivalent number of confessions, thus increasing the confession rate.

THE FUTURE OF *MIRANDA*

Outcome 1: *Miranda* Reduces Confessions

The first outcome, that *Miranda* would cause a significant reduction in confessions, is the one expected by both supporters and detractors of *Miranda* in 1966. But it raises ethical concerns that are surprisingly difficult to rebut. The question is how much we are willing to pay in terms of lost confessions for the practical benefits of the *Miranda* warnings plus the belief (hope?) that police pressure is less of a factor in the confessions that do result.[6]

Assume, for example, that the national confession rate with *Miranda* magically removed is 50 percent for serious crimes.[7] Now assume that we add *Miranda* and give police time to adjust to its strictures. If suspects listen closely to the *Miranda* warnings and often act in ways consistent with their self-interest, the confession rate will fall. Let us assume a robust *Miranda* effect—that the post-*Miranda* confession rate permanently dips to the level Cassell and Hayman claim for their Salt Lake County data: 33 percent of the interrogated suspects. (See Chapter 16.) The number of arrests for FBI index crimes—the most serious crimes—is roughly three million per year.[8] Applying a 17 percent reduction in confessions to the total number of arrests would mean a loss of around 500,000 confessions. Of course, not all arrests involve questioning, but we need only a rough estimate to allow a judgment on the *Miranda* ethical issue.

The number of lost confessions, however, does not tell us how many lost *convictions* would result. Police usually have other evidence (which is why they are questioning the suspect), and the other evidence is often sufficient to trigger "ameliorative mechanisms" that tend to ensure a conviction of some offense.[9] These mechanisms include plea bargaining, in which the prosecution almost always has more leverage than the defendant. Of course, to the extent a serious crime is plea-bargained to a lesser crime on account of a lost confession, this, too, is a cost of *Miranda*. "Lost convictions" thus include those cases where the suspect was never convicted of anything and those where the suspect served less time than he otherwise would have served. Because a rough estimate will suffice, we can take Stephen Schulhofer's conservative estimate that 20 percent of lost confessions will produce a lost conviction—either no conviction or conviction of a lesser offense than would otherwise result.[10]

Using this estimate, 500,000 lost confessions means 100,000 lost convictions. The cost to society of 100,000 lost convictions includes the new crimes that will be produced by having the offenders back on the street more quickly. The next step requires an estimate of the number of index crimes committed by the "average" criminal. Though estimates vary widely—some are as high as 187 total felonies per year—a reasonable estimate is approximately fifteen per year.[11]

We also need to know how much time in prison is lost because of the lost convictions. A rough average of prison time actually served for index crimes is about two years.[12] It is necessary, however, to discount this average sentence because the estimate of "lost" convictions included an undetermined number of convictions with shorter sentences. A reasonable assumption is that the loss of a confession reduces the average sentence by one-half. After all, a confession is powerful evidence. Without a confession, some charges will be dismissed and more favorable plea bargains seem likely in many cases. On this assumption, an estimate for the cost of each lost conviction is one year of actual incarceration. With an estimated 100,000 lost convictions, this becomes 100,000 more "years" added to the criminal population. If each criminal commits fifteen crimes per year, that is an additional 1.5 million crimes.

In reaching these estimates, two additional assumptions are made. One assumption, widely held among criminologists, is that the "supply" of crime victims is relatively elastic and thus having more criminals on the street will produce more crime and more victims.[13] The other assumption is that the effect of *Miranda* is spread evenly among all FBI index crimes rather than concentrated in certain crimes (such as murder and burglary). Because the 1.5 million figure is so heavily dependent on estimates and assumptions, it makes sense to talk about a range of additional crimes, say from one to two million.

The question is: What does *Miranda* provide to justify the acceptance of that level of new crimes? As we have seen, one answer is that the police, prosecutors, and courts can more easily decide the voluntariness issue under *Miranda*. Assuming that to be true, it is a pretty limp response. If we could prevent one to two million serious crimes per year by having a different rule about confessions, wouldn't society be justified in telling police, prosecutors, and judges that they will just have to work harder?

So the answer, to be defensible, must include prevention of compelled confessions. This argument assumes that the traditional voluntariness test will permit the introduction of some compelled confessions, crediting Lawrence Herman's argument in Chapter 10 that the voluntariness test is not very discriminating. Let us assume that one-half of the

500,000 lost confessions were compelled, in Fifth Amendment terms, but would have been admitted under the voluntariness test. This is a robust assumption, but I will show later that it does not matter what assumption we make if the sole *Miranda* effect is to reduce confessions. On the assumptions made thus far, we must choose between one and two million new crimes per year, and 250,000 compelled confessions admitted into evidence.

Now the question becomes: Is it worth all these serious crimes to avoid 250,000 compelled confessions? Reducing both sides of this "equation," is it worth compelling a single confession if we could expect thereby to prevent four to eight additional crimes? Answering this question requires a difficult ethical judgment, in part because compelled confessions and serious crimes do not seem commensurable. One way to compare the two is to note that victims of crime do not choose their status, while our system of justice assumes that criminals choose to commit crimes. We might then say that the harm of compelling a confession from a guilty suspect, someone who has chosen to violate the criminal law, is less than the harm of inflicting four to eight additional crimes on society, each crime having a victim who reasonably expects to be protected from crime.

At least as long as we are talking only about guilty suspects (and keeping in place all the other assumptions noted so far), it would be plausible to conclude that *Miranda* cannot ethically stand. If the only cost of overruling *Miranda* was compelling guilty suspects to confess, our concern with the dignity and autonomy of suspects might very well be subordinated to our wish to prevent one to two million new crimes each year. But we cannot avoid Richard Leo's concern in Chapter 20 with false confessions.

If we add false confessions to the mix, the ethical question becomes even more difficult. It is almost impossible to weigh the cost of an innocent defendant being convicted. Note, however, that there are two categories of false confessions, and the ethical question is different in each context. The category that first comes to mind, but which is likely quite rare, is a confession given by a suspect who is innocent of any criminal wrongdoing relevant to the police investigation. Such a person is in the interrogation room because someone made a mistake (the police, a witness) or someone has acted with malice toward the suspect.

Although mistakes are often made and people often act maliciously toward others, the conventional wisdom is that almost no one who is completely innocent of relevant wrongdoing can be convinced to confess by the kind of pressure permitted by the voluntariness test. Though no one has succeeded in giving much content to the voluntariness test, it is clear that it forbids torture and other types of physical compulsion. In the absence of the rack and the screw, it seems unlikely that a wholly innocent person would confess.

Richard Leo's contribution in Chapter 20 makes us rethink the conventional wisdom on this issue, but Leo's charge is directed against *Miranda* itself. He argues that *Miranda* fails to facilitate inquiry into the aspects of police interrogation that produce psychologically induced false confessions. Leo argues that matters may even be worse under *Miranda* than under the voluntariness test because courts do not tend to dig beneath the surface of a facially valid *Miranda* waiver, while in the pre-*Miranda* days judges had to inquire into the conditions of interrogation.

There is much here we do not know. For the moment, it is reasonable to assume that *Miranda* has no effect (positive or negative) on the number of "wholly innocent" false confessions. That leaves the second category of false confessions—when a suspect makes a confession that exaggerates his guilt. If, for example, the true facts would disclose a case of manslaughter, a confession that suggests murder would be a false confession, but the confessor would not be innocent in the sense the word is usually used. This suspect is innocent of murder, to be sure, but we do not know whether he will be found guilty of murder. Given the pressures on the system to produce guilty pleas, the lack of clarity of many offense definitions, and the vagaries of the process by which prosecutors choose charges, we simply do not know if the suspect will be convicted of the more serious (false) charge. We do know, however, that our hypothetical suspect has confessed to something he did not do, and this has to be judged a cost of police interrogation. Again we are not capable of assessing the total cost because we do not know how often this occurs with *Miranda* in place, nor do we know how often it would occur if we returned to the due process voluntariness test.

Until we have more information about false confessions, any ethical balance must remain tentative. It seems likely, however, that the increase in false confessions, including both senses of "false," will be so small that it should make a difference only if the balance was otherwise close. Is the choice between 250,000 compelled confessions and one to two million new crimes a close one? I think not. It seems unlikely that a sensible society would choose even one million new crimes in exchange for suppressing 250,000 generally reliable (but compelled) confessions.

If this is right, false confessions would change the ethical balance only if they increased markedly in a world without *Miranda*.

There are three critical assumptions to the very tentative ethical judgment just made: (1) the number of new crimes for each criminal, (2) the prison time lost for each lost conviction, and (3) the ratio of "hidden" compelled confessions to total lost confessions. The assumptions made earlier about (1) and (2) are defensible. No one knows the size of (3). But if (1) and (2) hold constant, (3) can almost be ignored. If we assume that every single confession suppressed by *Miranda* is a hidden compelled confession—which seems extremely unlikely—and hold both (1) and (2) constant, we can then ask whether it is worth suffering one to two million new crimes to keep 500,000 compelled (but hidden) confessions out of evidence. Again, it is difficult to argue that even two crimes (using the low end of the estimate) is a reasonable price to keep one guilty suspect from being compelled to confess by the inherent compulsion of police interrogation (but without actual compulsion that would be picked up by the voluntariness test).

One assumption we have not examined is whether *Miranda* actually prevents 500,000 suspects from confessing. It turns out that the number of "lost" confessions does not matter, as long as we hold constant assumptions (1) and (2). Each lost confession will produce, on average, the same number of new crimes. The ratio of new crimes to lost confessions will thus remain the same. If the *Miranda* effect is larger, causing more suspects not to confess, that only increases the number of new crimes produced by *Miranda*. If the effect is smaller, then *Miranda* plays a smaller role in reducing police compulsion and is correspondingly less beneficial. So any assumption about the magnitude of *Miranda*'s effect in deterring confessions leads (tentatively) to the same ethical judgment: *Miranda* is not ethically justified.

Outcome 2: *Miranda* Has No Effect

As Chapter 17 makes plain, although it is difficult to imagine that *Miranda* is wholly without effect, I am nevertheless skeptical that *Miranda* actually causes a measurable decrease in the confession rate. Given the self-interest that suspects have in not confessing, and the relative clarity of the *Miranda* warnings, why would not a measurable number of suspects decide to say nothing? The no-effect hypothesis incorporates an account of human volition that is more complex than the traditional understanding: It assumes that suspects are caught in a web of deterministic forces from which they cannot be saved by the mere giving of ritualized warnings.

Even if this account of human volition is less likely than the traditional understanding—that humans act rationally in their self-interest—it is hardly an inconceivable portrait of human motivation, particularly when humans are in the highly stressful situation of being under arrest and facing police interrogation. On this deterministic account, *Miranda* changes nothing about the behavior of suspects.

This is an easy outcome to evaluate as an ethical proposition. If *Miranda* causes no change in the behavior of suspects, it cannot claim credit for preventing the admission of *any* compelled statements. Moreover, even if *Miranda* causes the police to act differently, the difference in police behavior has (by definition in the no-effect outcome) no effect on suspects. Why would we care that the police act more fairly or more professionally if suspects remain unaffected by the change in police behavior? In effect, it is artificial to separate police behavior from the behavior of suspects. We care about police behavior only because we think it affects how suspects behave. If that link is severed (as it is in the context of *Miranda* if we assume that the warnings have no effect on any suspect), we would no longer care about police professionalism. If *Miranda*'s benefits are measured by asking whether suspects more often act in their self-interest, it would be fair to conclude that *Miranda* offers no benefits in the no-effect scenario.

Of course, on the assumptions made so far (that police always comply with *Miranda*), *Miranda* causes no harm, either: there will be no confessions to suppress if police always comply and thus no cost to the system in terms of lost evidence against guilty suspects. Given our simplifying assumptions, the no-effect outcome is an ethical draw—no discernible benefit or harm. In this no-effect world, it makes sense to talk about the symbolic value of *Miranda*. Perhaps the no-effect outcome is the empirical reality that the defenders of *Miranda* assume when they rest their case largely on its symbolism.

Outcome 3: A "Steady-State" Theory of *Miranda*

The third possible outcome is the one sketched in Chapter 17. Maybe *Miranda* persuades some suspects to make voluntary statements that sometimes turn out to be incriminating, at the same time that it permits roughly the same number of suspects to resist the inherent compulsion of police interrogation. This is a "win-win" situation for *Miranda* because

it fulfills the Court's promise of lessening the coercive effect of police interrogation without, on balance, costing the system any lost convictions. If this outcome can be empirically demonstrated, it would put to
rest the ethical question. *Miranda* would have no overall harmful effect,
because of the steady-state level of confessions, but could claim credit
for the reduction in compelled confessions.

Outcome 4: *Miranda* Increases Confessions

There is a darker possibility. The *Miranda* warnings may persuade
suspects to babble to police, and thus to incriminate themselves more
often than would have been the case prior to *Miranda*. To see this pos-
siblity, consider that the warnings have become a ritualistic event—
widely publicized on television—which signals that the police believe
the suspect is the guilty party. When the police give *Miranda* warnings, the suspect may understand the police to be saying, "You have the
right to remain silent; if you do, you will pay the penalty of continued
custody."

The suspect may now be more likely to answer. He feels the threat of
continued custody more acutely now that he has "official" confirmation
that the police believe him guilty, and he also likely perceives a greater
benefit from answering. He now has good reason to believe he will stay
in jail until he "clears" himself—until he tells the police a story that is
close enough to the truth to be believable and also minimizes his involvement in the crime. Since the warnings tell him he need not answer,
he could easily believe that a demonstrated willingness to answer will
help clear him. Moreover, he knows full well from living in Western culture what you and I know—that faced with listeners who will accept his
decision about whether to talk, his silence will itself be incriminating.

It is thus possible (and deeply ironic) that a substantial number of
suspects may incriminate themselves *because* they are given *Miranda*
warnings. Whether this persuasion is compulsion is a difficult question.
A case can be made that the warnings function as a sort of implicit
threat that the police will continue to hold the suspect in custody until
he cooperates by answering questions. If the suspect answers, it is likely
at least in part the result of this new threat, which would then make the
answer compelled at least on some accounts of coercion.[14] If this is
right, then some of the additional incriminating statements are compelled by *Miranda*.

But it is possible that a substantial number of the "persuaded" statements are noncompelled on standard accounts of compulsion. Perhaps many suspects do not feel the threat of continued custody as much as they feel freer to talk to the police now that they know they can stop talking whenever they wish. On this account of why some suspects babble to police, the resulting statements appear noncompelled.

The ethical implications here depend on the mechanism that causes the increase in confessions. If *Miranda* operates principally to compel confessions, on the account given above, *Miranda* would then be part of the coercive interrogation environment rather than part of a solution, and it would have failed in one of its central purposes. On the other hand, if *Miranda*'s principal effect is to make suspects feel free to talk to police, we can identify ethical benefits—more suspects feeling free to talk and more confessions from guilty suspects. A world in which we have both *Miranda* and more confessions seems likely to be, on balance, ethically beneficial.

Indeed, the fourth outcome is just the "steady-state" outcome writ large. Whatever ethical gain we perceive in the "steady-state" outcome is simply enhanced if *Miranda* produces more noncompelled confessions than it deters. These outcomes avoid not only the ethical critique of Grano and Cassell, but also the "mere symbolism" critique of David Simon.[15] Maybe, finally, a conceptual defense can turn back *Miranda*'s critics. But can we gather evidence of either "steady-state" theory of confessions? Paul Cassell and Bret Hayman conclude that such evidence will be virtually impossible to obtain.[16]

While it is true that several assumptions underlying the ethical analysis in this chapter lack rock-solid evidence, my intuition tells me that they clearly are plausible. And intuition ought to count for something when setting a research agenda. I now know what evidence I would like to see. Two research strategies might prove fruitful. One is to compare jurisdictions or departments that apply *Miranda* differently. For example, the Cassell/Hayman Salt Lake County study reported that one department required its officers to warn even noncustodial interviewees, while other departments trained officers not to give warnings prematurely.[17] Comparing the two noncustodial groups—those that were given *Miranda* warnings and those that were not—might provide evidence of both halves of my "steady-state" *Miranda* effect. We might find, after controlling for the type of crime, that suspects who were given *Miranda* warnings were both more likely to say nothing and more likely to incriminate themselves when they did answer. This would indicate that some suspects understand the warnings and adjust their behavior, albeit in different ways. Some act in their self-interest and remain silent, while others are moved by the warnings to talk more than they otherwise would.[18]

A more ambitious research project would make use of the increasing use of videotaped interrogations. More than one chapter in this book concludes that videotaping of confessions is a valuable supplement to *Miranda*. We note in the introduction to Part IV that two states have videotaping requirements (Alaska and Minnesota). William Geller reports in Chapter 23 that as of 1990 about one-third of the police departments serving populations of 50,000 or more were videotaping "at least some interrogations." These videotapes, either alone or in conjunction with interviews of defendants who confessed and whose convictions have become final, are a rich source of potential data about how different suspects react to the warnings. The defendants could be shown the videotape and asked why they answered questions at a particular juncture. We would also want to know what the suspect's strategy was in answering questions when and how he did. With a large stockpile of videotaped interrogations, researchers could control for sex, race, age, education, prior contact with the criminal justice system, intoxication, self-reported understanding of the warnings, reactions to particular styles of giving the warnings and seeking waivers, and many other factors that might be of potential importance in making the waiver decision.

There are difficulties with both research designs, to be sure, but this is not the place to argue about methodology. I call on researchers to be both creative and determined. Let's abandon ideology and old grudges, and turn to the worthy task of uncovering how *Miranda* really works in the police interrogation room. Until we know the answer to that question, any proposal to overrule or expand *Miranda* must be rejected.

We can now finish the story of Miranda—Ernest Miranda, that is. After Miranda was paroled for the rape of Mary Adams, he returned to Phoenix, and worked for a time as an appliance store deliveryman.[19] On January 31, 1976, he played poker with two illegal Mexican immigrants in La Ampola, a "dusty bar in the Deuce section of Phoenix."[20] A fistfight escalated into a knife attack on Miranda. He was stabbed twice and was dead on arrival at Good Samaritan Hospital.[21] Miranda was thirty-four years old. The police apprehended one of the immigrants, later charged as an accomplice in the killing of Miranda. The officers read the suspect his *Miranda* rights.[22]

Ernest Miranda is dead. Will the twenty-first century be a world without *Miranda?* It is not too late to gather the evidence that will permit policymakers to decide that difficult question.

NOTES

1. For an excellent critique of *Miranda*'s symbolic function that is different from that of Caplan, see Louis Michael Seidman, Brown and Miranda, 80 Cal. L. Rev. 673 (1992).

2. Telephone conversation with Yale Kamisar, March 5, 1997.

3. See chapter 17.

4. Oregon v. Elstad, 470 U.S. 298, 306 (1985).

5. *Id.* at 307.

6. *See* Joseph Grano, Confessions, Truth, and the Law (1994); George C. Thomas III, *An Assault on the Temple of* Miranda, 85 J. Crim. L. & Criminology 807 (1995) (reviewing Grano).

7. This figure is within my estimated pre-*Miranda* range (45–53 percent) and close to that of Cassell and Hayman (55–60 percent). See chapter 16.

8. Uniform Crime Reports 208 table 29 (1995) (showing for 1995 a total of 2,924,800).

9. Stephen J. Schulhofer, Miranda's *Practical Effects: Substantial Benefits and Vanishingly Small Social Costs,* 90 Nw. U. L. Rev. 500, 542–44 (1996) [excerpted in chap. 14].

10. *Id.* at 540–44. I rounded to 20 percent Schulhofer's actual estimate of 19 percent. Paul Cassell's estimate is only slightly higher—24–26 percent. See Paul G. Cassell, Miranda's *Social Costs: An Empirical Reassessment,* 90 Nw. U. L. Rev. 387, 433 (1996) [excerpted in chap. 13].

11. Steven D. Levitt, *The Effect of Prison Population Size on Crime Rates: Evidence from Prison Overcrowding Litigation,* National Bureau of Economic Research Working Paper No. 5119 (1995). See also Samuel Walker, Sense and Nonsense about Crime and Drugs 79 (3d. ed. 1994).

12. See Walker, *supra* note 11, at 49 (table 3.2) (average of twenty-five months for all felonies). Two years is probably somewhat low, because Walker's table includes felonies less serious than the index crimes. Only a rough estimate is needed to provide guidance on the ethical question.

13. The alternative, controversial assumption is a fixed "demand" for crime, created by the availability of victims, with the potential criminals simply dividing the fixed pool of victims into smaller shares if more criminals come on line. While the latter thesis is intriguing, its robust form causes many ethical issues in criminal justice policy to disappear. If the number of criminals on the street is only at best marginally relevant to the crime rate, the debate about using prison to incapacitate dangerous criminals, for example, is a waste of time.

14. For a fuller discussion of the possibility that *Miranda* may coerce suspects into incriminating themselves, see George C. Thomas III, *A Philosophical Account of Coerced Self-Incrimination,* 5 Yale J. L. & Human. 79 (1993).

15. See chapter 4. To be sure, Simon's critique may be too robust. He seems to imply that *Miranda* permits trickery and deception as a way to produce a valid waiver, but the Court has never held, or intimated, that this is true.

16. See chapter 16.

17. Paul G. Cassell and Bret S. Hayman, *Police Interrogation in the 1990s: An Empirical Study of the Effects of* Miranda 43 UCLA L. Rev. 839, 882 (1996) [excerpted in chap. 16—Eds.].

18. On the theory tentatively developed in this chapter, the group of "talkers" would include those who are compelled by the threat of continued custody and the fear of remaining silent and being thought guilty, and those whose responses are encouraged by these factors but nonetheless voluntary. Disaggregating these groups would be a conceptual and empirical challenge.

19. Liva Baker, *Miranda*: Crime, Law and Politics 408 (1983).

20. *Id.*

21. *Id.*

22. *Id.*

The Contributors

Janet Ainsworth is Professor of Law, Seattle University.

Albert Alschuler is Wilson-Dickinson Professor, University of Chicago Law School.

Gerald M. Caplan is Dean, McGeorge University School of Law.

Paul Cassell is Professor of Law, University of Utah.

William A. Geller is Associate Director of the Police Executive Research Forum.

Joseph D. Grano is Distinguished Professor of Law, Wayne State University.

Bret Hayman received his J.D. from University of Utah College of Law in 1996.

Lawrence Herman is Professor Emeritus of Law, The Ohio State University.

Phillip E. Johnson is Professor of Law, University of California, Berkeley.

Yale Kamisar is Clarence Darrow Distinguished University Professor of Law, The University of Michigan.

Richard A. Leo is Assistant Professor of Criminology, Law and Society, University of California, Irvine.

Patrick Malone is a partner is the law firm of Stein, Mitchell & Mezines, Washington, D.C.

Irene Merker Rosenberg is Royce R. Till Professor of Law, University of Houston.

Yale Rosenberg is A. A. White Professor of Law, University of Houston.

Stephen J. Schulhofer is Julius Kreeger Professor of Law and Criminology and Director of the Center for Studies in Criminal Justice, University of Chicago.

David Simon is a journalist with the *Baltimore Sun*.

George C. Thomas III is Professor of Law, Rutgers University.

Index

INDEX